EU FOREIGN RELATIONS LAW

This book reappraises the constitutional fundamentals of EU foreign relations law. The essays in the book examine and reassess the basic principles of EU foreign relations law that have emerged over 50 years of incremental Treaty-based and judicial development and explore the particular character of the EU's 'external constitution'. They have been written against a background of change and debate: the deliberation over the character of the appropriate constitutional framework which has surrounded the drafting of the Constitutional and Reform Treaties, the increasingly cross-pillar nature of much EU external action, and renewed interest in the accountability of foreign relations policy and practice to democratic and judicial review within and outside the EU. This collection will be of interest not only to EU foreign relations law specialists but also to those concerned with broader constitutional issues within EU law. In exploring the legal context in which the EU seeks to develop an international identity, and to structure and execute policies at the international level, the collection will also interest those working in international relations.

Essays in European Law: Volume 13

EU Foreign Relations Law

Constitutional Fundamentals

Edited by

Marise Cremona and Bruno de Witte

·HART·
PUBLISHING

OXFORD AND PORTLAND, OREGON
2008

Published in North America (US and Canada) by
Hart Publishing
c/o International Specialized Book Services
920 NE 58th Avenue, Suite 300
Portland, OR 97213–3786
USA
Tel: +1 503 287 3093 or toll-free: (1) 800 944 6190
Fax: +1 503 280 8832
E-mail: orders@isbs.com
Website: www.isbs.com

Hart Publishing, 16c Worcester Place, OX1 2JW
Telephone: +44 (0)1865 517530 Fax: +44 (0)1865 510710
E-mail: mail@hartpub.co.uk
Website: http://www.hartpub.co.uk

British Library Cataloguing in Publication Data

Data Available

ISBN: 978–1-84113–757–5

Typeset by Columns Design Ltd, Reading
Printed and bound in Great Britain by
TJ International Ltd, Padstow, Cornwall

Acknowledgements

The editors would like to thank the Academy of European Law for its support for the workshop at which the papers included in this book were first presented. We would also like to thank the participants in that workshop, discussants as well as paper-givers, for their essential contribution to this project. Dr Gracia Marín Durán has helped us to prepare the manuscript, way beyond reasonable expectations and with exceptional efficiency and good humour. Thank you finally to the editorial staff at Hart for their patience and understanding.

Marise Cremona
Bruno de Witte

Contents

List of Contributors

Marise Cremona is Professor of European Law at the European University Institute and Co-Director of its Academy of European Law. She was formerly Professor of European Commercial Law at the Centre for Commercial Law Studies, Queen Mary University of London.

Alan Dashwood is Professor of European Law at Cambridge and a Fellow of Sidney Sussex College; he is also a barrister. Previously, he was a Director in the Legal Service of the Council.

Bruno de Witte is Professor of European Law at the European University Institute, Florence. He is also co-director of the Academy of European Law at the EUI.

Christoph W Herrmann, LLM European Law (London), Wirtschaftsjurist (Univ Bayreuth) is Assistant Professor at the Chair for Public Law and European Law at the University of Munich and during 2006–07 was Jean-Monnet Fellow at the Robert Schuman Centre for Advanced Studies of the European University Institute, Florence.

Christophe Hillion is professor of European law and co-director of the Europa Institute, Faculty of Law, University of Leiden, the Netherlands.

Christine Kaddous studied at Neuchâtel University, Cambridge University (GB) and at the Institut d'études européennes of the Université libre de Bruxelles. She is professor of European Union Law at Geneva University and director of the Centre d'études juridiques européennes (CEJE) of the same University.

Panos Koutrakos is Professor of European Union Law and Jean Monnet Chair in EU Law at the University of Bristol.

Päivi Leino has worked at the Finnish Prime Minister's Office and was responsible for the legal aspects of the 2007 Intergovernmental Conference. She is associated with the Centre of Excellence for Global Governance Research at the Erik Castrén Institute of International Law and Human Rights, University of Helsinki, where she defended her doctoral thesis in 2005.

Eleanor Spaventa is Reader in Law at Durham University and Director of the Durham European Law Institute. She previously held positions at Birmingham University, where she was a lecturer, and at the University of Cambridge, where she was a Norton Rose European Law Lecturer and Director of Studies at New Hall.

Daniel Thym is a senior researcher at the Walter-Hallstein-Institute for European Constitutional Law at Humboldt-University in Berlin and the coordinator of the graduate school 'Constitutionalism Beyond the State: European Experiences and Global Perspectives'.

Ramses A Wessel is Professor of the Law of the European Union and other International Organizations and Co-Director of the Centre for European Studies of the University of Twente, The Netherlands.

Introduction

Marise Cremona and Bruno de Witte

This volume of essays reappraises what we call the constitutional fundamentals of EU foreign relations law. We use the term foreign relations law
to cover all EU external relations law, including each of the three pillars of
the existing European Union architecture. Indeed, one important factor
that explains the publication of this volume at this particular time is the
planned entry into force, in 2009, of the Treaty of Lisbon which creates a
modified and much more unified framework for the whole of the EU's
foreign relations. One of the most obvious characteristics of the Treaty of
Lisbon is the formal absorption of the European Community by the
European Union, the advantage of which will be particularly tangible in
the external domain, since it will put an end to the rather absurd situation
in which the 'group of 27' addresses the outside world with changing
personalities, often as 'European Community' but also sometimes as
'European Union'. The reasons for this chameleonic behaviour were rather
bemusing for that outside world, as well as for the European Union's own
citizens.

Apart from the end result of the reform process, which is enacted in the
Treaty of Lisbon, that process itself, because of its length and mostly
inclusive nature (except in the very last phase), provided an occasion for
political deliberation and academic debate about the character of the
Union's overall legal framework, and the external dimension occupied a
prominent place in the reform debates.

However, this volume is not proposed by us as a commentary on the
recent Treaty changes. It devotes at least as much, if not more, attention to
the incremental change in the Union's foreign relations law that has taken
place in recent years. Indeed, at the same time as the Treaty reform process
unfolded, the EU institutions and the Member State governments have
carried forward a series of important changes in the form and content of
the Union's foreign relations. A first element of relative novelty is the
ever-increasing cross-pillar nature of much EU external action, which is
giving rise to a growing number of inter-pillar disputes and questions over
the relationships between the pillars, some of which have been put before
the European Court of Justice for their resolution. Secondly, unprecedented
legal questions are arising over the implications of the changing nature of
the external action of the Union and its Member States and the international obligations weighing on them: typical examples are the adoption
and enforcement of anti-terrorism legislation, the conclusion of human

rights sensitive bilateral agreements in the field of migration, border crossing and criminal justice, and the increasing number of EU military and civilian missions abroad. This abundant practice has, thirdly, revived the debate on structural issues related to the accountability of foreign relations policy and practice to democratic and judicial review within the EU framework and at the national level.

In the light of these new developments and rekindled debates, we propose in this volume to re-examine and reassess the basic principles of EU foreign relations law that have emerged over almost 40 years of incremental Treaty-based and judicial development. Of course, the original text of the EEC Treaty already devoted some space to external relations, and the European Communities quickly started to enact externally directed measures and to conclude international agreements, some of which were truly important; one could mention, for example, the association agreement with Turkey, concluded in 1963, which is still politically and legally very relevant today because of its promise of ultimate EC membership of Turkey and because it is the source of the rich case-law of the ECJ dealing with the equal treatment rights of Turkish citizens residing in the Union. However, very little attention was paid in those initial years to the constitutional dimension of the Community's external relations, with some few exceptions, most notably the course presented at The Hague Academy by the later ECJ judge Pierre Pescatore in 1961.[1] Only in the early 1970s does this constitutional interest emerge, following two important European Court of Justice rulings: the *ERTA* judgment in 1971 dealt with the legal framework for treaty-making in the EC, and in particular the division of competences between the EC and its Member States, whereas the *International Fruit* judgment, one year later, dealt with the other side of the coin, namely the effects of external agreements in both 'domestic' legal orders, that of the EC itself and that of its Member States.

Since the mid-1980s, we have seen a major expansion of the Treaty provisions dealing with foreign relations due to the Single European Act and the Treaty of Maastricht which, taken together, multiplied the number of externally flavoured Treaty articles and thereby also the questions raised by overlapping legal basis provisions. At the same time, we have seen a rapid thickening of judge-made constitutional law relating to the respective roles of the Commission, the Council and the Parliament, to the intricate division of competences between the EC and the Member States, and their respective duties, and to the protection of individual rights and the right to invoke norms of external EU law before the ECJ and the national courts, to name just the principal areas of judicial law-making.

---

[1] P Pescatore, 'Les relations extérieures des Communautés européennes: contribution à la doctrine de la personnalité des organisations internationales' (1961) 103-II *Recueil des cours* 1.

As a result of this development, the EU's foreign relations has grown massively in volume and complexity and this has given rise, in recent years, to the publication of a number of comprehensive textbooks wholly devoted to the external dimension of EU law. It has also revived the need to reflect on the underlying principles of this legal regime, in other words: its *constitutional fundamentals*.

The use of that term in the title of this volume requires, perhaps, some justification. The founding Treaties of the European Union entrench institutional and other legal norms by putting them beyond the reach of the EU legislator, thus creating a rather strict distinction in EC and EU law between 'primary law' and 'secondary law'. It is tempting to use the 'domestic analogy' to describe this distinction, and therefore to consider the Treaties as forming the constitutional law of the EU. Indeed, the European Court of Justice itself called the EC Treaty the constitutional charter of the Community and many of its members, in their extra-judicial writings, have advocated the use of the domestic analogy long before the political actors embarked, in 2002, on their effort to enact an instrument that would have replaced the current Treaties and be named a Constitutional Treaty.

Despite the fact that the political actors at the European Council of Brussels in June 2007 abjured the use of this constitutional language, and carefully removed it from what became the Lisbon Treaty, it is quite likely that legal authors (and the members of the European Court) will continue to speak of the constitutional law of the EU based on the domestic analogy: since the Treaties occupy a higher rank in the legal hierarchy than the acts of the EU institutions, and since the Treaties fulfil several of the functions which a constitution fulfils at the national level, it is proper to consider the Treaties as forming the Union's constitutional instrument, and to consider that its now numerous provisions dealing with foreign relations form the Union's *droit constitutionnel externe*.

However, this formal definition is not entirely satisfactory, because it is both under- and over-inclusive. It is under-inclusive since it has become clear, in the course of the past decades, that the written norms of the founding Treaties are complemented by another judge-made source of higher law, namely the general principles of Community and Union law. Most notably, the protection of the fundamental rights of the individual against interference by the EU institutions is based on this complementary source of primary law and its impact on external relations has been very notable in recent years. The formal definition is also over-inclusive, since the text of the founding Treaties contains many (indeed, too many) detailed provisions which one would not normally find in a national constitutional text. Therefore, by focusing on the constitutional *fundamentals*, this book aims to identify the main norms and principles of the written and unwritten primary law of the European Union, with particular attention to the way in which these norms and principles are being reshaped by current changes in the Union's internal regime and in its external environment.

A recurring theme in the chapters of this volume is that of the distinctiveness of the 'external constitution'. Does it make sense to talk about an external constitution which is somehow separate or different from the Union's internal constitution? Similarly, in what sense does the EU's nature as an international organisation of conferred, but expanding, powers require a different approach to foreign relations law from that traditionally adopted by its Member States? With reference to this double distinctiveness question (the external versus the internal, and the EU constitution versus the national constitutional traditions), the themes of this book can, roughly speaking, be divided in three broad categories.

After an introductory chapter in which *De Witte* wonders whether the European Union has an overabundance of constitutional norms, compared to what one typically finds at the national level, a *first group* of chapters addresses the 'idiosyncratic' themes, namely those that are really specific to EU foreign relations law, and do not arise in a comparable way either at the internal EU level, or in the external relations constitutions of the Member States. This is, of course, primarily the case for the current distinction between the EU and the EC, and the related questions of the dividing line between the first and second pillars in the practice of foreign relations, which are addressed respectively by *Herrmann* and *Dashwood*. The chapter by *Hillion and Wessel* examines the little-studied question of the legal limitations which EU action in the 'intergovernmental' second pillar imposes on the Member States.

This chapter forms a transition to the *second group* of contributions which examine the 'external' counterpart of central constitutional questions of EU law that also have an important internal dimension. This is clearly the case with *Cremona*'s chapter on the duties of cooperation and compliance; although these duties originated in the domain of 'internal' EC law, they now play a probably more important role in shaping the nature of the relations between the EU and its Member States in the field of their international relations. Another closely related general question of EU constitutional law is the division of competences between the EC/EU and its Member States, and the question of the choice of legal basis, discussed in the chapter by *Koutrakos*. Although some of the key principles in this matter are identical to those applying to the internal policies of the EU, the external side presents its own problems, if only because of the presence of third states and the wish of the EU Member States to continue to appear, as much as possible, in their own right on the international scene.

The remainder of the chapters deal with themes that are 'classically constitutional', in the sense that they also arise, in roughly similar terms, in the constitutional order of the contemporary nation state. This is true for the question of parliamentary accountability in international relations, examined in the chapter by *Thym*; the protection of fundamental rights in the context of foreign policy, a very topical question at the European level examined by *Spaventa*; for the role of normative values in the shaping of foreign policy (the contribution by *Leino*); and for the traditional question of the 'domestic' effect of international treaty law in the legal order of the EC for which *Kaddous*, in her chapter, presents us with the current state of the art. These four themes may well echo traditional themes of the national constitutional law, but these chapters strikingly show the extent to which the law of the European Union offers some original answers to these traditional questions and is, indeed, very much in the forefront of developments, for good and for bad, compared to the law of the Member States.

Part I

EU Foreign Relations: Law and Constitution

1

Too Much Constitutional Law in the European Union's Foreign Relations?

BRUNO DE WITTE

I. CONSTITUTIONAL LAW AS A BURDEN FOR THE EUROPEAN UNION

ULYSSES PLUGGED HIS companions' ears and asked them to tie him to the mast of their ship while they were crossing the sea passage near the rocks on which the Sirens lived, so that he would not be tempted by their beautiful songs to steer the ship against those rocks. In his book entitled *Ulysses and the Sirens*, Jon Elster uses Homer's story in order to explain a psychological and social phenomenon consisting of binding oneself for the future. Such a precommitment can, in some circumstances such as those of Ulysses, be a form of (imperfect) rationality. Elster extends the notion into the domain of politics, and examines the role of constitutions as mechanisms of political precommitment.[1] The constitution, among other functions, protects the ship of state by tying the hands of the representatives of the people to prevent them from doing harm; constitutional limits serve to keep presidents from becoming dictators, to keep governments from trampling on fundamental rights, etc.

It is equally important, though, that Ulysses should not remain tied to the mast for too long. He remains the captain and must be able to steer the future course of the ship after they have passed the Sirens' rocks. Indeed, there can be a situation of constitutional overabundance in a given State,

---

[1] J Elster, 'Imperfect Rationality: Ulysses and the Sirens' in *Ulysses and the Sirens: Studies in Rationality and Irrationality* (Cambridge, CUP, 1979) 37; for a later contribution which focuses more specifically on constitutions, see J Elster, 'Ulysses Unbound: Constitutions as Constraints' in *Ulysses Unbound: Studies in Rationality, Precommitment and Constraints* (Cambridge, CUP, 2000) 88. For a historical discussion of the precommitment dimension of constitutionalism, see S Holmes, 'Precommitment and the Paradox of Democracy' in J Elster and R Slagstad (eds), *Constitutionalism and Democracy* (Cambridge, CUP, 1988) 195.

when too many matters are put beyond the reach of ordinary legislative, executive or judicial decision making by being entrenched at the constitutional level. This is either caused by a written constitutional text which is overly long and detailed, or by the detailed interpretative glosses added by a constitutional court to a constitutional document which, by itself, is succinct. The Portuguese Constitution adopted after the carnations revolution in 1974 is often cited as an example of the former,[2] and the case law of the German Constitutional Court is often accused of the latter. Of course, whether there is too much constitutional law, or too little, or just enough, depends on one's taste, and in particular on the ends which a given constitution is aimed to achieve, but the question of the 'right measure' of constitutional law is undoubtedly an important though neglected question of democratic theory. As Fossum and Menéndez put it, a constitution 'which exhausts the political space' becomes an 'asphyxiating straight-jacket'.[3]

The question of constitutional overload is directly related to the degree of 'constitutional inertia', that is, the existence of rules that guarantee that constitutions cannot be modified too easily. These rules include (in all kinds of combinations): special majorities in parliament; confirmation by a later vote; delay; a referendum; confirmation by sub-national government; the exclusion of certain matters from constitutional reform.[4] The more difficult it is to change a constitution, the worse the consequences of constitutional overload. In a legal order such as that of Austria, in which the procedural requirements for amending the constitution are very light, it does not matter too much that there is a large volume of constitutional law. Conversely, the great difficulty to change the Constitution of the USA is compensated by the fact that its text is short and often vague. When, however, there is a very large volume of constitutional law, and a very rigid procedure for modifying the constitution, there can be a problem.

This is, arguably, the case for the European Union (EU). The primary law of the EU, which has the same entrenchment effect as national constitutions have, namely that of shielding a number of matters from ordinary EU decision making, is very voluminous for two cumulative reasons: because the text of the instruments of primary law (essentially, now, the EC Treaty and the EU Treaty) is very long and sometimes

---

[2] In its current version (that is, after the seventh revision, which took place in 2005), the Portuguese Constitution has 296 Articles and takes up 91 pages on the Portuguese Parliament's internet site.

[3] JE Fossum and AJ Menéndez, 'The Constitution's Gift? A Deliberative Democratic Analysis of Constitution Making in the European Union' (2005) 11 *European Law Journal* 380, 409.

[4] See, for a short comparative survey, JE Lane, *Constitutions and Political Theory* (Manchester, Manchester University Press, 1996) 114–17.

extremely detailed,[5] and also because the Court of Justice has added to this a large amount of court-made constitutional law through the dynamic interpretation of written norms and through the creation of new, unwritten, norms of primary law (namely, the general principles of Community law). The EU does not only have a large volume of constitutional law, but it also has the most rigid rules of change (that is, of treaty revision) of any constitutional system. The various treaty reforms that have nevertheless occurred in the course of the last 20 years have mainly *added* new constitutional rules, but almost never did the Member States agree to '*de-constitutionalise*' particular norms, so as to put back in the democratic arena matters which had previously been entrenched in the founding Treaties. Thus, there has been a constant trend to increase the volume of constitutional law, accompanied by an increasing difficulty in modifying those constitutional rules. This detailed regulation of institutional procedures and sector-specific policies by the European Treaties unduly reduces the scope for democratic deliberation and for effective institutional responses to new policy challenges.

This problem can be described, in a nutshell, as the fact that the EU's constitutional law is often more of a burden than a support for the functioning of the EU. This issue surfaced occasionally during the ongoing constitutional reform process of the EU (which started in 2001 and may come to an end in 2009), but has not been addressed by it in a comprehensive or satisfactory way. Whereas the adoption of a Constitutional Treaty for the EU was seen, by its initiators and drafters, as a means to give new impetus to the European integration process and help the EU to address current challenges in a more efficient and democratic way, it can be argued that, in fact, the constitutional law of the EU, both in the past and in the future, has been and will be more of a burden than a stimulus for the integration project. The argument that there is 'too much constitutional law' in the EU is mainly based on the overabundance of primary law norms, which unduly constrains the normal democratic process. It is made worse by two other elements, namely the structural complexity of EU constitutional law which leads to a lack of 'legibility' for citizens, and the rigidity of the EU's rules of change which makes it difficult to adapt this complex and overabundant mass of norms to changing needs and circumstances.

During the long *pause de réflexion* which followed the negative referenda in France and the Netherlands of May–June 2005, one often heard

---

[5] The EC Treaty has 314 Articles, and the EU Treaty has 53 Articles. In addition, there are 36 Protocols to those two Treaties, and there is the separate Euratom Treaty. When counting the number of Articles (and, indeed, the number of words) one would most probably find that the primary law of the EU is more voluminous than any of the national constitutions of European states.

the view that Part III of the Constitutional Treaty was much too detailed and unwieldy, and had for that reason alone (leaving aside numerous other reasons) provoked negative feelings among the Dutch and French voters. These misgivings about the sheer volume of Part III point to a broader problem which predates the elaboration of the Constitutional Treaty (indeed, most of Part III was based on the existing text of the EC and EU Treaties), namely the fact that primary EU law contains detailed description of policies of the kind that one normally does not find in constitutions. The structural problem of the overload of constitutional law in and for the EU has been around for some time, and will stay around even if some reconfigured and suitably de-constitutionalised version of the Constitutional Treaty eventually enters into force.

Why this abundance and complexity? Much of it reflects the basic tension between the EU and its Member States. Constitutional rules—whether expressed in the Treaty texts or developed by the Court of Justice—tend to entrench and guarantee a specific and delicate equilibrium in those relations. In the words of the Council's *jurisconsulte* Jean-Claude Piris, 'the Member States, authors of the Treaty, want it detailed, because they want to control exactly how much competence they give to the EU and how much power they give to its institutions to exercise these competences'.[6] This shows that, in the case of the EU, enactment of constitutional rules is not so much a case of self-commitment (of Ulysses asking to be tied to the mast) but a means for the Member States' governments to bind others, namely the EU institutions. However, by doing so, they also limit the possibility for those institutions to act effectively for the defence of the common national interests; one could therefore modify the metaphor and describe this as Ulysses tying his best sailor to the mast.

The European 'rule-book' has thus grown at the same pace as the European Community's and the EU's role and policy responsibilities became more prominent. Each widening of the EU's policy remit since the Single European Act 1986 (SEA) was accompanied by a confirmation of the control powers of the national governments and of their remaining scope for autonomous action. The tracing of the boundary between integration and Member State autonomy was expressed not only in the vertical division of competences, but also in the horizontal division of competences, most crucially in the definition of the role and internal decision-making rules of the Council. Therefore, the constitutional rules which define the vertical and the horizontal division of powers are both very complex and detailed, full of specifications and derogations.

---

[6] JC Piris, *The Constitution for Europe: A Legal Analysis* (Cambridge, CUP, 2006) 59.

However, not all the constitutional complexity can be justified by this need to fix the 'integration balance' at any given moment in time. It would have often been possible, both for the Treaty reformers and for the Court, to devise simpler rules and to strive for greater constitutional parsimony. The constitutional law of *external relations* provides, in my view, a particularly clear illustration of this problem. Many other fields of EU law and policy could be examined in the same light, but external relations are particularly interesting for the clear contrast between the traditional scarcity of relevant provisions that one finds in *national* constitutions, and the overabundance of norms in *EU* primary law.

II. A PARTICULARLY COMPLEX EXTERNAL RELATIONS CONSTITUTION

The European constitutional provisions on foreign relations were not always abundant. The external relations provisions in the EEC Treaty, prior to the adoption of the SEA, were few and far-between. Some provisions, like the one allowing the EC to conclude association agreements (originally Article 238 EEC, now Article 310 EC), were (and still remain) particularly laconic. The origin of the current complexity of the Treaty rules on external relations lies in the early 1980s, when the EU governments started to show concern about the fragmentation between the EC system and the newly developed and institutionally separate European Political Cooperation (EPC) in foreign affairs.[7] One of the aims of the SEA (an aim expressed by the use of the word 'single') was to connect these two institutional strands more closely, but the Act did not effectively achieve that aim.[8] The transformation of EPC into the Common Foreign and Security Policy (CFSP) by the Treaty of Maastricht was a much more important step towards narrowing the gap with the European Community system, but the gap remained. The Treaty of Maastricht marked, indeed, the start of a new and more vigorous debate about 'Treaty architecture' due to its pillar approach and to the various opt-outs provided for single countries and groups of countries.

---

[7] The amalgamation of the Community and EPC structures was one of the central aims of the so-called Genscher/Colombo proposals made jointly by the German and Italian governments in November 1981; see P Neville-Jones, 'The Genscher/Colombo Proposals on European Union' (1983) 20 *CML Rev* 657. On the institutional practice of those early years, see S Nuttall, 'Interaction between European Political Cooperation and the European Community' (1987) 7 *Yearbook of European Law* 211.

[8] On the links between the two institutional settings after the Single European Act, see M Lak, 'Interaction between European Political Cooperation and the European Community (external): Existing Rules and Challenges' (1989) 26 *CML Rev* 281. On the weakness of the EPC legal regime even after the Single European Act, see R Dehousse and JHH Weiler, 'EPC and the Single Act: From Soft Law to Hard Law?' in M Holland (ed), *The Future of European Political Cooperation: Essays on Theory and Practice* (Basingstoke, Macmillan, 1991) 121.

These reforms accomplished by the SEA and the Treaty of Maastricht were essentially member-state-driven and their concerns were pragmatic. The states were facing the question of how to use the treaty instrument for creating European institutional structures that would optimally fit the foreign policy developments that had happened in a piecemeal and uncoordinated way over the years. All subsequent treaty revisions continued along the same line of the institutional fine-tuning of what, in Maastricht, became known as the CFSP. We have thus seen a gradual but far-reaching 'legalisation' of EU foreign policy[9] which is in fact a 'constitutionalisation'.

Obviously, once foreign policy competences were entrusted to a separate organisation, the EU, the need for a set of constitutional rules defining that organisation's competences and its decision-making procedures became obvious. But the choice itself of establishing a separate international organisation alongside the EC and building the complicated pillar structure, was not a necessary one. One could have integrated the ex-EPC (as well as cooperation in justice and home affairs) within the framework of the EC Treaty with exceptions and derogations to the Treaty's normal rules, as was done with Economic and Monetary Union, which also has very idiosyncratic institutional rules but was nevertheless integrated in the EC Treaty. One took, instead, the more complicated route, namely that of building a baroque legal construction whereby two new areas of cooperation were covered by a new treaty (the EU Treaty) linked to the existing treaties through the mechanism of a few enigmatic common provisions.

The disjunction between the EC and the EU does not seem satisfactory any more. The fact that CFSP could not, in its development, rely on long-standing legal principles and practices developed within the first pillar, has raised a host of legal issues for which the wording of the EU Treaty was not very helpful, including questions relating to the legal nature and binding effect of CFSP instruments, and to the effect of CFSP law in the domestic legal systems of the Member States. A particularly frustrating issue was that of the autonomous treaty-making capacity of the EU, which the Maastricht Treaty did not recognise in so many words, and which had to be affirmed step by step through practice.[10] There are also frequent situations of overlap between CFSP and EC external relations competence,[11] and sometimes this uncertainty leads to almost ridiculous situations, like when a third country is told that an agreement was wrongly

---

[9]   ME Smith, 'Diplomacy by Decree: The Legalization of EU Foreign Policy' (2001) 39 *Journal of Common Market Studies* 79.

[10]   For an exhaustive survey of the evolution of EU treaty-making law and practice since Maastricht, see D Thym, 'Die völkerrechtlichen Verträge der Europäischen Union' (2006) 66 *Zeitschrift für ausländisches öffentliches Recht und Völkerrecht* 863.

[11]   See R Baratta, 'Overlaps between European Community Competence and European Union Foreign Policy Activity' in E Cannizzaro (ed), *The European Union as an Actor in*

concluded by the European Community whereas it should have been by the EU (as happened after the Passenger Name Records judgment)[12] or that a planned agreement should, after all, be concluded with both the EU and European Community rather than with one of them or each of them separately (as in the case of the Schengen cooperation agreement with Switzerland).[13] Clearly, the merger of the legal personalities of the EC and the EU, as envisaged by the Constitutional Treaty and confirmed by the Lisbon Treaty, would considerably simplify the conduct of foreign relations and strengthen the external identity of the EU, even though it would not eliminate the legal need to distinguish between CFSP-agreements and non-CFSP agreements of the EU.

More generally (beyond the question of the pillar structure), there is a degree of detail in dealing with the external relations of the EC/EU which cannot be found in any national constitution—which are notoriously and perhaps overly laconic in dealing with foreign relations. Contemporary European constitutions tend to pay more attention to foreign relations than in earlier times, but they are still overwhelmingly 'internal' in their outlook. For example, the completely revised Swiss Constitution of 1999 only has some 10 articles (of a total of 197) that deal mainly with foreign relations. Also, membership of the EU is not mentioned in so many words in a large part of the EU Member States' constitutions. Generally speaking, contemporary European constitutions deal with some or all of the following foreign relations questions (either directly in the text or through additional court-made constitutional law):

a) The horizontal division of powers between the head of state, the government and parliament in matters of war and peace, in treaty-making and sometimes in other matters.

b) In federal or quasi-federal states, the vertical division of powers between the central government and the Member States or regions.

International Relations (The Hague, Kluwer Law International, 2002) 51; M Cremona, 'External Relations of the EU and the Member States: Competence, Mixed Agreements, International Responsibility, and Effects of International Law', *EUI Working Papers* LAW No. 2006/22, 9 ff. See also the chapter by Hillion and Wessel in this volume.

[12] Joined Cases C–317/04 and C–318/04 *European Parliament v Council and Commission*, judgment of 30 May 2006.

[13] The Commission had opposed the conclusion of this inter-pillar agreement, preferring the conclusion of two separate agreements with Switzerland on this matter, one by the EC and another by the EU. On this discussion, see C Kaddous, 'La place des Accords bilatéraux II dans l'ordre juridique de l'Union européenne' in C Kaddous and M Jametti Greiner (eds), *Accords bilatéraux II Suisse–UE et autres Accords récents* (Helbing & Lichtenhahn, Bruylant, LGDJ, 2006) 63, 73–4. For a general analysis of inter-pillar fragmentation, see R Wessel, 'Fragmentation in the Governance of EU External Relations: Legal Institutional Dilemmas and the New Constitution for Europe' in JW de Zwaan *et al*, *The European Union: An Ongoing Process of Integration—Liber Amicorum Alfred E Kellermann* (The Hague, TMC Asser Instituut, 2004) 123.

c) Limitation of sovereignty clauses, which specify the conditions on which state powers may be transferred to international organisations or more specifically to the EU.

d) The effects of international and European law in the domestic legal order.

e) The values and objectives that must inspire the country's foreign policy.

f) The specific role of the (constitutional) courts in controlling the exercise of foreign relations powers.

These various elements that form the common denominator of foreign relations rules in national constitutional law can also be found in the constitutional law of the EU, although some of the relevant EU rules are formulated in an indirect way (for example, the implicit exclusion of the European Court's role in CFSP matters by Article 46 EU Treaty), and others were developed entirely through case law rather than through the written text of the Treaties (for example, the question of the transfer of powers by the EC to other international organisations is not mentioned in the EC Treaty but was dealt with by the ECJ).[14] However, EU primary law tends to deal with many of these issues in a much more detailed way than national constitutions. In purely quantitative terms, a greater proportion of articles of the founding Treaties deal, entirely or in part, with foreign relations. This overabundant written text is complemented by an unusually abundant case law which has designed a fine pattern of rules on such foreign relations matters as the implied powers doctrine, the distinction between exclusive and shared competences, the duty of sincere cooperation in the context of mixed agreements, and the conditions under which international agreements have direct effect in the EC legal order—questions which are addressed in several contributions to this volume.

A feeling of uneasiness emerges from reading some recent European Court judgments on the EU's foreign relations, as well as the recent attempts, in the Constitutional Treaty, at constitutional codification and reform of foreign relations. That uneasiness is, to put it simply, that things really get too complicated, and that we now definitely have too much confusing and unhelpful constitutional law of foreign relations in the EU.

To start with the European Court's case law, there is a strikingly large number of recent judgments dealing with aspects of external relations. There is nothing wrong with that, and it helped to spark a revival of academic writing on the external constitutional law of the EU. However, some of the judgments seem almost unreal. They deal with arcane issues of

---

[14] See in particular the two Opinions of the ECJ on the European Economic Area Agreement: *Opinion 1/91* [1991] ECR I–6079, and *Opinion 1/92* [1992] ECR I–2821, and also *Opinion 1/00* [2002] ECR I–3493. For a discussion of this question, see the case comment by F Castillo de la Torre, (2002) 39 *CML Rev* 1373.

shared or exclusive competences, and legal basis and inter-pillar disputes, which rarely seem to be connected with the normative content or direction of foreign policy. They are often impenetrable for anyone but the specialists of external relations law. They sometimes complicate matters further rather than giving clear direction for the future. One traditional example of complicated judge-made constitutional law is the question of implied powers in the external domain. The Court's case law on that matter is so complex that, when the members of the Convention on the Future of the Union set out to codify the Court's case law on this point, they failed to get it right and the combined reading of Article I-13(2) and Article III-323(1) is neither a correct codification of the case law nor otherwise satisfactory.[15]

A recent example of judge-made complexity is the outcome of the Rotterdam Convention case.[16] The ongoing dispute between the institutions on where the borderline lies between trade agreements and environmental agreements was given a new twist by the Court of Justice, which came up with the unprecedented solution that this particular agreement— the Rotterdam Convention on international trade in hazardous chemicals—was *on* the borderline between the two policy fields and therefore needed to be based on both legal bases (the one for trade and the one for the environment) at the same time. None of the institutions involved in the dispute before the Court had contemplated this possibility, and they are now faced with the unenviable task of guessing whether an envisaged agreement is *more* about trade, or *more* about environment or *almost equally* about both. As Koutrakos notes in his comment on this judgment: 'Whilst a degree of uncertainty is inevitable within the constitutional landscape of EC primary law, it is regrettable that the Court should not seek to diminish the appetite of the Community institutions for legal basis disputes.'[17]

There are other cases in which a court action seemed to raise important questions of constitutional substance, but where the ECJ judgment disappointingly remains focused on the more arcane institutional issues. This happened in the Passenger Name Records judgment of June 2006.[18] The European Parliament raised a number of legal arguments to challenge the validity of the Commission and Council decisions on which the agreement with the USA on the transmission of passenger data was based. The Court

---

[15] See M Cremona, 'The Union's External Action: Constitutional Perspectives' in G Amato, H Bribosia, B de Witte (eds), *Genesis and Destiny of the European Constitution* (Brussels, Bruylant, 2007) 1173, 1183 ff.

[16] Case C–94/03 *Commission v Council*, judgment of 10 January 2006; see the critical case comment by P Koutrakos, (2007) 44 *CML Rev* 171.

[17] P Koutrakos, above n 16, 194.

[18] Joined Cases C–317/04 and C–318/04 *European Parliament v Council and Commission*, judgment of 30 May 2006; see comments by M Mendez, (2007) 3 *European Constitutional Law Review* 127, and by G Gilmore and J Rijpma, (2007) 44 *CML Rev* 1081.

only examined the competence argument, namely that the wrong legal basis (Article 95 EC) had been used for the agreement, and annulled the decisions on that ground. The Court stopped there and did not continue to examine the alleged violation of the fundamental right to privacy. As a result of the judgment, the EU had to beg the USA to sign an identical agreement, based this time on the correct legal basis, and the US Government used the opportunity to obtain even wider availability of passenger data than in the original agreement.[19] The serious fundamental rights issue raised by making numerous personal data available to US Government services has remained unresolved.

This is an unfortunate outcome, caused by a constitutional text which is too complex and by a court being sidetracked by the technical-legal part of the complaint from examining its genuinely constitutional part. This choice for 'judicial economy'—to address only those legal arguments which the Court must consider in order to reach a decision—is frequent in the ECJ's jurisprudence. It compares unfavourably with the attitude of the German Constitutional Court in a national security case which it decided on 15 February 2006. When examining the constitutionality of § 14 (3) of the Air Transport Security Act (*Luftsicherheitsgesetz*), which allowed the minister of defence to order that a passenger aeroplane be shot down in order to prevent a terrorist attack by that aeroplane, the Court first declared the provision to be unconstitutional for being *ultra vires* (internal security being a competence reserved to the *Länder* rather than the *Bund*), but it chose not to stop there and continued to examine whether the challenged provision also violated the fundamental rights of the German Constitution, and found that it did so.[20]

Turning now to the Constitutional Treaty of the EU (and its avatar, the Lisbon Treaty which was signed on 13 December 2007), it can be declared guilty of continuing the relentless accumulation of constitutional law. The Convention on the Future of the Union produced a vast number of both broad and detailed reform proposals in the field of external relations. The main objective of those proposals was to improve the decision-making capacity of the EU institutions in foreign policy but they have, arguably, also helped to tie the hands of the EU institutions more firmly than before. The total number of words spent on external relations is staggering, entirely unprecedented for a 'Constitution', and could be seen as the unfortunate result of 'constitutional fetishism', the belief that social reality

---

[19]   Gilmore and Rijpma, above n 18, 1085.
[20]   The text of the Constitutional Court decision is published in (2006) *Neue Juristische Wochenschrift* 751. See the case comment by O Lepsius, 'Human Dignity and the Downing of Aircraft: The German Federal Constitutional Court Strikes Down a Prominent Anti-Terrorism Provision in the New Air-Transport Security Act', (2006) 7 *German Law Journal* 761 (online journal).

can effectively be steered by just putting words in a constitutional document.[21] In addition to the rearrangement of the existing Treaty provisions on external relations,[22] the Constitutional Treaty adds much more new detail. This is most striking in the field of defence policy, on which the current Treaties say little. In the Constitutional Treaty, we first of all find a very long article (Article I-41) in Part I dealing with security and defence, followed by five fairly long articles in Part III (Articles II-309 to 313). According to one commentator, 'the Constitution's provisions on defence are clear and realistic, but it cannot be said that their entry into force is essential to further progress towards a European defence policy'.[23] But, if the new provisions were not essential to allow further progress towards defence policy, what was the justification for including them in the Constitution of the EU? The relevant articles do not contain rules that are, arguably, missing in the EU Treaty today, namely rules on judicial control and guarantees of fundamental rights in defence matters. They rather set out a detailed blueprint of defence tasks and, above all, detailed institutional and financial arrangements.

Outside the domain of defence, the Constitutional Treaty also contained numerous new provisions which are entirely dispensable. For example, why was it necessary to provide in the constitutional document of the EU that 'in order to establish a framework for joint contributions from young Europeans to the humanitarian aid operations of the Union, a European Voluntary Humanitarian Aid Corps shall be set up'?[24] In most states, such an initiative would be announced in a press statement of the government, and not in the Constitution!

In fact, the drafting process of the Constitutional Treaty, particularly because of the excessive leeway given to the Convention's working groups on external relations and defence, proved to be an occasion for the experts to push through a policy reform programme rather than an occasion for constitutional reflection.[25] The drafters of the Constitutional Treaty did not take a step back to consider which provisions *must* be included in a

---

[21] I use the term 'constitutional fetishism' in the sense proposed by N Walker, 'The Idea of Constitutional Pluralism', (2002) 65 *Modern Law Review* 317, 319 and 324 ff.

[22] This rearrangement, admittedly, would render the EU's external relations law somewhat more consistent and integrated than it currently is; see M Cremona, above n 15, 1173–82, and E Cannizzaro, 'Unity and Pluralism in the EU's Foreign Relations Power' in C Barnard (ed), *The Fundamentals of EU Law Revisited—Assessing the Impact of the Constitutional Debate* (Oxford, OUP, 2007) 193, 227–34.

[23] E Denza, 'Current Developments—External Relations' (2005) 54 *ICLQ* 995, 998.

[24] Art III–321(5) of the Constitutional Treaty.

[25] See the account of the *travaux préparatoires* by G Grevi, 'The Common Foreign, Security and Defence Policy' in G Amato, H Bribosia and B de Witte (eds), *Genesis and Destiny of the European Constitution* (Brussels, Bruylant, 2007) 807; and J Howorth, 'The European Draft Constitutional Treaty and the Future of the European Defence Initiative: A Question of Flexibility?' (2004) 9 *European Foreign Affairs Review* 483.

rigid Constitution that will be set in stone for an undefined number of years, and which other provisions could more appropriately be laid down in an informal policy document that is easily adaptable to changing priorities. The Lisbon Treaty, despite its professed aim of 'simplifying' the Constitutional Treaty, will not change this. It will spread the external relations provisions again over two separate Treaties (the EU Treaty, and the Treaty on the Functioning of the European Union), but this undoing of the merger of the Treaties will no longer entail a split legal personality—so, the existence of two separate Treaties will just be a gratuitous legal complication. In addition to this complication, all the constitutional overkill contained in the Constitutional Treaty will remain there also in the Lisbon Treaty.

The complexity of the EU constitutional rules spills over into the relations with third states. A well-known example of this is the practice of the mixed agreements, where it is seldom very clear to the third states which, among the EC or its Member States, is responsible for what, within the framework of a given agreement. Sometimes, the third states insist on requiring from the EC and its Member States a 'competence declaration' specifying the allocation of competences and responsibilities between them, but these declarations usually do not clarify much.[26] More often, they express the inability on the Community side to make sense of its own constitutional imbroglios. Examples of this are the Declaration made by the European Community regarding the WHO Framework Convention on Tobacco Control, and the Declaration regarding the UNESCO Convention on cultural diversity.[27] They consist of a vague indication of EC competence in the field, and a list of Community acts which are 'illustrative of the Community's sphere of competence in accordance with the provisions of the Treaty establishing the European Community'[28]—but are illustrative examples good enough? One commentator noted, with respect to the UNESCO Convention, that 'the declaration of competence included in this document, which refers in detail to EC legislation, risks to be too difficult to be comprehended by UNESCO Member States which are not members of the EC'.[29] Third states are indeed left with the unenviable task of relating the long list of EC acts and competences with the content of the UNESCO Convention, and of trying to guess what must be done by the EC, and what is left to the Member States. How could they know if the EC

---

[26]   M Cremona, 'External Relations of the EU and the Member States: Competence, Mixed Agreements, International Responsibility and Effects of International Law', *EUI Working Papers* LAW No. 2006/22, 21–2.
[27]   [2004] OJ L/213/23 and Council doc. 8668/1/06 REV 1 (en).
[28]   [2004] OJ L/213/23.
[29]   L Cavicchioli, 'The European Community at UNESCO: an Exceptionally Active Observer?' in J Wouters, F Hoffmeister, T Ruys (eds), *The United Nations and the European Union: An Ever Stronger Partnership* (The Hague, Asser Press, 2006) 135, 153.

legal experts do not know themselves? Perhaps one could consider this case to be 'illustrative' of the fact that the constitutional law of the EU's foreign relations is out of control?

III. CONCLUSION

Whereas the overall theme of this volume is to explore the constitutional fundamentals of the EU's external relations, the theme of this contribution is to argue that there are too many 'un-fundamentals' in the foreign relations constitution of the EU. The formal constitutional law of the EU, which consists of the primary law of the Treaties as interpreted by the Court of Justice and supplemented by general principles, contains many norms that are not constitutional in their substance. They do not serve the useful purpose of constitutional rules, namely to limit and steer the activity of the institutions, but are merely obstructive. Whereas strengthening the EU's external role is currently an important political priority of many governments, and whereas this aim became very prominent during the process of elaboration of the Constitutional Treaty,[30] the drafters of that Treaty (and of its successor the Lisbon Treaty) have not sufficiently reflected on the need for constitutional parsimony. This need is particularly pressing in the case of the EU, which is equipped with rules of constitutional change that are extremely rigid. Once the Lisbon Treaty has entered into force, there will presumably be no occasion for further treaty revisions for many years to come, and the governments may come to regret that they failed to take the opportunity for some genuine constitutional simplification—in the field of external relations, but also more generally.

---

[30] See G de Búrca, *The EU Constitution: In Search of Europe's International Identity*, Fourth Walter van Gerven Lecture (Groningen, Europa Law Publishing, 2005).

Part II

Foreign Relations Law in a Multi-Pillar Era

2

Much Ado about Pluto?
The 'Unity of the Legal Order of
the European Union' Revisited

CHRISTOPH HERRMANN*

Contemporary observations are changing our understanding of legal systems, and it is important that our nomenclature for norms reflects our current understanding. This applies, in particular, to the designation 'legal order'.

Modified excerpt of Resolution 5 of the International Astronomical Union of 24 August 2006.

I. INTRODUCTION

S INCE ITS DISCOVERY in 1930, Pluto has been considered a planet. However, this is no longer the case. Pluto has lost its prominent status following a—highly controversial[1]—resolution of the International Astronomical Union (IAU) of 24 August 2006 that defines what constitutes a planet in a contemporary astronomical sense.[2] Given its name, one is inclined to think that Pluto may have been doomed from the very beginning of its recognised existence. Of course, this is not a paper on astronomy, but one on European law. References to mythology

---

* Dr jur Christoph W Herrmann, LLM European Law (London), Wirtschaftsjurist (Univ Bayreuth) is Associate Professor at the Chair for Public Law and European Law at the University of Munich and was Jean-Monnet Fellow at the Robert Schuman Centre for Advanced Studies of the European University Institute, Florence. I am very grateful to Marise Cremona, Christoph Ohler and Rudolf Streinz for their fruitful comments on earlier versions of this paper. All remaining errors are of course my sole responsibility.
[1] More than 300 scientists signed a petition protesting against the definition by the IAU, see K Chang, 'Debate Lingers Over Definition For a Planet' *New York Times* (New York, 1 September 2006) 13.
[2] See http://wwwiauorg/fileadmin/content/pdfs/Resolution_GA26–5-6pdf.

and astrology are, however, very popular and virtually omnipresent in European politics and scholarship alike. Depending on the circumstances, they may be more or less useful.[3] Pluto has not been used in this regard so far, and of course its chances have further dropped with its recent demotion to a 'dwarf planet'.[4]

So why have I chosen to use Pluto as a metaphor in the title of this Chapter? It was certainly not (only) because of a feeling of sympathy for some small something that has been treated disrespectfully. Instead, it was because of the clarity with which the example displays the importance of definitions for our perception of the world around us. In reflecting on the 'unity of the European legal order', it becomes necessary to reveal the meaning of terminology that underpins it. This is particularly important in dealing with one of the most widely used metaphors of European integration scholarship, which lies at the heart of the matter: the 'pillar structure' of the European Union.

To describe the European Union as a Greek temple based on three 'pillars' is so common among European lawyers that it does not require any explanation.[5] It usually goes along with the perception of the EC Treaty and the EU Treaty as forming two legal orders, based on two different treaties, separate from each other with dissimilar central features. However, some scholarly contributions have always argued that EC and EU law form part of one single and unitary legal order, going along with the claim of an international legal personality for the EU or even the fusion of the former Communities and the EU by the Treaty of Maastricht. The aim of this Chapter is to re-analyse this 'unity thesis' against the backdrop of the recent case law of the ECJ. In an increasing number of cases during the last years, the Court has had to deal with issues that—naughtily enough—disregarded our beloved pillar-picture, due to a growing trend of 'cross-pillarisation' of the policies of the EU/EC.

Does the description of the European Union as a single legal order make any difference, when it comes to solving legal questions? I will argue in this Chapter that a lot depends on the perspective that you adopt with regard to the meaning of notions like 'legal order' and 'unity', but that the claim of unity does not contribute a great deal to the resolution of interpretative questions that occur with regard to the relationship between the different

---

[3] It seems doubtful, whether it is, eg, really necessary that an Advocate General devotes two out of 17 pages of conclusions to references to the myth of Sisyphus and its perception in contemporary European literature, when these remarks are irrelevant to the case, but must nevertheless be translated. See Conclusions of AG Colomer in C–461/03 *Gaston Schul Douane-expediteur* [2005] ECR I–10513. For a critical comment see C Herrmann, 'Die Reichweite der gemeinschaftsrechtlichen Vorlagepflicht in der neueren Rechtsprechung des Europäischen Gerichtshofs' (2006) *Europäische Zeitschrift für Wirtschaftsrecht* 231.

[4] See http://wwwiauorg/fileadmin/content/pdfs/Resolution_GA26–5-6.pdf.

[5] It has even found its way into wikipedia, cf www.wikipedia.org.

pillars of the European Union. In doing so, I will attempt to redesign our Greek temple and to abstain from architecturally unacceptable—since statically dangerous—drawings of a 'cross-pillarised' building, in which 'eroding pillars of sculpted sandstone'[6] are 'hijacked'[7] by 'Russian dolls'.[8]

II. THE RELATIONSHIP OF THE EC AND EU LEGAL ORDERS—CONSERVATIVE WISDOM RELOADED

Traditional doctrine does not perceive European law as consisting of one single and unitary legal order. Moreover, the EC and EU Treaties are deemed to form two separate legal orders, a view supplemented by the description of the EU as a temple-like construction. The perception of the European Union as a roof resting on three pillars is grounded in Article 1(3) TEU, which stipulates:

> The Union shall be founded on the European Communities, supplemented by the policies and forms of cooperation established by this Treaty.

The semantic differentiation between the 'European Communities' and the 'policies and forms of cooperation' lays the basis for the dichotomy between supranational EC law and intergovernmental EU law. Upon this—as well as other provisions of the TEU—rests the negation of an organisational character of the European Union—not to speak of legal personality—and its description as a mere permanent intergovernmental conference (Regierungskonferenz), or conference of governments. Consequently, acts adopted under the second or third pillar are described as agreements between the Member States, ie as traditional public international treaty law and not as secondary law of an international organisation. The key argument put forward is that the EU is not equipped with international legal personality, since the TEU lacks an explicit proviso to that end, and contains no provisions from which one could derive legal personality under the implied powers doctrine.

---

[6] See B de Witte, 'The Pillar Structure and the Nature of the European Union: Greek Temple or French Gothic Cathedral?', in T Heukels, N Blokker and M Brus (eds), *The European Union after Amsterdam—A Legal Analysis* (The Hague, Kluwer Law International, 1998) 51.

[7] See B de Witte, *ibid*; see also D Curtin, 'The Constitutional Structure of the Union: A Europe of Bits and Pieces' (1993) *CML Rev* 17.

[8] See D Curtin and I Dekker, 'The EU as a "Layered" International Organization: Institutional Unity in Disguise', in P Craig and G de Búrca (eds), *The Evolution of EU Law* (Oxford, Oxford University Press, 1999) 83.

This view, which has been most strongly advocated by Pechstein and König,[9] has recently gained new support by the German Bundesverfassungsgericht in its decision of 18 July 2005, which held the German legislation transposing the Council Framework Decision on the European Arrest Warrant[10] (European Arrest Warrant Act[11]) unconstitutional. The second Senate of the Bundesverfassungsgericht reasoned:

> As a form of action of European Union law, the Framework Decision is situated outside the supranational decision-making structure of Community law ... In spite of the advanced state of integration, European Union law is still a partial legal system that is deliberately assigned to public international law. This means that a Framework Decision must be adopted unanimously by the Council, it requires incorporation into national law by the Member States, and incorporation is not enforceable before a court. The European Parliament, autonomous source of legitimisation of European law, is merely consulted during the lawmaking process (see Article 39.1 of the Treaty on European Union), which, in the area of the 'third pillar', meets the requirements of the principle of democracy because the Member States' legislative bodies retain the political power of drafting in the context of implementation, if necessary also by denying implementation.[12]

This position reinforces the view already expressed by the Bundesverfassungsgericht in its Maastricht decision 14 years ago, in which it emphasised the differences between EC law and EU law.[13] This current reasoning is particularly striking, however, because the decision was handed down only one month after the ECJ had extended the principle of consistent interpretation to Framework Decisions in *Maria Pupino*,[14] since there can be no doubt that the duty developed by the ECJ in that case does also apply to constitutional courts of the Member States.[15] However, contrary to the Polish Constitutional Court two months before the Pupino ruling, the Bundesverfassungsgericht made no attempt to interpret the German Basic Law in a way that would have saved the German legislation from nullification, even though this would have been possible even without

---

[9]   M Pechstein and C Koenig, *Die Europäische Union*, 3rd edn (Tübingen, Mohr Siebeck, 2000) 28–78; *cf* also A Haratsch, C Koenig and M Pechstein, *Europarecht*, 5th edn (Tübingen, Mohr Siebeck, 2006) 29–45.

[10]   Council Framework Decision of 13 June 2002 on the European arrest warrant and the surrender procedures between Member States—Statements made by certain Member States on the adoption of the Framework Decision, 2002/584/JHA, [2002] OJ L/190/1.

[11]   Europäisches Haftbefehlsgesetz (2004) *Bundesgesetzblatt* I, 1748.

[12]   BVerfGE 113, 273 (300 *et seq*); English version provided by the Bundesverfassungsgericht available at http://wwwbundesverfassungsgerichtde/en/decisions/rs20050718_2bvr223604enhtml, para 82.

[13]   BVerfGE 89, 155 (195); English translation published in (1994) 31 *CML Rev* 1.

[14]   Case C–105/03 *Maria Pupino* [2005] ECR I–5285.

[15]   *Cf* W Cremer, 'Vorabentscheidungsverfahren nach Art 177 EGV und mitgliedstaatliche Verfassungsgerichtsbarkeit' (1999) *Bayerische Verwaltungsblätter* 266–70.

referring to a principle of consistent interpretation.[16] This reluctance to do so has been widely criticised, not only by Judges Lübbe-Wolff and Gerhardt in their dissenting opinions,[17] but also in academic writings.[18]

However, the Bundesverfassungsgericht did not only disregard the duty of consistent interpretation. It also sent—in the words of Judge Lübbe-Wolff—'dark signals' to the Court of Justice, by debating whether the limited extradition of Germans amounted to an Entstaatlichung (a loss of core elements of statehood) of the Federal Republic of Germany, which would be inadmissible under the German Constitution. Incidentally, it also emphasised the positive effect of the different character of the third pillar:

> Due to the area-specific restriction of the European ban on discrimination on grounds of Member State citizenship, a loss of the core elements of statehood, which would be inadmissible pursuant to the regulations of the Basic Law, cannot be established in this context as concerns the extradition of German citizens to other Member States.
>
> In particular with a view to the principle of subsidiarity (Article 23.1 of the Basic Law), the cooperation that is put into practice in the 'third pillar' of the European Union in the shape of limited mutual recognition, which does not provide for a general harmonisation of the Member States' systems of criminal law, is a way of preserving national identity and statehood in a single European judicial area.

One can read this part of the decision as a warning to the Court of Justice that it should not disregard the differences between the TEC and the TEU, something the Court might have been tempted to do in order to break the then constitutional deadlock and bring about some of the changes envisaged by the Constitutional Treaty through the back door.[19] The decision thus builds upon the claims of a potential unconstitutionality of the TEU if the second and third pillar were interpreted as true competences of the EU. In that case, the transfer of the sovereign rights of the Member States would be so all-embracing, Pechstein and Koenig contend, that the EU could only be described as a State. That would mean dismantling the

[16] On the difference between the two judgments see A Hinarejos Parga (2006) 43 *CML Rev* 583 and D Leczykiewicz (2006) 43 *CML Rev* 1181.

[17] See dissenting opinions of Judge G Lübbe-Wolff (above n 14, paras 155–84) and of Judge M Gerhardt (*ibid*, paras 185–202).

[18] See R Streinz, *Europarecht*, 7th edn (Heidelberg, CF Müller, 2005), para 231; A Hinarejos Parga, above n 16, 586 *et seq*; see also S Mölders, 'European Arrest Warrant is Void—The Decision of the German Federal Constitutional Court of 18 July 2005' (2006) 7 *German Law Journal* 45, with further references to German writings.

[19] On the possibility of an interpretation 'consistent with the Constitutional Treaty' see M Krajewski, 'Die institutionelle Gleichgewicht in den auswärtigen Beziehungen' in C Herrmann, H Krenzler and R Streinz (eds), *Die Außenwirtschaftspolitik der Europäischen Union nach dem Verfassungsvertrag* (Baden-Baden, Nomos, 2006) 63, 82 *et seq*; D Thym, 'Weiche Konstitutionalisierung—Optionen der Umsetzung einzelner Reformschritte des Verfassungsvertrags ohne Vertragsänderung' (2005) *Integration* no 4/2005 307, 311.

statehood of the Member States, an Entstaatlichung which would run contrary to the German constitution as interpreted by the Bundesverfassungsgericht.[20]

The theme of an alleged Enstaatlichung of Germany also lies at the heart of the actions against the ratification of the Constitutional Treaty brought by the German MP Peter Gauweiler.[21] It is noteworthy that one of the Judge Rapporteurs in this case, Judge Broß, in his dissenting opinion in the European Arrest Warrant Act case, had already argued that the European Arrest Warrant Act was in breach of the limits to European integration imposed by Article 23.1 German Basic Law.[22] However, the Bundesverfassungsgericht was obviously deeply divided about the issue. This can be inferred from the announcement made by Judge Broßin late 2006 that he will not work any further on the action against the Constitutional Treaty as long as its future remains uncertain. According to Broß, the Bundesverfassungsgericht thus wanted to abstain from interfering with the constitutional process of the EU, which was increasingly precarious after the failed referenda in France and the Netherlands and a period of reflection that had lapsed without any noticeable result. However, what had appeared as an exercise of a rather unorthodox kind of judicial self-restraint probably found its true reason for being in a substantial disagreement between the two different Judge Rapporteurs who were responsible for the two different types of action that had been brought by Mr Gauweiler.

III. THE 'UNITY THESIS'—CONTENT, FOUNDATION AND ALLEGED CONSEQUENCES

According to many other legal scholars, the European Union constitutes a single legal system, of which the Communities, the CFSP and the CPJC are mere subsystems.[23] Among the multitude of supporting arguments the

---

[20] *Cf* M Pechstein and C Koenig, *Die Europäische Union*, 3rd edn (Tübingen, Mohr Siebeck, 2000) 36 *et seq* and 47 *et seq*. *Cf* also E Denza, 'Lines in the Sand: Between Common Foreign Policy and Single Foreign Policy' in T Tridimas and P Nebbia (eds), *European Union Law for the Twenty-First Century—Rethinking the New Legal Order*, vol 1 (Oxford, Hart Publishing, 2004) 259, 272: 'To introduce into the Treaties uncertainties over primacy in the conduct of foreign affairs and over whether the Member States retain any power of independent action in foreign affairs would call into question the separate nation status of the Member States.'

[21] 2 BvR 839/05. Full text (in German) available at http://wwwpetergauweilerde/pdf/themen/EU-Verf-Klage-27–5.pdf.

[22] See BVerfGE 113, 279, 319 *et seq*.

[23] See eg D Curtin and I Dekker, 'The EU as a 'Layered' International Organization: Institutional Unity in Disguise' in P Craig and G de Búrca (eds), *The Evolution of EU Law* (Oxford, Oxford University Press, 1999) 83–136; S Kadelbach, 'Einheit der Rechtsordnung als Verfassungsprinzip der Europäischen Union?' in A von Bogdandy and C-D Ehlermann (eds), *Konsolidierung und Kohärenz des Primärrechts nach Amsterdam* Europarecht Beiheft 2

usual elements are the 'new stage' clause of Article 1(2) TEU, the objectives of the Union (Article 2 TEU), the single institutional framework (Article 3 TEU), the European Council as an organ of the Union (Article 4 TEU), the consistent references to 'the Union' and 'its Members' in the TEU, the provisions on enhanced cooperation (Article 43 *et seq* TEU) and last but not least on the amendment of the Treaties and accession to the Union as a whole (Article 48, 49 TEU), to name only the most prominent ones. Increasingly, the thesis goes hand in hand with the claim of an international legal personality of the EU, based in particular but not exclusively on Article 24 TEU. However, the different authors adhering to this view do not always concur with regard to the conclusions that might be drawn from the perceived unity. In general, this position seems to have become the 'middle ground' within the discussion.[24]

Some German authors go even further. Von Bogdandy and Nettesheim in particular argue that the various European institutions may be considered institutions of the 'European Union', constituting a single organisation with legal personality, and having absorbed the former three Communities (EC, ECSC, EAEC).[25] In the words of von Bogdandy,

[t]he terms 'Communities' and 'pillars of the European Union' do not demarcate different organizations, but only different capacities with partially specific legal instruments and procedures. All the Treaties and the secondary law form a single legal order.[26]

The centrally claimed legal consequence is that the legal principles that the ECJ developed under the TEC could more or less also be applied to the TEU and secondary instruments adopted thereunder. Primarily, this concerns the supremacy of EU law,[27] but it may also apply to the principles of loyalty, non-discrimination and the direct effect of Community law as well as to the applicability of general principles of law within the second and

(Baden-Baden, Nomos 1998) 51–66; W Schroeder, 'Verfassungsrechtliche Beziehungen zwischen Europäischer Union und Europäischen Gemeinschaften' in A von Bogdandy (ed), *Europäisches Verfassungsrecht* (Berlin, Springer, 2003) 373–414; J Wichard, 'Wer ist Herr im europäischen Haus' (1999) *Europarecht* 170–84; B de Witte, above n 6, 51–67.

[24] See B de Witte, above n 6, 58, who, however, at the time of writing considered the position denying a legal personality of the EU to be the 'middle ground'.

[25] See A von Bogdandy, 'The Legal Case for Unity: The European Union as a Single Organization with a Single Legal System' (1999) 36 *CML Rev* 887; A von Bogdandy, 'Die Europäische Union als einheitlicher Verband' in A von Bogdandy and C-D Ehlermann (eds), above n 23, 165–83; A von Bogdandy and M Nettesheim, 'Die Verschmelzung der Europäischen Gemeinschaften in der Europäischen Union' (1995) *Neue Juristische Wochenschrift* 2324–8; A von Bogdandy and M Nettesheim, 'Die Europäische Union, Ein einheitlicher Verband mit eigener Rechtsordnung' (1996) *Europarecht* 3–26; A von Bogdandy and M Nettesheim, 'Ex pluribus Unum fusion of the European Communities into the European Union' (1996) 2 *European Law Journal* 267–89.

[26] A von Bogdandy, 'The Legal Case for Unity: The European Union as a Single Organization with a Single Legal System' (1999) 36 *CML Rev* 887, 887.

[27] *Ibid*, 889.

third pillar. Furthermore, the 'unity thesis' is considered to be the only legal construction capable of explaining the 'landmark decision' of the ECJ in the Airport Transit Visa case,[28] in which the Court, on the basis of Article 47 TEU, held itself competent to annul a measure under the TEU insofar as this encroached upon the competences vested in the EC,[29] a decision described as a misjudgment (*Fehlurteil*) by Pechstein, the main proponent of a strict separation between EC and EU law.[30]

IV. THE INCREASING CROSS-PILLARISATION OF EU POLICIES

Recent times show a clear trend towards the integration of those policies falling under the TEC and those falling under the TEU.[31] This development is driven by an increasing number of civil operations under the framework of the Common Foreign and Security Policy (CFSP), which might also be considered as a matter of technical cooperation under Article 181a TEC; the ever-broader notion of international security, which especially brings development policies into the realm of 'high' foreign policy[32]; the closely related fight against terrorism including sanctions directed against private individuals instead of third countries; the growing awareness for the security dimension of energy policy; and finally, the artificial division of the Area of Freedom, Security and Justice between the TEC and the third pillar brought about by the Treaty of Amsterdam.

The process of 'cross-pillarisation', which resembles an increased inter-connectivity between different EC external policies,[33] makes the choice of a correct legal basis, consistently treated as a 'constitutional question' by the ECJ,[34] increasingly troublesome. Furthermore, ensuring a 'coherence' (compare Article 3 (2) TEU) of action taken by the EC and the EU requires an increasing number of interdependent measures under both treaties or even measures resting upon complementary legal bases in both treaties.

---

[28] Case C–170/96 *Commission v Council* [1998] ECR I–2763.

[29] A von Bogdandy, above n 26, 888 *et seq*.

[30] Cf M Pechstein (1998) *Juristenzeitung* 1008.

[31] *Cf* M Cremona, 'External Relations of the EU and the Member States: Competence, Mixed Agreements, International Responsibility, and Effects of International Law', *EUI Working Paper* LAW No 2006/22, 9 *et seq*; R Wessel, 'The Inside Looking Out: Consistency and Delimitation in EU External Relations' (2000) 37 *CML Rev* 1135, 1145 *et seq*.

[32] *Cf* A Secure Europe in a better World—European Defence Strategy, 13.12.2003.

[33] On that see C Herrmann, 'Gripping Global Governance—The External Relations of the EU between the Treaty of Nice and the Convention on the Future of Europe' in T Tridimas and P Nebbia (eds), *European Union Law for the Twenty-First Century—Rethinking the New Legal Order*, vol 1 (Oxford, Hart Publishing, 2004) 291–302.

[34] *Opinion 2/00 (Cartagena Protocol)* [2001] ECR I–9713, paras 5 *et seq*.

This causes problems with regard to the common reading of Article 47 TEU, which stipulates that nothing in the TEU 'may affect' the TEC.[35]

V. LEGAL UNITY AND LEGAL DIVERSITY—RECENT APPROACHES OF THE EUROPEAN COURTS

After some 12 years during which the legal problems caused by the 'cross-pillarisation' of EU policies played almost no role before the ECJ, they have arrived there within the last few years en masse. Many of the issues brought before the Court concern the choice of legal basis. However, together with this, the effect of EU legal instruments has also been raised, as has the question of fundamental rights protection in the domain of the second and third pillar.

A. Delimitation of Competences—Airport Transit Visa, Criminal Sanctions and Passenger Name Records

It was in the Airport Transit Visa case[36] that the ECJ first came across the problem of the delimitation of the EC Treaty and the EU Treaty. The case concerned a joint action regarding airport transit visas, which the Council had adopted on the basis of the third pillar, *in concreto* K3 (now Article 31) TEU. The measure aimed at the harmonisation of the Member States' policies regarding the requirement of airport transit visa. The Commission brought an action for annulment pursuant to then Article 173 (now Article 230) TEC, claiming that the joint action was in breach of then Article 100c TEC (rescinded), which would have been the correct legal basis for the measure. The United Kingdom submitted that the action was inadmissible, because the act had been adopted under the third pillar and the Court had no jurisdiction over third pillar measures under then Article L TEU. AG Fenelly in his conclusions had pointed to a number of prior cases in which the Court had opted for a 'functional approach' in the sense that the pure formal branding of an act designed to have legal effects would not be decisive for its classification.[37] The ECJ, applying a much shorter reasoning and referring to then Article M (now Article 47) TEU, held that it was

---

[35] On coherence cf Communication from the Commission to the European Council of June 2006—Europe in the World—Some Practical Proposals for Greater Coherence, Effectiveness and Visibility, COM (2006) 278, 6 *et seq.*

[36] Case C–170/96 *Commission v Council* [1998] ECR I–2763.

[37] Conclusions of AG Fenelly, C–170/96 *Commission v Council* [1998] ECR I–2763, para 7 *et seq.*

the task of the Court to ensure that acts which, according to the Council, fall within the scope of Article K.3(2) of the [TEU] do not encroach upon the powers conferred by the EC Treaty on the Community.[38]

The same matter came before the Court again in 2003, in a case concerning criminal sanctions for the protection of the environment.[39] Following an initiative of the Danish Government, the Council had adopted a Framework Decision on the basis of Articles 29, 31(1)(e) and 34(2)(b) TEU, requiring the Member States in its core provision 'to ensure that serious environmental crime is punishable under criminal law'. At the same time, the Council rejected a similar proposal for a Directive on the basis of Article 175 TEC, which the Commission had presented one year after the Danish Government. The Commission then brought an action under Article 35 TEU, asking for an annulment of the Framework Decision as it was in breach of a Community competence.[40]

Whereas in the Airport Transit Visa case, the Commission had lost on the merits, since the measure in question could not have been adopted on the basis of the TEC, this time the ECJ found that the EC indeed had a competence to impose an obligation on the Member States to provide for criminal sanctions for specific crimes against the environment. As predicted earlier,[41] the ECJ, quoting its ruling in the Airport Transit Visa case, followed a 'reasoning'[42] of 'what could that should' and declared the Framework Decision void under Article 35 TEU for encroaching upon the powers of the EC,[43] despite the fact that the competence under Article 175 TEC only was concurrent and not exclusive.

However, problems do not only occur when the Council decides to act under the second or third pillar instead of the Community pillar. On the contrary, a similar conflict can arise where action is taken on the basis of the TEC, where the EC has no competence to do so. An example of this is the Passenger Name Record case decided 30 May 2006.[44] Within the framework of the fight against terrorism, the United States passed some legislation providing that airlines operating flights to, from, or across the United States' territory had to provide the US customs authorities with electronic access to the data contained in their reservation and departure

---

[38] Case C–170/96 *Commission v Council* [1998] ECR–I 2763, para 16.

[39] Case C–176/03 *Commission v Council* [2005] ECR I–7879.

[40] See H Weiß, 'EC Competence for Environmental Criminal Law—An Analysis of the Judgment of the ECJ of 13.9.2005 in Case C–176/93, Commission v Council' (2006) *Zeitschrift für europarechtliche Studien* 381, 385 *et seq*.

[41] See eg P Eeckhout, *External Relations of the European Union* (Oxford, Oxford University Press, 2004) 150.

[42] Neither the AG nor the ECJ made any effort to argue the question what 'affects' in Art 47 TEU actually means in any detail.

[43] Case C–176/03 *Commission v Council* [2005] ECR I–7879, paras 38–55.

[44] Joined Cases C–317/04 and C–318/04 *Parliament v Council* [2006] ECR I–4721.

control systems, the so-called passenger name records. Since the provision of these data is problematic under European data protection regulations, an agreement was finally concluded between the EC and the United States on the basis of Articles 25 and 26 of Directive 95/46/EC.[45] The Directive itself was based on Article 95 TEC.[46] It explicitly excluded the processing of data

> ... in the course of an activity falling outside the scope of Community law, such as those provided for by Titles V and VI of the Treaty on European Union and in any case to processing operations concerning public security, defence, State security ... and the activities of the State in areas of criminal law.[47]

Since the purposes for which the US customs authorities required the passing on of the data were clearly related to State security, the ECJ annulled the decision to conclude the agreement, holding that it did not fall under the scope of the Directive. The EU subsequently concluded a new agreement on the basis of Articles 38 and 24 TEU.[48] However, given the clear wording of the Directive, the importance of the judgment for the determination of the relationship between the TEU and the TEC should not be overestimated. One could easily think of a similar exclusion of data processing with regard to policies inside the TEC, eg environmental policies.

B. Interconnecting Treaty Objectives—*Yusuf* and *Kadi*

Of much greater importance is the judgment delivered by the Court of First Instance in the cases of *Yusuf* and *Kadi*.[49] The cases concerned the freezing of assets within the framework of the fight against terrorism. In order to implement UN Security Council regulations on the matter, the EU and EC had adopted a number of legal instruments, among them EC Regulations based upon Articles 60, 301 and 308 TEC. One of the issues before the CFI was whether Article 308 TEC could have served as the sole legal basis for sanctions directed against private individuals who were not related to the rulers of any third country. For the use of Article 308 TEC, however,

---

[45] Decision 2004/496/EC, [2004] OJ L/183/83.

[46] For an account of the factual and legal background of the case see conclusions of AG Léger in Joined Cases C–317/04 and C–318/04 *Parliament v Council* [2006] ECR I–4721, paras 1–42.

[47] Art 3(2), first indent.

[48] See Council Decision 2006/729/CFSP/JHA of 16 October 2006 on the signing, on behalf of the European Union, of an Agreement between the European Union and the United States of America on the processing and transfer of passenger name record (PNR) data by air carriers to the United States Department of Homeland Security, [2006] OJ L/298/27.

[49] Case T–306/01 *Yusuf and Al Barakaat International Foundation v Council and Commission* [2006] ECR II–3533 and Case T–315/01 *Kadi v Council and Commission* [2006] ECR II–3649.

the measure in question must be adopted with a view to attaining one of the aims of the Community. In this respect, the Commission had claimed that one of the general objectives of the Community was to ensure international peace and security. The CFI rejected this line of reasoning, emphasising the coexistence of Community and Union law:

> Contrary to what the Commission maintains, indeed, nowhere in the preamble to the EC Treaty is it stated that that act pursues a wider object of safeguarding international peace and security. Although it is unarguably a principal aim of that treaty to put an end to the conflicts of the past between the peoples of Europe by creating 'an ever closer union' among them, that is without any reference whatsoever to the implementation of a common foreign and security policy. The latter falls exclusively within the objects of the Treaty on European Union which, as emphasised in the preamble thereto, seeks to mark a new stage in the process of European integration undertaken with the establishment of the European Communities.

> While, admittedly, it may be asserted that that objective of the Union must inspire action by the Community in the sphere of its own competence, such as the common commercial policy, it is not however a sufficient basis for the adoption of measures under Article 308 EC, above all in spheres in which Community competence is marginal and exhaustively defined in the Treaty.

> Last, it appears impossible to interpret Article 308 EC as giving the institutions general authority to use that provision as a basis with a view to attaining one of the objectives of the Treaty on European Union. In particular, the Court considers that the coexistence of Union and Community as integrated but separate legal orders, and the constitutional architecture of the pillars, as intended by the framers of the Treaties now in force, authorise neither the institutions nor the Member States to rely on the 'flexibility clause' of Article 308 EC in order to mitigate the fact that the Community lacks the competence necessary for achievement of one of the Union's objectives. To decide otherwise would amount, in the end, to making that provision applicable to all measures falling within the CFSP and police and judicial cooperation in criminal matters (PJC), so that the Community could always take action to attain the objectives of those policies. Such an outcome would deprive many provisions of the Treaty on European Union of their ambit and would be inconsistent with the introduction of instruments specific to the CFSP (common strategies, joint actions, common positions) and to the PJC (common positions, decisions, framework decisions).[50]

Despite finding that the TEU and the TEC constituted two 'integrated but separated legal orders', the CFI continued, interpreting the special provisions of Articles 60 and 301 TEC, which bridge the divide between the TEU and the TEC:

---

[50] Case T–306/01 *Yusuf and Al Barakaat International Foundation v Council and Commission* [2006] ECR II–3533, paras 154–6.

In the circumstances, account has to be taken of the bridge explicitly established at the time of the Maastricht revision between Community actions imposing economic sanctions under Articles 60 EC and 301 EC and the objectives of the Treaty on European Union in the sphere of external relations.

It must be held that Articles 60 EC and 301 EC are quite special provisions of the EC Treaty, in that they expressly contemplate situations in which action by the Community may be proved to be necessary in order to achieve, not one of the objects of the Community as fixed by the EC Treaty but rather one of the objectives specifically assigned to the Union by Article 2 of the Treaty on European Union, viz., the implementation of a common foreign and security policy.

Under Articles 60 EC and 301 EC, action by the Community is therefore in actual fact action by the Union, the implementation of which finds its footing on the Community pillar after the Council has adopted a common position or a joint action under the CFSP.[51]

On the basis of this reasoning, and referring also to the single institutional framework and the obligation of consistency laid upon the institutions by Article 3 TEU, the CFI held the use of Articles 60, 301 and 308 TEC as a combined legal basis for the contested Regulation to be legitimate. The reference to Article 3 TEU is particularly interesting, since Article 46 TEU does not grant the Court of Justice jurisdiction over this provision, and therefore jurisdiction is also denied to the CFI. The ECJ had hence refused to interpret then Article B (now Article 2 TEU) as being clearly outside its jurisdiction.[52]

C. EC Law Principles Applied to EU Law—*Maria Pupino*

In another recent case, the ECJ was confronted with the question whether the principle of consistent interpretation also applied to Framework Decisions enacted under the third pillar. An Italian court had referred a question under Article 35(3)(b) TEU concerning the interpretation of Framework Decision 2001/220/JHA on the standing of victims in criminal proceedings. France and Italy had questioned the admissibility of the request for a preliminary ruling, arguing that the answer could have no relevance for the case to be decided by the Italian court. The main arguments put forward were that Framework Decisions had no direct

---

[51] *Ibid*, paras 159–61. See also Case T–228/02 *Organisation des Modjahedines du peuple d'Iran*, judgment of 12 December 2006, paras 105 *et seq*, where the CFI held that the powers of the EC under Art 301 and 60 TEC did not constitute 'powers circumscribed by the will of the Union', ie that the EC has discretion whether or not to take the measures foreseen in the CFSP instrument.

[52] Case C–167/94 *Grau Gomis*, [1995] ECR I–1023, para 6.

effect, and that because of the difference between Directives and Framework Decisions, a principle of consistent interpretation could not exist with regard to Framework Decisions, or if it existed, it could not oblige a national court to construe national legislation *contra legem*. The UK and Sweden also emphasised the intergovernmental nature of the cooperation between Member States in the context of Title VI of the TEU.[53]

The ECJ, following the conclusions of AG Kokott in principle, decided to the contrary. In the view of the Court, the wording of Article 34(2)(b) TEU is closely inspired by Article 249(3) TEC. The Court went on:

> Irrespective of the degree of integration envisaged by the Treaty of Amsterdam in the process of creating an ever closer union among the peoples of Europe within the meaning of the second paragraph of Article 1 EU, it is perfectly comprehensible that the authors of the Treaty on European Union should have considered it useful to make provision, in the context of Title VI of that treaty, for recourse to legal instruments with effects similar to those provided for by the EC Treaty, in order to contribute effectively to the pursuit of the Union's objectives.[54]

The ECJ then emphasised the importance of its jurisdiction under Article 35 TEU, which would be deprived of most of its useful effects if individuals were not entitled to invoke Framework Decisions in order to obtain a consistent interpretation of national law. Furthermore, the Court rejected the argument that the duty of loyalty did not exist with regard to the TEU because of the lack of a provision similar to Article 10 TEC, and that hence the principle of consistent interpretation could not be 'extended' to the third pillar. Moreover, the Court found that:

> [i]t would be difficult for the Union to carry out its task effectively if the principle of loyal cooperation, ..., were not also binding in the area of police and judicial cooperation in criminal matters ....[55]

However, even adopting the conclusion drawn by AG Kokott that the principle of loyalty also applied with regard to EU law, the Court abstained from a more detailed analysis of its fundamental character. This contrasts with the conclusions of the Advocate General, who had explicitly distinguished the TEU from the EEA Treaty, by stating:

> Unlike the EEA Agreement, which is concerned only with the application of rules on free trade and competition in economic and commercial relations between the Contracting Parties, but provides for no transfer of sovereign rights to the inter-governmental institutions which it sets up, the Treaty on European Union, as stated in the second paragraph of Article 1, marks a new stage in the process of creating an ever closer union among the peoples of Europe. To that end it supplements the activities of the Community with new policies and forms of

---

53 Case C–105/03 *Maria Pupino* [2005] ECR I–5285, para 26.
54 Case C–105/03 *Maria Pupino* [2005] ECR I–5285, para 36.
55 Case C–105/03 *Maria Pupino* [2005] ECR I–5285, para 42.

cooperation. The term policies indicates that, contrary to the view of the Swedish Government, the Treaty on European Union includes not only inter-governmental cooperation, but also joint exercise of sovereignty by the Union. Moreover, the first paragraph of Article 3 EU obliges the Union to respect and build upon the acquis communautaire.

The increasing degree of integration expressed in the phrase 'ever closer cooperation' is also shown by the development of the Treaty on European Union which, after its creation by the Treaty of Maastricht, was brought ever more closely into line with the structures of Community law by the Treaties of Amsterdam and Nice and is to be merged fully with Community law by the Constitutional Treaty.[56]

The explicit disregarding of the legal nature of the TEU demonstrated by the ECJ ('irrespective of the degree of integration') is, on the one hand, regrettable. On the other, the view taken by the ECJ is fully in line with its general approach towards the interpretation of international agreements and the exploration of their character, eg with a view to a possible direct effect, including the interpretation of the TEC in *Van Gend en Loos*.[57]

As we have seen, the European Courts are increasingly frequently confronted with questions related to the character of the second and third pillar of the TEU as well as with questions regarding their relationship with the first pillar, Community law. However, the cases decided so far do not reveal any clear theoretical underpinning with regard to the nature of and relations between the different pillars of European law.

VI. THE 'UNITY THESIS' REVISITED—DOES IT MAKE ANY DIFFERENCE?

A. Theoretical Foundations

Having emphasised the importance of definitions at the outset of this paper, we must now clarify the meaning of 'legal order' and its 'unity'. The term 'legal order' (*Rechtsordnung*) usually refers to a given set of norms that belong together, eg because they are applicable in a given territory as law of the land or to certain subjects of law. The term implies that there are 'ins' and 'outs', ie some legal norms that belong to the legal order and some others that do not. At the same time, the notion 'order' refers to a certain degree of structure, arrangement or system. The idea of 'unity'

---

[56] Conclusions of AG Kokott in Case C–105/03 *Maria Pupino* [2005] ECR I–5285, paras 32–3.

[57] Case 26/62 *Van Gend en Loos* [1963] ECR I–3, paras 8 *et seq.*

appears with regard to both the question of belonging as well as the question of the internal structure of the legal order. However, the meaning in either case is not quite the same.

The notion 'unity of the legal order' has been used in manifold senses in legal theory.[58] Two different meanings deserve attention but must also be distinguished in the present context.[59] First, the concept of unity is closely related to Hans Kelsen's Pure Theory of Law (*Reine Rechtslehre*).[60] According to this theory, every legal order is based on a basic norm (*Grundnorm*), which constitutes the highest norm in a hierarchically structured pyramid of norms (*Stufenbau der Rechtsordnung*).[61] All norms that form part of the legal order formally derive their validity from the basic norm, since they were generated in accordance with the rules adopted on the basis of the *Grundnorm*. In this formalistic sense, the basic norm serves to identify the belonging of a multiplicity of norms to a unitary legal order. Second, the 'unity of the legal order' constitutes a claim of substantive, normative unity, ie the absence of lacunae and contradictions within an identified legal system. This claim is considered as contributing to the peacemaking and integrating function of the legal order, traditionally associated with the State and the constitution if one confines this notion to documents that not only limit existing power, but also constitute and regulate all the exercising of sovereign power.[62] In this sense, the idea of unity is based on the assumption of a theoretical single will of the sovereign, this even being the people or the nation, which is free of contradictions, or to put it differently: which is coherent or consistent.[63]

---

[58] M Baldus, *Die Einheit der Rechtsordnung Bedeutung einer juristischen Formel in Rechtstheorie, Zivil- und Staatsrechtswissenschaft des 19 und 20 Jahrhunderts* (Frankfurt am Main, Duncker & Humblot, 1995). For a current overview of the different usages in the context of European law *cf* J Bast and P Dann, 'European Ungleichzeitigkeit: Introductory Remarks on a Binational Discussion about Unity in the European Union' in P Dann and M Rynkowski (eds), *The Unity of the European Constitution* (Berlin, Springer, 2006) 1–9.

[59] For a similar differentiation cf S Kadelbach, 'Einheit der Rechtsordnung als Verfassungsprinzip der Europäischen Union?' in A von Bogdandy/C-D Ehlermann (eds), above n 23, 52 *et seq*.

[60] H Kelsen, *Reine Rechtslehre*, 2nd edn (Vienna, Verlag Franz Deuticke, 1960).

[61] *Ibid*, 228 *et seq*.

[62] Cf N Krisch, 'Die Vielheit der europäischen Verfassung' in Y Becker *et al* (eds), *Die Europäische Verfassung—Verfassungen in Europa*, 45 Assistententagung Öffentliches Recht (Baden-Baden, Nomos, 2005) 61–89.

[63] The difference between the wording of Arts 1(3) and 3(1) and (2) TEU in the English language and in other languages has been pointed out elsewhere (see C Tietje, 'The Concept of Coherence in the Treaty on European Union and the Common Foreign and Security Policy' (1997) 2 *European Foreign Affairs Review* 211 *et seq*. On the concept of coherence in the framework of European law see in greater detail S Bartea, 'Looking for Coherence within the European Community' (2005) 11 *European Law Journal* 154 *et seq*; P Gauttier, 'Horizontal Coherence and the External Competences of the European Union' (2004) 10 *European Law Journal* 23, 24 *et seq*; see also S Besson, 'From European Integration to European Integrity: Should European Law Speak with Just One Voice' (2004) 10 *European Law Journal* 257–81, who uses Dworkin's concept of integrity instead of coherence.

Given this, it is worthwhile considering using uniformity (*Einheitlichkeit*) instead of unity (*Einheit*) when claiming the internal coherence of a legal order. As a postulate, unity is a powerful tool in the construction of legal rules within a legal system, eg in order to avoid or solve conflicts. However, it is a theoretical construction and cannot answer every interpretative question; nor must it be used to overcome differing regulatory ideals embodied in different legal subsystems of the same legal order. Whether and to what extent a legal order envisages unity or preserves diversity is a question of interpretation in its own right. One may criticise legal systems for their low degree of uniformity and may argue that this puts their legitimacy at risk. However, there is no legal rule that requires a *pouvoir constituant* to create uniformity and avert diversity.[64] Furthermore, to claim the substantive unity of a legal order, one must first prove the connectedness of the respective norms first. There is no point in arguing that two norms that belong to different legal systems must be interpreted in conformity on the ground of unity. On the other hand, the diversity of legal rules is not a decisive sign that two norms do not belong to the same legal order.

The two different meanings of 'unity' laid out above, despite their differences, are closely related. As already pointed out, 'unity' in the sense of the peaceful resolution of conflicts is served by a legal order providing complete and coherent answers. The available legal rules will most probably be more coherent where they can be traced back to a single source of legitimacy. Lastly, this will be the easiest case, where a theoretical *Grundnorm* is mirrored by a Constitutional or Supreme Court as the ultimate arbiter of legal conflicts.

It is not always crystal clear in what sense the notion 'unity' is used by different authors with regard to the EU legal order. Sometimes the different layers of analysis appear to be admixed. This picture becomes even more complicated when sociological or political science arguments are added to the analysis. The behaviour of the different actors may very well serve as an indication of their specific understanding of the legal framework. However, the normative quality of such behaviour is highly questionable outside the accepted categories of 'subsequent practice' or 'customary law',[65] the relevance of both of which concepts is rather unsettled in European law. The overwhelming practice of the 'single institutional framework' seems to make a clear-cut case for speaking of the EU as a

---

[64] *Cf* S Kadelbach, 'Einheit der Rechtsordnung als Verfassungsprinzip der Europäischen Union?' in A von Bogdandy/C-D Ehlermann (eds), above n 23, 55, who argues that the *pouvoir constituant* must not rebut the assumption of the reasonableness of the constitution by over-fragmentation.

[65] See O Dörr, 'Noch einmal: Die Europäische Union und die Europäischen Gemeinschaften' (1995) *Neue Juristische Wochenschrift* 3161, 3163 *et seq*; M Pechstein and C Koenig, *Die Europäische Union*, 3rd edn (Tübingen, Mohr Siebeck, 2000) 31.

single organisation or a single actor from a social science perspective. However, in a *Rechtsgemeinschaft* (Community built on the rule of law), which the EC at least constitutes,[66] we should be extremely careful about arguing on the basis of mere practice that does not have any normative foundation. I will hence deliberately confine myself in the following to developing a legal—some would say legalistic—argument. Only by doing this, I believe, can we derive methodologically correct answers to legal questions, ie to questions of interpretation and application of the law to a given or hypothetical case. In the following, then, I will turn to the most important questions connected with the theme of the 'unity of the legal order', in order to test its validity, necessity and utility.

B. The Common Source of the European Union Legal Order

The aim of this Chapter is not to contribute to the complex theoretical debate about the *Grundnorm* or the ultimate point of recognition of European law, its replacement or shifting, or who would ultimately decide in case of a constitutional crisis.[67] Many of these questions remain indeed unsolved. However, to answer the question whether the EU is a single legal order or simply a franchiser who organises the 'corporate identity' of EC law and the second and third pillar legal systems, it is necessary to find the ultimate legal source inside the legal system of the EU. The question of unity from this perspective would thus be, whether all EU law, enacted under any of the pillars, derives its validity from the same legal norm. In order to answer this, we must treat all acts of the institutions, be these Regulations, Directives, Joint Actions, Common Positions or anything else, like threads poking out of a confused ball of wool. If we unroll the ball and follow all ends, will we find that all the threads are tied together into a knot in the middle?

Under the Treaties, it is clear that all secondary and tertiary instruments derive their legitimacy from being enacted on the basis of and according to the procedures laid down by the respective Treaty, but what about the TEC and Titles V and VI of the TEU? Do they stem from the same source? At first glance, it seems obvious that the existence of two different Treaties means that they do not share their source of legitimacy, but rest on separate acts of the constituent power of the Member States. However, such a description would have to leave out the fact that the different Treaties are firmly tied together, especially by Articles 48 and 49 TEU:

---

[66] See recently ECJ, judgment of 6 October 2006 in Case C–232/05, *Commission v France*, para 57.

[67] For an account of the different positions see M Schroeder, *Das Gemeinschaftsrechtssystem* (Tübingen, Mohr Siebeck, 2002) 223–55, who argues that the validity of Community law cannot be explained by the Pure Theory of Law.

neither amendment nor accession can take place with respect to only the TEC or the TEU.[68] Of course, during the IGC it may be decided to amend only provisions of Title V or VI of the TEU, but this would include a deliberate decision not to change the TEC or vice versa. The ultimate rule of recognition within the legal system of the EU is, consequently, the collective will of the Member States, as 'Masters of the Treaty'.[69] How they establish the legality of their respective ratifications is, however, not a matter of EU law, despite the requirements vis-a-vis the internal constitutional order that can be derived from Articles 6, 7 and 49 TEU. However, this does not mean that the EU derives its legitimacy directly from the peoples of the Union, as sometimes purported in academic writings.[70] The peoples of Europe are only a formal source of legitimacy, as they have a say in the respective ratifications of their countries. So, we can trace back the whole body of EC and EU law to a single source, the collective will of the Member States, which means that in a formalistic sense EC and EU law belong to the same legal order, even though the linkage is one on the highest possible level of the legal order: the ultimate source of the legal order as such.

C. The Question of Legal Personality

An analysis of the unity of the EU's legal order cannot completely avoid the question of the EU's legal personality. However, I do not intend to add any substantive argument to a discussion which I consider—in this case rightly on the basis of international practice—a fait accompli.[71] Even a naïve reading of the post-Amsterdam TEU, speaking of 'the Union', 'its identity' and 'its Members' makes one wonder how one could ever have questioned the existence of an entity independent of its Members. That such an entity, insofar as it is capable of acting independently also in relation to third

---

[68] For the importance of that argument see also B de Witte, above n 6, 59; D Curtin and I Dekker, 'The Constitutional Structure of the European Union: Some Reflections on Vertical Unity-in-Diversity' in P Beaumont, C Lyonis and N Walker (eds), *Convergence and Divergence in European Public Law* (Oxford, Hart Publishing, 2002) 59, 63 *et seq*.

[69] See BVerfGE 89, 155, 190: 'Herren der Verträge'. English translation published (1994) *CML Rev* 1.

[70] A von Bogdandy, 'The Legal Case for Unity: The European Union as a Single Organization with a Single Legal System' (1999) 36 *CML Rev* 887, 900.

[71] For a detailed discussion of the issue of international legal personality of the EU see P Eeckhout, *External Relations of the European Union* (Oxford, Oxford University Press, 2004) 154 *et seq*; M Schroeder, 'Verfassungsrechtliche Beziehungen zwischen Europäischer Union und Europäischen Gemeinschaften' in A von Bogdandy (ed), *Europäisches Verfassungsrecht* (Berlin, Springer, 2003) 373, 386 *et seq*; R Wessel, 'Revisiting the International Legal Status of the EU' (2000) 5 *European Foreign Affairs Review* 507–37. The opposite view is most strongly presented by M Pechstein, 'Rechtssubjektivität für die Europäische Union?' (1996) *Europarecht* 137–44.

countries, or could at least be perceived as doing so, would be attributed
international legal personality from the perspective of public international
law, seems equally obvious and follows a fundamental necessity of law,
which requires the attribution of rights and duties to those who actually
appear to act.[72] On the other hand, the wording of the Treaties is so clear
in its distinction between the EC and the EU that the artificial claim of a
single legal person EU into which the EC and the European Atomic Energy
Community (EAEC) have been merged, should be renounced. The current
treaty-making practice of the EC and the EU confirms the distinction
between the two.

Furthermore, the question of the legal personality of the EU is relatively
unimportant for the assessment of the unity of the legal order. Whether or
not a political entity as a whole enjoys legal personality within its own
legal system or whether it always acts through organs which are equipped
with separate legal personality is an issue of the construction of that legal
order, but does not answer the question whether the legal order presents
itself as a formal and substantive unity.[73]

D. Conflicts of Norms in the European Union Legal Order

One of the central features of a legal order is its capacity to solve the
conflicts that arise from contradictions between different rules of the
system. The commonly applied interpretative principles such as interpretation in conformity with higher-ranking norms, *lex specialis derogat legi
generali*, and *lex posterior derogat legi priori* serve this purpose. Where
conflicts cannot be solved by applying these principles, one of the norms
must be disregarded. If a hierarchy between the rules can be established,
this will normally be the inferior norm. The same principles can also apply
to whole legal subsystems, eg different legal regimes for different policy

---

[72]   See R Wessel, 'The Inside Looking Out: Consistency and Delimitation in EU External
Relations' (2000) 37 *CML Rev* 1135, 1138 *et seq*. A similar development has taken place in
German company law, where the *Bundesgerichtshof* held the *Gesellschaft bürgerlichen Rechts
(GbR)* to be *rechtsfähig* (having legal capacity) after more than a hundred years during which
legal doctrine thought of the GbR as being just a framework for the joint rights of its
partners, which meant, eg, that you had to sue all the partners, etc. This form of association
is widespread among the free professions in Germany; see BGH (2001) *Neue Juristische
Wochenschrift* 1056.

[73]   For a more detailed discussion of this issue see A von Bogdandy, 'The Legal Case for
Unity: The European Union as a Single Organization with a Single Legal System' (1999) 36
CML Rev 887, 891 *et seq*; A von Bogdandy and M Nettesheim, 'Die Europäische Union, Ein
einheitlicher Verband mit eigener Rechtsordnung', (1996) *Europarecht* 3, 15 *et seq*; M
Schroeder, 'Verfassungsrechtliche Beziehungen zwischen Europäischer Union und
Europäischen Gemeinschaften' in A von Bogdandy (ed), *Europäisches Verfassungsrecht*
(Berlin, Springer, 2003) 373, 382 *et seq*; cf also B de Witte, above n 6, 61 *et seq*, who also
points to the difference between equipping an international organization with legal personality vis-a-vis third countries and its Member States.

areas with different goals, or within federal legal systems between the federal and the state level. Where no explicit rules provide for the resolution of conflicts, they must be established by interpretation. This is more likely to happen where a single superior court has the ultimate jurisdiction to rule on these matters.[74]

Applying this very basic methodology to the relationship between the TEU and the TEC, we can easily see that no general hierarchy between the pillars or the Treaties can be established.[75] Neither of the Treaties derives its validity from the other, since both rest upon the collective will of the Member States. However, there are several 'bridges' between the two Treaties, which establish specific validity relationships between the two components, eg Article 301 TEC, but the existence of these bridges does not mean that they constitute two separate legal orders, nor that they form two parts of just one order. Similarly, the existence of provisions governing the effect of rules of public international law within the German legal order is interpreted as supporting monist as well as dualist thinking. To which reading one adheres depends upon whether one considers the respective rules as being constitutive (supporting a dualist view) or declaratory (supporting a monist view).[76] Many of the possible conflicts between the TEC and the second and third pillar are sufficiently solved by the explicit provisions.

The absence of a general hierarchy in the sense of a validity relationship between the two main Treaties[77] does not necessarily mean that they do not belong to the same legal order. As pointed out above, they are firmly linked together by the final provisions of the TEU. The claim of unity is, however, not appropriate to solve horizontal conflicts. Indeed, for the application of the two most important principles, *lex specialis* and *lex posterior*, it is not even necessary to consider the two systems as a 'unity'. This is because even if it is assumed that both Treaties constitute two completely separate legal orders, they still would have a mutual interpretative influence if one applied the customary rules of interpretation of public international law as laid down in the Vienna Convention on the Law of Treaties, in particular in Article 31(2)(a) and (3)(c) thereof. According to these provisions, any norm of public international law applicable between

---

[74] Cf also S Kadelbach, 'Einheit der Rechtsordnung als Verfassungsprinzip der Europäischen Union' in A von Bogdandy and C-D Ehlermann (eds), above n 23, 54; R Wessel, 'The Inside Looking Out: Consistency and Delimitation in EU External Relations' (2000) 37 *CML Rev* 1135, 1137 *et seq*.

[75] See M Pechstein and C Koenig, *Die Europäische Union*, 3rd edn (Tübingen, Mohr Siebeck, 2000) 57 *et seq*.

[76] Cf M Schweitzer, *Staatsrecht III*, 8th edn (Heidelberg, CF Müller, 2004) 15 *et seq*.

[77] Art 47 TEU, to which we will turn below, does not—in my submission—establish a supremacy of the TEC over the TEU (nor the other way around), but only a safeguard mechanism that operates very similarly to a *lex specialis* rule of interpretation.

the parties has to be taken into account for the interpretation of a Treaty. Under the *lex posterior derogat legi priori* principle, which is also to be found in Article 30(2) of the Vienna Convention, the TEU could even have partially derogated the TEC without any formal connection being established between the two Treaties, simply because the parties to the Treaties are identical. To prevent this *lex posterior* effect was one of the key functions of Article 47 TEU, to which we will now turn.

E. Demarcation of Competences between the Pillars: Article 47 TEU

One of the most important conflicts between the pillars is the possible overlap between the different legal bases that can be used for the pursuance of the objectives of the EU and the EC. The necessary demarcation between the two is governed by Article 47 TEU. As pointed out above, this provision is not the only one that is relevant for the determination of the relationship between the TEC and the second and third pillar of the TEU, nor is the delimitation of competences its only area of application. However, it is one of the key provisions and its reading has a significant impact on the construction of the EU's legal order.

In *Environmental Criminal Sanctions*, the ECJ found that the Council was in breach of Article 47 TEU when it enacted a Framework Decision under the third pillar, since the EC had a competence to act under Article 175 TEC. At first glance, this seems odd, given that the EC competence under the environmental policy is not an exclusive one, ie the Member States could still act independently in the field of the environment. However, the Court had already taken the same position in Airport Transit Visa and it was predictable that—assuming a Criminal Sanctions Competence of the EC—it would arrive at the conclusion that the Framework Decision was in breach of Article 47 TEU. Arguably, the remaining concurrent competence of the Member States included the joint intergovernmental exercise under the third pillar and did not 'affect' the TEC.[78] If, on the other hand, action under the second or third pillars is considered as an action by the European Union as an organisation in its own right, acting through one of its organs, there is no such thing as an intergovernmental exercise of Member State competence. The competences under the TEU would then be (non-exclusive) competences of the EU. Alternatively could the Member States have subsequently transferred part of the competence they had retained when entering into the TEC, to the EU, creating a parallel competence of the EC and EU?

[78] P Eeckhout, *External Relations of the European Union* (Oxford, Oxford University Press, 2004) 150.

Two arguments seem possible to support the approach of the ECJ. First, one could argue that the power the Member States retained was categorically non-transferable. However, to make this argument, one would need to distinguish between transferable and non-transferable competences and it is difficult to see the basis for such distinction. However, on the basis of Article 47 TEU, it can be put forward that the Member States, when entering into the Treaties of Maastricht, Amsterdam and Nice, waived by virtue of Article 47 TEU their right to transfer competences to the EU which they had—even non-exclusively—already transferred to the EC, because the creation of 'parallel competences' of the EC and the EU would indeed 'affect' the TEC. The reason for this is that the institutional setup of the second and third pillar deviates significantly from the setup under the TEC. This institutional balance would thus indeed be affected; especially the right of initiative of the Commission and the rights of the European Parliament under Article 251 TEC, if the second and third pillar had established competences parallel to those already existing, since they would have created a way to circumvent the rules governing the exercise of the competence under the TEC. This reading of Article 47 TEU is supported by Article 1(3) TEU, which states:

> The Union shall be founded on the European Communities, *supplemented* by the policies and forms of cooperation established by this Treaty (emphasis added).

The word 'supplemented' refers to something that is added to something else in order to complete the latter. This suggests a subordination of the second and third pillar, because, wherever the TEC already provided for legal rules, it was not incomplete and so did not need to be supplemented.[79] This interpretation is also in line with Article 11(1) TEU despite the broadly worded catch-all description of the CFSP to be found therein, since the broad scope is still very useful as to whether or not a specific issue falls into the scope of the CFSP when it comes to vertical conflicts with the Member States. Furthermore, the CFSP can be read as a fall-back competence for all cases not yet covered by the TEC. For such a *lex generalis*, it makes perfect sense to be formulated as broadly as possible.[80] Lastly, this reading of Article 47 TEU is supported by Article 30(2) of the Vienna Convention on the Law of Treaties.

The bottom line of the argument is as simple as this: whatever could already be done under the TEC did not need to be, and therefore could not be, assigned to the European Union, the integrationist character of which is

---

[79] See the argument made by R Wessel, 'The Inside Looking Out: Consistency and Delimitation in EU External Relations' (2000) 37 *CML Rev* 1135, 1146 *et seq*.

[80] *Ibid*, 1148 *et seq*, who considers the TEC external competences to constitute *lege speciali* to the *lege generalis* of the CFSP.

much weaker. The effect of Article 47 TEU is thus to render the competences in the second and third pillar subordinate to the competences in the TEC, ie to make their use dependent on the non-existence of competences under the first pillar. This type of subordination is, however, not unheard of inside the TEC itself. Article 308 TEC can only be used as a legal basis if there is no other legal basis in the TEC to be found and if some additional conditions are met.[81]

The perception of the competences under the second and third pillar as subordinate to those under the TEC does not make the demarcation unnecessary. However, the criteria for this exercise, in particular with regard to the demarcation of the CFSP and the first pillar external relations, are not clear. The pending case on Small Arms and Light Weapons[82] may shed light on this question. Given the broadly worded goals of the CFSP as laid down in Article 11(1) TEU, as well as the mix of goals found in the reality of external relations, the 'aims and content' test used by the ECJ to delineate the different legal bases under the TEC[83] is not well suited in that regard. More convincingly, the choice of legal basis should be founded on the different kinds of instruments that are available to the EU and the EC for the conduct of their external relations, once it has been established that the measure has a foreign policy goal in a broad sense. It is obvious that there are wide differences between the catalogue of acts of the organs found in Article 249 TEC and in Article 12 TEU. Furthermore, the descriptions of Joint Actions and Common Positions under the second pillar are very specifically directed at typical foreign policy measures. According to Article 14 TEU, 'Joint actions shall address *specific situations* where *operational action* by the Union is deemed to be required' (emphasis added). Similarly, Article 16 TEU stipulates: 'Common positions shall define the approach of the Union to a *particular matter* of a geographical or thematic nature' (emphasis added). Both provisions reflect the ad hoc nature of foreign policy, which is determined by operational activities and non-legislative diplomatic activity. The possibility of international agreements—a further classic instrument of foreign policy—within the sphere of the CFSP does not contradict this submission. Moreover, the fact that international agreements are not mentioned as genuine measures by which the CFSP is to be pursued (compare Article 12 TEU) confirms the view that the CFSP is mainly designed as a policy which does not require truly legal instruments, ie instruments designed to be applied by a court of law. On the other hand, the increasing use of Article 14 TEU for the

---

[81]   On the details of Art 308 TEC see M Bungenberg, *Artikel 235 EGV nach Maastricht* (Baden-Baden, Nomos, 1999).

[82]   Case C–91/05 *Commission v Council* (pending), [2005] OJ C/115/10.

[83]   See eg Case C–281/01 *Commission v Council* [2003] ECR I–12049, para 33.

establishment of agencies equipped with separate legal personality[84] may be seen as evidence that an institutionalisation of foreign policy might be necessary. Nevertheless, at present this practice is arguably illegal under the current TEU. However, to find that there might be situations in which neither the EC nor the EU can take the necessary foreign policy measures does not militate against the submitted approach towards demarcation of competences. Moreover, it would be peculiar if no gaps occurred in a system that is built on the principle of limited attribution of powers.

However, the real problems of demarcation between the pillars are to be found

elsewhere. It is the relationship between the competences of the EC under Article 308 TEC and the competences of the EU under the second and third pillar that is particularly troublesome. Article 308 TEC has been given a rather lax interpretation by the Court of Justice, rendering the requirement that action should prove necessary 'in the course of the operation of the common market' virtually meaningless. At least some of the current overlap between the TEU and the TEC would disappear if a more restrictive stance was taken on Article 308 TEC.[85] This holds true, for example, for the problems created by the RRM,[86] which was enacted on the basis of Article 308 TEC but has hardly any relation to the operation of the common market, a view that is supported by the fact that the Lisbon Treaty provides for an explicit competence for a similar instrument in Article 213 TFEU.

F. Unity and Coherence

The separation of powers between the EC and the EU and the different institutional setup of both areas make contradictory behaviour possible if not likely, in particular with regard to external relations. Hence, coherence is written into Article 1(3) and Article 3 and Article 13(3) TEU as a goal to strive for. The obvious problem from the perspective of the 'unity of the legal order' theme is that the obligation to ensure coherence between EU and EC policies is laid down in the TEU only, with no provision of the TEC incorporating the duty. On the other hand, Article 47 TEU is interpreted as a prohibition to read implied Treaty amendments into the TEU or TEC. This view is mainly based on the wording of Article 47 TEU, which replicates the heading of Title II of the TEU and is therefore

---

[84] See eg Joint Action 2004/551/CFSP of 12 July 2004 on the establishment of the European Defence Agency, [2004] OJ L/245/17.

[85] See Case T–306/01 *Yusuf and Al Barakaat International Foundation v Council and Commission* [2006] ECR II–3533, para 156.

[86] Council Regulation (EC) No 381/2001 creating a rapid-reaction mechanism [2001] OJ L/57/5.

interpreted as meaning that except for Article 8 TEU and the Final Provisions, nothing in the TEU shall affect the TEC, including Articles 1 to 7 TEU.[87] If this is the correct reading of Article 47 TEU, the Commission in particular would be under no obligation to ensure coherence when acting on the basis of its TEC powers. However, this would render the obligation almost meaningless, as has already correctly been pointed out.[88] However, to arrive at this conclusion that changes to the TEC may have been made implicitly by the TEU as well, one does not have to have recourse to the unity argument, but the submission can solely be based on the existing Treaty provisions.[89]

G. EU Law as Part of the 'New Legal Order'?

So far we have established that the EU legal order can be described as a single legal order from a formal point of view, though being made up of three different legal subsystems. These subsystems are tightly connected by Articles 48 and 49 TEU and are based on the collective will of the Member States. At the same it has been shown that a general hierarchy cannot be established between the subsystems, and that the claim of unity is not capable of resolving the conflicts between the different legal subsystems, embedded in the different treaties, nor even within these subsystems themselves.

So is it really irrelevant to speak of the EU legal order as a single legal order? In my submission, the key question is not primarily a question of unity, but one as to the legal character of EU law: does EU law share the features of the 'new legal order' established by the Court of Justice in *Van Gend en Loos*? As pointed out above, the application of central principles of EC law to EU law—direct effect, primacy and loyal cooperation amongst them—is the purported key legal consequence of the unity thesis. Having been swirling around ever since the creation of the EU,[90] the question as to the nature of EU law has been increasingly raised in more recent writings, even though not necessarily as a question regarding the

---

[87] See H-J Cremer, 'Artikel 47 EU-Vertrag' in C Calliess and M Ruffert (eds), *Kommentar zu EU-Vertrag und EG-Vertrag*, 2nd edn (Neuwied, Luchterhand, 2002); H Herrnfeld, 'Artikel 47 EUV, para 7' in J Schwarze (ed), *EU-Kommentar* (Baden-Baden, Nomos, 2000).

[88] See R Wessel, 'The Inside Looking Out: Consistency and Delimitation in EU External Relations' (2000) 37 *CML Rev* 1135, 1148, who points to other provisions of the TEU implicitly modifying the TEC.

[89] M Pechstein and C Koenig, *Die Europäische Union*, 3rd edn (Tübingen, Mohr Siebeck, 2000) 58 *et seq.*

[90] Cf U Everling, 'Reflections on the Structure of the European Union' (1992) 29 *CML Rev* 1053, 1064, who considers the TEU to belong to the category of integration treaties whose construction would in the first place be oriented to the objectives of integration.

unity of EU and EC law.[91] Given the deliberate placing of the second and third pillar outside the Community framework by the Member States, it would be difficult to argue in favour of an identical legal nature of the pillars only on the basis of a claimed unity. Moreover, some of the authors that contend most strongly the intergovernmental nature of the second and third pillar and who even deny the legal personality of the EU, go much further than others with regard to the substantive connectivity of the two Treaties by accepting that the TEU may have changed the TEC implicitly despite the wording of Article 47 TEU.[92]

The discussion had gained additional momentum with the Constitutional Treaty, which integrated all pillars, made reference to the 'Community basis' (Article I-1(1)) for the exercise of competences and declared all EU law to have primacy over the law of the Member States (Article I-6). Which exact consequences were to be derived thereof for the provisions on the CFSP was heatedly debated in academic writings.[93] However, the Constitutional Treaty as a single legal document integrating all pillars has finally found its place in European legal history, which makes it even more important to take a look at the developments that are really taking place, in particular the more recent case law of the Court of Justice. The Maria Pupino case has given a first indication of the position of the ECJ, even though the Court did not make it clear whether it considers EU law to be a 'new legal order' in the sense of the *Van Gend en Loos* case. However, some of the arguments that it put forward supporting the duty of consistent interpretation closely resemble those used more than 40 years ago, among them the effectiveness of the carrying out of the EU's objectives and the jurisdiction of the Court of Justice. The mentioning of the 'similar effect' of the legal instruments available under the TEU and the extension of the principle of loyalty to the third pillar—instead of a foundation on provisions in the TEU itself—support the assumption that the ECJ in principle recognises the integrationist character of the TEU. Also, the very claim of a duty of national courts deriving from the Treaty implies that the TEU (not the framework decisions themselves) does not only impose obligations on the Member States as subjects of public international law, but also on their organs—the executive and the judiciary—directly. The

---

[91] See D Curtin and I Dekker, 'The Constitutional Structure of the European Union: Some Reflections on Vertical Unity-in-Diversity', in P Beaumont, C Lyons and N Walker (eds), *Convergence and Divergence in European Public Law* (Oxford, Hart Publishing, 2002) 59, 67 *et seq*; C Timmermans, 'The Constitutionalization of the European Union' (2001/2002) 21 *Yearbook of European Law* 1, 8 *et seq*.

[92] M Pechstein and C Koenig, *Die Europäische Union*, 3rd edn (Tübingen, Mohr Siebeck, 2000), 5 *et seq* and 58 *et seq*.

[93] Cf M Cremona, 'A Constitutional Basis for External Action? An Assessment of the Provisions on EU External Action in the Constitutional Treaty', *EUI Working Paper* LAW No 2006/30, 21 *et seq* with further references to the discussion.

duty of consistent interpretation as a duty of EU law thus partly deprives the Member States of their choice as to how to conform to their obligations flowing from the TEU. That is, it bears the presumption of a direct applicability of the TEU in the legal order of the Member States,[94] although this does not mean that the secondary instruments adopted under the TEU share these features, or, in the case of Framework Decisions, direct effect is explicitly ruled out by Article 34(2)(b) TEU. Moreover, in the case of the CFSP, it seems hard to imagine how an instrument of foreign policy could have a direct effect on individuals, especially if the legal restrictions on the possible character of the instruments as laid out above were obeyed.[95] Nevertheless, if the Court had the opportunity to rule on how to resolve a conflict between an EU legal instrument and the law of the Member States (most possibly with regard to an EU agreement under the third pillar), it is hard to see the Court ruling in favour of the law of the Member States instead of declaring the primacy of EU law.[96] Ultimately, this would mean, then, that Member States' laws would have to be disapplied insofar as they are in conflict with EU law.

VII. THE UNITY OF THE LEGAL ORDER, THE CONSTITUTIONAL TREATY AND THE LISBON TREATY

At first glance, the Constitutional Treaty[97] seemed to solve all the legal questions surrounding the 'unity question'. It had brought together EC and EU law under one single treaty and had established a new legal person called 'European Union'. As pointed out above, the Constitutional Treaty also had extended the principle of primacy of EC law to the areas of the current second and third pillar. Nevertheless, besides the persistent questions with regard to the actual meaning of primacy in the realm of the CFSP, unity-related problems had persisted, as demonstrated by Article III-308 Constitutional Treaty, which stipulated:

> The implementation of the common foreign and security policy shall not affect the application of the procedures and the extent of the powers of the institutions laid down by the Constitution for the exercise of the Union competences referred to in Articles I-13 to I-15 and I-17.

[94]   See C Herrmann, (2005) *Europäische Zeitschrift für Wirtschaftsrecht* 436, 438.

[95]   C Timmermans, 'The Constitutionalization of the European Union' (2001/2002) 21 *Yearbook of European Law* 1, 9.

[96]   For the arguments supporting that view see D Curtin and I Dekker, 'The Constitutional Structure of the European Union: Some Reflections on Vertical Unity-in-Diversity', in P Beaumont, C Lyons and N Walker (eds), *Convergence and Divergence in European Public Law* (Oxford, Hart Publishing, 2002) 59, 67 *et seq*; C Timmermans, 'The Constitutionalization of the European Union' (2001/2002) 21 *Yearbook of European Law* 1, 10.

[97]   [2004] OJ C 310/1.

Similarly, the implementation of the policies listed in those Articles shall not affect the application of the procedures and the extent of the powers of the institutions laid down by the Constitution for the exercise of the Union competences under this Chapter.

Article III-308 of the Constitutional Treaty was mostly regarded as replacing Article 47 TEU. It was then pointed out that, contrary to Article 47 TEU, Article III-308 CT had a Janus face, since it protected not only the traditional EC external policies from the CFSP, but also vice versa.[98] This analysis of Article III-308 CT was, of course, correct, given the clear wording of its paragraph 2. However, attention must also be drawn to the significant difference in the identification of what shall not affect or be affected. It is in this regard that Article III-308 CT deviated significantly from Article 47 TEU, which stipulates that 'nothing in this Treaty shall affect the Treaties establishing the European Communities ...'. Because of this wording, Article 47 TEU is widely read as a collision norm, derogating the application of the *lex posterior derogat legi priori* rule in relation between the TEU and the TEC. Within the Constitutional Treaty, which would have entered into force in all parts at the same time, it would have lost this function completely. Consequentially, Article III-308 of the Constitutional Treaty could not be read as meaning that the provisions on the CFSP could not have changed the provisions on the former EC external policies.

Furthermore, despite the unification of the pillars into one Treaty, the demarcation of competences would have become even more troublesome with regard to the possible overlaps between the CFSP and other external policies, since the provisions on the CFSP would no longer have contained separate objectives and the CFSP would have applied to 'all areas of foreign policy'. This not only suggests that the presumption in favour of 'EC competences' under the Constitutional Treaty should have been upheld,[99] but also that it would not have been the objectives that should have been used but the legal character of the measures in question, in order to demarcate the CFSP from other external policies once it had been established that they fall into the sphere of external action.

The Lisbon Treaty, the mandate for which was agreed upon by the Brussels European Council of 21 and 22 June 2007 has deliberately abolished the 'constitutional concept' of a single treaty. Instead, the TEU will be amended significantly by putting into it Part I and IV of the Constitutional Treaty, and the TEC will significantly be changed and

[98] M Cremona, 'A Constitutional Basis for External Action? An Assessment of the Provisions on EU External Action in the Constitutional Treaty', *EUI Working Paper* LAW No 2006/30, 21 *et seq.*

[99] See *ibid*, 21 *et seq.* See also P Eeckhout, *External Relations of the European Union* (Oxford, Oxford University Press, 2004) 151.

renamed in order to incorporate most of what was Part III of the Constitutional Treaty before. At the time of writing, there was no actual text available of the Treaty envisaged, so it was too early to make any substantial comments on it. However, the mandate that was agreed upon by the European Council touched upon some of the matters discussed in this paper. First, it is intended to replace the current Article 47 TEU with the wording contained in Article III-308 CT.[100] Another very interesting point is that an additional paragraph was added to Article 308 TEC (as amended by the Constitutional Treaty), which is designed to clarify that Article 308 TEC cannot serve as a legal basis for attaining objectives pertaining to the CFSP.[101] Thereby, one of the most problematic overlaps between the first and the second pillar could indeed be reduced, as suggested above. The new Article 308 is further accompanied by a provision in the new TEU which contains further clarification, including that no legislative acts may be adopted in the area of the CFSP.[102] This confirms the position taken above that CFSP measures, owing to their operational character, do not require legislative activity.

VIII. CONCLUDING OBSERVATIONS

Given the intensity of the debate about the unity of the EU legal order, one would expect that the question had a greater effect on the interpretation of EU law. However, on the contrary, there is hardly any question of interpretation that can be solved having recourse to the concept. The possible conflicts between the Treaties are mostly horizontal in nature and are dealt with explicitly by the Treaties. The application of the *lex posterior* rule is not applicable with regard to TEU and TEC by virtue of Article 47 TEU and in applying the *lex specialis* principle, the concept of unity is neither of great help nor is it necessary for actually deciding which rule is more specific. Applying customary rules of interpretation of public international law would create similar results in many cases. Furthermore, the cases so far decided by the ECJ are in many respects comparable with those decided under the TEC in situations that have a relationship with different EC policies. Given this, it is hardly surprising that the 'merger of the pillars' under the Constitutional Treaty had little impact on the questions discussed above.[103] What we arrive at is the conclusion that it makes little sense to claim the 'unity of the legal order' with regard to the

---

[100]   See Article 40 TEU as amended by the Lisbon Treaty.
[101]   See Article 352(4) TFEU.
[102]   See Article 24(1)(2) TEU as amended by the Lisbon Treaty.
[103]   This concurs with the fact, that during the Maastricht negotiations, the structure of the Treaty was perceived more as a matter of representation than of substance, see B de Witte, above n 6, 51–67.

relationship between the TEC and the TEU. From a formalistic point of view, there is indeed a strong case for perceiving the TEU and TEC as subsystems of one single legal order. However, confronted with a great diversity of institutional designs—between the pillars as well as in-between them—there is hardly any room for a substantive claim of unity. As stated above, the formal unity of a legal order only allows for the presumption of a single will of the rule enactor, coherent and free of contradictions. However, this presumption may be rebutted by the very wording of the rules actually enacted. Such is the case for the EU legal order: it is a single, unitary, but very incoherent legal order of a constitutional character or, as the CFI put it in the *Yusuf* case, 'integrated but separate'[104] legal orders. It is a mere play on words to deny it characterisations such as constitution, legal order, legal system or similar, for the sole reason that it does not mirror our state-experience-shaped expectations in all aspects. This being said, one should abstain from drawing too heavily on such notions as 'unity of the legal order' when making a legal argument.

The true questions to answer hence seem to be different, among them the vanishing issue of the 'legal personality' of the EU and, for the future, the question whether the second and third pillar share the character of the TEC as a 'new legal order of public international law' as well as the role and rights of private individuals under the second and third pillars.[105] And yet again: to answer these, we do not need to put forward a concept of such unclear bearing as the 'unity of the legal order'. The answers instead lie in the provisions of the TEU itself.

However, for the time being, holding EU law to constitute a 'new legal order' would require a significant amount of political will, as well as juridical capability. The Convention on the Future of Europe and the IGC 2004 had this political will and the Constitutional Treaty left unresolved almost only the questions of primacy and judicial oversight with regard to the CFSP. However, France and the Netherlands failed to deliver the ratifications needed for it to enter into force. The assessment for the Lisbon Treaty, which seems to have good chances to be ratified in all Member States, is not different from the one for the Constitutional Treaty. The fact that the Treaty leaves untouched the separation of EU law into two treaties does not seem to make any difference, especially since they are declared to be of the same importance and legal standing. It is obvious, of course, that the legal system established by both treaties would be incomplete if the

---

[104] CFI, Case T–306/01 *Yusuf and Al Barakaat International Foundation v Council and Commission* [2006] ECR II–3533, para 156.

[105] See Conclusions of AG Mengozzi of 26 October 2006 in C–354 and 355/04 P *Segi and others v Council*, judgment of 27 February 2007.

other one was taken away. Nevertheless, what does this mean for the legal character of the CFSP, its demarcation from other external policies and judicial control?

So what does it matter at the end of the day whether we call Pluto a planet or a 'dwarf planet'? To me as an astronomical layman, it does not seem to have too many consequences, especially not for the question of whether it exists or not. The same seems to be true for the question whether or not to describe the legal order established by the TEU and the TEC as a unity or not. As I have tried to show, it is more of a *façon de parler* than anything else, at least beyond the sphere of pure legal theory, ie in the real world of European law, where interpretations are born, live, work and die.

A. The Architecture—Greek Temple, Gothic Cathedral or …?

According to customary rules of European legal scholarship, a treatise of the structure of the EU must conclude with some metaphor, ideally drawn from architecture. So what do we see now, when we stand in front of this peculiar building called 'European Union'? Is it still a temple structure, resting on three pillars? Or does it instead resemble a French gothic cathedral with the similarity with the EU being one with regard to its floor plan?[106] A lot depends, of course, on the perspective which distorts our image of an object as we come up close to it. This simple truth was rediscovered by Filippo Brunelleschi, one of the most brilliant architects of the Renaissance, if not of all times, in 1410. Maybe we should instead describe Brunelleschi's masterpiece, the cupola of the Florentine dome Santa Maria del Fiore, as the best-suited metaphor for the EU, in particular for its future shape under the Lisbon Treaty. The cupola was built without any pillars or scaffolding supporting the growing structure, which consists of a thick inner and a much thinner outer layer. At the beginning of the work, which took 14 years for the cupola alone, it was not certain if it could be built, nor were the necessary instruments already invented. Indeed, how exactly the beautiful construction was achieved remains an unresolved mystery of architecture. Spanning a diameter of 47 metres, the cupola is the greatest brick-structure roof ever built in the world.[107]

As regards the European integration process, we still seem to be in the critical phase of construction, with a high degree of uncertainty as to whether or not the roof will hold up and with quite some judicial masonry

[106] For this metaphor see B de Witte, above n 6, 64 *et seq*.
[107] See R King, *Brunelleschi's Dome: How a Renaissance Genius Reinvented Architecture* (Penguin, 2001).

works still ahead of us. Given that the foundations of the EU's philosophical underpinnings were laid with the re-interpretation of the human condition during the Renaissance, the cupola does not seem to be the worst of architectural metaphors for the ongoing endeavour of European integration and the EU. Last but not least: the dome and the cupola still exist after more than 500 years and they attract admirers from all over the world, just as the EU does! Not to mention the hundreds permanently queuing to get into it …

3

The Law and Practice of CFSP Joint Actions*

ALAN DASHWOOD

I. INTRODUCTION

PRACTICE WITH RESPECT to the instruments of the common foreign and security policy (CFSP) has varied over the years since the inception of the policy following the entry into force of the Treaty on European Union on 1 November 1993. This Chapter focuses more particularly on the period from January 2001, when the infrastructure for developing and managing the European Security and Defence Policy (ESDP) was put in place, pursuant to decisions taken at the European Council of Nice in December 2000.[1]

The two substantive parts of the Chapter explore different kinds of choice that have to be made by the EU institutions when they are engaged in formulating and implementing the external relations policy of the Union. The first part considers, in the light of the post-Nice practice, the criteria that ought to guide the choice of joint actions as the appropriate form of legal instrument for the adoption of measures in pursuance of the objectives of the CFSP. The second part considers the constraints imposed by Article 47 TEU on the choice for the institutions between implementing external relations policy by way of a CFSP joint action, or by way of a Community measure adopted under one of the legal bases in the EC Treaty.

* The writer is grateful to Dr Christoph Herrmann for his trenchant and constructive comments on the version of this Chapter that was presented as a paper at the EUI Workshop of 10/11 November 2006 on 'EU Foreign Relations Law: Constitutional Fundamentals', and also to Professor Bruno De Witte for making a number of helpful suggestions.
[1] See the Report of the French Presidency, with its seven annexes, which was approved by the European Council of Nice in December 2000.

II. THE CHOICE BETWEEN JOINT ACTIONS AND OTHER CFSP INSTRUMENTS

A. Article 14 TEU

Joint actions (JAs) are defined by Article 14 (1) TEU in these terms:

> . . . Joint actions shall address specific situations where operational action by the Union is deemed to be required. They shall lay down their objectives, scope, the means to be made available to the Union, if necessary their duration, and the conditions for their implementation.

From that definition, it appears that JAs have two salient features: they 'address specific situations'; and they are for use 'where operational action by the Union is deemed to be required'. In other words, JAs do not have a normative character. Their essential function is to organise international action, which it has been decided should be taken in the name of the Union. Nevertheless, as we shall see, they have been used, presumably as the least inappropriate instrument available, for certain legislative purposes.

Other provisions of Article 14 describe rather fully the obligations that JAs impose on Member States. According to paragraph (2), JAs 'commit the Member States in the positions they adopt and in the conduct of their activity'. Prior information must be provided to the Council of any position or action that a Member State contemplates taking pursuant to a JA, in sufficient time to allow, if necessary, for consultations within the Council.[2] In the face of changes in the situation to which it relates, a JA will continue to bind the Member States unless and until the Council has adopted any necessary decision[3]; however, '[i]n cases of imperative need . . . and failing a Council decision', an individual Member State 'may take the necessary measures as a matter of urgency', though in so doing it must have regard to the general objectives of the JA, and the Council must be informed immediately of any such measures.[4]

JAs are not stated by Article 14 to be binding upon the EU institutions. Indeed, with regard to the Commission, Article 14(4) implies the opposite, by providing: 'The Council may *request* the Commission to submit to it any appropriate proposals relating to the common foreign and security policy to ensure the implementation of a joint action'.[5] That wording safeguards the independence of the Commission, even in the context of the CFSP, where it does not have a monopoly of the initiative. However, as

---

[2]   Art 14(5).
[3]   Art 14(2).
[4]   Art 14(6).
[5]   Emphasis added.

Eeckhout has pointed out,[6] the Commission is responsible, together with the Council, for ensuring the consistency of the Union's external activity as a whole, and the two institutions are bound to cooperate to that end.[7]

Are JAs capable of producing any legal effects for individuals? It seems clear from Article 14 that the obligations to which they give rise are binding only upon Member States; if the implementation of a JA calls for action to be taken by or against individuals, this must be achieved through national measures.[8] It would follow that the authorities of a Member State would not be able to rely upon the provisions of a JA to validate action that would otherwise be contrary to national law. What of the converse case, that it may be possible for JAs to have some degree of vertical direct effect? Could it be argued before a national court that action taken by a Member State was unlawful, because incompatible with obligations imposed by a JA? Unlike the provisions of Article 34(2)(b) and (c) TEU relating, respectively, to Title VI framework decisions and decisions, Article 14 does not state explicitly that JAs shall not entail direct effect. However, for Title V instruments to have direct effect, when Title VI instruments do not, would seem to be contrary to the system of the Treaties, more particularly in view of the exclusion of the Court of Justice from the domain of the CFSP.

The writer does not agree with Lenaerts and Corthaut that, because JAs (and common positions) have binding force, they must be included, along with EC directives, among the rules available to courts in the Member States for the purposes of judicial review of national measures.[9] This view is apparently based on the primacy of EU law, which is taken to extend to instruments adopted under the Second and Third Pillars.[10] In the writer's submission, the issue as to whether an instrument is capable of having direct effect is logically prior to that of its status relative to national law. In other words, a provision must first be cognisable by Member State courts, before there can be any conflict with the applicable national rules, which might lead to the disapplication of the latter.

---

[6]   P Eeckhout, *External Relations of the European Union* (Oxford, Oxford University Press, 2004) (hereinafter, 'Eeckhout'), p 400.

[7]   Art 3(2) TEU.

[8]   See Eeckhout, above n 6, p 402, where it is stated: 'The ill-defined nature of joint actions therefore appears to permit virtually any type of government activity, *with the exception of general normative action creating rights and obligations for citizens*' (emphasis added).

[9]   K Lenaerts and T Corthaut, 'Of Birds and Hedges: the Role of Primacy in invoking Norms of EU Law' (2006) 31 *EL Rev* 287, 391.

[10]   Despite sharing the qualms that are widely felt about the image of the EU as a classical Greek façade with three pillars joined by a pediment, the writer will follow the convention of referring to the First (EC), Second (Title V TEU)) and Third (Title VI TEU) Pillars, where this provides a convenient shorthand.

All of which is only to say that JAs are not required, *as a matter of EU law*, to be directly applied by national courts in either vertical or horizontal situations. This does not exclude the possibility that they may be recognised as capable of producing certain direct effects, under the constitutional law of some of the Member States.

A question that remains is whether national courts are bound by a duty of consistent interpretation with respect to JAs,[11] as it was held in *Pupino* that they are with respect to Third Pillar framework decisions.[12] On the one hand, the existence of the duty is explained in the *Pupino* judgment by the necessary implication, to enable the Union to carry out its task effectively, of a principle of loyal cooperation under the Third Pillar, analogous to the principle which finds expression in Article 10 EC[13]; in view of the explicit wording of Article 11(2) TEU, which closely echoes that of Article 10 EC,[14] it might be thought that the Court's reasoning in *Pupino* applies *a fortiori* to the Second Pillar. On the other hand, the absence from Title V TEU of a preliminary rulings jurisdiction, even of the truncated kind provided by Article 35 TEU for the purposes of Title VI, might be thought to militate against a positive duty of consistent interpretation imposed as a matter of EU law, since national courts would have no way of obtaining authoritative guidance as to how they should discharge such a duty.

At all events, once again it may be possible, under the constitutional law of a Member State, for its courts to use a JA (or other CFSP instrument) as a tool for the interpretation of the applicable national provisions, for instance on the basis of a presumption, such as that of English law, that the legislature intends to comply with the State's international obligations.

B. Joint Actions Distinguished from other CFSP Instruments

Article 12 TEU lists five means of pursuing the objectives identified by the preceding Article:

defining the principles of and general guidelines for the CFSP;

deciding on common strategies;

---

[11] On the duty of consistent interpretation as regards EC directives, see Case C–14/83 *Von Colson* [1984] ECR 1891; Case C–106/89 *Marleasing* [1990] ECR I–4135; Case C–160/01 *Mau* [2003] ECR I–4791; Joined Cases C–397/01 to C–403/01 *Pfeiffer* [2004] ECR I–8835.

[12] Case C–105/03 [2005] ECR I–5285.

[13] *Ibid*, para 42.

[14] Art 11(2) provides: 'The Member States shall support the Union's external and security policy actively and unreservedly in a spirit of loyalty and mutual solidarity. The Member States shall work together to enhance and develop their mutual political solidarity. They shall refrain from any action which is contrary to the interests of the Union or likely to impair its effectiveness as a cohesive force in international relations . . .'.

adopting joint actions;

adopting common positions;

strengthening systematic cooperation between Member States in the conduct of policy.

The first and last of the indents in Article 12 refer to ways of furthering the objectives of the CFSP that do not entail the adoption of specific forms of instrument. The instrument-types mentioned in the Article from which it is necessary to distinguish joint actions are common strategies and common positions.

(i) Common Strategies

According to Article 13(2) TEU, the European Council has power to 'decide on common strategies to be implemented by the Union in areas where the Member States have important interests in common'. These must 'set out their objectives, duration and the means to be made available by the Union and the Member States'. While the definition provided by Article 13(2) is distinctly meagre, it seems clear—from their designation, from the fact that they are decided upon by the European Council and from the reference to '*areas* where the Member States have important interests in common'[15]—that common strategies are intended to be programmatic instruments, and this has been confirmed by the rather limited practice.[16] They are thus sharply distinguishable from joint actions, which are instruments decided on by the Council, where operational measures are needed to respond to or address a specific situation.[17]

(ii) Common Positions

Article 15 TEU says that common positions (CPs):

... shall define the approach of the Union to a particular matter of a geographical or thematic nature. Member States shall ensure that their common policies conform to the common positions.

---

[15] Emphasis added. It is submitted that 'areas' is not to be understood in a purely geographic sense but as covering 'policy areas'. *Cf* the reference in Art 28(1) TEU to 'the areas referred to in this Title'. The possibility of defining common strategies on 'thematic subjects' was explicitly envisaged by the Vienna European Council of December 1998: see Presidency Conclusions, para 74.

[16] Only three common strategies have been decided upon, relating respectively to Russia, [1999] OJ L/157/1, Ukraine, [1999] OJ L/331/1, and the Mediterranean Region, [2000] OJ L/183/5).

[17] The nature and legal effects of common strategies are more fully considered by the writer in 'Decision-making at the Summit' (2000) 3 *CYELS* 79, 84–8.

The distinction between JAs and CPs seems clear in principle. CPs are the appropriate instrument for the institutions to choose where the object is merely to bind the Member States to an agreed policy stance. If action is necessary in pursuance of a CFSP objective, then the correct instrument is a JA.

Nevertheless, the line between JAs and CPs may sometimes be a fine one. This can be illustrated by the practice with respect to the imposition of economic sanctions on third States. Under the cross-pillar mechanism of Articles 60 and 301 EC, the political decision to adopt measures of economic coercion in respect of a given country is recognised as a matter for the CFSP; but the measures themselves, where they involve interrupting financial or economic relations governed by the EC Treaty, fall to be adopted under Community powers. In the consistent practice of the Council, CPs are used for the CFSP decision, despite the fact that the purpose is evidently to set operational steps in motion. Given that those steps are to be taken, not by the Union pursuant to Title V TEU but by the Community under the EC Treaty (or, in some cases, eg an arms embargo, by the Member States), the choice of instrument is justifiable. However, the use of a JA might be thought equally appropriate, and the drafting of Article 301 assumes that both forms of instrument are available to the Council. Thus, for instance, where country X was suspected of fomenting civil unrest in a neighbouring country, Y, it would be convenient, and surely unobjectionable, for decisions on the imposition of economic sanctions against X and on the dispatch of a police mission to help restore order in Y to be combined within a single JA.

(iii) Decisions sui generis

This form of instrument came to be recognised under the First Pillar, in order to fill a gap resulting from the narrow definition of a 'decision', in the fourth paragraph of Article 249 EC, as 'binding in its entirety upon those to whom it is addressed', ie an act having one or more specific addressees. A number of EC Treaty provisions appeared to confer power on the institutions to adopt legally binding acts that were neither aimed at specific addressees nor designed to lay down general rules. Familiar examples include: decisions, in areas of 'complementary' Community competence such as those of education, vocational training and culture,[18] on the adoption of programmes comprising incentive measures, such as the

---

[18]   See, respectively, Arts 149, 150 and 151.

Socrates Action Programme;[19] decisions on the internal organisation of the institutions, such as those establishing rules of procedure; and instruments of appointment.[20]

Decisions *sui generis* have been taken over from Community law into the field of the CFSP. They are regularly used for the adoption of measures implementing JAs, as well as for making certain appointments; and it was by instruments of this kind that, even before the entry into force of the Treaty of Nice, the Council set up the Political and Security Committee (PSC) as 'the standing formation' of the former Political Committee, and defined its remit, as was also done with respect to the Military Committee and the Military Staff of the EU.[21]

The constitutionality of this practice may appear questionable. By the time Article 12 was inserted into the TEU by the Treaty of Amsterdam, decisions *sui generis* had long been recognised as useful First Pillar instruments. If it had been intended they should be available for the purposes of the Second Pillar, would they not have been included in the Article 12 list?

Article 13(3) TEU provides that '[t]he Council shall take the *decisions* necessary for defining and implementing the [CFSP] on the basis of the general guidelines defined by the European Council'.[22] It might be thought that the word 'decisions' should be understood in this context in the generic sense of any measure required for giving concrete effect to the policy guidelines the European Council lays down. Nevertheless, the Council appears to regard Article 13(3) as authorising recourse to decisions *sui generis*, since the provision is cited as one of the legal bases for the important Council Decision establishing the mechanism, known as 'ATHENA', to administer the financing of the common costs of EU operations having military or defence implications.[23]

There is more solid textual support for the use of decisions *sui generis* as Second Pillar implementing measures. This can be found in Article 23(2)

---

[19] Decision no 253/2000/EC of the European Parliament and the Council of 24 January 2000 establishing the second phase of the Community action programme in the field of education 'Socrates' [2000] OJ L/28/1.

[20] See the analysis of the practice with respect to decisions *sui generis* in the paper on ' Simplification of legislative procedures and instruments', which was presented by the Director-General of the Council's Legal service, Mr J-C Piris, to Working Group IX of the Convention on the Future of Europe (Working document 06 of 6 November 2002). A list of examples is given in n 10 on p 7. Piris notes, at p 10 of his paper, the useful terminological distinction which is drawn in German legal parlance between an *Entscheidung* (addressed decision) and a *Beschluss* (unaddressed decision).

[21] See Council Decision 2001/78/CFSP, 2001/79/CFSP and 2001/80/CFSP, all of 22 January 2001, at, respectively, [2001] OJ L/27/1, L/27/4 and L/27/7.

[22] Emphasis added.

[23] Council Decision 2004/197/CFSP of 23 February 2004, [2004] OJ L/63/68. The other legal basis is Art 28(3) TEU, which provides for the financing of CFSP expenditure. A similar view of Art 13(3) TEU is taken at p 10 of the paper referred to above, note 20.

TEU, which identifies the situations where the Council is empowered to act for the purposes of the CFSP by a qualified majority. The first indent of Article 23(2) refers to the Council's 'adopting joint actions, common positions or *taking any other decision* on the basis of a common strategy' and the second indent to its 'adopting *any decision* implementing a joint action or a common position'.[24] That drafting may be taken as an indication that 'decisions' constitute an available instrument, distinct from the common strategies, JAs or CPs that are being implemented. As regards the establishment of the PSC and other Council bodies, it is submitted that adopting decisions *sui generis* for such purposes can be seen as incidental to the power of self-organisation of the EU institutions, which is extended to the Second Pillar by Article 28(1) TEU.[25] As regards appointments, these may be an aspect either of the implementation of a JA or of the organisation of internal Council bodies.

With no guidance obtainable from the Court of Justice, all that can be said with complete confidence as to the distinction between decisions *sui generis* and JAs under the Second Pillar is that JAs must be used for exercising the *primary* competence conferred by the TEU when operational action is called for in pursuance of CFSP objectives.

C. Joint Actions in Practice—a (Rough) Typology

A typology is a tool of analysis. Its function is to bring out distinctions and similarities between the elements that comprise a given field of knowledge or experience, in a way that aids understanding of those elements, of their interrelationship and of the field as a whole. That aim can be achieved even by a rough and ready set of categories, which is all the present typology of JAs claims to be.

The typology is designed to highlight the different purposes for which JAs have been used in the post-Nice practice. The discussion of the various categories focuses on the typical content of measures, their legal basis (or bases) and the suitability of the choice of instrument. There are two main categories, into which the great majority of JAs fall, and two much smaller categories, which it will be suggested are anomalous.

(i) JAs that Organise ESDP Operations

A catalogue of ESDP civilian, police and military operations, including ones now completed, can be found on the Council's website. The distinguishing feature of such operations is that they are planned and executed

---

[24] Emphasis added.
[25] Art 28(1) is cited as the legal basis of the decisions in question.

within the Council's ESDP infrastructure. A typical action will entail the implementation of a mission in a third country by personnel seconded by EU Member States or institutions, subject to a chain of command that leads, by way of a Head of Mission (or, in military operations, by way of an Operation Commander and a Force Commander) to the PSC. The latter will be charged with providing political control and strategic direction of the operation, and will be authorised by the Council, pursuant to Article 25(3) TEU, to take any relevant decisions.[26] In military operations, the EU Military Committee will be given a monitoring role. There may be provision for participation by third countries, in which case the PSC will be authorised to make the necessary arrangements, including the establishment of a Committee of Contributors, if appropriate.

JAs organising ESDP operations have a fairly standard content. They normally include: a definition of the mission, sometimes elaborated in a mission statement; provisions relating to the structure of the operation and the chain of command, as well as to staffing and the status of personnel; provisions relating to political control and strategic direction by the PSC and, where appropriate, to military direction; and financial arrangements. Recent examples of JAs, showing the variations to be expected between those relating, respectively, to civilian, police and military operations, would be: the JA on the European Union Integrated Rule of Law Mission for Iraq (EUJUST LEX);[27] the JA on the European Union Police Mission for the Palestinian Territories (EUPOL COPPS),[28] and the JA on the European Union military operation in support of the United Nations Organisation Mission in the Democratic Republic of the Congo (MONUC) during the election process.[29] An unusual example of an instrument structured so as to take account of the combined civilian (police) and military components of the operation in question is the JA on the European Union civilian-military supporting action to the African Union mission in the Darfur region of Sudan.[30]

Practice with respect to the citation of legal bases in JAs of this type has stabilised, although it is not yet fully consistent. It is submitted that in the legal order of the Union express reference to a legal basis is only necessary to indicate a choice that has been made between power-conferring options that are available under the applicable Treaty.

In contrast to the EC Treaty, Title V TEU does not employ the method of the specific attribution of competences. The substantive scope of the

---

[26] As measures implementing JAs, decisions of the PSC taken under powers delegated by the Council pursuant to Art 25 are adopted—correctly—in the form of decisions *sui generis*.

[27] Council Joint Action 2005/190/CFSP of 7 March 2005, [2005] OJ L/62/37.

[28] Council Joint Action 2005/824/CFSP of 14 November 2005, [2005] OJ L/300/65.

[29] Council Joint Action 2006/319/CFSP of 27 April 2006, [2006] OJ L/116/98.

[30] Council Joint Action 2005/557/CFSP of 18 July 2005, [2005] OJ L/188/46.

Union's competences under Title V is defined by the list of CFSP objectives in Article 11 TEU. Article 17 TEU does not constitute a separate legal basis, since it merely clarifies the scope of security policy, as provided for by Article 11. Since there could only be one substantive legal basis for action under CFSP powers, there is no need for it to be explicitly identified.

Current practice is to cite, at least, Article 14 TEU (identifying the instrument as a JA) and Article 25(3) TEU (as the basis for the Council's grant of decision-making power to the PSC).[31] In my submission, that is both necessary and sufficient. Some JAs, which specify tasks for the Secretary General / High Representative for the CFSP (SGHR), also mention Article 26[32]; I see no need for this, since the SGHR always has responsibility under the Article for 'contributing to the . . . implementation of policy decisions'. Similarly, the citation of Article 28(3) TEU in some JAs[33] seems pointless, since the paragraph refers to the financing of CFSP operational expenditure in all cases, both the normal case where expenditure is charged to the Community budget and also where, exceptionally, it is charged to the Member States or some of them.[34]

In the light of the definition in Article 14(1) TEU, there can surely be no question that JAs are the appropriate form of CFSP instrument for organising action by the Union, which is considered by the Council to require planning and execution within the its ESDP infrastructure.

(ii) JAs that Provide Financial or other Assistance

The function of JAs falling into this second main category is to organise contributions by the EU—in cash or kind, or by way of technical assistance—towards the realisation of projects that are not managed within the ESDP infrastructure, although they accord with established goals of the CFSP.

The structure of such instruments is generally simpler than that of the JAs in the first category. It will usually be sufficient to identify the project to be supported (or particular aspects of a given project, of which a detailed description may be given in an annex), the nature of the proposed assistance and the entity to which this is to be provided, while also making suitable internal arrangements for overseeing the implementation of the JA and setting a financial reference amount. Examples include: the considerable number of JAs in support of projects that are seen as furthering the

---

[31]   See, eg, the JA on EUPOL COPPS, above note 28.

[32]   See, eg, Council Joint Action 2004/523/CFSP of 28 June 2004 on the European Union Rule of Law Mission in Georgia, EUJUST THEMIS [2004] OJ L/228/21.

[33]   See, eg, the JA on EUJUST LEX, above note 27.

[34]   The exceptional cases are where expenditure arises from operations having military or defence implications or where the Council acting unanimously decides against charging expenditure to the Community budget.

implementation of the EU Strategy against the Proliferation of Weapons of Mass Destruction[35]; successive JAs that have contributed financially to OSCE operations in Georgia[36]; and the JA on helping to provide the Democratic Republic of the Congo with the law-enforcement equipment, arms and ammunition needed for setting up an Integrated Police Unit in Kinshasa.[37]

In current practice, JAs of this kind invariably have Article 14 as their sole legal basis. The analysis undertaken above, with respect to the legal bases of the first category of JAs, would indicate the correctness of that choice.

The question may be asked whether such JAs meet the criteria laid down by the definition of a JA in Article 14(1) TEU; or should they rather have been adopted in the form of CPs? In the writer's submission, the provision of financial or other assistance in furtherance of a concrete project, even one that is managed by a body external to the Union, can properly be regarded as 'operational action' within the meaning of Article 14(1). The point can be made by contrasting the JA in support of the Biological and Toxin Weapons Convention, under which a financial contribution is authorised towards certain projects identified in an annex,[38] with the CP relating to the Review Conference of the same Convention, which lays down the policy objectives to be pursued by the EU within the Conference.[39]

An interesting case that calls for brief consideration is that of Joint Action 2002/589/CFSP on the EU's contribution to combating the destabilising accumulation and spread of small arms and light weapons (SALWs).[40] Title I of the JA requires the Union to work for the building of consensus in relevant international and regional bodies on a number of stated principles and measures, designed to prevent the further destabilising accumulation of SALWs and to reduce existing accumulations. Title II is about the provision of financial and technical assistance to programmes and projects which make a direct and identifiable contribution to the principles and

---

[35] For instance, Council Joint Action 2006/418 CFSP of 12 June 2006 on support for IAEA activities in the areas of nuclear security and verification and in the framework of the implementation of the EU Strategy against the Proliferation of Weapons of Mass Destruction, [2006] OJ L/165/20.

[36] For instance, Council Joint Action 2006/439/CFSP of 27 June 2006 regarding a further contribution of the European Union to the conflict settlement process in Georgia/South Ossetia, [2006] OJ L/174/9.

[37] Council Joint Action 2004/494/CFSP of 17 May 2004 on European Union support to the establishment of the Integrated Police Unit in the Democratic Republic of the Congo (DRC), [2004] OJ L/182/41.

[38] Council Joint Action of 27 February 2006, [2006] OJ L/65/61.

[39] Council Common Position of 20 March 2006, [2006] OJ L/88/65.

[40] Council Joint Action of 12 July 2002, [2002] OJ L/191/1. This replaced an earlier JA with a slightly narrower scope: see Council Joint Action 1999/34/CFSP of 17 December 1998, [1999] OJ L/9/1.

measures referred to in Title I. The Council is empowered to decide on the principle, arrangements and financing of such projects. The JA does not itself address any specific situation; it establishes a legal and policy basis, authorising and organising the operational implementing decisions through which the Union's fight against SALWs is to be conducted. This two-stage approach, bringing coherence to the prosecution of an aspect of the CFSP, appears to be fully consistent with Article 14 TEU.[41]

(iii) Some Anomalous JAs

In a few instances, JAs have been used for the adoption of measures that are quasi-legislative in character. These are the JAs of July 2001 establishing a European Union Institute for Security Studies (EUISS)[42] and a European Union Satellite Centre (EUSC),[43] and that of 18 July 2005 establishing a European Security and Defence College (ESDC).[44] There can scarcely be any doubt that bodies of this kind, possessed of decision-making organs, and in the case of the EUISS and the EUSC of legal personality, would have been created, under the legal order of the Community, by means of a regulation. The use of JAs, *faute de mieux*, seems unsatisfactory, in view of the drafting of Article 14 EC, which defines the legal effects of joint actions in terms purely and simply of the obligations they impose upon Member States. However, it is submitted, to have resorted in these cases to decisions *sui generis* would have been even less appropriate, in view of the uncertainty, which was noted above, as to the extent of the availability of such instruments under the Second Pillar, except in the situations covered by Article 23(2) and Article 28(1) TEU. In particular, the establishment of the bodies here in question—in contrast to the PSC, for instance—cannot be regarded as an act of internal self-regulation by the Council.

Of less concern, perhaps, is the practice of using JAs for the appointment of special representatives, pursuant to Article 18(5) TEU,[45] though this also seems inappropriate. To treat an appointment as an instance of addressing a specific situation calling for operational action by the Union puts a strain on language. In other cases, such as the appointment of the Chairman of the Military Committee, the Council acts by way of a

---

[41] A different issue, to which this Chapter returns below, is whether the adoption of measures to combat the accumulation and spread of SALWs constitutes a prohibited encroachment on the competence of the Community, protected by Art 47 TEU.

[42] Council Joint Action 2001/554/CFSP, [2001] OJ L/200/1.

[43] Council Joint Action 555/CFSP, [2001] OJ L/200/5.

[44] Council Joint Action 2005/575/CFSP, [2005] OJ L/194/15.

[45] Eg Council Joint Action 2006/468/CFSP of 5 July 2006 renewing and revising the mandate of the Special Representative of the European Union for Sudan, [2006] OJ L/184/38.

decision *sui generis*.[46] There is no obvious reason why, simply because the possibility of appointing special representatives is specifically provided for by the TEU, recourse to a decision *sui generis* for this purpose should not be open to the Council.

As a final example of an anomalous instrument, mention should be made of the JA identified on the Council's website as the legal basis of the EU Border Assistance Mission to Moldova and Ukraine.[47] It might have been expected that this would have taken the standard form of a JA organising action within the ESDP infrastructure. Instead, it is presented as an amendment to the mandate of the EU Special Representative for Moldova, designed to incorporate various new elements into the mandate, relating to the oversight of developments on the Moldova–Ukraine state border. Inquiries indicate that this should be considered an isolated oddity, designed to circumvent disagreements as to competence between the Council and the Commission.

III. THE CHOICE BETWEEN JOINT ACTIONS AND COMMUNITY MEASURES

A. The Issue

Article 47 TEU provides:

> Subject to the provisions amending the [EC and EURATOM Treaties], and to these final provisions, nothing in this Treaty shall affect the Treaties establishing the European Communities or the subsequent Treaties and Acts modifying and supplementing them.

Evidently, the function of Article 47 is to preserve the integrity of the Community legal order. It follows that, in spite of the reference in the introductory sentence of Article 11(1) TEU to a CFSP 'covering all areas of foreign and security policy', the scope of the Union's competence under Title V TEU does not extend to matters such as the regulation of external trade, development cooperation or economic, financial and technical cooperation with third countries other than developing countries ('general cooperation'), for which legal bases have been provided by the EC Treaty.[48]

Thus Article 47 confirms what can be gathered from the text of Article 11(1) itself. It seems clear, particularly since the reformulation of Article 11

---

[46] Eg Council Decision 2006/451CFSP of 27 June 2006, [2006] OJ L/179/59.

[47] Council Joint Action 2005/776/CFSP, [2005] OJ L/292/13.

[48] Respectively, Art 133, Arts 177 to 181 and Art 181a.

by the Treaty of Amsterdam, that the generality of the introductory sentence is qualified by the list of CFSP objectives in the five indents that follow, namely:

– to safeguard the common values, fundamental interests, independence and integrity of the Union in conformity with the principles of the United Nations Charter;

– to strengthen the security of the Union in all ways;

– to preserve peace and strengthen international security, in accordance with the principles of the United Nations Charter, as well as the principles of the Helsinki Final Act and the objectives of the Paris Charter, including those on external borders;

– to promote international cooperation;

– to develop and consolidate democracy and the rule of law, and respect for human rights and fundamental freedoms.

When Article 11(1) is considered as a whole, it can be seen that the competence attributed under Title V TEU is intended to cover the foreign policy of the Union in a restrictive sense, namely the political, security and defence aspects of external relations, as distinct from their economic, social and environmental aspects, which remain the preserve of the Community.[49]

The issue addressed here is whether the protection afforded to the EC Treaty by Article 47 would go so far as to preclude the adoption of a JA that was genuinely designed to further one or more of the Article 11(1) objectives, merely because the operational action it provides for might conceivably have been adopted in furtherance of an EC external relations objective, and regardless of whether action has actually been taken by the Community, or is even contemplated. More concretely, does the fact that a certain course of action might help to create the conditions for successfully achieving the socio-economic aims of development cooperation, say, or those of general cooperation, mean that such action cannot be taken by way of a Second Pillar JA, although this is deemed to be necessary in order to strengthen the security of the Union or to preserve peace and strengthen international security? May there not be situations in which it would be permissible to adopt a broadly similar measure under one competence or the other—or, indeed, complementary actions under both of them together—the choice to be determined by policy priorities and by what is the more convenient and practical in a given political conjuncture?

That issue will be considered in relation to a concrete example, the JA on the EU Rule of Law Mission in Georgia, designated 'EUJUST THEMIS',

---

[49] The definition of the scope of the CFSP in Art 11(1) is amplified, with regard to the Union's competence in the security field, by Art 17(1) and (2) TEU.

which has now been completed.[50] It seemed appropriate to focus on a JA that was wholly civilian in character, since manifestly the Community has no power to launch military operations, so that there can be no possibility of parallel CFSP and EC competences with respect to the latter.

According to its mission statement:

EUJUST THEMIS shall, in full coordination with, and in complementarity to, EC programmes, as well as other donors' programmes, assist in the development of a horizontal governmental strategy guiding the reform process for all relevant stakeholders within the criminal justice sector, including the establishment of a mechanism for coordination and priority setting for the criminal justice reform.[51]

Among other more specific activities, it was stated that EUJUST THEMIS could provide guidance to Georgia's new criminal justice reform strategy, support the planning for new legislation, eg a Criminal Procedure Code, and support the development of international as well as regional coopera- tion in the area of criminal justice.[52] The mission was structured as a typical ESDP operation, with a Head of Mission and a staff of experts seconded by EU Member States or institutions, and with the PSC exercis- ing political control and strategic direction.

Shortly after the adoption of the JA establishing EUJUST THEMIS, the Commission announced various projects designed to reinforce the rule of law and democratic processes in Georgia, which were to be financed on the basis of the Community's Rapid Reaction Mechanism (RRM).[53] Those projects, said the Commission, echoing the words of Article 2 of the JA, would be 'closely coordinated with . . . EUJUST THEMIS in order to ensure full complementarity between all the EU actions in support of the rule of law in Georgia'.

That looks like a textbook example of the exercise of parallel CFSP and EC competences in conformity with the duty of consistency laid on the institutions by Article 3 TEU. However, whether such an eminently reasonable set of arrangements was lawful depends on the view that is taken as to the constraints Article 47 TEU places on the competence of the Union under the Second Pillar. If, as the action taken by the Commission under the RRM would indicate, a measure having similar content could have been adopted by the Community under Article 181a EC, does it follow that the establishment of EUJUST THEMIS must be regarded as a violation of Article 47, even though at the time it escaped legal challenge?

---

[50] Council Joint Action 2004/523/CFSP, [2004] OJ L/228/21.
[51] Art 2(1).
[52] Art 2(2).
[53] See Council Regulation (EC) no 381/2001of 26 February 2001 creating a rapid reaction mechanism, [2001] OJ L/57/6.

B. Case Law on Article 47 TEU

To date, the Court of Justice has given judgment in three cases where the application of Article 47 TEU has been directly in issue, all of them relating to legislative instruments adopted under Third Pillar competences.[54]

In the Airport Transit Visas case, Advocate General Fennelly expressed the view that 'Article [47] was inserted in the Treaty on European Union with the very purpose of ensuring that, in exercising their powers under Titles V and VI of that Treaty, the Council and the Member States do not *encroach on* the powers attributed to the Communities under the respective founding and amending Treaties'.[55] Adopting the metaphor used by Mr Fennelly, the Court of Justice defined its task under Article 47 as being 'to ensure that acts which, according to the Council, fall within the scope of . . . the Treaty on European *Union do not encroach upon the powers conferred by the EC Treaty on the Community*'.[56] In the event, it was held by the Court, following its Advocate General, that there was no encroachment on Article 100c EC, because the situation governed by the Joint Action did not involve the crossing of Member States' external borders by third country nationals, and was therefore beyond the scope of the competence conferred on the Community by that provision. However, it seems clear that, had there been Community competence under Article 100c to lay down arrangements on airport transit visas, the Joint Action would have been found to 'affect' the EC Treaty within the meaning of Article 47 TEU.

The Environmental Penalties case was about a Title VI instrument in the form of a Framework Decision laying down a number of environmental offences, in respect of which the Member States were required to prescribe criminal penalties. The Commission considered that the correct legal basis for imposing criminal penalties for environmental offences was Article 175(1) EC; indeed, it had put forward a proposal for a directive on the protection of the environment through criminal law, which the Council had chosen not to adopt.

Advocate General Ruiz-Jarabo Colomer dealt only briefly with Article 47 TEU; he referred to the duty of the Council to refrain from exercising its Title VI powers 'by virtue of the primacy of Community law established

---

[54]   Case C–170/96 *Commission v Council* [1998] ECR I–2763 (Airport Transit Visas case); Case C–176/03, *Commission v Council* [2005] ECR I–7879 (Environmental Penalties case) Case C–440/05 *Commission v Council*, nyr (*Ship-source pollution* case).

[55]   Opinion of Advocate General Fennelly in Case C–170/96 *Commission v Council*, para 8. Emphasis added.

[56]   Case C–170/96 Airport Transit Visas case, para 16. Emphasis added.

by [the Article]',[57] and to the existence of a legal basis for the Community to act with respect to the matters in question as 'cancelling out the powers of the Union'.[58]

The Court of Justice reiterated the definition of the task imposed upon it by Article 47 TEU as being to prevent encroachment upon the powers conferred by the EC Treaty on the Community,[59] which meant in the instant case that it was necessary to ascertain whether the relevant provisions of the Framework Decision ought to have been adopted on the basis of Article 175 EC.[60] It recalled that the protection of the environment 'constitutes one of the essential objectives of the Community', as indicated by the express provisions of Articles 2 and 3(1), as well as by Article 6 EC[61]; and that legal bases for Community action on the environment were to be found in Articles 174 to 176 EC.[62] The Court then referred to its settled case law according to which 'the choice of legal basis for a Community measure must rest on objective factors which are amenable to judicial review, including in particular the aim and the content of the measure'.[63] It was clear, the Court said, from the title and the first three recitals of the Framework Decision in question, that 'its objective is the protection of the environment'.[64] As to the content of the Framework Decision, while criminal law and procedure did not generally fall within the Community's competence, that did not prevent measures relating to the criminal law of the Member States from being taken where this was considered necessary to ensure that Community rules on environmental protection were fully effective.[65] It followed that 'on account of both their *aim* and their *content*, Articles 1 to 7 of the framework decision have as their main purpose the protection of the environment and they could have been properly adopted on the basis of Article 175 EC'.[66] Since, therefore, those provisions encroached upon powers that had been conferred on the Community, and they were not severable, the Framework Decision as a whole was found to infringe Article 47 EC and had to be annulled.[67]

---

[57] Opinion of Advocate General Ruiz-Jarabo Colomer in C–176/03, Environmental Penalties case, para 26.

[58] *Ibid*, para 27.

[59] *Ibid*, para 39.

[60] *Ibid*, para 40.

[61] *Ibid*, paras 41 and 42.

[62] *Ibid*, para 43.

[63] *Ibid*, para 45, citing Case C–300/89, *Commission v Council* [1991] ECR I–2867 and Case C–336/00, *Huber* [2002] ECR I–7699.

[64] *Ibid*, para 46.

[65] *Ibid*, paras 48 and 49. As will be noted below, the point is dealt with more superficially than in the Opinion of the Advocate General.

[66] *Ibid*, para 51. Emphasis added.

[67] *Ibid*, para 53. The provisions of the Framework Decision other than Arts 1 to 7 were held by the Court not to be severable.

In the *Ship-source Pollution* case, the Court of Justice, following Advocate General Mazák, reiterated its reasoning in Environmental Penalties. However, it held that, in specifying in some detail the type and level of penalties to be applied, the Framework Decision in question had exceeded the Community's competence in environmental matters.

Case 91/05, which was still pending at the time of writing, has provided the Court of Justice with a possible opportunity of considering the application of Article 47 TEU in relation to Second Pillar measures.[68] The proceedings were brought by the Commission to obtain the annulment of Council Decision 2004/833/CFSP,[69] one of the several implementing Decisions adopted on the basis of Joint Action 2002/589 on combating the accumulation and spread of SALWs, which was briefly considered above.[70] The disputed Decision provides for the EU to contribute towards implementing projects in the framework of the Moratorium on the Import, Export and Manufacture of SALWs, which is operated by the Economic Community of West African States (ECOWAS). It authorises a financial contribution and technical assistance to set up the Light Weapons Unit within the ECOWAS Technical Secretariat and also to convert the Moratorium into a Convention on SALWs between the Member States of ECOWAS.[71]

As indicated in the summary of its Application that was published in the *Official Journal*, the Commission's argument in Case C–91/05 is essentially that Decision 2004/833 encroaches upon the powers of the Community in the field of development cooperation, thereby infringing Article 47 TEU. The outcome of the case may, therefore, shed some light on what it means for the EC Treaty to be 'affected' in the sense of Article 47[72].

C. Application of the Case Law to the Interaction between CFSP and EC Competences

In the writer's submission, there are crucial aspects of the relationship between EC and CFSP competences which differentiate a measure like EUJUST THEMIS (or, indeed, Decision 2004/833) from the Third Pillar

---

[68]   Case 91/05, *Commission v Council*, [2005] OJ C/115/10.

[69]   [2004] OJ L/359/65.

[70]   At the same time as attacking Decision 2004/883, the Commission has asked the Court to make a declaration of illegality, pursuant to Art 241 EC, against Joint Action 2002/589.

[71]   See Art 1(2).

[72]   Judgment in Case 91/05 was given on 20 May 2008. The implications of the judgment are briefly considered in the Post Scriptum, below.

measures that were the subject of the proceedings in the Environmental Penalties and *Ship-source Pollution* cases, and previously in the Airport Transit Visas case.

(i) No Identity of Objectives between the First and Second Pillars

As the provisions of Article 61 EC and Article 29 TEU expressly indicate, the First and Third Pillars share the establishment of an area of freedom, security and justice as a common objective; hence the need for the opening phrase of Article 29 to make clear that the provisions of Title VI TEU are '[w]ithout prejudice to the powers of the European Community'. The authors of the TEU evidently saw no need to include such a phrase in Article 11(1), because the objectives set for the CFSP by that provision are ones that cannot, in themselves, be the specific object of action taken under the EC Treaty. The task and activities of the Community, as defined by Articles 2 to 4 EC, are purely socio-economic. It is true that Article 177(2) EC requires that Community policy in the area of development cooperation 'shall *contribute* to the general objective of developing and consolidating democracy and the rule of law, and to the objective of respecting human rights and fundamental freedoms'; and there is a similar requirement in Article 181a(1), second paragraph, with respect to general cooperation. However, this is not a free-standing competence but rather a consideration that must inform the Community's policy in pursuing the socio-economic objectives of the envisaged cooperation.[73]

Confirmation of the divide between EC external relations competence and the CFSP was recently provided by the Court of First Instance in its *Yusuf* and *Kadi* judgments.[74] Rejecting a Commission argument that ensuring peace and security was a 'general objective' of the Community, the Court roundly stated:

> Although it is unarguably a principal aim of [the EC Treaty] to put an end to the conflicts of the past between the peoples of Europe by creating 'an ever closer union' among them, that is without any reference whatsoever to the implementation of a common foreign and security policy. The latter falls exclusively within the objects of the TEU which, as emphasised in the preamble thereto, seeks to 'mark a new stage in the process of European integration undertaken with the establishment of the European Communities'.[75]

---

[73] As to which, in the case of development cooperation, see Art 177(1). The socio-economic character of the measures provided for by Art 181a is clear from the reference to 'economic, financial and technical cooperation' and the requirement that such measures 'be consistent with the development policy of the Community'.

[74] Case T–306/01 *Yusuf v Council and Commission* [2005] ECR II–3533 and Case T–315/01 *Kadi v Council and Commission* [2005] ECR II–3649; on appeal as, respectively, Case 415/05P and Case 402/05P.

[75] *Yusuf* judgment, para 154; *Kadi* judgment, para 118.

It follows that there can be no precise identity of objectives between acts adopted under CFSP competences or under EC competences, even where their content may be similar. EUJUST THEMIS provides an illustration. The objectives of the operation, as defined by recitals (2) and (3) of the JA, were to support the transition process in Georgia, more particularly by bringing local standards with regard to the rule of law closer to international and EU standards, and to help avoid any deterioration in the security situation in Georgia, '*with potentially serious repercussions on regional and international security*'. Those are objectives going to the preservation of peace and the strengthening of international security, mentioned in the third indent of Article 11(1) TEU, as well as to developing and consolidating democracy and the rule of law, mentioned in the fifth indent; and arguably also to strengthening the Union's own security, mentioned in the second indent. On the other hand, the measures taken pursuant to the RRM had to be linked to the Community's cooperation policy.

Thus EC and CFSP actions that may appear similar in content will usually be found on analysis to be pursuing objectives that are, at least partially, dissimilar. This is significant, because of the emphasis that was placed by the Court of Justice in the Environmental Penalties case on the fact that both the aim and the content of the provisions of the Framework Decision in question were such as to indicate that the main purpose of those provisions fell within the scope of the legal basis provided by the EC Treaty for the protection of the environment; in other words, the very same measure could have been adopted on that legal basis. The case is, therefore, authority for the proposition that Article 47 TEU protects the EC Treaty against being 'affected' through the direct substitution of a TEU instrument for a Community instrument. The adoption of an act under the TEU will be found to infringe Article 47, where an identical act—that is to say, one having not only the same *content* but also the same *aim*—could be adopted under one of the legal bases in the EC Treaty.

The lack of identity of objectives means that such will rarely, if ever, be the case, as between acts adopted under First or Second Pillar competences.

(ii) Non-pre-emptive Character of the First Pillar/Second Pillar Interaction

Another point of distinction, as compared with the situation in Airport Transit Visas and in Environmental Penalties, lies in the nature of the competences in question, and hence of any possible interaction between them.

CFSP competence and the EC competences with which it is most likely to interact, namely those for development cooperation and general cooperation, are non-pre-emptive in character. They are not in a race to occupy the field, because exercise of the one competence leaves open the full range of possibilities for exercise of the other—subject, of course, to the principle of consistency in Article 3 TEU.

There is a sharp contrast with the nature of the interaction between First and Third Pillar competences that was held to fall within the prohibition of Article 47 TEU in the circumstances of the Environmental Penalties case. Owing to its regulatory character, the Title VI Framework Decision, if it had been valid, would have had the effect of pre-empting an area of potential legislative activity. So long as it remained in force, no regulation or directive relating to the punishment of the environmental offences in question could have been adopted on the basis of Article 175 EC, since the existence of two pieces of legislation with the same subject-matter would infringe the principle of legal certainty. Here, therefore, a Title VI competence was 'in competition' with an available Community competence, in the sense that whichever was exercised first would occupy the field for the time being, excluding or restricting the exercise of the other. There would have been a similar effect in the Airport Transit Visas case, if the Community's competence under Article 100c EC had extended to the regulation of such visas, since the adoption of the Joint Action would have prevented that competence from being exercised within the occupied field.

A possibly helpful analogy can be found in the case law showing that action by the Community in the field of development cooperation and humanitarian aid does not have the consequence of precluding autonomous action by the Member States with respect to the same subject-matter, as would be the case in other policy areas.[76] Because operations undertaken in those areas are non-pre-emptive, there is no need for the Community order to be protected by the AETR principle.[77]

Similarly, the protection afforded to the EC Treaty by Article 47 TEU can be regarded as redundant, where the exercise of a TEU competence does nothing to inhibit the subsequent exercise of an available Community competence. It will rarely, if ever, be the case that the adoption of a measure designed to further the foreign policy objectives of the CFSP prevents action from being taken that is deemed to be appropriate in pursuance of the socio-economic objectives of EC external relations. There was certainly no such occupation of the field by EUJUST THEMIS, as the complementary action under the Community's RRM demonstrated.

---

[76] Joined Cases C–181/91 and C–248/91 *Bangladesh* [1993] ECR I–3685; Case C–316/91, *EDF* [1994] ECR I–625. See also Art 14 (3) and (4) of the Treaty establishing a Constitution for Europe.
[77] Case 22/70 *Commission v Council* [1971] ECR 263 (AETR case).

D. Parallelism between CFSP and EC Competences

It appears from the foregoing analysis that the reasoning in the Environmental Penalties judgment presents no obstacle to the adoption of measures like EUJUST THEMIS (or Decision 2004/833). The way remains open to an interpretation of Article 47 TEU recognising that a degree of parallelism exists between the competence of the Union under Title V TEU and the competence of the Community under the EC Treaty. There may, in other words, be a partial overlap between the respective competences, in the sense that certain actions genuinely undertaken for the purposes of the one might genuinely be undertaken for the purposes of the other, without this representing a threat to the integrity of either.

Such an interpretation would be consonant with the *effet utile* of the CFSP. It must be assumed that the authors of the TEU meant what they said, when they set the European Union the task of asserting its identity on the international scene, 'in particular through the implementation of a common foreign and security policy'[78]; or when they set the objectives of the CFSP in Article 11(1) in terms indicating that it is to extend to all the aspects of foreign and security policy defined by the five indents that follow, including the strengthening of the Union's security 'in *all* ways'.[79] The plenitude of Union competence in the security field is further emphasised by Article 17(1) TEU, which says that the CFSP 'shall include *all* questions relating to the security of the Union'.[80] It would defeat the clear intention of those provisions, if Article 47 prevented the Council from adopting a JA which it considered necessary in the interests of the security of the Union and the wider interests of international peace and security, merely because the possibility existed of adopting a measure having similar content in the framework of economic, financial and technical cooperation with the third country concerned.

IV. CONCLUSION

The two parts of this Chapter have examined different aspects of the post-Nice practice with respect to the implementation of the CFSP through JAs as it has developed within the legal framework provided by Title V TEU.

---

[78]   Art 2(1), second indent TEU. See also the reference, in the tenth recital of the preamble to the TEU, to the framing of a CFSP as the means of 'reinforcing the European identity and its independence in order to promote peace, security and progress in Europe and in the world'.
[79]   Art 11(1), second indent. Emphasis added.
[80]   Emphasis added.

The analysis in the first part indicates that the practice makes it possible to identify two main categories of JAs and tends to confirm the viability of the distinction between JAs and the other forms of CFSP instrument. However, it also suggests that the instruments expressly provided for by Article 12 TEU may not be suited to all of the purposes for which the adoption of binding legal acts in the sphere of the CFSP may be required. The importation of decisions *sui generis* into the sphere of the Second Pillar may be seen as a practically useful development; though it is of uncertain legality, other than for implementing one of the instruments provided for by Article 12 TEU or in the exercise of the Council's power of self-organisation. There are some matters, notably the establishment of bodies like the EUISS and the EUSC, where the absence of a form of legislative instrument is felt—a lacuna which, it may be recalled, the Treaty establishing a Constitution for Europe would have done nothing to fill.

In the second part of the Chapter, an attempt is made to understand the nature of the 'effect' on the EC Treaty that Article 47 TEU is designed to guard against. The Airport Transit Visas, Environmental Penalties and Ship-source Pollution cases have established that Third Pillar (and by extension Second Pillar) competences cannot be used to adopt measures, both the aim and content of which are identical to those of measures that could be taken by the Community under one of the legal bases of the EC Treaty. On the other hand, it has been argued, those authorities have nothing to say about the validity of an instrument like the JA on EUJUST THEMIS, which pursues the foreign, security or defence objectives of Article 11 TEU by way of action that might also be open to the Community in pursuance of the different objectives of the EC Treaty. Article 47 must be interpreted in context and in a sense that allows full value to be given to other provisions of the TEU, notably the ambitious aim of enabling the Union to assert its identity on the international scene, for which the CFSP is the designated vehicle. There is no legal impediment to recognising the parallel nature of the Union's CFSP competence and those Community competences with which it has a likely interface; and such recognition would provide the basis for the development of a more effective EU foreign policy, in conformity with the principle of consistency.

POST SCRIPTUM

Since this paper was written, judgment has been given on 20 May 2008 in Case 91/05, commonly referred to as 'the *ECOWAS* case'.[81] Contrary to

---

[81] See n 69. In Case 91/05, the writer acted for the United Kingdom, which was one of six Member States intervening in support of the Council. The views expressed in this postscript and throughout the paper are exclusively his own. A brief account of Case 91/05, in similar

the opinion of A G Mengozzi, the Court of Justice held that Decision 2004/833 ('the contested Decision') ought to have been adopted under the Community's competence for development cooperation policy instead of as a CFSP measure, and that it must accordingly be annulled.

The ruling turned on the Court's interpretation of the contested Decision as pursuing simultaneously both CFSP objectives and development cooperation objectives, without either of these being incidental to the other; while the particular action that was contemplated (providing funds and technical assistance) was capable of serving both sets of objectives. In a similar situation, where several legal bases in the EC Treaty were concerned, the solution would be to found the instrument in question on all of them; however, in the Court's view, the solution of a cumulative legal basis was precluded by Article 47 TEU. Since, considered in the light of its aim as well as of its content, the Decision could have been adopted as a development cooperation measure, that was what, the case law indicated, should have been done.

If the *ECOWAS* judgment had been available sooner, the main thrust of the argument in this chapter would have been no different. However, it would have been necessary to address some of the unexpected elements of the Court's reasoning, such as the reliance placed on policy documents (notably the 2006 'Consensus' text)[82], in arriving at a conception of the demarcation between development cooperation competence and CFSP competence that is hard to reconcile with the clear language of Article 177 EC and Article 11 TEU.

Most importantly, there would have been no reason to resile from the contention as to the existence of an area of potential 'overlap' between first and second pillar competences, where a measure having a certain *content* may be adopted in furtherance either of a *Community aim* or of a *CFSP aim*. The trouble with the contested Decision, as understood by the Court of Justice, was that it was pursuing CFSP and development cooperation objectives at *the same time*. Future accidents could thus be avoided, as long as Article 47 remains in force, by language making crystal clear that the specific and only aim of an arms control measure is the strengthening of international peace and security.

In the writer's submission, therefore, EUJUST THEMIS would not have been vulnerable in the same way as the *ECOWAS* Decision. There was no

---

terms to the above, will be included in the writer's contribution to Dashwood and Maresceau, *Recent Development in the Law and Practice of EU External Relations: Salient Features of a Changing Landscape* (Cambridge: CUP, forthcoming); this piece, entitled 'Article 47 TEU and the relationship between first and second pillar competences' develops and elaborates some ideas put forward here.

[82] Joint Statement by the Council and the representatives of the governments of the Member States meeting within the Council, the European Parliament and the Commission on European Union Development Policy, OJ 2006 C 46/1.

language in the JA that could have been interpreted as suggesting that objectives of general cooperation policy pursuant to Article 181a EC were intended to be given the same prominence as that of enhancing the security of Georgia, a near neighbour of the Union. Moreover, the exclusively CFSP focus was strengthened by the structuring of EUJUST THEMIS as a typical ESDP operation under the political control and strategic direction of the PSC.

At all events, the significance of the *ECOWAS* judgment is likely to be short-lived. The primacy accorded to the Community under the existing Treaties will not be carried over into the constitutional order as re-configured by the Treaty of Lisbon. In particular, Article 47 TEU is to be replaced by Article 40 of the amended TEU, providing equal mutual protection for the Union's CFSP and TFEU competences. Once that happens, the Court's reasoning in *ECOWAS*, based on the notion of 'encroachment' upon Community competence that was developed in Airport Transit Visas and applied in Environmental Penalties and Ship-source Pollution, will cease to be tenable.

4

Restraining External Competences of EU Member States under CFSP

CHRISTOPHE HILLION AND RAMSES WESSEL*

'On security matters, the Treaty allocates sovereignty to member states. But that sovereignty has to be compatible with our general interests in security.'

Javier Solana, 29 March 2007, European Parliament, EU Observer, 29 March 2007.

I. INTRODUCTION

WHILE THE IMPACT of Community policies on Member States' external powers has been extensively studied,[1] the effect(s) of another important area of the Union's external action, namely the foreign and security policy, has hitherto been virtually neglected. One reason for this oversight could be that many Member States originally conceived the Common Foreign and Security Policy (CFSP) as an *intergovernmental* form of cooperation which, as such, would do no harm to States' freedom to conduct their own foreign policy in general, and to their sovereign powers to conclude international agreements in particular.

On the occasion of the 15th anniversary of the Treaty on European Union (TEU), there are at least two reasons for reconsidering this basic proposition. First, it may be argued that CFSP has, since its inception,

---

* Christophe Hillion is Professor of European Law at the University of Leiden (thanks to Anne Myrjord for all her suggestions and support); Ramses A Wessel is Professor of the Law of the EU and other International Organisations at the University of Twente, the Netherlands.

[1] See P Eeckhout, *External Relations of the European Union: Legal and Constitutional Foundations* (Oxford, Oxford University Press, 2004); P Koutrakos, *EU International Relations Law* (Oxford, Hart Publishing Ltd, 2006); A Dashwood and C Hillion (eds), *The General Law of EC External Relations* (London, Sweet & Maxwell, 2000); M Dony and JV Louis, *Commentaire J Mégret: Le droit de la CE et de l'Union européenne—Relations extérieures*, vol 12 (Brussels, éd. de l'Université de Bruxelles, 2005).

developed into a set of procedural and substantive notions that come increasingly close to those which characterise the Community legal order. Second, it has become clear over the past 15 years that rather than being completely separate, the EC and CFSP interact within a unitary EU legal order.[2]

This Chapter envisages the impact of the CFSP normative framework on Member States' freedom to conclude international agreements, either *inter se* or with third parties. A first part examines the potential restraints that are based on CFSP primary and secondary norms. The second part analyses the nature of the EU competence to conclude international agreements in the field of CFSP, and the effects such EU agreements may have on Member States' foreign policy powers. The third part studies the possible influence that principles of the EU legal order more generally may have on the CFSP normative content, and the latter's ability to constrain Member States' foreign policy power.[3]

II. CFSP NORMS AS RESTRAINTS ON MEMBER STATES' EXTERNAL COMPETENCES

Possible restraints on Member States' freedom to conclude international agreements in CFSP fields can stem from CFSP treaty norms (A) and CFSP secondary measures (B).[4] The degree of restraining effect of those CFSP norms is also determined by the potential role that the judiciary may play in ensuring that those norms are enforced (C), as well as the interpretation given to the specific CFSP principle of loyal cooperation (D).

---

[2] See also R Gosalbo Bono, 'Some Reflections on the CFSP Legal Order' (2006) 43 *CML Rev* 337, who refers to 'progressive supranationalism' in relation to the development of CFSP (at 349); and P Koutrakos, *Trade, Foreign Policy & Defence in EU Constitutional Law* (Oxford, Hart Publishing, 2001); E Denza, *The Intergovernmental Pillars of the European Union* (New York, OUP, 2002); E Denza, 'Lines in the Sand: Between Common Foreign Policy and Single Foreign Policy' in T Tridimas and P Nebbia (eds), *European Union Law for the Twenty-first Century* (Oxford, Hart Publishing, 2004) 259.

[3] We will only occasionally refer to the Treaty of Lisbon, which is expected to enter into force in 2009. For an assessment of the impact of earlier, but on this terrain quite similar, Constitutional Treaty, see, eg, M Cremona, 'A Constitutional Basis for Effective External Action? An Assessment of the Provisions on EU External Action in the Constitutional Treaty', *EUI Working Paper*, LAW no 2006/30; as well as her 'The Draft Constitutional Treaty: External Relations and External Action' (2003) 40 *CML Rev* 1347.

[4] The question of whether a CFSP legal order exists will not be dealt with in this Chapter. On the basis of earlier research, we accept that CFSP norms are legal norms and that they can therefore be envisaged as such. See in this regard RA Wessel, *The European Union's Foreign and Security Policy: A Legal Institutional Perspective* (The Hague, Kluwer Law International, 1999); MR Eaton, 'Common Foreign and Security Policy' in D O'Keeffe and P Twomey (eds), *Legal Issues of the Maastricht Treaty* (London, Chancery Law Publishing, 1994) 221; F Terpan, *La Politique étrangère et de sécurité commune de l'Union européenne* (Brussels, Bruylant, 2003), and more recently Gosalbo Bono, above n 2, 367.

A. The Binding Nature of Primary CFSP Norms

In addressing the question of whether the CFSP *treaty* provisions may limit Member States' contractual competences, the cardinal CFSP obligation of 'systematic cooperation' falls to be examined. According to Article 16 TEU: 'Member States shall inform and consult one another within the Council on any matter of foreign and security policy of general interest in order to ensure that the Union's influence is exerted as effectively as possible by means of concerted and convergent action.'[5]

In principle, the scope of issues covered by the obligation of systematic co-operation is not subject to any limitation regarding time or space, as the provision talks of 'any matter of foreign and security policy [...]'. However, Article 16 immediately qualifies that obligation by adding the phrase '*of general interest*'. No further specification has been provided of what the notion of 'general interest' stands for in the context of CFSP.[6] Hence, on the one hand, Member States are obliged to inform and consult one another whereas, on the other hand, they appear to enjoy individual discretion to decide whether or not a matter is of 'general interest'.[7]

Be that as it may, Member States nonetheless remain *obliged* to inform and consult one another whenever issues are of general interest, in the sense that they reach beyond national interests. Indeed, and as recalled by Article 12 TEU, the Member States have accepted this obligation as one of the means to achieve the CFSP objectives set out in Article 11 TEU.[8] The binding nature of this obligation is indeed supported by the use of the word 'shall' in Article 16 TEU.[9]

Given the nature of the Member States' duty to inform and consult, it is unfortunate that the Treaty does not further articulate this obligation. In

[5] There was an early consensus on the content of Art 16 (J2(2)) TEU; it was not modified throughout the negotiations of the TEU and already formed part of the Luxembourg Draft of 18 June 1991 (Art G of the CFSP provisions).
[6] The legal nature of the CFSP obligations has been amply discussed ever since their creation but in view of the absence of judgments by the ECJ, conclusive answers have not yet been presented.
[7] The principle of attributed competences as reflected in Art 5 TEC (but which is a general principle in international institutional law), implies that whatever has not been attributed to the organisation remains in the hands of the Member States.
[8] Art 12 TEU reads:
The Union shall pursue the objectives set out in Article 11 by:
– defining the principles of and general guidelines for the common foreign and security policy;
– deciding on common strategies;
– adopting joint actions;
– adopting common positions;
– strengthening systematic cooperation between Member States in the conduct of policy.'
[9] *Cf* also Gosalbo Bono, above n 2, 342, who argues that this language indeed imposes 'binding legal duties for the member States and the institutions and which contrast with the soft law nature of the EPC provisions in the SEA'.

order to establish its *content*, it is therefore necessary to turn to general descriptions of the obligation of consultation in international law. Broad definitions underline the duty not to adopt a position as long as the other partners have not been consulted.[10] There appears to be no reason to assume that the notion of consultation used in Article 16 TEU deviates from these general definitions. EU Member States must therefore refrain from making national positions on CFSP issues of general interest public before having discussed them in the framework of the CFSP cooperation.

Hence, international agreements concluded by EU Member States *inter se*, or with third states, can be left out of the systematic CFSP cooperation *only if* the content of such agreements is of purely bilateral interest to the parties, and when no general (read: EU) interest is at stake. In view of the broad scope of CFSP envisaged in Articles 11 and 12 TEU, it can be suggested that most international agreements to be concluded by individual Member States should be notified and, if necessary, discussed by Council working parties. Arguably, this proposition is further supported by the loyalty that Member States must demonstrate towards the Union's CFSP, as stipulated in Article 11(2) TEU. This provision notably states that Member States 'shall work together to enhance and develop their mutual political solidarity' and 'refrain from any action which is contrary to the interests of the Union or likely to impair its effectiveness as a cohesive force in international relations'. The provisions of Article 16 TEU, and the obligations they encapsulate, ought to be understood in the light of that principle.[11]

B. The Binding Nature of Secondary CFSP Norms

CFSP treaty norms are largely procedural in nature. Further restraints on Member States' external (or *inter se*) competences could depend on secondary CFSP measures. While the binding nature of common positions, joint actions (JAs) or other decisions is only marginally dealt with in the Treaty,[12] the language used by the relevant Treaty provisions nonetheless

---

[10] *Cf* Th Jürgens, *Die gemeinsame Europäische Aussen- und Sicherheitspolitik* (Köln, Carl Heymanns Verlag, 1994) 210: 'das Gebot, von der endgültigen Festlegung einer eigenen Position Abstand zu nehmen, solange nicht die Anhörung des Konsultationspartners stattgefunden hat'.

[11] The principle of loyal cooperation is examined in detail below under section 2.D.

[12] No interpretation may be expected from the Court of Justice given that Art 46 TEU excludes Title V from its jurisdiction; as confirmed by, eg, Case T–201/99 *Royal Olympic Cruises Ltd and others v Council and Commission* [2000] ECR II–4005; Case T–228/02 *Organisation des Modjahedines du peuple d'Iran*, judgment of 12 December 2006 (para 49); Case C–354/04 P *Gestoras Pro Amnistía and Others v Council*, judgment of 27 February 2007 (para 50).

suggests that those CFSP acts, once adopted,[13] do limit the freedom of Member States in their individual policies.[14] In particular, joint actions 'shall commit the Member States in the positions they adopt and in the conduct of their activity' (Article 14(3)) and 'Member States shall ensure that their national policies conform to the common positions' (Article 15).[15]

Hence, Member States are not allowed to adopt positions or otherwise to act contrary to JAs. This was already clear in the first Luxembourg Draft, which stipulated that 'each Member State shall be bound by the joint line of action in the conduct of its international activity'.[16] It is indeed notable that the vague notion of 'joint line of action' was replaced by that of 'joint action', which more clearly entails a concrete decision by the Council. Moreover, the adjective 'international' before 'activity' was removed in the final text, thereby suggesting that *all* Member States' activities should be aligned with the JAs. The reason may have been that the word 'international' gave the impression that Member States' activities were relevant only where relations with third states were involved. This would have excluded relations *within* the Union. Arguably, such removal is an indication of Member States' full awareness, at the time of the negotiations, of the binding nature of JAs. Indeed, some Member States' insistence on unanimous voting provides additional evidence of such awareness.[17]

The nature of CFSP decisions as concrete norms of conduct, demanding a certain unconditional behaviour from the Member States, is typified by the strict ways in which exceptions to JAs are envisaged. A first possibility to depart from adopted JAs is offered by Article 14(2) TEU, which is

[13] The publication in the Official Journal of CFSP autonomous acts is decided on a case-by-case basis, by unanimous decision of the Council or the Coreper: see Art 17 of the Council Rules of Procedure; [2002] OJ L/230/7.

[14] On CFSP Joint Actions specifically, see A Dashwood, 'The Law and Practice of CFSP Joint Actions', ch 3, this volume; also: RA Wessel, *The European Union's Foreign and Security Policy: a Legal Institutional Perspective* (Dordrecht, Martinus Nijhoff, 1999) 154; F Dehousse, 'La politique étrangère et de sécurité commune' in JV Louis and M Dony (eds), *Relations Extérieures—Commentaire J Mégret, Le droit de la CE et de l'Union européenne* (Brussels, Institut d'Etudes Européennes, 2005) 441, 475; P Koutrakos, above n 1, 399ff.

[15] In the same vein, EU Common Strategies, envisaged in Art 13 TEU, bind not only the EU institutions but also the Member States. For instance the European Council 1999 CS on Ukraine provided that the Council, the Commission and Member States shall review, according to their powers and capacities, existing actions, programmes, instruments, and policies to ensure their consistency with that Common Strategy; see pt 41, Common Strategy on Ukraine; [1999] OJ L/331/1.

[16] Draft Treaty on the Union from the Luxembourg Presidency, 18 June 1991, Article K in F Laursen and S Vanhoonacker, *The Intergovernmental Conference on Political Union: Institutional Reforms, New Policies and International Identity of the European Community* (Maastricht, EIPA, 2002) 401.

[17] See, eg, the speech made by Prime Minister John Major in the House of Commons on 20 November 1991; *ibid*, 424.

similar to, but at the same time clearly departs from, the *rebus sic stantibus* rule as foreseen in Article 62 of the Vienna Convention on the Law of Treaties (VCLT).[18] According to Article 14(2) TEU:

> If there is a change in circumstances having a substantial effect on a question subject to Joint Action, the Council shall review the principles and objectives of that action and take the necessary decisions. As long as the Council has not acted, the Joint Action shall stand.[19]

Hence, even if the original circumstances constitute an essential determinant of the parties' consent to be bound, and even if the effect of the change is likely to transform radically the extent of obligations still to be performed, Member States may not invoke the change in circumstances as a ground for not complying with the particular decision. In that sense the CFSP provision cannot be regarded as a clausula *rebus sic stantibus*. Article 14(2) TEU provides that it is up to the Council to decide on possible modifications of the effect of the JA. Pending the Council's decision, no Member State is allowed to deviate from the JA.[20]

On the other hand, the Treaty does not completely rule out that 'changes in the situation' may have an impact on the effects of the JA. Under certain strict conditions, such changes may constitute a valid reason for Member States to take 'necessary measures'. According to Article 14(6) TEU:

> In cases of imperative need arising from changes in the situation and failing a Council decision, Member States may take the necessary measures as a matter of urgency having regard to the general objectives of the Joint Action ...

In this case, '[t]he Member State concerned shall inform the Council immediately of any such measures' (paragraph 6, last sentence). While this provision comes again close to the *rebus sic stantibus* rule of Article 62 VCLT already mentioned, the criteria to be met are strict: (1) there must be a case of *imperative need*; (2) the situation must have been changed; (3) the Council has not (yet) come up with a decision to solve the matter; (4)

---

[18] Vienna Convention on the Law of Treaties, Art 62, paras 1(a) and (b). The criteria to justifiably invoke this provision include: the fundamental change of circumstances was not foreseen by the parties and (a) the existence of those circumstances constituted an essential basis of the consent of the parties to be bound by the treaty; and (b) the effect of the change is radically to transform the extent of obligations still to be performed under the treaty.

[19] This is a much stronger provision than the one originally foreseen by the Luxembourg Presidency: 'The Council shall adapt Joint Action to changes in the situation'. Luxembourg Draft, Article J, para 2, in Laursen and Vanhoonacker, above n 17, 410.

[20] After the entry into force of the treaty, Zoller pointed to an inherent practical danger of this procedure: 'Certes, en principe, l'État membre qui envisage de se désolidariser d'une action commune ne peut le faire qu'à défaut d'une décision du Conseil et en tenant compte des objectifs généraux de l'action commune. Mais les garde-fous semblent bien fragiles et il n'est pas exclu qu'en cas de crise grave, le Conseil soit paralysé et dans l'impossibilité de prendre une décision.' E Zoller, 'Titre V: Dispositions concernant une politique étrangère et de sécurité commune' in V Constantinesco *et al*, *Traité sur l'Union Européenne: Commentaire article par article* (Paris, Economica, 1995) 781, 794.

measures will have to be *necessary*; and (5) must be taken as a *matter of urgency*; (6) the general objectives of the JA should be taken into consideration; and (7) the Council shall be immediately informed. It seems that the formulation of these explicit conditions purports to rule out any valid appeal to Article 62 VCLT to justify deviations from JA.

While in the case of common positions (generally used for measures lacking an operative dimension) the effects are not presented in detail by the Treaty makers, they too are meant to guide the behaviour of Member States in their external relations.[21] It is clear, on the one hand, that a common position commands Member States *to do* something ('bring your conflicting national policies into line with the Common Position'), while, on the other hand, it requires them to *refrain* from doing something ('do not adopt any national positions that do not conform to the Common Position'). In this sense, the term 'position' is different from its usual meaning of (an attitude on) a state of affairs.[22] The phrase 'shall ensure' in Article 15 TEU makes it clear that the provision does not simply envisage an inducement, but that it establishes a concrete obligation to create a particular situation or, what amounts to the same thing, to prevent a particular situation from occurring.[23]

Given their characteristics, can CFSP secondary measures limit Member States' ability to engage in international agreements (either *inter se* or with third states), where the latter's content conflict with adopted CFSP decisions? In answering this question, it is important to recall that the existence of secondary CFSP norms does not automatically block the possibility for Member States to take individual policy initiatives in the same issue area. Practice reveals that, in most cases, the scope of CFSP decisions is limited, thereby leaving ample space for national policies. Thus, in practice, conflicts are primarily to be expected when Member

---

[21] Another indication of the normative nature of Common Positions can be found in Art 19(1): 'Member States shall co-ordinate their action in international organizations and at international conferences. They shall uphold the Common Positions in such fora. In international organizations and at international conferences where not all Member States participate, those which do take part shall uphold the Common Positions.' This provision adds an external dimension to the basically internal obligations of the Member States.

[22] *Cf* for the early discussion already I MacLeod, ID Hendry and S Hyett, *The External Relations of the European Communities: A Manual of Law and Practice* (Oxford, Clarendon Press, 1996) 416 and 421, who observe that this formal type of common position in practice has taken the form of a Council decision *sui generis* ('*Beschluß*' instead of an Art 249 EC '*Entscheidung*'). However, according to Zoller (above n 20, 788), a Common Position may still lack 'normative effects' when Member States have not expressed a clear consent. Nevertheless, she sees a Common Position as 'un acte juridique unilatéral qui leur [la Communauté (*sic!*) et ses États Membres] est imputable'.

[23] See in general on this issue, eg, O Schachter, *International Law in Theory and Practice* (Dordrecht, Martinus Nijhoff Publishers, 1991) 98: 'There is an obvious difference between a text that uses language of obligation ('shall') in regard to future conduct and one that only "intends" or "plans" to take some action.'

States' agreements directly violate core parts of CFSP decisions, or when Member States' existing agreements clash with a subsequent CFSP decision.

In a recent article, Thym argued that the special nature of CFSP entails that Member States remain free to enter into international agreements—either *inter se* or with third states—even where these agreements conflict with their CFSP obligations, and that in the absence of a transfer of sovereign competences, the binding nature of Union norms should not easily be presumed.[24] While this conclusion would allegedly do justice to the intergovernmental dimension of CFSP, the above considerations nonetheless suggest that Member States have been prepared to accept restraints on their foreign policy competences. It is indeed questionable whether one can still maintain that under CFSP, no sovereign rights were transferred to the Union, and that therefore Member States have retained unfettered freedom to enter into international agreements on issues already covered by EU decisions.[25]

C. The Role of the Judiciary in enforcing CFSP Norms

In order to determine whether and how the CFSP primary or secondary norms can effectively restrict Member States in their external relations, the role of the judiciary falls to be examined. In this respect, it is well established that Article 46 TEU does not extend the jurisdiction of the European Court of Justice to the provisions of Title V of the TEU on CFSP. Nevertheless, Article 47 TEU offers the only basis for the Court to review CFSP acts, for the purposes of ascertaining that EU institutions have not acted in a way that would encroach upon the *acquis communautaire*.[26] Article 47 TEU provides that 'nothing in [the TEU] shall affect the Treaties

---

[24] D Thym, 'Die völkerrechtlichen Verträge der Europäischen Union' (2006) 66 *Zeitschrift für ausländisches öffentliches Recht und Völkerrecht* 904: 'Hiernach besitzen die Mitgliedstaaten die rechtliche Möglichkeit, innerstaatlich und im völkerrechtlichen Verkehr auch Regelungen zu treffen, die im Widerspruch zu ihren unionsrechtlichten Verpflichtungen stehen [...]'; cp K Lenaerts and T Corhaut, 'Of Birds and Hedges: the Role of Primacy in Invoking Norms of EU Law' (2006) 31 *EL Rev* 287. See also below section III. B.

[25] In this regard, see M Brkan, 'Exploring the EU Competence in CFSP: Logic or Contradiction?' (2006) 2 *Croatian Yearbook of European Law and Policy* 173; *cf* the current position of the Member States, as reflected in the 'Draft IGC Mandate', annexed to the Presidency Conclusions, 21–22 June 2007, and particularly the insistence on the specificity of the CFSP in fns 6 and 22.

[26] On the interpretation of the *acquis communautaire*, see, eg, S Weatherill, 'Safeguarding the acquis communautaire' in T Heukels, N Blokker and M Brus (eds), *The European Union after Amsterdam: A Legal Analysis* (The Hague, Kluwer Law International, 1998) 153; or C Curti Gialdino, 'Some Reflections on the Acquis Communautaire' (1995) 32 *CML Rev* 1089.

establishing the European Communities or the subsequent Treaties and Acts modifying and supplementing them'.[27]

The Court's control, based on Article 47 TEU, was first exercised in the Airport Transit Visas case. *In casu*, the Commission sought the annulment, pursuant to Article 230(2) EC, of a Council Joint Action on airport transit arrangements, which was adopted under Title VI of the TEU. The Commission contended that the Council should have acted on the basis of the provisions of Title IV of the EC Treaty, and by not doing so, infringed the provisions of Article 47 TEU. In response, the Court held that it had jurisdiction under Article 47 TEU 'to ensure that acts which, according to the Council, fall within the scope of [Title VI] of the Treaty on European Union do not encroach upon the powers conferred by the EC Treaty on the Community'.[28] In the event, the judges found that the Council was justified in choosing Title VI TEU as the relevant decision-making framework for adopting the measure under review, since the situation governed by the Joint Action did not entail the crossing of Member States' external borders by third country nationals, a domain that is covered by Community competence.

By contrast, in the Environmental Penalties case,[29] the Court annulled a Council Framework Decision laying down environmental offences, in respect of which the Member States were required to lay down criminal penalties. The Court found that 'on account of both their aim and their content, Articles 1 to 7 of the framework decision have as their main purpose the protection of the environment and they could have been properly adopted on the basis of Article 175 EC'. Since the Framework Decision encroached upon powers conferred upon the Community, it infringed Article 47 EC, and was therefore annulled.

While the Airport Transit Visas and the Environmental Penalties cases concerned measures adopted on the basis of Title VI TEU, the pending ECOWAS case involves Commission proceedings against two Council acts adopted in the context of Title V TEU.[30] This case thus represents the first

---

[27] Even before the establishment of the Union, the preservation of the *acquis communautaire* was already applied by the Court in relation to the external competences of Member States when in *Centro-Com* it held that these 'must be exercised in a manner consistent with Community law'; see Case C–124/95 *Centro-Com* [1997] ECR I–81, para 41.

[28] Case C–170/96 *Commission v Council* [1998] ECR I–2763, paras 15–16.

[29] C–176/03 *Commission v Council* [2005] ECR I–7879 (Environmental Penalties case).

[30] Namely a Joint Action on the Union's contribution to combating the destabilizing accumulation and spread of small arms and light weapons (2002/589/CFSP) and the Decision implementing this Joint Action (2004/833/CFSP) with a view to the European Union contribution to the West African organization ECOWAS (Case C–91/05, pending: see [2005] OJ C/115/10). It is interesting to note that the Commission refers to the joint action as 'an act of general legislative nature'. While it is tempting to regard this as a general qualification by the Commission of the legal nature of CFSP acts, the present authors realise that it may very well be a pragmatic argument.

opportunity for the Court to control the institutions' compliance with Article 47 TEU in a case involving the interplay between the first and second pillars.[31]

As it has been established, Article 47 allows the Court to protect the *acquis communautaire* against PJCC encroachment, and if need be to annul the contentious act. Though it may have been argued otherwise,[32] the Court should most probably confirm that its jurisdiction under Article 47 TEU includes the review of CFSP measures to ascertain that they do not affect Community powers.

Recent case law also provides some additional indications of a possible outcome of the ECOWAS case. In its *Yusuf* and *Kadi* pronouncements, the Court of First Instance not only addressed the vertical hierarchy between the national, EU and UN legal order, but also the horizontal relation between the Union's pillars. At least in relation to the imposition of economic and financial sanctions to individuals (which is not expressly foreseen by Articles 60 and 301 TEC), the CFI held that the Union's objectives could only be attained by making use of Community competences and that:

> [u]nder Articles 60 EC and 301 EC, action by the Community is therefore in actual fact action by the Union, the implementation of which finds its footing on the Community pillar after the Council has adopted a common position or a joint action under the CFSP.[33]

The CFI *Yusuf* and *Kadi* judgments offer a clear example of an explicit, albeit exceptional, subordination of the Community to CFSP decision making, and an indication that the unity of the Union's legal order cannot be neglected by the Court.[34] At the same time, it recalls that the EU

---

[31] In Cases T–349/99 *Miskovic* and T–350/99 *Karic*, the Court of First Instance missed the opportunity when the Council amended the decision challenged by two individuals who had been refused a visa on the basis of a CFSP act.

[32] It has been argued that it is 'doubtful whether the combined effect of Arts 46(e) and 47 may result in the conferral upon the ECJ, in respect of provisions of Title V of the EU Treaty, of the same powers of judicial review which it enjoys under the Community Treaty'; see M-G Garbagnati Ketvel, 'The Jurisdiction of the European Court of Justice in Respect of the Common Foreign and Security Policy' (2006) *ICLQ* 77–120, 90; see also R Baratta, 'Overlaps between European Community Competence and European Union Foreign Policy Activity' in E Cannizzaro (ed), *The European Union as an Actor in International Relations* (The Hague, Kluwer Law International, 2002) 51, who suggested that the Court could also rule on the 'irrelevance or inefficacy of such an act in the Community order'.

[33] Cases T–306/01, *Ahmed Ali Yusuf and Al Barakaat International Foundation v Council and Commission* [2005] ECR II–3533; and T–315/01, *Yassin Abdullah Kadi v Council and Commission* [2005] ECR II–3649, (para 161 *Yusuf* case).

[34] See more extensively on this issue RA Wessel, 'The Inside Looking Out: Consistency and Delimitation in EU External Relations' (2000) 37 *CML Rev* 1135; as well as RA Wessel, 'Fragmentation in the Governance of EU External Relations: Legal Institutional Dilemmas

judiciary can only adjudicate *indirectly* on CFSP provisions.[35] While these cases suggest a certain willingness from the Courts not to ignore CFSP when related to Community law, it still does not provide any answer to the question of the extent to which it is competent to review actions by Member States if these conflict with established Union policies.

The case law examined hitherto consists of cases involving judicial review by the Court of Justice on the basis of Article 230 EC. This leaves open the question of whether *national courts* have complete freedom to decide on the validity of a CFSP act whenever the legal basis of a national implementation measure is being questioned. Obviously, they are not bound by a *Foto-Frost* duty to refrain from invalidating EU decisions as this case law is clearly related to Community law.[36]

In that respect, the recent judgment of the Court in the *Segi* case is instructive. The case concerns an appeal by Segi (and in a similar case by another Basque organisation, Gestoras Pro Amnistía) to set aside an earlier order of the Court of First Instance.[37] The decision under attack in this case is a Common Position (2001/931/CFSP) with a legal basis in both the second (Article 15 TEU) and the third pillars (Article 34 TEU). Although Article 35(1) does not enable national courts to refer a question to the Court for a preliminary ruling on a common position, the relevant question according to the Court is whether or not the decision produces legal effects in relation to third parties. In the event, the two organisations were placed on a list of terrorist organisations, annexed to Common Position 2001/931/CFSP. The Court thus found that that common position had produced legal effects in relation to the two organisations, and concluded:

> As a result, it had to be possible to make subject to review by the Court a common position which, because of its content, has a scope going beyond that assigned by the EU Treaty to that kind of act. Therefore, a national court hearing

and the New Constitution for Europe' in JW de Zwaan *et al*, (eds), *The European Union—An Ongoing Process of Integration*, Liber Amicorum Fred Kellermann (The Hague, TMC Asser Press, 2004) 123.

[35] This is also reflected in cases such as *Hautala*, in which the Court of First Instance argued that it could adjudicate on the legality of a Council decision on the public access to documents even if this decision extended to CFSP documents: Case T–14/98 *Hautala v Council* [1999] ECR II–2489, paras 41–2; see also earlier with respect to third-pillar documents Case T–174/95 *Svenska Journalistförbundet* [1998] ECR II–2289.

[36] Case C–314/85 *Foto-Frost v Hauptzollamt Lübeck-Ost* [1987] ECR 4199. See, however, for arguments to apply the *Foto-Frost* reasoning to Union law: DM Curtin and IF Dekker, 'The EU as a "Layered" International Organization: Institutional Unity in Disguise' in P Craig and G De Búrca (eds), *The Evolution of EU Law* (Oxford, Oxford University Press, 1999) 83, 123. See, for this question and others in relation to the impact of the 2004 Constitutional Treaty, also 'The CFSP under the EU Constitutional Treaty—Issues of Depillarization, Editorial Comments' (2005) 42 *CML Rev* 325.

[37] See Cases C–355/04 P *Segi and Others v Council* and C–354/04 P *Gestoras Pro Amnistía and Others v Council*, judgments of 27 February 2007, nyr.

a dispute which indirectly raises the issue of the validity or interpretation of a common position adopted on the basis of Article 34 EU [...] and which has serious doubt whether that common position is really intended to produce legal effects in relation to third parties, would be able, subject to the conditions fixed by Article 35 EU, to ask the Court to give a preliminary ruling. [...] The Court would also have jurisdiction to review the lawfulness of such acts when an action has been brought by a Member State or the Commission under the conditions fixed by Article 35(6) EU.[38]

In addition, the Court confirmed for the first time the binding nature of common positions, examined earlier:[39]

A common position requires the compliance of the Member States by virtue of the principle of the duty to cooperate in good faith, which means in particular that Member States are to take all appropriate measures, whether general or particular, to ensure fulfilment of their obligations under European Union law.[40]

It is tempting, though not perhaps entirely justified, to transpose the above findings to the second pillar. On the one hand, the common position in question could also be regarded as a CFSP decision since it was equally based on both Article 15 and Article 34 TEU. Indeed, as suggested by previous practice, the subject matter—economic and financial sanctions against groups and individuals—is primarily a second pillar issue, and in that capacity closely linked to the Community legal order (viz *Yusuf*).[41] On the other hand, the only reason why the Court concludes on a legal remedy in this case seems to be the presence of a judicial competence in the third pillar in relation to other instruments (decisions and framework decisions). There is no comparable role for the Court in relation to acts with a single CFSP legal basis.

The *Segi* judgment therefore only partly helps in answering the question of the possible legal restraints on the Member States' external actions.[42] As the Court's jurisdiction on CFSP provisions is likely to remain limited in the future Treaty settlement,[43] and given the ambiguity of the possible application of the principles of primacy and direct effect to CFSP,[44] a

---

[38] Case C–355/04 P *Segi and Others v Council*, judgment of 27 February 2007, paras 54–55.

[39] See above section II.A.

[40] Case C–355/04 P *Segi and Others v Council*, judgment of 27 February 2007, para 52.

[41] This would also be in line with Art 275 of the new TFEU, which confers jurisdiction on the ECJ to review 'the legality of European decisions providing for restrictive measures against natural or legal persons [...]'.

[42] See further below, part IV.B.

[43] See the reference in n 41 above.

[44] Most commentators have argued that there are many reasons (including the special nature of CFSP, the general absence of ECJ jurisdiction, the relation with established case law and the probable absence of direct effect) not to apply the principle of primacy to CFSP. See in particular A Dashwood, 'The Relationship between the Member States and the European Union/European Community' (2004) 41 *CML Rev* 355, 363 and 379; as well as his 'The EU

relationship with either Community law or the third pillar will continue to be helpful to interpret the scope of the CFSP legal restraints.

One way of approaching this issue could be to focus on what the Court in *Segi* referred to as 'the principle of the duty to cooperate in good faith'. While the Court used this line to establish the binding nature of common positions, the EU Treaty formulates this as a general principle in the second pillar.

D. The Principle of Loyal Cooperation under Title V TEU

The potential constraining character of primary and secondary CFSP obligations, analysed above, ought to be examined also in the light of the specific principle of loyal cooperation, included in Title V TEU. Article 11(2) TEU provides:

> The Member States shall support the Union's external and security policy actively and unreservedly in a spirit of loyalty and mutual solidarity.

> The Member States shall work together to enhance and develop their mutual political solidarity. They shall refrain from any action which is contrary to the interests of the Union or likely to impair its effectiveness as a cohesive force in international relations.[45]

Placed in the first Article of Title V, this loyalty principle appears to underpin the whole development of CFSP, and govern the relationship between the Member States and the Union in this area. Hence, Member States' specific obligations under the CFSP title should be interpreted in the light of that general obligation to support the Union's CFSP. Indeed, the inclusion of 'shall' makes Member States' loyalty and cooperation clearly mandatory, while suffering little exception, as suggested by the expressions 'actively' and 'unreservedly'.

Although it may be conceived as a mere expression of the general international law principle of *pacta sunt servanda*,[46] the principle of loyalty enshrined in Article 11(2) nevertheless seems more specific. Member States are bound by a *positive* obligation actively to develop the

Constitution: What will Really Change?' (2004–2005) 7 *Cambridge Yearbook of European Legal Studies* 33, 34. See also Editorial Comments (2005) 42 *CML Rev* 325, 327. In this respect, see the Declaration concerning primacy, adopted by the Lisbon Intergovernmental Conference.
    [45] The principle returns in the new TEU in Art 24(3) in even stronger terms: 'Member States shall actively and unreservedly support the Union's common foreign and security policy in a spirit of loyalty and mutual solidarity and shall comply with the Union's action in this area. They shall refrain from action contrary to the Union's interests or likely to impair its effectiveness'. See also M Cremona, above n 3, 19, on the confusion between this provision and the general statement of the principle in Art 4(3) new TEU.
    [46] H Wehberg, 'Pacta Sunt Servanda' (1959) 53 *AJIL* 775.

Union's CFSP, which since the Amsterdam Treaty encompasses the Member States' duty to 'work together to enhance and develop their mutual political solidarity'. In addition, Article 11(2) contains a *negative* obligation for the Member States not to undertake 'any action which is contrary to the interests of the Union or likely to impair its effectiveness as a cohesive force in international relations'. Article 11(2) TEU also foresees in its last indent that the Council is to ensure that these principles are complied with.

Indeed, it is notable that these positive and negative obligations echo the obligations related to the principle of loyal cooperation expressed in Article 10 EC which,[47] falling within the jurisdiction of the Court of Justice, have been extensively explicated and developed.[48] Suffice to recall that the principle of loyal cooperation expressed in Article 10 EC has been held by the Court to include: (1) the obligation to take all appropriate measures necessary for the effective application of Community law; (2) the obligation to ensure the protection of rights resulting from primary and secondary Community law; (3) the obligation to act in such a way as to achieve the objectives of the Treaty, in particular when Community actions fail to appear; (4) the obligation not to take measures which could harm the *effet utile* of Community law; (5) the obligation not to take measures which could hamper the internal functioning of the institutions; and (6) the obligation not to undertake actions which could hamper the development of the integration process of the Community.[49]

[47] 'Member States shall take all appropriate measures, whether general or particular, to ensure fulfilment of the obligations arising out of this Treaty or resulting from action taken by the institutions of the Community. They shall facilitate the achievement of the Community's tasks. They shall abstain from any measure which could jeopardise the attainment of the objectives of [the EC] Treaty'. This subsection is partly based on RA Wessel, above n 4, Section 4.3.1.2.

[48] See further J Temple Lang, 'The Core of the Constitutional Law of the Community—Art 5 EC' in L Gormley (ed), *Current and Future Perspectives on EC Competition Law* (The Hague, Kluwer Law International, 1997) 41; K Mortelmans, 'The Principle of Loyalty to the Community (Art 5 EC) and the Obligations of the Community Institutions' (1998) 5 *Maastricht Journal of European and Comparative Law* 67; M Blanquet, *L'article 5 du traité CEE—Recherches sur les obligations de fidélité des Etats membres de la Communauté* (Paris, LGDJ, 1994).

[49] See rather extensively A Hatje, *Loyalität als Rechtsprinzip in der Europäischen Union* (Baden-Baden, Nomos, 2001). Central to Hatje's conception is the thesis that loyalty serves the creation of unity, which is characterised by the general institutional autonomy of both the Member States and the EU on the one hand and the duty of cooperation in order to implement the objectives of the EU on the other. The mediation of conflicts on the political and legal levels thus becomes one of the most important tasks of the principle of loyalty; see S Bitter, 'Loyalty in the European Union—A Review' (2002) 3 *German Law Journal*; see also Case C–339/00 *Ireland v Commission* [2003] ECR I–11757, paras 71 and 72, and case law cited.

Moreover, in relation to the conclusion and implementation of international agreements in particular, recent case law points to various procedural obligations based on Article 10 EC. For instance, Member States have an obligation to consult the EU institutions when they negotiate bilateral agreements in a sphere where the Community has not yet concluded an agreement, but where 'there is a start of a concerted Community action at international level'.[50] Procedural obligations derived from Article 10 EC in relation to Member States' international commitments also encompass, within the specific framework of a mixed agreement, a duty to inform and consult the competent Community institutions.[51]

Given the proximity between the provisions of Article 11(2) TEU and Article 10 EC respectively, there are reasons to interpret the former in the light of the latter's interpretation. As illustrated by the *Pupino* judgment, the Court seeks inspiration in its interpretation of EC provisions to interpret similar EU provisions.[52] Indeed, the same judgment suggests that the principle of loyal cooperation, expressed particularly in Article 10 EC, may have a trans-pillar application. In particular, the Court held that:

> [i]t would be difficult for the Union to carry out its task effectively if the principle of loyal cooperation, requiring in particular that Member States take all appropriate measures, whether general or particular, to ensure fulfilment of their obligations under European Union law, were not *also* binding in the area of police and judicial cooperation in criminal matters, which is moreover entirely based on cooperation between the Member States and the institutions.[53]

Unconvinced by the Italian and United Kingdom Governments' argument that the TEU contains no obligation similar to that laid down in Article 10 EC, the Court held that the principle of loyal cooperation binds the Member States in relation to the Union, 'in order to contribute effectively to the pursuit of the Union's objectives'.[54] The Court thereby suggested that the principle of loyalty has a trans-pillar definition and application. A fortiori, the principle of loyal cooperation should apply also in the context

---

[50] In Case C–266/03 *Commission v Luxembourg* [2005] ECR I–4805, the Court held that: '[t]he adoption of a decision authorising the Commission to negotiate a multilateral agreement on behalf of the Community marks the start of a concerted Community action at international level and requires, for that purpose, if not a duty of abstention on the part of the Member States, at the very least a duty of close cooperation between the latter and the Community institutions in order to facilitate the achievement of the Community tasks and to ensure the coherence and consistency of the action and its international representation'; see also C–433/03 *Commission v Germany* [2005] ECR I–6985.

[51] Case C–459/03 *Commission v Ireland (MOX Plant)* [2006] ECR I–4635.

[52] Case C–105/03 *Pupino* [2005] ECR I–5285, paras 19, 21 and 28 (similarity between the system established by Art 234 EC and that of Art 35 TEU); paras 33–34 (similarity in the wording of Art 249 and Art 34(2)(b)).

[53] Case C–105/03 *Pupino* [2005] ECR I–5285, para 42. Emphasis added.

[54] *Ibid*, para 36.

of CFSP given the inclusion in Title V of a specific provision containing obligations similar to those laid down in Article 10 EC.[55]

Transposed to the CFSP context, the Court's interpretation of the principle of loyal cooperation could entail far-reaching obligations for the Member States, particularly with respect to their power to conclude international agreements in the field of CFSP. In the light of the Court's 2005 pronouncement in *Commission v Luxembourg*,[56] it could be argued that, although not prevented from acting, Member States are expected under Article 11(2) TEU to inform and consult the EU institutions in areas where there is the start of a concerted Union CFSP action at international level.[57] Indeed, given that each CFSP instrument in principle expresses a concerted action of the Union at the international level, the procedural obligations linked to the CFSP principle of loyal cooperation would not only apply in situations where negotiations of an agreement based on Article 24 TEU are envisaged by the Presidency,[58] it could also apply where the start of a concerted action leads notably to a JA or a common position. Thus, Member States should inform and consult EU institutions, even prior to the adoption of a CFSP autonomous act or the conclusion of an EU agreement, as soon as an EU concerted action at international level emerges.

Although the application of the principle of loyal cooperation to the CFSP context appears to be supported both by the terminology of Article 11(2) TEU and by the Court's case law, it could be argued that the inclusion in Title V TEU of a *specific* expression of such principle of cooperation prevents, or at least qualifies the full transposition of the Court's interpretation of the principle of loyal cooperation expressed on Article 10 EC to the CFSP context. After all, the application of the principle of loyal cooperation as a principle of Union law may be explained by the absence of any specific expression of that principle in the context of Pillar III. In other words—and following the Court's line of reasoning in *Pupino*—the default principle of loyal cooperation based on the interpretation of Article 10 EC would apply where the Treaty does not provide for a specific expression of such principle. Conversely, the inclusion of a specific duty of cooperation in the CFSP context would prevent the *full* transposition of the interpretation of Article 10 EC therein. Thereby, Member States and the EU institutions would be subject, in the context of

---

[55]   Further on the *Pupino* ruling: E Spaventa, 'Opening Pandora's Box: Some Reflections on the Constitutional Effects of the Decision in *Pupino*' (2007) 3 *Eu Const* 5.

[56]   Case C–266/03 *Commission v Luxembourg* [2005] ECR I–4805; also C–433/03 *Commission v Germany* [2005] ECR I–6985. See further M Cremona, 'Defending the Community Interest: the Duties of Cooperation and Compliance', ch 5, this volume.

[57]   Such a procedural obligation would indeed echo the obligation of systematic cooperation foreseen in Art 16 TEU.

[58]   See further below.

CFSP, to obligations derived from Article 11(2) TEU specifically, to be interpreted taking account of the specific objectives and nature of, and place within the system of, Title V.

Indeed, the proposition that the interpretation of Article 10 EC is not automatically transferable to the context of CFSP seems to be supported by the provisions of the post-Lisbon Treaties. Despite the formal 'depillarisation' of the Union that it intends to operate, the Lisbon Treaty will maintain a distinction between the principle of loyal cooperation expressed notably in Article 4 of new TEU, therein re-branded 'sincere cooperation',[59] and the specific principle related to CFSP, foreseen in Article 24 new TEU.[60] At first sight, this dual loyalty is surprising given the Community's amalgamation with the Union,[61] which should have entailed that the principle of sincere cooperation would have generally applied between the Member States and the *Union institutions*, over all areas corresponding to the objectives of the Union, thus including CFSP. Arguably, the inclusion of the CFSP principle of loyalty, alongside the general principle of Article 4, in the new treaty typifies the intent still to distinguish the CFSP and other EU provisions, and suggests that the two principles are perhaps meant to operate differently.[62]

While this *lex specialis* duty of cooperation could lead to a more specific interpretation of the Member States' duty of cooperation in relation to CFSP, it does not mean that the latter may prevent or limit the application of the principle of Article 10 EC itself. In view of the general primacy of Community law over the law of the other two pillars, based on Article 47 TEU, Article 11(2) cannot, in principle, serve as a tool to limit or prevent the application of the principle of loyal cooperation with the Community institutions. In other words, Member States could not rely on the specific provisions of Article 11(2) to justify an infringement of their obligations under Article 10 EC. Only in exceptional situations does the TEU foresee that EC law may be subject to CFSP instruments. As it will be suggested in

[59] 'Pursuant to the principle of sincere cooperation, the Union and the Member States shall, in full mutual respect, assist each other in carrying out tasks which flow from the Constitution. The Member States shall take any appropriate measure, general or particular, to ensure fulfilment of the obligations arising out of the Constitution or resulting from the acts of the institutions of the Union. The Member States shall facilitate the achievement of the Union's tasks and refrain from any measure which could jeopardise the attainment of the Union's objectives.'

[60] 'Member States shall actively and unreservedly support the Union's common foreign and security policy in a spirit of loyalty and mutual solidarity and shall comply with the Union's action in this area. They shall refrain from action contrary to the Union's interests or likely to impair its effectiveness.'

[61] See Arts IV–437 and IV–438 TCE.

[62] Even if the Court of Justice, which would have jurisdiction on both provisions, could give them an equivalent interpretation.

the last section of this paper, it could be argued, on the contrary, that Article 10 EC could serve to force Member States to comply with their CFSP obligations.[63]

Summing up, Title V on CFSP includes a specific expression of the duty of cooperation between the Member States and CFSP. If interpreted in the light of the general duty of loyal cooperation encapsulated in Article 10 EC,[64] the CFSP principle of loyalty, which constitutes another expression of the same principle, could entail far-reaching restrictions for the Member States' freedom in the fields covered by CFSP.

III. EU INTERNATIONAL AGREEMENTS AS RESTRAINTS ON MEMBER STATES' EXTERNAL COMPETENCES

Examining primary and secondary CFSP norms, it has become clear that Member States have accepted restraints on their autonomy. This section looks at the impact of the EU treaty-making competence (A), and the nature of this external power (B), on the Member States' foreign policy freedom.

A. The Treaty-making Competence of the EU

The EU competence to conclude agreements with third states and other international organisations in the non-Community areas has been the subject of intense debate ever since the negotiations on the Treaty of Maastricht. The controversy stems from the unclear legal status of the Union. While the abandoned 2004 TCE[65] as well as the Reform Treaty expressly confer international legal personality on the Union,[66] the current

---

[63] See Section IV.A below.

[64] Indeed, Art 10 EC is only but one expression of the general principle of loyal cooperation, operating within the EU legal order. See in this regard what the Court says about the principle in the context of mixed agreements; see eg *Opinion 2/91 (ILO Convention)* [1993] ECR I–1061; *Opinion 1/94 (WTO Agreement)* [1994] ECR I–5267; Case C–25/94 *FAO* [1996] ECR I–1469; C–459/03 *Commission v Ireland* [2006] ECR I–4635 (MOX Plant); *Opinion 1/03 (Lugano Convention)* [2006] ECR I–1145.

[65] Art I–7 TCE.

[66] Art 47 of the new TEU.

treaty remains silent in this respect.[67] Be that as it may, the EU has nonetheless engaged actively in legal relations with third states and other international organisations.[68]

The conclusion of international agreements by the Union is governed by the provisions of Article 24 TEU,[69] which are partly modelled on Article 300 TEC.[70] Cross-references included in Articles 24 (CFSP) and 38 (PJCC) TEU indicate that the procedure foreseen in Article 24 TEU is used also for concluding EU international agreements in the PJCC sphere. In other words, Article 24 TEU represents the general legal basis for the Union's treaty-making power, including for concluding cross-pillar (second and third) agreements.[71]

---

[67] Nevertheless, 'As time goes by, the debate seems ever more irrelevant', as Eeckhout rightly observes. Eeckhout also points to the consensus on this issue in academic circles. P Eeckhout, above note 1, 155. *Cf* also the views by (the Council's Legal Counsel) Gosalbo Bono, above n 2, 354–5.

[68] By now (early 2007) the Union has become a party to some 90 international agreements. See more extensively RA Wessel, 'The European Union as a Party to International Agreements: Shared Competences, Mixed Responsibilities', in A Dashwood and M Maresceau (eds), *Law and Practice of EU External Relations* (Cambridge, Cambridge University Press, forthcoming). Parts of this section have been based on that article. The Agreements may be retrieved through the Council's Agreements Database.

[69] Art 24 TEU provides:
'1. When it is necessary to conclude an agreement with one or more States or international organisations in implementation of this Title, the Council, acting unanimously, may authorise the Presidency, assisted by the Commission as appropriate, to open negotiations to that effect. Such agreements shall be concluded by the Council acting unanimously on a recommendation from the Presidency.
2. The Council shall act unanimously when the agreement covers an issue for which unanimity is required for the adoption of internal decisions.
3. When the agreement is envisaged in order to implement a joint action or common position, the Council shall act by a qualified majority in accordance with Art 23(2).
4. The provisions of this Article shall also apply to matters falling under Title VI. When the agreement covers an issue for which a qualified majority is required for the adoption of internal decisions or measures, the Council shall act by a qualified majority in accordance with Art 34(3).
5. No agreement shall be binding on a Member State whose representative in the Council states that it has to comply with the requirements of its own constitutional procedure; the other members of the Council may agree that the agreement shall nevertheless apply provisionally.
6. Agreements concluded under the conditions set out by this Article shall be binding on the institutions of the Union.'

[70] Cp Art 24(6) TEU with Art 300(7) TEC. Art 24 has undergone changes with the Nice Treaty revision, namely the inclusion of para 6 and an extension of qualified majority voting. See, eg, Editorial Comments (2001) 38 *CML Rev* 825; E Regelsberger and D Kugelmann, 'Art 24 EUV para 1' in R Streinz, *EUV/EGV* (Munich, Beck, 2003); as well as I Österdahl, 'The EU and Its Member States, Other States, and International Organizations—the Common European Security and Defence Policy after Nice' (2001) 70 *Nordic Journal of International Law* 341.

[71] See the 2006 Agreement between the European Union and the United States of America on the processing and transfer of passenger name record (PNR) data, which is based on Decision 2006/729/CFSP/JHA of the Council of 16 October 2006 (OJ, 2006, L 298, 27.10.2006) and refers to both Arts 24 and 38 TEU.

The provisions of Article 24 TEU epitomise the multi-level character of the EU external relations regime in which both the Union and the Member States have a role to play.[72] The Nice Treaty foresees the distinct competence of the Union to conclude international treaties. According to modified paragraphs 2 and 3 of Article 24, the Council shall act unanimously when the agreement covers an issue for which unanimity is required for the adoption of internal decisions, but it will act by a qualified majority whenever the agreement is envisaged to implement a JA or common position. Moreover, paragraph 6 sets out that the agreements concluded by the Council shall be binding on the institutions of the Union. In other words, the Union is capable of contracting obligations under international law that are distinct from those of the Member States.[73]

Indeed, the debate on whether agreements concluded on the basis of Article 24 TEU are concluded by the Council on behalf of the Union or on behalf of the Member States[74] has been superseded by practice. In effect, the Union has become a party to an increasing number of international agreements based on Article 24 TEU.[75] One of the main issues in the debate relates to the provisions of Article 24(5) TEU:

> No agreement shall be binding on a Member State whose representative in the Council states that it has to comply with the requirements of its own constitutional procedure; the other members of the Council may agree that the agreement shall nevertheless apply provisionally.

---

[72] See more extensively RA Wessel, 'The Multilevel Constitution of European Foreign Relations' in N Tsagourias (ed), *Transnational Constitutionalism: International and European Perspectives* (Cambridge, Cambridge University Press, 2007).

[73] Nevertheless, some Member States (still) hold on to the view that the Council concludes agreements on their behalf, rather than on behalf of the Union. See on this issue also S Marquardt, 'La capacité de l'Union européenne de conclure des accords internationaux dans le domaine de la coopération policière et judiciaire en matière pénal', in G De Kerchove and A Weyembergh (eds), *Sécurité et justice: enjeu de la politique extérieure de l'Union européenne* (Brussels, Edition de l'Université de Bruxelles, 2003) 179, 185. See the same contribution for arguments underlining the view that the Council can only conclude these agreements on behalf of the EU. *Cf* also S Marquardt, 'The Conclusion of International Agreements under Art 24 of the Treaty on European Union' in V Kronenberger (ed), *The European Union and the International Legal Order: Discord or Harmony?* (The Hague, TMC Asser Press, 2001) 333; D Verwey, *The European Community, the European Union and the International Law of Treaties: a Comparative Legal Analysis of the Community and Union's External Treaty-making Practice* (The Hague, TMC Asser Press, 2004) 74; and RA Wessel (2000), above n 34.

[74] See more extensively RA Wessel, 'The International Legal Status of the European Union' (1997) 2 *EFA Rev* 109; as well as 'Revisiting the International Legal Status of the EU' (2000) 5 *EFA Rev* 507.

[75] And even before that, it was clear that 'it would hardly be persuasive to contend that such treaties are in reality treaties concluded by individual Member States'; see C Tomuschat, 'The International Responsibility of the European Union' in E Cannizzaro (ed), above n 32, 181. *Cf* also Eeckhout, above n 1, 159; P Koutrakos, above n 1, 406–9 and Gosalbo Bono, above n 2, 354–6. It should, however, be recalled that some early agreements mentioned 'The Council of the European Union' as the contracting party, including the 1999 Agreement with Republic of Iceland and the Kingdom of Norway, and the 2000 Agreement with the Republic of Iceland and the Kingdom of Norway.

This provision was often read in conjunction with Declaration no 4 adopted at the Amsterdam IGC:

> The Provisions of Article J.14 and K.10 [now Articles 24 and 38] of the Treaty on European Union and any agreements resulting from them shall not imply any transfer of competence from the Member States to the European Union.

However, neither in theory nor in practice have these provisions limited the EU treaty-making capacity. Article 24 TEU provides that the Council concludes international agreements after its members (the Member States) have unanimously agreed that it can do so.[76] On the basis of paragraph 5, Member States may invoke their national constitutional requirements to prevent becoming bound by the agreement, but this does not affect the conclusion of the agreement by the Union.[77] While on some occasions the issue was raised,[78] it has obviously not prevented the conclusion of such agreements.

Indeed, one may argue that when agreements are not binding on Member States that have made constitutional reservations, *a contrario*, agreements *are* binding on those Member States that have not made this reservation. While this may hold true for the relation between the Member State and the EU, it cannot be maintained vis-a-vis the third state or other international organisation. After all, no treaty relationship has been established between the Member States and this party, and unless the agreement explicitly involves rights and/or obligations for Member States in relation to the other party, there is no direct link between them. In case Member States' participation is necessary for the Union to fulfil its treaty obligations, the other party seems to have to address the Union, which, in turn, will have to address its Member States.[79]

The above-mentioned Declaration no 4 does not seem to conflict with the EU distinct treaty-making capacity. Since the right to conclude treaties

---

[76] The explicit reference to the unanimity rule (as a *lex specialis*) seems to exclude the applicability of the general regime of constructive abstention in cases where unanimity is required as foreseen in Art 23 TEU. Furthermore, as indicated by G Hafner, 'The Amsterdam Treaty and the Treaty-Making Power of the European Union: Some Critical Comments' in G Hafner *et al*, *Liber Amicorum Professor Seidl-Hohenveldern—in Honour of his 80th Birthday* (The Hague, Kluwer Law International, 1998) 279, the application of the constructive abstention to Art 24 would make little sense, since Art 24 already provides the possibility of achieving precisely the same effect insofar as Member States, by referring to their constitutional requirements, are entitled to exclude, in relation to themselves, the legal effect of agreements concluded by the Council.

[77] Art 17 of the Council Rules of Procedure foresees that, in principle, international agreements concluded in accordance with Art 24 TEU are published in the OJEU, 'unless the Council decides otherwise on the grounds of Arts 4 and 9 of Regulation (EC) No 1049/2001 of the European Parliament and of the Council of 30 May 2001 regarding public access to European Parliament, Council and Commission documents', [2002] OJ L/230/7.

[78] See S Marquardt (2003), above n 73, 182, who refers to Germany and France.

[79] See more extensively on these issues D Verwey, above n 73.

is an original power of the Union itself, the treaty-making power of the Member States remains unfettered and, indeed, is not transferred to the Union. Therefore, the Declaration can only mean that this right of the Union must not be understood as creating new substantive competences for it.[80] Through the Council Decision, Member States have been provided with an opportunity to set limits to the use by the Union of its treaty-making capacity, both from a procedural and a substantive perspective.

The fact that the EU becomes a party to the agreement (and not its Member States) is underlined by the way the agreements come into force. Many agreements use the following provision in this respect[81]:

> This agreement shall enter into force on the first day of the first month after the Parties have notified each other of the completion of the internal procedures necessary for this purpose.

However, so far, the 'internal procedures' on the side of the Union seem to relate to the necessary decision of the Council and not to any national constitutional procedure in the Member States. In other cases, the entry into force is even simpler[82]: 'This Agreement shall enter into force on the first day of the month after the Parties have signed it.'

It goes beyond the scope of this Chapter to investigate the parliamentary procedures related to Article 24 agreements in all 27 Member States. Suffice to say that Member States generally do not consider it expedient to submit EU external agreements to their regular parliamentary procedure.[83] As ratification by the governments of the Member States is not required for agreements concluded by the Union, their constitutional requirements simply do not apply. In the Netherlands for instance, parliamentary approval of Article 24 agreements is not considered necessary given that the Kingdom of the Netherlands is not party to those agreements. For the same reason, EU agreements are not published in the *Traktatenblad*, which is the national review of treaties concluded by the Kingdom. An exception was made for two agreements concluded with the United States in the area of PJCC, for these could be considered to complement or even amend existing bilateral treaties with the US. However, the position of the

---

[80]   As also submitted by Hafner, above n 76, 272. In this respect, see the Declarations on the CFSP annexed to the Lisbon final Act.

[81]   See, eg, the 2005 Agreement between Romania and the European Union on security procedures for the exchange of classified information, [2005] OJ L/118/48.

[82]   See, eg, the 2006 Agreement between the International Criminal Court and the European Union on cooperation and assistance, [2006] OJ L/115/50.

[83]   This is confirmed by G De Kerchove and S Marquardt, 'Les accords internationaux conclus par l'Union Européenne' (2004) *Annuaire Français de Droit International* 803, 813: '[...] dans la pratique suivie jusqu'à présent, aucun État membre n'a invoqué le respect de ses règles constitutionnelles lors de la conclusion par le Conseil d'accords dans le domaine de la PESC.'

Netherlands was not exceptional: all Member States—save Austria, Estonia, France, and Greece—made a constitutional reservation. The same situation occurred in relation to the conclusion of the EU agreements with Iceland and Norway, while eight Member States invoked Article 24(5) TEU in relation to the agreement with Switzerland.[84] This clearly differentiates the third-pillar agreements from the ones concluded under CFSP.[85]

While on the basis of the current treaty regime the *existence* of an EU treaty-making power is established, the provisions of Article 24 TEU do not, in themselves, shed any light on the *scope* of such EU power. Paragraph 1 of Article 24 TFEU merely stipulates that 'conclud[ing] an agreement with one or more States or international organisations in implementation of this Title' must be '*necessary*',[86] leaving it the Member States to establish that necessity. The scope of the EU treaty-making power thereby remains undetermined, in contrast to that of the Community, which is legally provided by the EC Treaty itself.[87]

In what appears to merge the two scenarios of Article 24 TEU and Article 300 EC respectively, Article 216 new TEU not only foresees that the 'conclusion of an agreement is necessary in order to achieve [...] one of the objectives', but also establishes a competence when the conclusion of an agreement 'is provided for in a legally binding Union act or is likely to affect common rules or alter their scope'. Although this provision does not give any guidance as to the limits of this competence, it seems that it should, at least, be read in conjunction with the principle of conferral in 5 new TEU.[88] Indeed, as argued by Cremona, the new treaty-making provision 'introduces a confusion between the existence of competence and exclusivity' as it does not address the situation where, although an agreement is perhaps not necessary to achieve a Union objective, its conclusion *by a Member State* might 'affect common rules or alter their scope'.[89] Therefore in a situation of parallel competences, the nature of the EU competence should first and foremost be considered and in particular its possible pre-emptive exclusivity.

---

[84]   *Ibid*, 813 and 823. In these cases the Council decided to have a procedure in two stages, allowing for Member States to follow domestic parliamentary procedures. See Conclusions of the Council of 6 June 2003, Doc 10409/03 of 18 June 2003. *Cf* also J Monar, 'Editorial Comment—Mostar: Three Lessons for the European Union' (1997) 2 *EFA Rev* 1; and T Georgopoulos, 'What Kind of Treaty-Making Power for the EU?' (2005) 2 *EL Rev* 190, 193.

[85]   In these cases, it may be wondered why the Union and its Member States have not opted for the same construction that has proved its value under Community law: the 'mixed agreement'.

[86]   Emphasis added.

[87]   The provisions of Art 300 EC stipulate that the Community concludes agreements with one or more States or international organisations 'where this [ie EC] Treaty provides'.

[88]   See more extensively on the possible interpretations of Art 216 TFEU, M. Cremona (2006), above n 3, 9–12.

[89]   *Ibid*, 11.

B. The Nature of EU Competence to conclude International Agreements

The potentially broad scope of EU treaty-making power based on Article 24(1) TEU raises the question of whether, and to what extent, the exercise of EU competence may pre-empt Member States' powers in a particular area. Put differently, what if international agreements concluded by Member States 'affect CFSP rules or alter their scope'?

With respect to EC external powers, the Court of Justice emphasised, notably in its Opinion 1/75, that Community policies consist of the combination and interaction of internal and external measures.[90] Stressing that it was impossible for the Member States to exercise powers concurrent to those of the Community, as this would risk compromising the effective defence of the latter's common interests, the Court established the exclusive Community power over the common commercial policy (CCP).[91] The rationale behind the Court's decision was to prevent Member States' individual actions from infringing a common policy that was deemed necessary to make the system work.[92] The Court also stressed the principle of Member States' loyalty towards the Community. The exclusivity of Community powers in relation to a key area of Community competence—trade—was thereby conceived as an essential device to ensure consistency in Community external relations. While Opinion 1/75 was specifically related to the CCP, the way the Court handled the question posed there could perhaps help addressing a similar problem under CFSP.

Like the CCP, CFSP consists of a coherent set of rules aimed at establishing a common policy. Indeed, the 'common commercial policy was conceived in (current) Article 133 EC in the context of the operation of the common market, for the defence of the common interests of the Community, within which the particular interests of the Member States had to endeavour to adapt to each other'.[93] This description comes close to the purpose of CFSP, in which Member States' particular interests are also subjected to the notion of a common policy.

However, the question of division of competences between the Union and the Member States is more difficult to characterise than the division of competence between the Community and the Member States. The Court's

---

[90]   *Opinion 1/75 (re Understanding on a Local Cost Standard)* [1975] ECR 1355.
[91]   In particular, the Court found that unilateral Member States' actions would lead to unacceptable distortions of competition in the internal market. Moreover, accepting the possibility that Member States adopt positions which differed from intended Community positions, would distorting the institutional framework call into question the mutual trust within the Community and prevent the latter from fulfilling its task in the defence of the common interest (Opinion 1/75, 1363–4)? See more extensively A Dashwood and C Hillion, 'Introduction' in A Dashwood and C Hillion (eds), above n 1, v–vi; and P Eeckhout, above n 1, 12–14.
[92]   *Opinion 1/75 (re Understanding on a Local Cost Standard)* [1975] ECR 1355.
[93]   P Eeckhout, above n 1, 13.

jurisprudence related to effects of EC law on Member States' powers derives explicitly from its view that the EC Treaty establishes a new legal order. Given the specific regime governing the non-Community parts of the Union, that Court's jurisprudence cannot be applied, *mutatis mutandis*, to the interplay between the EU and the Member States. Indeed, the CFSP obligations are largely procedural in nature and only foresee a common policy (read: Union policy) to the extent that this is desired and supported by the Member States.[94] The key principle underlying CFSP is encapsulated in Article 16 TEU, which provides enough leeway for the Member States to prevent issues from being placed on the Union's agenda altogether. Irrespective of the obligation for Member States to 'inform and consult one another within the Council on any matter of foreign and security policy', the subsequent words 'of general interest' indicate, as suggested earlier, a large margin of discretion on the side of (individual) Member States. Indeed, although there is an obligation to try and reach a Union policy, in case of failure, the Member States remain free to pursue their own national policies.

While 'mixity' has become the solution to overcome the division of competences between the EC and its Member States,[95] the international agreements concluded under CFSP are—perhaps ironically[96]—*exclusively* concluded by the European Union.[97] This is in line with the Amsterdam amendment to Article 11 TEU, on the basis of which CFSP is no longer

---

[94] *Cf* P Koutrakos, 'Constitutional Idiosyncrasies and Political Realties: The Emerging Security and Defence Policy of the European Union' (2003) 10 *Columbia Journal of European Law* 69.

[95] On mixity, see J Heliskoski, *Mixed Agreements as a Technique for organizing the International Relations of the European Community and its Member States* (The Hague, Kluwer, 2001); P Eeckhout, above n 1, ch 7; A Dashwood, 'Why Continue to Have Mixed Agreements At All?' in JHJ Bourgeois *et al* (eds), *La Communauté européenne et les accords mixtes* (Brussels, Presses Interuniversitaires Européennes, 1997) 93–9; A Rosas, 'Mixed Union—Mixed Agreements', in M Koskenniemi (ed), *International Law Aspects of the European Union* (The Hague, Martinus Nijhoff Publishers, 1998) 125–48; NA Neuwahl, 'Joint Participation in International Treaties and the Exercise of Power by the EEC and its Member States: Mixed Agreements' (1991) 28 *CML Rev* 717–40; and on responsibility in these cases in particular E Neframi, 'International Responsibility of the European Community and of the Member States under Mixed Agreements' in E Cannizzaro (ed), above n 32, 193–205.

[96] Indeed, the multilevel dimension is at least as self-evident as in the Community, with regard to which Dashwood rightfully held: 'It is an inescapable aspect of the constitutional character of the Community that the competence conferred by the EC Treaty in external as well as internal matters is limited, and usually shared with the Member States. Mixed agreements are a natural and practical mechanism to enable the Union, with its character as a constitutional order of States, to function effectively on the international plane.' A Dashwood, 'Opinion 2/00, Cartagena Protocol on Biosafety' (2002) 39 *CML Rev* 367–8.

[97] As the 2004 Agreement with the Swiss Confederation concerning the latter's association with the so-called Schengen *acquis* shows, combined EC/EU agreements are possible (see below section 4.C). A similar construction has been debated for the 2006 Cooperation Agreement with Thailand. In the end, however, the agreement was concluded as a traditional Community/Member States mixed agreement; see D Thym, above n 24, 909. A similar debate

defined and implemented by 'the Union and its Member States', but merely by the Union. Nevertheless, it would be going too far to conclude on an exclusive competence for the Union on this basis, in the line of Opinion 1/75. In fact, the whole system of CFSP as described above seems to point to the existence of 'shared', if not 'parallel' competences: both the Union and its Member States appear to be competent to conclude treaties in the area of CFSP (including ESDP). In that sense, the effect of CFSP norms on Member States' powers could be envisaged in the light of the Court's pronouncements on the effects of Community powers in the fields of development cooperation or humanitarian aid. This case law suggests that since the Community competence in these fields is not exclusive, the Member States are accordingly entitled to enter into commitments themselves vis-a-vis non-Member States, either individually or collectively, in the Council or outside it, or even jointly with the Community.[98]

Does this mean that the 'exclusivity' issue plays no role at all in relation to CFSP? Lisbon Treaty envisages the application of the principle of pre-emption to shared competences (Article 2(2) TFEU). However, the CFSP competence is therein described separately from the other types of EU competences, and is not listed under the shared competences. As Cremona argues, this would amount to acknowledging that Member States under CFSP are not pre-empted from concluding international agreements in areas already covered by Union agreements. In other words, it is unlikely that the conditions contained in Article 3(2) on exclusive Union competences would apply in a CFSP context.[99] Article 3(2) TFEU reads: 'The Union shall also have exclusive competence for the conclusion of an international agreement when its conclusion is provided for in a legislative act of the Union or is necessary to enable the Union to exercise its internal competence, or insofar as its conclusion may affect common rules or alter their scope'. Indeed, CFSP rules will not find their basis in a 'legislative act'.

That being said, when this provision is read in conjunction with the loyalty principle enshrined in Article 28(4) new TEU, it seems too early completely to rule out exclusivity in the field of CFSP, particularly in view of the fact that the Court would have jurisdiction in respect of this Article. After all, even in the current period, the Union's external activities in the form of the conclusion of international agreements are booming and

---

took place on the EU accession to the ASEAN Treaty of Amity and Cooperation. As the relevant documents (such as Council Doc 15772/06) are not in the public domain, these developments are difficult to follow.

[98] Joined Cases C–181/91 and C–248/91 *European Parliament v Council of the European Communities and Commission of the European Communities* [1993] ECR I–3685 (Bangladesh case); Case C–316/91 *European Parliament v Council of the European Union* [1994] ECR I–625 (EDF case).

[99] M Cremona (2006), above note 3, 18–19.

Member States' actions increasingly risk affecting common rules or altering their scope. While the creation of CFSP norms depends on the political will of the Member States, once these norms have been established, their very purpose is to restrict the freedom Member States traditionally enjoy in their external relations. Allowing Member States to affect—or even act contrary to—common norms established by EU international agreements would amount to rendering most of the provisions in Title V of the EU Treaty nugatory.

The emerging question, then, is whether a hierarchy of competences can be established: to what extent are Member States bound by agreements concluded by the Union, and do these agreements restrict their individual freedom in external relations? In this respect, there appears to be no reason not to apply the so-called *Haegeman* doctrine to EU agreements and to regard them as forming 'an integral part of Union law'.[100] This view is supported by the reference in Article 24(6) TEU that the agreements bind the institutions.[101] The question remains, however, whether the Member States are automatically bound by the agreements as a matter of EU law, and indeed whether perhaps a 'direct effect' of the agreements could even be construed. This would place the Member States in a different position towards the agreements than in other international organisations.

In the EC, Member States do have special obligations on the basis of agreements concluded by the Community.[102] Article 300(7) TEC clearly provides that agreements shall be binding on the institutions *and* the Member States and, in *Kupferberg*, the Court held:

> In ensuring respect for commitments arising from an agreement concluded by the Community Institutions the Member States fulfil an obligation not only in relation to the non-member country concerned but also and above all in relation to the Community which has assumed responsibility for the due performance of the agreement.[103]

Irrespective of the fact that the past 15 years have blurred the distinction between Community law and the law of the other Union pillars, Court judgments such as *Haegeman* and *Kupferberg* explicitly referred to the 'autonomous legal order' of the Community. Such jurisprudence cannot therefore be easily transposed to the law of the other EU sub-orders, since

---

[100] As provided by the ECJ in relation to international agreements concluded by the European Community: Cases C–181/73 *Haegeman* [1974] ECR 449 and C–104/81 *Kupferberg* [1982] ECR 3641. See in the same line Thym, above n 24, 900.

[101] *Ibid.*

[102] See in general on this issue for instance V Lowe, 'Can the European Community Bind the Member States on Questions of Customary International Law?' in M Koskenniemi, above note 95, 149–68.

[103] Case C–104/81 *Kupferberg* [1982] ECR 3641, para 13.

all differences between the pillars have not disappeared.[104] Notwithstanding the *Pupino* line of case law,[105] Union law can still be distinguished from Community law, thereby suggesting that the legal nature of agreements that form part of Union law should be judged, first and foremost, with due regard to the specific nature of the Union legal order.

In other words, Article 300(7) TEC and Article 24(6) TEU cannot be interpreted in a similar fashion. The latter provides that EU agreements are binding on the institutions, and no reference is made to the Member States. While there are good reasons to assume that decisions in the non-Community sub-orders of the Union are also binding on Member States, and that such decisions cannot be ignored in their domestic legal orders,[106] particularly in view of the principle of Article 11(2) TEU, it is not obvious that the principles of 'direct effect' and 'supremacy' form part of Union law.[107] This implies that the domestic effect (applicability) of the agreements depends on national (constitutional) arrangements. As we have seen, the practice of the PJCC agreements indeed reveals that Article 24(5) TEU is used in a way to allow national parliaments to let their governments approve the treaty before the Union adopts the final ratification decision.

A related question concerns whether the EU *acquis* (viz CFSP and/or PJCCM *acquis*) runs the risk of being affected through the conclusion of agreements by the Union and/or its Member States. Indeed, 'much of the external relations case law of the Court serves to shield the *acquis communautaire* [...].'[108] In fact, as recently confirmed by the Court in Opinion 1/03: 'The purpose of the exclusive competence of the Community is primarily to preserve the effectiveness of Community law and the proper functioning of the systems established by its rules'.[109] In a recent study, Klabbers pointed out that to shield the *acquis*, the Community makes use of a variety of primacy clauses in mixed agreements, either by providing that in cases of conflict between the external agreement and Community law, Community law shall prevail, or by inserting a clause to assure that Member States in their mutual relations apply Community law rather than the external agreement.[110]

---

[104] Irrespective of the *prima facie* Union-wide application of the principle of primacy in the 2004 Constitutional Treaty (Art I–6), one may doubt whether CFSP measures may produce direct effect and enjoy supremacy over national norms on the basis of the Lisbon Treaty. See also 'Editorial Comments' (2005) 42 *CML Rev* 325.

[105] Case C–105/03 *Pupino* [2005] ECR I–5285; see further below.

[106] See more extensively RA Wessel (1999), above n 4, ch 5.

[107] *Cf* also K Lenaerts and T Corhaut, 'Of Birds and Hedges: the Role of Primacy in Invoking Norms of EU Law' (2006) 31 *EL Rev* 287.

[108] J Klabbers, 'Safeguarding the Organizational *Acquis*: the EU's External Practice' (2007) 4 *International Organizations Law Review* 57.

[109] Above n 54, para 131.

[110] J Klabbers (2007), above n 108.

About nine different '*acquis*-saving clauses' can thus be found in the agreements, ranging from a 'disconnection clause' (in their relations *inter se*, the Member States shall continue to apply Community law) to a 'conditioned territorial application clause' (restricting the scope of application of the agreement to the territory of the Community and the third partner). Similar clauses may be located in EU agreements as well. Hence, the 2003 EU–US Extradition Agreement provides that it 'shall not preclude the conclusion, after its entry into force of bilateral Agreements between a Member State and the United States of America consistent with this agreement'. Indeed, as Klabbers observes: 'The Member States remain free to add further refinements with the treaty partner (in this case the US), but the basic regime is laid down by the Union: the Union determines, in conjunction with its treaty partner, what room to move the Member States have left.'[111]

A CFSP example is formed by the Agreement between the EU and Ukraine on the Security Procedures for the Exchange of Classified Information, which foresees that '[t]his Agreement shall in no way prevent the parties from concluding other agreements relating to the provision or exchange of classified information subject to this Agreement *provided that they do not conflict with the provisions of this Agreement.*'[112] A similar 'consistent further agreement clause' may also be found in the NATO–EU Agreement on Security of Information.[113]

It should, however, be kept in mind that in these cases, the 'parties' referred to in the clause do not include the EU Member States. Again, any possible restriction on Member States' freedom to conclude agreements in the same area would have to be based on internal Union law. Perhaps on that basis we could agree with Klabbers that '[...] while not parties to the agreements strictly speaking, nonetheless departing from such treaties by individual Member States would be difficult to justify; therewith, such clauses would also provide the limits as to what individual Member States can legitimately do'.[114] After all, if—as in Community law—shielding the *acquis* is the primary purpose of these clauses, then they would be deprived

---

[111] *Ibid*. See Art 18 of the EU–US Extradition Agreement, [2003] OJ L/181/27; as well as the EU–US Agreement on Mutual Legal Assistance, OJ L 181/34, 19.7.2003. See more extensively Georgopoulos, above n 84.

[112] Art 14 (emphasis added); [2005] OJ L/172/86. Similar clauses can be found in the security of information agreements concluded between the EU and other states, including Croatia ([2006] OJ L/116/74) and Macedonia ([2005] OJ L/94/39).

[113] [2003] OJ L/80/36.

[114] *Cf* Klabbers (2007), above n 108. See earlier with a focus on Community law his 'Restraints on the Treaty-Making Powers of Member States Deriving from EU Law: Towards a Framework for Analysis' in E Cannizzaro, above n 32, 151–75.

of any effect if they would allow Member States to conclude agreements, either *inter se* or with third parties, which would depart from established Union law.[115]

IV. THE NORMATIVE CHARACTER OF CFSP IN THE LIGHT OF ITS PLACE WITHIN THE EU LEGAL ORDER

The foregoing sections scrutinised the potential restraining effects of CFSP norms (treaty provisions, secondary measures and agreements) on Member States' foreign policy powers, by interpreting Member States' obligations in the light of the Court's case law and legal scholarship. This section examines whether the inclusion of CFSP into the broader EU legal order could affect its normative character. It will be argued that Member States' CFSP obligations might be coloured by provisions of the other two EU sub-orders, the Community and the third pillars, respectively. First, Article 10 EC itself could compel the Member States to comply with their CFSP obligations, at least in some specific circumstances (A). Second, the restraining effect of EU agreements on Member States powers might be strengthened by the Court's widening jurisdiction on third pillar instruments (B). This, in turn, may have an effect on the use of external competences Member States have retained on the basis of the EC Treaty (C).

A. The Effect of Article 10 EC on Member States' CFSP Obligations

It has been suggested earlier that the duty of loyal cooperation expressed in Article 10 EC may inspire the way in which the Member States' duty of loyal cooperation under Article 11(2) TEU could be conceived. This section suggests that Article 10 EC *itself* may oblige Member States to comply with their CFSP obligations, as a way to fulfil their EC obligations.

As established by the Court of Justice, notably in the *Centro-Com* judgment,[116] Member States must comply with their obligations under EC law, even when they act in the context of their reserved powers. They have

---

[115] See on the role of the *acquis* in external relations also L Azoulai, 'The *Acquis* of the European Union and International Organisations' (2005) 11 *ELJ* 196.

[116] Case C–124/95, *Centro-Com* [1997] ECR I–81. See also Case 466/98 *Commission v UK* [2002] ECR I–9427, para 41; also in Case C–221/89 *Factortame and Others* [1991] ECR I–3905, para 14 and Case C–264/96 *ICI v Colmer* [1998] ECR I–4695, para 19.

to act consistently with, and respect, Community law.[117] These Community law obligations include those derived from Article 10 EC. As emphasised by the Court, the duty of cooperation of Article 10 EC 'is of general application and does not depend either on whether the Community competence concerned is exclusive *or on any right of the Member States to enter into obligations towards non-member countries*'.[118] This case law entails that, even outside the sphere of Community powers, Member States must not only refrain from infringing EC law, they must also abstain from acting in a way which would make the Community's tasks more difficult or jeopardise the attainment of the objectives of the EC Treaty.[119]

Hence, if Member States' acted, or omitted to act, in violation of their CFSP obligations with the effect of making the Community's achievement of its tasks more difficult, those actions or omissions would, arguably, also constitute an infringement of Article 10 EC. For example, if the conclusion by a Member State of a bilateral agreement with a third country was to contradict the CFSP provisions of an existing EC–EU cross-pillar agreement concluded with the same country, the Community could ultimately suffer from this Member State's infringement of the CFSP instrument. In particular, given the customary absence, in mixed agreements, of a clause defining the precise division of powers on the EU side,[120] the third party could, if the dispute settlement consultations failed to reach an amicable settlement, decide to take retaliatory measures against the EU and EC jointly,[121] or even specifically in areas relating to Community powers,[122]

---

[117] On this point, see M Cremona, 'External Relations and External Competence: the Emergence of an Integrated Policy' in P Craig and G de Búrca (eds), *The Evolution of EU Law* (Oxford, OUP, 1999), 137; see also Opinion of AG Jacobs in the *Centro-Com* case, above note 27, paras 40–4.

[118] Emphasis added. Cases C–266/03, *Commission v Luxembourg* [2005] ECR I–4805 and C–433/03 *Commission v Germany* [2005] ECR I–6985.

[119] On the application of Art 10 EC beyond the scope of Community competence, see eg Blanquet, above n 48, 306; CWA Timmermans, 'Organising joint participation of EC and Member States' in A Dashwood and C Hillion (eds), above n 1, 239.

[120] In this regard, see eg HG Schermers, 'The Internal Effect of Community Treaty-Making' in D O'Keeffe and H Schermers (eds), *Essays in European Law and Integration* (Deventer, Kluwer, 1982) 167, 170; J Heliskoski, above n 95, 11 and 69.

[121] In the absence of clear allocation of powers between the Community and the Member States, it has been suggested that the principle should be that Community and Member States are jointly liable; see, eg, Opinion of Jacobs AG in Case C–316/91 *European Parliament v Council* [1994] ECR I–625, para 69, Case C–53/96 *Hermès* [1998] ECR I–3603, para 24. Further: C Tomuschat, 'Liability for Mixed Agreements' in D O'Keeffe and HG Schermers (eds), *Mixed Agreements* (Deventer, Kluwer, 1983) 125; G Gaja, 'The European Community's Rights and Obligations under Mixed Agreements' in D O'Keeffe and HG Schermers (eds), *Mixed Agreements* (Deventer, Kluwer, 1983) 133, 137ff; and R Kovar, 'La participation des Communautés européennes aux conventions multilatérales' (1975) 20 *AFDI* 903, 916–17.

[122] As Christian Tomuschat pointed out, if the Community and its Member States wilfully and purportedly refrain from formally publicising their demarcation line between their respective areas of jurisdiction, their partners cannot be expected to make the necessary inquiries themselves; see C Tomuschat, above n 121, 130.

thereby affecting the Community rights under the agreement.[123] In these circumstances, the Member State's failure to comply with its CFSP obligations would make the achievement of Community's tasks more difficult, and would jeopardise the attainment of the objectives of the EC Treaty, in violation of the principle of loyal cooperation under Article 10 EC.

If this reasoning holds true, it could be argued that on the basis of Article 10 EC, the Member State concerned could be required, as a matter of Community law, to comply in good faith with its CFSP obligations, as they notably derived from the cross-pillar agreement, in order to forestall potential negative implications for the Community. Indeed, the Court emphasised in *Commission v Luxembourg* that the Member States also have 'to abstain from *any* measure which could jeopardise the attainment of the objectives of the [EC] Treaty'.[124] The Commission would thus be entitled, under the enforcement procedure of Article 226 EC, to sue the Member State for failing to comply with its Article 10 EC obligation, as a result of a violation of the CFSP obligations flowing from the cross-pillar agreement.[125] At any rate, it could be argued that the Member State concerned ought to consult and inform the EU institutions of its intentions,[126] in order to facilitate the achievement of the Community's tasks.[127] Indeed, as Article 10 EC not only binds the Member States, but also the institutions,[128] it could be argued that the Council is under an 'Article 10'

---

[123]   Indeed, if the Union itself was held liable as a result of a Member State violation of the EU-related provisions of the agreement, this liability could have implications for the Community. Art 28(3) TEU provides that, in principle, operating expenditure to which the implementation of CFSP measures gives rise is charged to the budget of the European Communities. Assuming that reparations are part of the implementation of the agreement, reparations resulting from EU non-compliance with the agreement resulting from a Member State's infringement would indirectly affect the Community.

[124]   Emphasis added. Cases C–266/03, *Commission v Luxembourg* [2005] ECR I–4805 and C–433/03 *Commission v Germany* [2005] ECR I–6985.

[125]   C-D Ehlermann, 'Mixed Agreements—A list of Problems' in D O'Keeffe and HG Schermers (eds), *Mixed Agreements* (Deventer and Boston, Kluwer, 1983), 3, suggests that the Community should thus have the right to take preventive steps against the Member State whose action risks engaging the Community's responsibility. In particular, he considers that 'it would be unavoidable to allow the Community to use the infringement procedure in spite of the fact that the Member State acts within its sphere of competence. As regards enforcement proceedings in situations involving Member States' obligations, under mixed agreements, which relate to areas that are not entirely covered by Community law, see Case C–239/03 *Commission v France* [2004] ECR I–9325, para 25; Case C–13/00 *Commission v Ireland* [2002] ECR 2943; Case C–459/03 *Commission v Ireland* [2006] ECR I–4635 (MOX Plant case).

[126]   Case C–266/03 *Commission v Luxembourg* [2005] ECR I–4805; see also case C–433/03 *Commission v Germany* [2005] ECR I–6985.

[127]   Indeed, given that the Member State action or omission has implications for the implementation of the cross-pillar agreement, the Member State action or omission would have a 'general interest' dimension in the sense of Art 16 TEU, and would thus entail that that Member State must inform and consult other Member States; see Section II.A above.

[128]   Further, see K Lenaerts and P van Nuffel, *Constitutional Law of the European Union* (London, Sweet & Maxwell, 2005), 115–23.

duty to ensure that the Member States comply with their CFSP obligations so as not to make the achievement of Community's tasks more difficult.

Similarly, if some Member States were to prevent the establishment by the Community of economic sanctions towards a third state, as required by a prior CFSP common position or joint action, it could be posited that the Commission would be entitled, not only to sue the Council on the basis of Article 232 EC for failing to adopt the relevant EC measure under Article 301 EC, but it could also rely on Article 10 EC against the recalcitrant Member States which, by failing to act in accordance with the CFSP instrument, prevented the Community from fulfilling its tasks.

The foregoing hypothetical examples typify the proposition that Member States have to comply with the duty of cooperation of Article 10 EC also when acting in the context of CFSP. In addition, on the basis of Article 10 EC, Member States might be sanctioned for infringing their CFSP obligations where such violation makes the achievement of Community tasks more difficult, or jeopardises the attainment of the objectives of the EC Treaty.[129] These examples also epitomise the interconnections between the different sub-orders within the Union, in the sense that failure to comply with obligations undertaken in one order could have effects on the law of another order.[130] The Community thus has an interest, not only in Member States' compliance with their EC obligations, but also in the observance of their CFSP obligations. To be sure, Member States' compliance with their CFSP obligations is not only a requirement under the provisions of Title V, Article 11(2) in particular, it is also a means to fulfil the overall objective of the EU, foreseen in Article 2 TEU, of asserting its identity on the international scene. As a constitutive part of the Union, the Community contributes to fulfilling this EU objective, through its external policy, within its sphere of competence.[131] Arguably, this contribution would be made more difficult if Member States, as actors in the system of EU external relations, infringed their EU obligations under CFSP. The principle of loyal cooperation based on Article 10 EC plays a key role in ensuring the consistency and coherence of the overall Union's external activities, as required by Article 3 TEU.[132] It could indeed be argued that a failure to comply with the requirement of Article 3 TEU could, at least in

---

[129]   See in this sense, Timmermans, above n 119, 241; see also M Cremona, 'Defending the Community Interest: the Duties of Cooperation and Compliance', ch 5, this volume.

[130]   Heliskoski, above n 95, 211; Gaja, above n 121, 140 also points out that matters can be interlinked, even if apparently relating to clearly different legal authorities.

[131]   Cases T–306/01, *Ahmed Ali Yusuf and Al Barakaat International Foundation v Council and Commission* [2005] ECR II–3533; and T–315/01, *Yassin Abdullah Kadi v Council and Commission* [2005] ECR II–3649, (para 161 *Yusuf* case).

[132]   Further: C Hillion, '*Tous pour un, un pour tous!* Coherence in the External Relations of the European Union' in M Cremona (ed), *Developments in EU External Relations Collected Courses of the Academy of European Law* (Oxford, OUP forthcoming).

certain cases, be seen as a breach of Article 10 EC, thus constituting grounds for the justiciability of consistency and coherence.[133]

The foregoing suggested that the normative character of the CFSP sub-order is not only determined by the CFSP provisions themselves, but that it is also coloured by other principles underpinning the EU legal order. In particular, the Member States' ability to conclude international agreements *inter se* or with third countries in areas of CFSP might be affected by the principle of loyal cooperation established by Article 10 EC. The next section argues that the third pillar can also have an impact on the Member States' obligations under CFSP.

B. Article 35 TEU and Member States' Obligations to comply with EU Agreements

As recalled earlier, Article 46 TEU does not extend the jurisdiction of the Court of Justice to the provisions on CFSP contained in Title V of the TEU.[134] In other words, Member States cannot be forced to the same extent as in the context of the EC external agreements to comply with their obligations under an EU agreement. However, the apparent freedom that Member States thereby enjoy should not be overstated. While the principle of loyal cooperation based on Article 10 EC constrains the Member States when acting in non-EC related fields, their freedom therein can also be limited by the Court's widening jurisdiction within the third pillar. As this section argues, the *Pupino* and *Segi* line of case law could have the effect of enhancing the effectiveness of Member States' obligations deriving from EU agreements concluded on the combined bases of Articles 24 and 38 TEU.

The *Segi* judgment explored earlier recalls that,[135] under Title VI of the TEU, the Court's jurisdiction is limited by the provisions of Article 35 TEU notably in terms of EU acts that can be the subject of preliminary references, or judicial review. It also points out that since the Union is founded on the rule of law principle and respects fundamental rights as general principles of Community law, institutions, just like the Member States when they implement Union law, are subject to review of the

---

[133] On the interactions between Art 10 EC and Art 3 TEU, see HG Krenzler and HC Schneider, 'The Question of Consistency' in E Regelsberger *et al*, *Foreign Policy of the European Union: From EPC to CFSP and Beyond* (Boulder, Lynne Rienner, 1997) 133, 147; Heliskoski, above n 95, 64; R Frid, *The Relations between the EC and International Organisations. Legal Theory and Practice* (The Hague, Kluwer, 1995) 149.

[134] Case C–354/04P *Gestoras Pro Amnistía and Others v Council*, judgment of 27 February 2007; Case T–228/02 *Organisation des Modjahedines du peuple d'Iran*, judgment of 12 December 2006.

[135] See Cases C–355/04 P *Segi and Others v Council* and C–354/04 P *Gestoras Pro Amnistía and Others v Council*, judgments of 27 February 2007, nyr.

conformity of their acts with the Treaties and the general principles of the law. In this context, Article 35(1) TEU establishes a preliminary procedure to guarantee observance of the law in the interpretation and application of the Treaty. Contending that it would be counter to that objective to interpret Article 35(1) narrowly, the Court found that the right to make a reference for a preliminary ruling must therefore exist 'in respect of all measures adopted by the Council, whatever their nature or form, which are intended to have legal effects in relation to third parties'.

Since the Court refers to 'all measures adopted by the Council, whatever their nature or form, which are intended to have legal effects in relation to third parties', it could be wondered whether third pillar instruments other than common positions, and notably EU agreements based on Articles 24 and 38 TEU, could equally be the subject of a preliminary reference. After all, such EU agreements are instruments concluded by the Council, and they may have legal effects in relation to third parties, as notably illustrated by the EU Agreement with the US on the processing and transfer of passenger name record (PNR) data by air carriers to the US Department of Homeland Security,[136] or the Agreements between the EU and the US on extradition and mutual legal assistance in criminal matters.[137]

Following the Court's approach, it cannot be excluded that the provisions of EU agreements based on Articles 24 and 38 TEU could also be the subject of a preliminary reference, at least in so far as the provisions relate to the third pillar, and they produce legal effects in relation to third parties. If that holds true, national courts would be in a position to obtain an interpretation, or indeed question the validity of such EU agreements. In the light of the Court's pronouncement in *Pupino*, and particularly in view of the principle of loyal cooperation, the national courts would then be compelled to refer to the content of the EU agreement when interpreting the relevant rules of its national law, or indeed international agreements.

In other words, the *Segi* jurisprudence, combined with the *Pupino* decision, could well entail that Member States' freedom to conclude external agreements might be affected by EU agreements based on Articles 24 and 38 TEU. Of course, the effect of an EU agreement, as envisaged above, would only concern the third-pillar-related provisions of that agreement but not its CFSP aspects, nor a fortiori the provisions of 'pure' second pillar agreements. If this reasoning holds true, it would become decisive to distinguish what belongs to CFSP and what belongs to PJCC in cross-pillar EU agreements, a task which arguably could be performed by the Court under Article 35 TEU.

---

[136] [2006] OJ L/288/27.
[137] [2003] OJ L/181/25.

It appears therefore that the 'judicialisation' of the third pillar may have implications for the second. It triggers a need to distinguish different categories of EU agreement, as their effects on Member States and the jurisdiction of the Court may differ from one to the other. Moreover, it could require that the outer limits of CFSP be policed, not only in relation to the EC Treaty on the basis of Article 47 TEU, but also in relation to the third pillar given the Court's jurisdiction on the basis of Article 35 TEU. More generally, the foregoing also supports the proposition that the interplay between CFSP and other norms of the EU legal order may influence, if not affect the nature or effects of, Member States' CFSP obligations, and their freedom to conclude international agreements in the areas covered by CFSP.

C. Member States' Interactions with the EC in Areas relating to CFSP

This final section raises the question of whether one may envisage situations in which CFSP norms engender restraints on Member States' actions in areas of external competence they have retained under the EC Treaty. Only limited external powers fall within the Community's exclusive competence. In most cases the Member States have retained at least part of their original external competences, resulting in 'mixity' as a key feature of the Community's external relations. The question then is whether the CFSP norms entail an obligation of conduct for the Member States to act through the CFSP machinery, thus *qua* Council of the EU in areas relating to foreign and security policy, and particularly when acting in relation to, or jointly with, the Community. In other words: do the Member States remain entirely free to ignore the procedural CFSP obligations in areas in which the EC Treaty does not affect their individual external competences? This question will be approached from three different angles. First, Member States' freedom will be tested when they take action in areas where the Community has no exclusive powers, actually or potentially (ie complementary powers). Member States' discretion will then be examined in the context of mixed agreements, classical or cross-pillar, covering inter alia foreign policy issues. Finally, it will be wondered whether Member States may be subject to CSFP obligations when they act in the context of Article 297 EC.

The first scenario relates to the question of whether, beyond their obligations to comply with Community law (including obligations derived from Article 10 EC), Member States have unlimited discretion when they act in areas where the Community cannot have exclusive competence, and where, as a consequence, they remain free to act alone or collectively. More particularly, do the CFSP norms force Member States to use the Council as an EU institution in areas where they have kept their ability to act *qua* Member States, individually or collectively? Or is there at least a possibility to use CFSP to this end?

This question could indeed be raised in the context of the pending ECOWAS case.[138] To recall the facts, the Commission notably challenges the legality of Council Decision 2004/833/CFSP, which provides for an EU contribution to the Economic Community of West African States (ECOWAS) in the framework of the Moratorium on Small Arms and Light Weapons. Because this decision has been adopted as a CFSP decision, the Commission argues that it infringes Article 47 TEU, since it affects Community powers in the field of development aid.[139] In particular, the Commission contends that Article 11(3) of the Cotonou agreement concluded with the ACP countries covers actions notably against the spread of small arms and light weapons. It also points out that it had concluded, pursuant to Article 10(2) of Annex IV of the Cotonou agreement, a Regional Indicative Programme for West Africa with the ECOWAS and the West African Economic and Monetary Union (WAEMU), which gives support to a regional policy of conflict prevention and good governance, and announces support in particular for the moratorium on the import, export and production of light weapons in West Africa.

In order to determine whether the impugned act should have been adopted as a Community act, the Court may follow its Environmental Penalties approach, and examine the aim and content of the measure in order to establish the main thrust of the measure, eventually to determine its appropriate legal basis. The outcome of the case would thereby depend on the scope of the development cooperation competence of the Community, and incidentally that of CFSP. Arguably, the outcome could also be determined by the nature of that Community competence, and of the potential existence of an *EU* (read CFSP) power to act in areas where competence is shared between the Community and the Member States. As evoked earlier, the Court has made clear in the EDF case that the Community does not have exclusive powers in the field of development cooperation, and that the Member States 'are accordingly entitled to enter into commitments themselves vis-à-vis non-member States, either collectively or individually, or even jointly with the Community'.[140] Similarly in relation to humanitarian aid, the Court pointed out that since the Community does not have exclusive competence in this field, 'Member States are not precluded from exercising their competence in that regard collectively

---

[138] C–91/05 *Commission v Council* (ECOWAS case), pending: see [2005] OJ C/115/10.

[139] The Commission is also seeking a declaration of illegality against Council Joint Action 2002/589/CFSP on the same basis and for the same reasons.

[140] Case C–316/91 *European Parliament v Council* [1994] ECR I–625 (EDF case); para 26.

in the Council or outside it'.[141] The Court was thus ready to admit that in those areas, Member States' and Community acts may co-exist. In the light of this case law, it may be wondered whether, in case the Court establishes that the aim and content of the measure do concern development aid, this would automatically entail that the measure ought to be adopted as an EC measure. Conversely, does the fact that development cooperation is an area where Member States are entitled to act individually or collectively or indeed within the Council, alongside the Community, entail that the measure could (or perhaps should) be adopted by the EU Council on the basis of Title V, instead of the Member States?[142]

Without attempting to give a full answer to this question, it would appear that, while the Member States remain free to act individually or collectively, including within the premises of the Council (ie meeting of the representatives of the Member States acting, as representatives of their governments, and thus collectively exercising the powers of the Member States, but not in their capacity as members of the Council), this freedom does not seem to include Member States' discretion to choose between a CFSP and an EC legal basis when action is to be taken at EU level.[143] In particular, the provisions of Articles 2, 3 and 47 TEU, read together, tend to suggest that should the Member States decide that action should be taken at EU level in the field of development policy, they may have to do it through the Community decision-making procedures, wherever the Community has the power to act. Conversely, and it may sound partly absurd, the logic of the Treaty provisions seems to suggest that Member States are still entitled to act on their own behalf, individually, collectively, in the Council or outside it, but not *qua* Council, acting on the basis of Title V. Once it becomes clear that there is an EU competence, it simply does not seem to be up to the Member States to opt for an EU (viz CFSP or PJCC) rather than an EC competence.

In a similar vein, one may wonder whether aspects of mixed agreements relating to Member States' powers could be, or even ought to be, dealt with by the EU *qua* CFSP, following the provisions of Article 24 TEU. For instance, if the Member States have the common wish to include a political dialogue, or an extensive cooperation in security and defence matters in an external agreement jointly concluded with the Community, should the CFSP/ESDP-related provisions *require* that the Union become party to the

---

[141] Joined Cases C–181/91 and 248/91, *European Parliament v Council and Commission* [1993] ECR I–3685 (Bangladesh case).

[142] A Dashwood, 'The Interface between EC External Relations and the CFSP' in A Dashwood and M Maresceau (eds), *Law and Practice of EU External Relations* (Cambridge, Cambridge University Press, 2007); A Dashwood, 'The Law and Practice of CFSP Joint Actions', ch 3, this volume.

[143] Cp the argument of the Danish Government in the *Airport Transit Visa* case referred to above, n 28 (Case C–170/96 *Commission v Council* [1998] ECR I–2763).

agreement rather than the Member States, alongside the Community? The advantage of that approach would be to allow the agreement possibly to be concluded as a cross-pillar EC/EU agreement, rather than a classical mixed agreement, and thus to avoid the heavy ratification process at the national level. However practical it may look, this approach would not mean that classical mixity would be disposed of. Indeed, EU participation does not seem to be legally mandatory.

First, a cross-pillar agreement could not replace a classical mixed agreement where the latter contains, alongside CFSP provisions, provisions related to powers shared between the Community and the Member States. In areas of shared powers, the EU cannot replace the Member States acting on the basis of Article 24 TEU, given the obligation enshrined in Article 47 TEU, and the objective of Article 2 TEU. As suggested above, in areas of shared powers, including areas of co-existent powers such as development cooperation, the Member States do not appear to have a choice between acting in the EC framework or in the CFSP framework.

Second, in relation to areas of a mixed agreement relating to CFSP, the provisions of Article 24 TEU and practice thereof suggest that using the CFSP treaty-making machinery is not mandatory. In legal terms, the EU concludes an agreement on the basis of Article 24 TEU when the Member States deem it 'necessary ... in implementation of [the CFSP] title', in contrast to the provisions of Article 300 EC which instead envisages the Community's exercise of its treaty-making power '[w]here this [EC] Treaty provides ...' Thus, the common will of the Member States to include provisions related to CFSP in a mixed agreement does not automatically lead to the negotiation and conclusion of an agreement partly based on Article 24 agreement, for it may not be deemed 'necessary' for the Union itself to conclude the agreement. Arguably, the Union's objective of asserting its identity on the international scene (Article 2 TEU), combined with the loyalty principle of Article 11(2) TEU, should nevertheless be considered, when assessing the 'necessity' of an Article 24 agreement.

Moreover, it should be noticed that since the introduction of Article 24 TEU by the Treaty of Amsterdam, there has only been one agreement concluded both by the Community and the Union on the bases of Articles 300 EC and 24 TEU, respectively.[144] Agreements involving areas of EC competence and cooperation in CFSP matters are still concluded as 'classical' mixed agreements by the Community and the Member States,

---

[144] Agreement between the European Union, the European Community and the Swiss Confederation concerning the Swiss Confederation's association with the implementation, application and development of the Schengen *acquis* concluded in 2004 by the EU, on the basis of Arts 24 and 38 TEU (Council Decisions 2004/849/EC; [2004] OJ L/368/26) and the EC, on the basis of Art 62, point 3 of the first subparagraph of Art 63, Arts 66 and 95, in conjunction Art 300(2) (Decision 2004/860/EC; [2004] OJ L/370/78). The Agreement (13054/04) is available at the Public Register of the Council only.

acting jointly. Indeed, both the Commission and some Member States tend to favour classical mixity. The Commission fears that the EU as a party may overshadow Community external powers while, on the other hand, some Member States fear that their international posture would be hampered by too prominent a Union.[145] One could also add that the conclusion of a mixed agreement by the EU in place of the Member States would have the effect of subtracting the areas covered by the EU from any democratic control. Presently this democratic control is still partly ensured at the level of ratification by the Member States' parliaments.

The last angle from which to study Member States' potential obligation to act in the framework of CFSP is that of Article 297 EC. This provision foresees situations where Member States have to consult each other with a view to taking together steps needed to prevent the functioning of the common market being affected by Member States measures, taken in the event of serious internal disturbances affecting the maintenance of law and order, in the event of war, serious international tension constituting a threat of war, or in order to carry out obligations it has accepted for the purpose of maintaining peace and international security.

Since a Member State may use these provisions as justifications for not complying with its internal market obligations, it may be suggested that such justification, particularly given the subject matter it relates to, ought to be discussed and assessed, if not addressed in the context of CFSP. In particular, it could be wondered whether that State's concerns ought to be validated by a decision taken in the context of CFSP for them to be lawfully invoked, in the EC context, as justification for derogations to the internal market rules.[146] On the other hand, one may argue that this debate is perhaps too academic as both Article 297 EC and Article 16 EU foresee a possibility for Member States to consult one another on these issues in the Council and there is no necessity to define the exact legal basis, or framework. In addition, both provisions use similar mandatory language ('Member States shall ...') to establish the consultation obligation. The only difference is that Article 297 seems to allow Member States to consult each other outside the Council.

This section has attempted to demonstrate that the inclusion of CFSP in the broader context of the EU legal order has implications for the normative content of CFSP. It has been suggested that the obligations of Article 10 EC may colour Member States' obligations under CFSP. It was

---

[145] This seems to be the background to the failure to conclude a cross-pillar agreement in the context of the EU accession to the ASEAN Treaty of Amity and Cooperation (TAC) as suggested by Council Doc 16042/06 of 30 November 2006 entitled 'Draft Council authorization to the Presidency and the Commission to negotiate the accession to ASEAN Treaty of Amity and Cooperation (TAC) by the EU and EC respectively'.

[146] Further on Art 297 EC, see P Koutrakos, 'Is Art 297 EC a "Reserve of Sovereignty"?' (2000) 37 *CML Rev* 1339.

also argued that the recent case law of the Court of Justice in relation to the third pillar instruments, developed in the context of Article 35 TEU, could also affect the way in which Member States apprehend their obligations under EU agreements, at least those agreements which include third pillar provisions. Finally, the section has attempted to shed light on the limits to Member States' discretion to use CFSP mechanisms where interacting with the Community.

V. CONCLUSION

The aim of this Chapter was to examine the possible restraints on the basis of the CFSP primary and secondary norms and—in the line of these general notions—to analyse the possible effects of agreements concluded by the EU on Member States' foreign policy competences. At the time of the conclusion of the Treaty on European Union—now 15 years ago—it was widely held that the very *rationale* underlying the creation of CFSP as a separate pillar within the new Union was to be found in the leeway offered to Member States to continue developing their own foreign policy. In fact, CFSP (just as the cooperation in the area of Justice and Home Affairs) was to develop outside the Community legal order, in order for it not to become affected by the notions characterising that order, notably primacy, direct effect and an allegedly 'unbounded' role of the European Court of Justice. At the same time, however, CFSP was legally connected to the European Community as both of them became part of a new entity, the European Union. Hence, the pillars were separate, but nonetheless clearly inseparable. It is this nearness that formed the basis of our analysis.

With the ongoing interplay between the pillars, the normative character of CFSP may increasingly be coloured by principles originating in the other pillars. While 'cross-pillar mixity' is scarce,[147] it is assumed that at least in those cases, for instance, the full scope of Article 10 EC is applicable. Similar 'spill-over' effects have proved to be possible from the third to the second pillar as revealed by the *Pupino*, and in particular the *Segi* line of case law. Hence, where a cross-pillar legal basis is used, developments in one pillar (either on the basis of legal practice or of case law) can hardly be blocked from the other pillar.

Partly on the basis of this case law we have argued, however, that this development is of a more general nature and is not confined to cross-pillar decision-making. Thus, in interpreting the CFSP loyalty obligation laid down in Article 11(2), its proximity to Article 10 EC should be taken into account, in particular in relation to the conclusion of agreements. The

[147] In this respect, see P Eeckhout, above n 1, 184.

potential impact of the loyalty principle (which despite existing 'pillar-specific' characteristics could be seen as a 'principle of Union law') on Member States' freedom under CFSP should not be underestimated.

On the basis of the limited availability of case law related to CFSP no final conclusions can be drawn on a number of issues. One of those issues concerns the primacy, direct effect and justiciability of CFSP decisions and agreements. While we have argued that EU agreements are to be regarded as forming 'an integral part of Union law', it is also clear that 'Union law' is not to be equated with 'Community law'. And even when 'Union law' is concerned, the far reaching *Segi* qualification of common positions with a partial CFSP legal basis indicates that specific pillar characteristics (in this case of the third pillar) should be taken into account. At the same time, however, *Segi* revealed (as *Pupino* did earlier) the Court's approach in interpreting the legal nature and scope of non-Community Union instruments in the light of the overarching Union legal order, for the development of which traditional Community principles prove to play an important role.

Our overall conclusion is that the CFSP normative order does indeed restrain the external competences of the Member States, thus putting its alleged 'intergovernmental' nature into perspective. First of all, the primary CFSP norms entail a consultation obligation which cannot be ignored by Member States without a complete denial of the *rationale* behind CFSP. In addition, Member States' specific obligations under the CFSP title should be interpreted in the light of the general loyalty obligation to support the Union's CFSP (Article 11(2) TEU). This obligation becomes more substantive once the Union has acted, and given the proximity between the provisions of Article 11(2) TEU and Article 10 EC respectively, there are reasons to interpret the former in the light of the latter's interpretation.

A second related conclusion concerns the competence of the Union to conclude international agreements with third states or other international organisations. We have argued that, in a situation of parallel competences, the nature of the EU competence involved should be considered, and in particular its possible pre-emptive effect. Indeed, it seems too early completely to rule out exclusivity in the field of CFSP. After all, the (international) legal status of agreements concluded by the Union could be deprived of any effect if they would allow Member States to conclude agreements, either *inter se* or with third parties, which would depart from established Union law.

Third, the interplay between the pillars reveals an increasing need to use cross-pillar instruments (or to connect different EU and EC instruments). This, in turn, makes it difficult to approach the CFSP obligations in isolation. Member States' CFSP obligations might be coloured by provisions of the other two EU sub-orders. While the connection between CFSP and EC issues in particular may lead to a different perception of CFSP constraints, it is nevertheless difficult to argue that Member States retained powers in the area of foreign affairs (eg development cooperation) should be exercised specifically in the framework of CFSP, as Member States are not able to choose between a CFSP and an EC legal basis when action is to be taken at EU level.

Part III

The EU and its Member States

5

Defending the Community Interest: the Duties of Cooperation and Compliance

MARISE CREMONA*

I. INTRODUCTION

THE PURPOSE OF this Chapter is to explore one specific aspect of the operation of EU foreign policy as a complex system, a system which includes the EC, the Member States and the second and third pillar competence fields, but which nevertheless seeks to represent itself as a unity, an identity on the international scene (Article 2 TEU).[1] The particular aspect that I want to discuss relates to the management of shared and overlapping competences[2]; more particularly, the ways in which the Member States are constrained in exercising their own foreign policy competences by the obligations which derive from their membership of the complex order of the European Union. There is a tendency sometimes to see exclusivity—the recognition of exclusive Community competence—as somehow the most perfect expression of the unity of the system—there is one actor and we therefore have one voice and a (better chance of a) coherent policy framework. Adopting this view, we should celebrate each

* Many thanks to the participants of the Workshop held at the EUI on 10–11 November 2006, and especially to Robert Schütze and Bruno de Witte, for their comments and constructive suggestions.

[1] RA Wessel, 'The Multilevel Constitution of European Foreign Relations' in N Tsagourias (ed), *Transnational Constitutionalism: International and European Perspectives* (Cambridge, Cambridge University Press, 2007).

[2] Competences are shared where both the Community and Member States have competence in relation to a particular field of activity (such as environmental policy), or in relation to a particular agreement (such as the WTO, or UNCLOS). I am here using the term overlapping competences to refer to the situation where the Community legal order impacts on the exercise by a Member State of its own foreign relations competence.

victory of exclusive competence and somehow regard shared competence as second-best, and (for example) mixed agreements as a 'necessary evil'.[3]

This Chapter will argue that exclusivity is not the only way to defend the Community interest,[4] nor necessarily the best solution. The Union does not operate as a zero sum game.[5] Shared competence exercised in the framework of the loyalty obligation defined in Article 10 EC and Article 11(2) TEU, and in conformity with the principle of primacy of Community law, may allow greater flexibility. This approach (based on the primacy principle and the loyalty obligation) may be conducive to a stronger unity than the unity of exclusivity,[6] in that it operates when the Member States are exercising their own competences whether or not shared with the EC or EU.

In what follows, then, the focus of the discussion will be the way in which the obligation on Member States to comply with Community law (Article 10 EC), from which both the principle of primacy and the duty of cooperation are derived, operates to constrain Member State action at the external level, both substantively (primacy) and procedurally (the duty of cooperation). The focus here will be on EC law, as it is in the creative application of Article 10 EC that we can find the fullest development of these ideas; a discussion by Hillion and Wessel of the extent to which Member States' foreign policy may be constrained by Union CFSP action can be found in Chapter 5 of this volume.

In what follows I will adopt Dashwood's distinction between the scope of Community competence and the scope of Community law. As Dashwood has said, the limits of Community powers are not the same as the boundaries to the scope of application of the Treaty, the objectives of the Treaty being attained through action not only of the Community itself but also by the Member States.[7] In the present context, the distinction is important as I will argue that it is in the light of the *scope of Community law* that we need to determine the Community's tasks and its objectives as well as the obligations of the Member States 'arising out of this Treaty', as expressed in Article 10 EC.

---

[3] JHH Weiler, 'The External Legal Relations of Non-unitary Actors: Mixity and the Federal Principle' in JHH Weiler, *The Constitution of Europe: Do the New Clothes Have an Emperor?* (Cambridge, CUP, 1999), 132.

[4] *Opinion 1/75* [1975] ECR 1355.

[5] J Klabbers, 'Restraints on the Treaty-Making Power of Member States Deriving from EU Law: Towards a Framework for Analysis' in E Cannizzaro (ed), *The European Union as an Actor in International Relations* (The Hague/London, Kluwer Law International, 2002). Not even, arguably, in the field of the CCP, but that is outside the scope of this Chapter.

[6] On unity linked to exclusivity, see *Opinion 1/2003*, judgment of 7 February 2006, para 122.

[7] A Dashwood, 'The Limits of European Community Powers' (1996) 21 *EL Rev* 113.

Bridging the two principles of primacy and the duty of cooperation is the concept of 'the Community interest'. We find this idea being used as early as *Opinion 1/75*:

[the common commercial] policy is conceived in that article [now Art 133] in the context of the operation of the common market, for the defence of the common interests of the Community, within which the particular interests of the Member States must endeavour to adapt to each other.[8]

In this case the Court goes on to hold that the Community interest could not be effectively defended were Member States able 'to ensure that their own interests were separately satisfied in external relations' by acting unilaterally, and so concludes that exclusivity is the only effective way to defend the Community interest. However, the obligation on the Member States to defend the Community interest even when acting within the scope of their own powers has since been recognised,[9] and the Community interest has become something to be defended both by the Community and its institutions and by the Member States. What is the Community interest? To say that the concept is in some sense a bridge between the principle of primacy and the duty of cooperation is to locate its basis in Article 10 EC:

Member States shall take all appropriate measures, whether general or particular, to ensure fulfilment of the obligations arising out of this Treaty or resulting from action taken by the institutions of the Community. They shall facilitate the achievement of the Community's tasks.

They shall abstain from any measure which could jeopardise the attainment of the objectives of this Treaty.

The Community interest is thus linked closely to the objectives and tasks of the Community and thus—in this context at least—is not simply an expression of the collective interest of the Member States but represents an aspect of the autonomy of the Community system. Arguably, then, it differs from the 'general interest' identified in Article 16 TEU as the focus of the obligation to inform and consult within the context of the CFSP.[10] Whether or not we can identify a 'Union interest', and what relationship this might have to the Community interest, is a broader question raised in other Chapters of this book.[11] Even if we confine ourselves to the concept of the Community interest the concept has been used in various contexts,

---

[8] *Opinion 1/75* [1975] ECR 1355. The Court reflects the words of what is now Art 131 EC, which refers to the aim of the Member States, through the CCP, 'to contribute, in the common interest, to the harmonious development of world trade, the progressive abolition of restrictions on international trade and the lowering of customs barriers'.

[9] See the discussions of Art 307 EC and of Reg 847/2004/EC below.

[10] See Chapter 5, this volume, for a full discussion of the implications of this provision, in which a link is made between the 'general interest' and the Union interest.

[11] *Ibid*; see also Chapters 3 and 4, this volume.

although all with a link to achieving the Community's objectives and tasks, the primacy and thus the scope of Community law. It appears to include:

—the policy interests of the Community, as in *Opinion 1/75* cited above, and Regulation 847/2004/EC discussed below. We also find this policy-oriented notion of the Community interest in the anti-dumping field where the Commission is instructed to take the Community interest into account in deciding whether to propose provisional or definitive measures;[12]

—an interest in ensuring that international agreements entered into by the Community are properly performed (*Commission v Ireland*,[13] *Commission v France*[14]);

—the collective exercise of Member State competence in the Community interest where Community participation in an international agreement is not possible (*Opinion 2/91*[15]);

—an interest in ensuring that Member States comply with their EC Treaty obligations when exercising their competence to conclude international agreements (Open Skies cases[16]);

—an interest in ensuring that Member States do not maintain in force international obligations that conflict with their Community law obligations (*Commission v Portugal*[17]);

—an interest in ensuring that international negotiations by Member States do not obstruct ongoing negotiations by the Community (Regulation 847/2004/EC, *Commission v Luxembourg*[18]);

—an interest in ensuring that the autonomy of the Community legal order is preserved (Sellafield case[19]).

One of the aims of this Chapter will be to explore to what extent the concept is a useful one in articulating the principles governing the management of shared and overlapping competences, and in particular identifying the boundaries of Member States' obligations. In doing so we

---

[12] Council Regulation 384/96/EC of 22 December 1995 on protection against dumped imports from countries not members of the European Community, [1996] OJ L/56/1. In Art 21 of the Regulation the Community interest is defined in terms of 'an appreciation of all the various interests taken as a whole' including the domestic industry, users and consumers; in spite of a reference to the particular importance of effective competition and elimination of trade distortion it is therefore primarily an expression of a collective interest rather than an autonomous interest of the Community separated from the 'interested parties'. *Cf* also the 'common European interest' and 'common interest' as it appears in the context of regulation of state aids, Art 87(3) EC.

[13] Case C–13/00 *Commission v Ireland* [2002] ECR I–2943 (Berne Convention case).

[14] Case C–239/03 *Commission v France* [2004] ECR I–9325 (Etang de Berre case).

[15] *Opinion 2/91 (ILO Convention No 170)* [1993] ECR I–1061, para 5. See also Case C–439/01 *Libor Cipra and Vlastimil Kvasnicka v Bezirkshauptmannschaft Mistelbach* [2003] ECR I–745, paras 5 and 23, referring to Council Regulation 2829/77/EEC ([1977] OJ L/334/11) and the AETR Agreement.

[16] See, eg, Case C–476/98 *Commission v Germany* [2002] ECR I–9855 (Open Skies case).

[17] Case C–62/98 *Commission v Portugal* [2000] ECR I–5171.

[18] Case C–266/03 *Commission v Luxembourg*, judgment of 2 June 2005.

[19] Case C–459/03 *Commission v Ireland* [2006] ECR I–4635.

will turn first to substantive compliance as an expression of the principle of primacy (II), followed by procedural compliance as expressed in the duty of cooperation (III).

II. SUBSTANTIVE COMPLIANCE AND THE PRINCIPLE OF PRIMACY

This section will approach the issue of substantive compliance from three perspectives. First (A), the obligations imposed by Community law on Member States when negotiating agreements within their own competence but 'in the shadow' of the Community legal order. Second (B), the issue of Member State responsibility *in Community law* for performance of their obligations under mixed agreements, and the relationship between that responsibility, the scope of Community law and the nature of the Community interest. Third (C), a reconsideration of the concept of the 'scope of Community law' in this context of substantive compliance.

A. Member State Agreements in the Shadow of the Community

Legislative (non-a priori) exclusivity[20] is based on the principle of primacy in the sense that Community legislation takes priority in the field. Where the field has been occupied or largely covered by common rules, 'Member States may not enter into international commitments outside the framework of the Community institutions, even if there is no contradiction between those commitments and the common rules.'[21] So compliance—in the sense of the need to avoid contradiction—should not arise where competence has become exclusive because the Member States are precluded from acting at all. In contrast, where competence is shared, or the Member States have retained competence in the field, their freedom to act—while recognised by the Court—is subject to the need to comply with Community law norms.

In *Kramer*, for example, the Court recognised the continuing (although temporary) competence of the Member States to conclude international agreements in the absence of Community legislation, while being clear that the Member States in so doing were subject to Community law obligations, including (what is now) Article 10 EC. This obligation the Court defined in both negative and positive, and in both substantive and procedural terms:

---

[20] By this term, I denote primacy which is based on the existence of Community legislation in the field, as opposed to a priori exclusivity (for example, the CCP), which does not depend on the existence of legislation. See further R Schütze, 'Supremacy Without Pre-Emption? The Very Slowly Emergent Doctrine of Community Pre-Emption' (2006) 43 *CML Rev* 1023.

[21] Case C–467/98 *Commission v Denmark* [2002] ECR I–9519, para 82; Case C–476/98 *Commission v Germany* [2002] ECR I–9855 (Open Skies case), para 108.

the obligation to refrain from entering into commitments which might hinder the Community in carrying out its tasks, as well as the obligation to proceed by common action and actively to promote Community participation in the relevant agreements.[22]

Kramer was a case in which the Member States had already decided to transfer competence to the Community, although the complete transfer, in the sense of actual exercise of that competence, had not taken place. However, the same principle applies in cases where competence remains with the Member States. Klabbers has expressed the position thus:

> For the activities of the Member States are not simply curtailed by the powers they have transferred or delegated to the Community, but may also be curtailed by the substance of the Community's activities: even where the formal power still remains with the Member States, they cannot use their power in any which way they please.[23]

Thus, under Article 133(5) EC (which deals with agreements in the fields of trade in services and commercial aspects of intellectual property):

> This paragraph shall not affect the right of the Member States to maintain and conclude agreements with third countries or international organisations *insofar as such agreements comply with Community law* and other relevant international agreements. (Emphasis added.)

This is a rule designed to prevent conflict rather than preclude Member State action[24] and is a specific statement of the more general obligation based on Article 10 EC. In *Centro-Com* the Court applies the principle to a field of activity (foreign policy) which falls outside Community competence altogether, albeit in a context involving autonomous action rather than the conclusion of an international agreement:

> The Member States have indeed retained their competence in the field of foreign and security policy. At the material time, their cooperation in this field was governed by *inter alia* Title III of the Single European Act. None the less, the powers retained by the Member States must be exercised in a manner consistent with Community law.[25]

How far does this obligation go? In what follows we will look at three specific examples relating to the conclusion by Member States of bilateral

---

[22]   Cases 3, 4, 6/76 *Kramer* [1976] ECR 1279, paras 39–45. The procedural aspect of the obligation will be considered further below.

[23]   J Klabbers, above n 5, p 175.

[24]   It indicates that the field of services and intellectual property has not been occupied as far as international agreements are concerned, and therefore the Member States are not pre-empted from acting, but, on the other hand, conflict between rules of Community and Member State origin should be avoided.

[25]   Case C–124/95 *R v HM Treasury and Bank of England ex parte Centro-Com* [1997] ECR I–81, paras 24–25.

agreements: the conclusion of bilateral double tax treaties by Member States; bilateral agreements on social security benefits; and the conclusion of bilateral open skies treaties. Before we turn to these examples relating to the conclusion of new agreements by the Member States, however, let us briefly look at the position of agreements concluded by Member States before the coming into force of the EEC Treaty (or the accession of the Member State to the Community/Union).

(i) Article 307 EC: Balancing Foreign Policy Interests of Member States and the Community Interest

What for simplicity we will call pre-accession agreements are covered by Article 307 EC. This provision takes into account the position of third countries, thus providing a limited 'defence' for Member States where there is a conflict. In its interpretation of Art 307 the Court has constructed a delicate balance between the rights and interests of third countries and Member States on the one hand, and on the other the Community interest and the requirements of the Community legal order.

> The rights and obligations arising from agreements concluded before 1 January 1958 or, for acceding states, before the date of their accession, between one or more Member States on the one hand, and one or more third countries on the other, shall not be affected by the provisions of this Treaty.
> To the extent that such agreements are not compatible with this Treaty, the Member State or States concerned shall take all appropriate steps to eliminate the incompatibilities established. Member States shall, where necessary, assist each other to this end and shall, where appropriate, adopt a common attitude. ...[26]

A pre-accession agreement that has been revised may become a new, post-accession agreement; in such cases Article 307 will cease to apply and instead the situation will be governed by the compliance principles discussed below. Thus, although Germany argued in the Open Skies case that its agreement with the USA was a prior agreement as it was originally concluded in 1955, it was decided by the Court that the amending protocol agreed in 1996 precluded the application of Article 307: '[Article 307] cannot apply to amendments which Member States make to such agreements by entering into new commitments after the entry into force of the Treaty.'[27]

---

[26] Art 307 EC, paras 1 and 2. The first paragraph was amended by the Treaty of Amsterdam to make it absolutely clear that the provision applies not only to pre-1958 agreements but also to those concluded by new Member States before the date of their accession.

[27] Case C–476/98 *Commission v Germany* [2002] ECR I–9855 (Open Skies), para 69.

The Article 'is of general scope and applies to any international agreement, irrespective of subject-matter, which is capable of affecting application of the Treaty.'[28] It is significant, therefore, that the provision is not limited to agreements which would themselves fall within Community competence; instead it is concerned, in its second paragraph, with the issue of compatibility with the EC Treaty. It is in this sense that the scope of Community law, and thus the Community interest, is engaged. This is borne out by the Court's interpretation of paragraph 1, making it clear that it is not concerned with any transfer of competence or responsibility to the Community. The 'rights and obligations' referred to in Article 307(1) means the *rights* of third countries and the *obligations* of the Member State(s). It thus implies:

> a duty on the part of the institutions of the Community not to impede the performance of the obligations of Member States which stem from a prior agreement. However, that duty of the Community institutions is directed only to permitting the Member State concerned to perform its obligations under the prior agreement and does not bind the Community as regards the non-Member country in question.[29]

We might compare here the approach of the Court in *International Fruit Company* with respect to the GATT, in which the transfer of exclusive competence in trade matters from the Member States to the Community entailed not only an obligation to permit the Member State to fulfil their GATT obligations, but also a positive obligation towards other Contracting Parties under the provisions of the GATT itself.[30] I am not here suggesting that *International Fruit Company* would apply in all cases of supervening exclusive competence; rather pointing to the difference in approach when the issue is one of competence rather than compatibility with Community law. Article 307 is not concerned with (transfers of) competence, but rather deals with possible conflicts of obligation, resolving them, ultimately, in favour of the Community legal order.

So a Member State may rely on Article 307(1) to provide a justification for failing to comply with Community law obligations, if doing so would be inconsistent with its obligations to a third State under a prior agreement. As only their obligations are 'protected', Member States cannot use this provision to justify giving priority to rights they might have under a

---

[28] Case C–62/98 *Commission v Portugal* [2000] ECR I–5171, para 43. See also cases 812/79 *Attorney General v Burgoa* [1980] ECR 2787, para 6, and C–158/91 *Levy* [1993] ECR I–4287, para 11.

[29] Case 812/79, *Attorney General v Juan C Burgoa* [1980] ECR 2787, para 9.

[30] Cases 22–24/72, *International Fruit Company* [1972] ECR 1219, para 18: 'In so far as under the EEC Treaty the Community has assumed the powers previously exercised by Member States in the area governed by the General Agreement, the provisions of that agreement have the effect of binding the Community.'

prior agreement over their EC Treaty obligations: 'When an international agreement allows, but does not require, a Member State to adopt a measure which appears to be contrary to Community law, the Member State must refrain from adopting such a measure.'[31]

Article 307(2) provides that 'all appropriate steps' must be taken to eliminate any incompatibility. Three points may be briefly made. First, conflict may be avoided by the principle of consistent interpretation.[32] Second, a pre-accession agreement may not conflict with Community law at the time of accession, but if Community law and policy develop subsequently to the point that an incompatibility arises, paragraph 2 will apply. Third, the obligation to take 'all appropriate steps' is stronger than a 'best efforts' obligation; it imposes an obligation of result. Renegotiation and even denunciation may be required:

> Although, in the context of Article 234 [now 307] of the Treaty, the Member States have a choice as to the appropriate steps to be taken, they are nevertheless under an obligation to eliminate any incompatibilities existing between a pre-Community convention and the EC Treaty. If a Member State encounters difficulties which make adjustment of an agreement impossible, an obligation to denounce that agreement cannot therefore be excluded.[33]

In this 1998 case, the obligation to phase out or adjust existing bilateral agreements by a specific date was contained in the (later) Regulation on maritime transport adopted by the Community, which concerned Community relations with third States as well as intra-Community trade. Where the Community develops an exclusive competence in the field in question, any renegotiation and conclusion of an external agreement may need to be carried out by the Community rather than the Member State(s).[34] It is significant that the Court, when discussing this obligation on the Member States in *Commission v Portugal*, specifically refers—as being reflected in Article 307—to the Community interest, and the balance between the Community interest and the foreign policy interests of the Member State(s):

> As regards the argument that such denunciation would involve a disproportionate disregard of foreign-policy interests of the Portuguese Republic as compared with the Community interest, it must be pointed out that the balance between

---

[31] C–324/93, *R v Secretary of State for Home Department, ex parte Evans Medical Ltd and Macfarlan Smith Ltd* [1995] ECR I–0563, para 32.

[32] '… the national court must ascertain whether a possible incompatibility between the Treaty and the bilateral convention can be avoided by interpreting that convention, to the extent possible and in compliance with international law, in such a way that it is consistent with Community law.' C–216/01 *Budvar v Rudolf Ammersin GmbH*, judgment 18 November 2003, para 169.

[33] Case C–62/98 *Commission v Portugal* [2000] ECR I–5171, para 49.

[34] This may, de facto, be more realistic even in cases of supervening shared competence (*cf* the Open Skies scenario, examined below).

the foreign-policy interests of a Member State and the Community interest is already incorporated in Article 234 [now 307] of the Treaty, in that it allows a Member State not to apply a Community provision in order to respect the rights of third countries deriving from a prior agreement and to perform its obligations thereunder. That article also allows them to choose the appropriate means of rendering the agreement concerned compatible with Community law.[35]

The national interest is defined not in broad terms of international comity but rather, in holding that the national interest is adequately reflected in Article 307(1), in terms of the need on the part of the Member States to perform their international obligations without giving rise to a possible conflict with Community law. Although the case in question concerned a field where there was (now exclusive) Community competence, the Court frames its reference to the Community interest in its interpretation of the Treaty provision quite generally, and as we have already seen Article 307 also covers cases where the national agreement is within the competence of the Member States. In this way it is of broader scope than the '*AETR* effect' in the sense that it does not require or lead to a finding of exclusive Community competence. Thus, even in cases where the full *AETR* effect would not apply, and the existence of Member State competence is not put into question, the Community interest reflected in Article 307(2) may affect the Member States' exercise of their own competence (the maintenance in force of national agreements) insofar as there is an incompatibility with the Community legal order.

Article 307 EC applies to agreements *between Member States and third countries*. In principle, as a result of the primacy of Community law, the EC Treaty (and secondary law) will take precedence in case of conflict over prior bilateral agreements *between Member States* in fields covered by that Treaty.[36] Even where a prior bilateral agreement between Member States 'falls outside the field of application of the Treaty' the Court has applied the general obligation in Article 10 EC; thus in cases where the application of an EC law provision might be impeded by such an agreement, 'every Member State is under a duty to facilitate the application of the provision and, to that end, to assist every other Member State which is under an obligation under Community law'.[37] In an agreement between two Member States there is no third state whose rights need to be protected, thereby providing a defence to what would otherwise be a breach of Community

---

[35] Case C–62/98 *Commission v Portugal* [2000] ECR I–5171, para 50.
[36] Case C–10/61 *Commission v Italy* [1962] ECR 1. This reflects the general international law rule that the later treaty between two parties will prevail: Art 30(3) of the Vienna Convention on the Law of Treaties.
[37] Case C–235/87 *Matteucci* [1988] ECR 5589, para 19.

law. Both Member States are under an obligation not to insist on rights under the agreement if to do so would impede the application of Community law.

(ii) Taxation and Extension of Benefits

We can now turn to the position of post-accession agreements, in fields where the Member States have retained competence. The first example is that of double tax agreements. The Member States retain external competence in tax matters:

> ... in the absence of unifying or harmonising measures adopted in the Community, in particular under the second indent of Article 220 of the EC Treaty (now the second indent of Article 293 EC), the Member States remain competent to determine the criteria for taxation of income and wealth with a view to eliminating double taxation by means, *inter alia*, of international agreements.[38]

That competence must, however, be exercised in conformity with EC law obligations:

> As far as the exercise of the power of taxation so allocated is concerned, the Member States nevertheless may not disregard Community rules. According to the settled case-law of the Court, although direct taxation is a matter for the Member States, they must nevertheless exercise their taxation powers consistently with Community law.[39]

This includes compliance with the Treaty provisions on establishment which 'guarantee nationals of Member States of the Community who have exercised their freedom of establishment and companies or firms which are assimilated to them the same treatment in the host Member State as that accorded to nationals of that Member State.'[40] Permanently established branches, which are not tax resident, must not be treated differently from resident companies, including subsidiaries.[41] In *Saint-Gobain* the Court held that the host Member State must extend to Community companies established in its territory (PEs), even where they are non-resident for tax purposes, the same (tax) advantages which it grants to its own resident companies under the terms of a double tax treaty with a third country:

> the national treatment principle requires the Member State which is party to [a double-taxation treaty concluded between a Member State and a non-member

---

[38] Case C–307/97 *Saint-Gobain v Finanzamt Aachen-Innenstadt* [1999] ECR I–6161, para 56.
[39] *Ibid*, para 57.
[40] *Ibid*, para 34.
[41] Case C–270/83 *Commission v France* [1986] ECR 273.

country] to grant to permanent establishments of non-resident companies the advantages provided for by that treaty on the same conditions as those which apply to resident companies.[42]

Thus, where an advantage is granted by a Member State under a bilateral agreement with a third country it must, on the basis of the equal treatment requirement in Article 43 EC, be extended to all Community companies established in that Member State.[43] In *Saint-Gobain* the Court argued that the unilateral extension of the advantage by Germany to non-tax-resident PEs would not affect the rights of the third country or impose obligations on it, so the 'balance and reciprocity' of this bilateral treaty would not be affected. Thus it is possible to argue that the Community obligation here described affects the Member States' internal operation of their tax laws but not their freedom of movement in negotiating with third countries.[44] However, in the Open Skies cases, considered below, the Court goes further and applies the same reasoning in a case where the advantage under the bilateral agreement is granted by the third country, and the bilateral agreement is thus directly implicated.

(iii) Social Security and Objective Justifications for Differential Treatment

In *Gottardo*[45] the Court held that a French national was entitled to the same treatment as an Italian national with respect to entitlement to an Italian old-age pension, the issue being whether she was entitled to have taken into account periods worked in Switzerland. Under an Italian–Swiss convention she would be so entitled if she were an Italian national, or a national of another Member State which also had a similar agreement with

---

[42]   Case C–307/97 *Saint-Gobain v Finanzamt Aachen-Innenstadt* [1999] ECR I–6161, para 58.

[43]   In Case C–376/03 *D v Inspecteur van de Belastingdienst / Particulieren / Ondernemingen buitenland te Heerlen* [2005] ECR I–05821, the Court clarifies the limits of this principle. In *Saint-Gobain* a company that is not resident but which has a taxable permanent establishment in a Member State was held to be in a equivalent situation to a company resident in that Member State and thus entitled to the same tax advantages, including those granted under a double tax treaty. In *D*, the Court took the view that a non-resident such as D was not in an equivalent situation to a resident for the purposes of applying a double tax treaty between two Member States and there is thus no discrimination in treating them differently. Whatever one thinks of the merits of this distinction (between resident/non-resident in *D*, and resident/non-resident but with a permanent establishment in *Saint-Gobain*) and the somewhat circular reasoning, the decision in *D* confirms the point being made here: that Member States' international agreements (eg double tax treaties) are subject to control for compliance with Community law.

[44]   This argument is perhaps not very convincing as far as new agreements are concerned: it may be hard to negotiate a reciprocal deal if the third country knows that whatever advantage it is given will automatically be extended to companies from all the other 24 Member States.

[45]   Case C–55/00 *Gottardo v INPS* [2002] ECR I–413.

Switzerland. The Court took the view that these advantages must also be extended by Italy to a Community national who was not entitled under the Italian–Swiss agreement.

> ... when giving effect to commitments assumed under international agreements, be it an agreement between Member States or an agreement between a Member State and one or more non-member countries, Member States are required, subject to the provisions of Article 307 EC, to comply with the obligations that Community law imposes on them. The fact that non-member countries, for their part, are not obliged to comply with any Community-law obligation is of no relevance in this respect.
>
> It follows from all of the foregoing that, when a Member State concludes a bilateral international convention on social security with a non-member country which provides for account to be taken of periods of insurance completed in that non-member country for acquisition of entitlement to old-age benefits, the fundamental principle of equal treatment requires that that Member State grant nationals of other Member States the same advantages as those which its own nationals enjoy under that convention unless it can provide objective justification for refusing to do so.[46]

As with the double tax treaty, the Member State was being asked to extend unilaterally the benefits granted to its own nationals as a result of an international agreement to nationals of other Member States. The existence of the bilateral agreement per se was not a valid reason for distinguishing between them. We should, however, note the phrase 'objective justification'. The Community law principle at stake is that of equal treatment; if there is an objective justification to distinguish between the two situations (*in casu*, the entitlement of the French national and the Italian national to an Italian old-age pension), then differential treatment may be justified. In a later passage in the same judgment, the Court accepts that 'the balance and reciprocity of a bilateral international convention' may amount to an objective justification; however, in this case (as in *Saint Gobain*) the unilateral extension of benefits by one Member State to nationals of other Member States would not compromise the rights of the third country or impose any additional obligation on it. The issue of objective justification (the denial of discrimination) was also raised in *D v Inspecteur van de Belastingdienst*, this time with more success.[47] This case, it should be remembered, involved an inter-Member-State agreement under which the reciprocal rights and obligations applied only to persons resident in one of the Contracting (Member) States (Belgium and the Netherlands). Thus, the differential treatment was based on residence: a Member State national taxpayer resident in (for example) Germany was not regarded (for the

---

[46] Case C–55/00 *Gottardo v INPS* [2002] ECR I–413, paras 33–34.
[47] See above n 43.

purposes of Netherlands wealth tax) as being in the same situation as a taxpayer resident in either the Netherlands or Belgium. Unlike *Saint-Gobain*, *Gottardo* and indeed also Open Skies, there was no permanent establishment in the Member State granting the advantage (the Netherlands), and the Court took the view that this provided an objective justification.[48] We cannot assume, therefore, that all advantages under bilateral agreements must automatically be extended to all other Community nationals; the principle is one of equal treatment and it may well be that those nationals are not in the same situation with respect to the benefits in question. These cases do all demonstrate, however, that a Member State will need to justify differential treatment, even where it flows from the existence of a bilateral agreement, and that the agreement does not in itself remove the application of Community law rules.

(iv) Open Skies and Benefits Granted by Third Countries

In the Open Skies cases[49] the principle of equality of treatment is taken further: the advantage withheld from other Community nationals, as compared with the Member State's own nationals, is an advantage granted by a third country and thus compliance would require the agreement of that third country (or the removal of the advantage—withdrawal from the agreement). The bilateral agreements in question contained ownership and control clauses which in the Court's view contravened Article 43 EC on rights of establishment, since, under the bilateral agreement, Community companies established in the Member State party did not have the same *rights of access to the US market* as companies regarded as having the nationality[50] of that Member State. Note that we are here not talking about access to the Community market, or pension or tax advantages in the Member State (as with *Gottardo, Saint-Gobain* or *D*), but access to a third country market. According to the Court, it did not matter that the advantages were granted by the third country:

> Community airlines suffer discrimination which prevents them from benefiting from the treatment which the host Member State, namely the Federal Republic of Germany, accords to its own nationals. … [T]he direct source of that

---

[48] Although Art 56 EC, which was at issue in this case, is not based upon discrimination (or residence), discrimination nevertheless comes into the justification in Art 58(1)(a) EC under which Art 56 on the free movement of capital is without prejudice to the right of Member States 'to apply the relevant provisions of their tax law which distinguish taxpayers who are not in the same situation with regard to their place of residence'. This justification does not permit Member States to take measures which 'constitute a means of arbitrary discrimination' (Art 58(3) EC). Hence the Court's attention to whether taxpayers resident in different Member States should be regarded as being in the same situation.

[49] Cases C–466/98, C–467/98, C–468/98, C–469/98, C–471/98, C–472/98, C–475/98 and C–476/98, judgments of 5 November 2002.

[50] That is, companies under the ownership and control of nationals of that Member State.

discrimination is not the possible conduct of the United States of America but the clause on the ownership and control of airlines, which specifically acknowledges the right of the United States of America to act in that way.[51]

Here, the bilateral agreement itself conflicted with Community law, since it effectively allowed the third country to discriminate; it was not possible for the problem to be resolved unilaterally by the Member State (by simply extending the benefits, as in *Saint-Gobain*), and renegotiation of the agreement would be required.

In addition, the aftermath of the Open Skies cases illustrates that even where competence is shared, it may be more politically realistic for the Member States to decide to negotiate as a Community, especially if they need to persuade powerful third countries to extend the benefits of any agreement to all Community companies. Despite the limited nature of Community exclusive competence in the field of air transport as found by the Court in the Open Skies cases, the Council decided (after years of refusal) to grant the Commission a mandate to negotiate with third countries, reflecting the difficulty for Member States of ensuring compliance with Article 43 EC in individual negotiations.[52] The compliance constraints, although not in themselves legally precluding Member State action, may make it de facto difficult to negotiate a Treaty-compliant agreement.

In all these cases, although Member States have not lost the competence to conclude bilateral agreements, their freedom of action was constrained, either in effectively extending the implementation of the agreement to other Community nationals, or in being required to insist that the third country extended the benefits of the agreement to Community nationals established in their territories. In effect, the ostensibly bilateral agreement acquires a Community dimension.

(v) Re-negotiating Bilateral Agreements

Thus we have seen that in the case of both pre-accession and post-accession agreements, where there is an incompatibility with Community law, re-negotiation of the agreement may be necessary. In such cases, the Open Skies agreements provide a concrete example of the application of the concept of the Community interest and the duty of cooperation. As we have just seen, following the Court judgments in the Open Skies cases the

[51] Case C–476/98 *Commission v Germany* [2002] ECR I–9855(Open Skies case), paras 153–4.

[52] Commission Communication on the consequences of the Court judgments of 5 November 2002 for European air transport policy COM(2002)649; Commission Communication on relations between the Community and third countries in the field of air transport COM(2003)94.

Council agreed that Community agreements should be negotiated with third countries which would replace bilateral Member State agreements. In addition, and pending the negotiation of the Community agreements, the Council adopted a Regulation which attempts to give effect to the duty of cooperation in a field of shared competence where Member States are under an obligation to bring existing agreements into line with Community law.[53] The Preamble to the Regulation refers to the duty of cooperation and confirms that the cooperation procedure established by the Regulation is 'without prejudice to the division of competencies between the Community and Member States' (recital 5). Nevertheless, Member States seeking to negotiate amendments to their existing bilateral agreements must ensure that they take into account 'broader Community interests' as well as strict compatibility, and this will include the need to operate consistently with Community-level negotiations.

> It is essential to ensure that a Member State conducting negotiations takes account of Community law, broader Community interests and ongoing Community negotiations. (Recital 8.)[54]

The Regulation imposes two main types of obligation on the Member States. One is procedural, and will be mentioned below.[55] The other is substantive: to include in national negotiations relevant standard clauses developed jointly by the Commission and the Member States; the obligation to treat all Community air carriers with an establishment in their territory equally in terms of consultation and participation in such negotiations; not to introduce any new arrangement which reduces the number of Community air carriers benefiting from the agreement; the obligation to treat all such carriers equally in terms of implementation of the agreement provisions on traffic rights. Thus the Regulation sets out in specific terms how the Member States' freedom to negotiate in an area of shared competence is constrained by the need to take into account not only compatibility with Community law but also the Community interest: the Commission will notify the Member States both if it sees a likely incompatibility and if it takes the view that the negotiations 'are likely to undermine the objectives of Community negotiations underway with the third country concerned'.[56] Even further, the conclusion of such a bilateral

---

[53] Regulation 847/2004/EC on the Negotiation and Implementation of Air Service Agreements between Member States and Third Countries, [2004] OJ L/157/7; Recital 6 of the Preamble states: 'All existing bilateral agreements between Member States and third countries that contain provisions contrary to Community law should be amended or replaced by new agreements that are wholly compatible with Community law.'

[54] On the relationship between national negotiations and the application of Art 10 where the Community has proposed to negotiate an agreement, see further below.

[55] See below, section III.C.

[56] Art 1(4).

agreement by a Member State is to be subject to 'authorisation'[57] and where the standard clauses are not incorporated into the agreement, such authorisation will depend on the terms of the agreement being found not to harm the object and purpose of the Community transport policy (Art 4(3)).

This is a particularly strong example, in that it is dealing with a (relatively) transitional period during which the Member States will maintain but attempt to adjust existing national/bilateral agreements and at the same time a programme of negotiation of new Community agreements is envisaged. The idea of a common negotiating position (standard clauses) has also been conceded. Indeed, the Member States have also agreed that the Community should negotiate, effectively on their behalf, amendments to their existing bilateral air transport agreements with third countries (so-called 'horizontal agreements').[58] It is also a field in which the standard international agreements contain provisions which fall partly within exclusive Community competence. As a result it can be claimed that Member States should no longer act autonomously. Nevertheless there are signs that the approach adopted in Regulation 847/2004 may well find application elsewhere.[59] It indicates the way in which, in a field which is clearly not fully one of exclusive competence, the primacy of Community law, the duty of cooperation and the Community interest may be reflected in procedures designed to balance continuing Member State involvement and developing Community competence.

---

[57] By the Commission assisted by the committee established under Reg 2408/92/EC.

[58] According to the Commission: 'Between June 2003 and May 2006, the method of separate bilateral negotiations has led to changes with 39 partner States, representing 69 bilateral agreements corrected. Under the second option, horizontal negotiations have led to changes with 23 partner States, representing an additional 342 bilateral agreements.' (http://ec.europa.eu/transport/air_portal/international/pillars/horizontal_agreements_en.htm) For an example of a horizontal agreement, see Proposal for a Council Decision on the conclusion of an agreement between the EC and Ukraine on certain aspects of air services, COM (2005) 368 final.

[59] For example, the JHA Council on 19–20 April 2007 discussed the approach to be adopted towards existing and future Member States' bilateral agreements in the field of enforcement of maintenance awards, following the coming into force of a projected Community instrument on the subject. The Council discussed a Presidency proposal that existing agreements would remain, subject to Art 307 EC. 'For future bilateral agreements and any amendment of existing bilateral agreements with particular third countries, the Presidency suggests introducing a procedure for the negotiation and conclusion of such agreements, inspired by existing precedents in Community law, *inter alia*, the procedure for air services. That procedure should establish criteria and conditions for assessing whether the conclusion of such an agreement is in the Community's interest. Where that is not the case, the procedure should establish criteria and conditions for the negotiation and conclusion of such agreements by Member States, particularly if the prospective agreement's provisions differ in content from Community rules, so as to ensure that agreements do not compromise the system established by the proposed Regulation.'

(vi) Intra-Member State Obligations: Disconnection Clauses

The foreign policy of Member States does of course include their relations, within an international law framework, with other EU Member States. Member States may conclude agreements with some of or all the other Member States, with or without third countries, and with or without the joint participation of the EC itself. Mixed agreements (to which the EC and third countries are party alongside the Member States) will be considered in the next section. Inter-Member-State agreements will not be considered in any detail in this Chapter, for lack of space, and as their legal implications have been explored systematically elsewhere.[60] Briefly, we may say that the principle of the primacy of Community law will apply, such that it will take precedence over conflicting norms in inter-Member-State agreements, whether or not these pre-date the EC Treaty or accession.[61] Where some or all Member States conclude an international agreement with third countries which may impact on the sphere of application of Community law, however, a particular technique is used which is designed to ensure the primacy of Community law obligations in relations between the Member States themselves.[62] These so-called disconnection clauses now follow a standard form:

> In their mutual relations, Parties which are members of the European Community shall apply Community rules and shall not therefore apply the rules arising from this Convention except in so far as there is no Community rule governing the particular subject concerned.[63]

The disconnection clause recognises that the Member States are part of the Community legal order and as such Community law obligations will apply

---

[60] B de Witte, 'Old-fashioned Flexibility: International Agreements between Member States of the European Union' in G de Búrca and J Scott (eds), *Constitutional Change in the EU—From Uniformity to Flexibility?* (Oxford, Hart Publishing, 2000); B de Witte, 'Chameleonic Member States: Differentiation by Means of Partial and Parallel International Agreements' in B de Witte, D Hanf and E Vos (eds), *The Many Faces of Differentiation in EU Law* (Antwerp/Oxford/New York, Intersentia, 2001).

[61] See above, section II.A(i).

[62] As Bruno de Witte points out, in the case of open multilateral treaties, such as many of the Council of Europe conventions, not all Member States may sign and ratify them, or not at the same time. The need for mechanisms to reduce legal differentiation is recognised and the disconnection clause considered here is one of those options, alongside other procedures mentioned by de Witte, such as encouraging all Member States to ratify the convention through a Council Recommendation. See B de Witte, 'Old-fashioned flexibility: International Agreements between Member States of the European Union' in G de Búrca and J Scott (eds), *Constitutional Change in the EU—From Uniformity to Flexibility?* (Oxford, Hart Publishing, 2000) 38–9.

[63] Art 27(1) of the European Convention on Transfrontier Television 1989, ETS No 132, as amended by Protocol ETS No 171. Other examples include Art 26(3) of the Council of Europe Convention on the Prevention of Terrorism, CETS No 196; Art 16*bis* of the Convention on Insider Trading, CETS No 130, as amended by Protocol CETS No 133. Disconnection clauses may be used both where the EC is and where it is not itself a party.

as between themselves, notwithstanding the commitments they take on with respect to third States. Although the Member States conclude the agreement independently, their status as members of the EU is recognised and the primacy of Community law takes effect in derogation from the normal priority given to provisions of a later treaty. To that extent the disconnection clause can be seen as a mechanism for the protection of the Community *acquis* from possible conflict with international law norms[64]; indeed as such they are a substantive counterpart to the obligation expressed in Article 292 EC whereby Member States undertake not to submit *inter se* disputes concerning the EC Treaty to external dispute settlement processes.[65] The disconnection clause is designed to avoid conflict and to preserve the primacy of Community law as between the Member States; in this it goes further than a rule of priority (ie a rule that in case of conflict between Community law and the agreement, priority is given to the former[66]), being rather a choice of law rule (Community law will apply between the Member States whether or not there is a conflict). A disconnection clause does not, however, remove the possibility of an 'effect' on the Community legal order such as to trigger pre-emption and exclusivity. The Court of Justice has taken the view that a conflict-avoidance rule such as a disconnection clause cannot be seen as an alternative to determining whether the conditions for pre-emption are satisfied: 'any initiative seeking to avoid contradictions between Community law and the agreement envisaged does not remove the obligation to determine, prior to the conclusion of the agreement, whether it is capable of affecting the Community rules'.[67] These clauses are not, therefore, an 'alternative answer' to the justification for exclusive Community competence based on the *AETR* effect, any more than is a priority rule[68]; rather they are one mechanism used, in cases where the Member States are exercising their own treaty-making competence, to ensure the primacy of Community law in intra-Member State relations.

---

[64] J Klabbers, 'Safeguarding the Organizational *Acquis*: The EU's External Practice' (2007) 4 *International Organizations Law Review* 57, which provides an examination of disconnection clauses in the context of other types of clause used to protect the *acquis*.
[65] See below for further discussion of Art 292 EC.
[66] See, eg, Art 134 of the Schengen Convention.
[67] *Opinion 1/2003 (Lugano Convention)* [2006] ECR I–1145, para 129. The Court goes on to make clear that a mechanism such as a disconnection clause 'is not in itself a decisive factor in resolving the question whether the Community has exclusive competence to conclude that agreement or whether competence belongs to the Member States', *ibid*, para 130.
[68] *Cf* Case C–467/98 *Commission v Denmark* [2002] ECR I–9519, para 82, cited above in text at note 21, and para 101 of the same judgment.

B. Mixed Agreements and the Community Interest

In what ways does the Member States' duty to comply with their Community law obligations impact on their participation in mixed agreements?[69] In this section we will consider some aspects of the Member States' responsibility *in Community law* for the performance of Community agreements which are also mixed agreements, and the relationship between that responsibility, the scope of Community competence, the scope of Community law and the Community interest.[70] Our starting point must be the *Community law obligation* to perform the agreement derived from Article 300(7) and Article 10 EC, which is separable from their obligations (in international law) as parties to mixed agreements. As the Court has said, the Member States 'fulfil an obligation not only in relation to the non-member country concerned but also and above all in relation to the Community which has assumed responsibility for the due performance of the Agreement.'[71] Whether the Community or the Member State actually implements the agreement will depend on 'the state of Community law for the time being in the areas affected by the provisions of the agreement'.[72] This depends on the internal division of competence, and does not necessarily depend on who concludes the agreement or on the legal base used.[73] To take one example in a field of shared competence, the Council Decision concluding the WIPO Copyright Treaty (WCT) and the WIPO Performances and Phonograms Treaty (WPPT) refers to the importance of synchronising ratification of these treaties by the Member States and conclusion by the Community, with a view to ensuring proper implementation of the obligations they contain.[74] The Decision spells out

---

[69]   This section is a revised version of Chapter 2.1 of 'External Relations of the EU and the Member States: Competence, Mixed Agreements, International Responsibility, and Effects of International Law', Report of M Cremona, Community Rapporteur, X Xenopoulos (ed), FIDE 2006 National Reports.

[70]   As far as their conclusion is concerned, agreements may be mixed either because they fall partly outside Community competence and Member State participation is thus required; alternatively, the agreement may fall partly within exclusive Community competence and partly within shared competence; finally, the agreement may lie entirely within shared competence, it being decided however to conclude the agreement jointly. The latter decision—to conclude the agreement as a mixed agreement even where the participation of both Community and Member States is not legally necessary—is, as Dashwood and Heliskoski put it, a political choice: see A Dashwood and J Heliskoski, 'The Classic Authorities Revisited' in A Dashwood and C Hillion (eds), *The General Law of EC External Relations* (London, Sweet & Maxwell, 2000), 17. Arguably, although Member States have a right to exercise their competence and conclude the agreement themselves, in doing so they should have regard to the need to facilitate the Community's tasks (Art 10 EC).

[71]   Case C–104/81 *Hauptzollampt Mainz v Kupferberg* [1982] ECR 3641, para 13.

[72]   Case C–104/81 *Hauptzollampt Mainz v Kupferberg* [1982] ECR 3641, para 12.

[73]   Case C–268/94 *Portugal v Council* [1996] ECR I–6177, para 47.

[74]   Council Decision 2000/278/EC of 16 March 2000 on the approval, on behalf of the European Community, of the WIPO Copyright Treaty and the WIPO Performances and

this link between Member States' and Community obligations in terms of the responsibility of Member States to implement Community Directives designed to ensure compliance:

> The President of the Council is hereby authorised to deposit the instruments of conclusion ... as from the date by which the Member States will have to bring into force the measures adopted by the European Parliament and the Council necessary to adapt the existing Community legislation to the obligations deriving from the WCT and the WPPT.[75]

The Commission has a role in ensuring compliance with Community agreements, as a Community obligation. In *Commission v Germany*,[76] for example, the Commission brought an infringement action against Germany under Article 226 [ex 169] EC, on the grounds of a German failure to comply with the International Dairy Arrangement concluded by the Community in 1980 under GATT (Tokyo Round). Germany argued that a disputed interpretation of IDA obligations had been referred to the '113 Committee' and that the Commission should have waited for its view. The Court disagreed, holding that the role of the Committee is purely advisory, and should not hinder the Commission's duty to enforce Community law under what is now Article 211 EC; responsibility for ensuring the uniform interpretation of Community agreements lies with the Court of Justice and is not a matter for political consensus.[77] In this decision the Court lays the foundation for its future positions as regards both the enforcement and the interpretation of agreements. Both this case and *Kupferberg* involved agreements which were not mixed; how do these principles apply in the case of mixed agreements?

> The Convention [UNCLOS] was concluded by the Community and all of its Member States on the basis of shared competence. ... [M]ixed agreements have

---

Phonograms Treaty, [2000] OJ L/89/6. According to the recitals, 'the approval of the WCT and the WPPT is a matter for both the Community and its Member States. ... The deposit of the instruments of conclusion of the Community should take place as far as possible simultaneously with the deposit of the instruments of ratification of the Member States'.

[75] *Ibid*, Art 2. The relevant legislation is Directive 2001/29/EC of the European Parliament and of the Council of 22 May 2001 on the harmonisation of certain aspects of copyright and related rights in the information society, [2001] OJ L/167/10. See also Statement by the Council on the Principles regarding the ratification by the European Community and its Member States of the 1996 WIPO Treaties, agreed by General Affairs Council, 23 July 2007, Council Doc 11517/07, setting out guiding principles for the ratification of the 1996 WIPO Treaties designed to ensure that 'Member States and the European Community should undertake the same commitments'.

[76] Case C–61/94 *Commission v Germany* [1996] ECR I–3989.

[77] 'The initiation of proceedings before the Court by the Commission cannot therefore depend on the outcome of consultations within the Article 113 Committee; a fortiori, it cannot hinge on whether a consensus between the Member States has first been found to exist within the Committee with regard to the interpretation of the Community's commitments under an international agreement.' (Case C–61/94 *Commission v Germany* [1996] ECR I–3989, para 15.)

the same status in the Community legal order as purely Community agreements, as these are provisions coming within the scope of Community competence ...[78]

This implies that a Member State has a Community law obligation (not just an international law obligation) to implement a mixed agreement, as its provisions are 'within the scope of Community competence' and an integral part of the Community legal order.[79] What does this mean? Similar statements have been made in three recent cases, with a small but significant difference in wording in the English language version of one of the three.[80] Following the French text, in which the language at the critical point in all three cases is identical, the Court holds that not only do the provisions of such agreements form an integral part of the Community legal order, but that the agreement as a whole has the same status in that legal order as Community agreements: 'Les accords mixtes ont le même statut dans l'ordre juridique communautaire que les accords purement communautaires, s'agissant des dispositions qui relèvent de la compétence de la Communauté.'[81]

The precise wording is important, because when the Community concludes a mixed agreement it is not always clear to what extent it is operating under Community competence and engaging Community responsibility. In the case of an agreement which is mixed because it contains provisions which are *outside* Community competence (and possibly others which are outside Member State competence), then it is comparatively clear, at least as far as internal Community law is concerned. However, if the agreement is one of concurrent competence, where

---

[78] Case C–459/03 *Commission v Ireland* [2006] ECR I–4635, paras 83–4.

[79] In Case 12/86 *Demirel* [1987] ECR I–3719, for example, the Court held that the provisions of the Association Agreement with Turkey on free movement of persons fell within Community competence (para 9), and also, citing *Kupferberg*, that 'in ensuring respect for commitments arising from an agreement concluded by the Community institutions the Member States fulfil, within the Community system, an obligation in relation to the Community, which has assumed responsibility for the due performance of the Agreement' (para 11).

[80] Case C–459/03 *Commission v Ireland* [2006] ECR I–4635, para 84 (cited in text at note 78); see also Case C–13/00 *Commission v Ireland* [2002] ECR I–2943 (Berne Convention), para 14, 'mixed agreements concluded by the Community, its Member States and non-member countries have the same status in the Community legal order as purely Community agreements, as these are provisions coming within the scope of Community competence'. However, the judgment in Case C–239/03 *Commission v France* [2004] ECR I–9325 (Etang de Berre), para 25, reads in its English version: '... mixed agreements concluded by the Community, its Member States and non-member countries have the same status in the Community legal order as purely Community agreements *in so far as* the provisions fall within the scope of Community competence' (emphasis added). Notwithstanding, in their French versions all three judgments contain an identical phrase: « s'agissant des dispositions qui relèvent de la compétence de la Communauté ». As the passage which differs in the English (para 25 of case C–239/03) expressly cites one of the other passages (para 14 of Case C–13/00), as does the most recent formulation in case C–459/03 cited above, the difference is likely to be an accident of translation.

[81] Case C–459/03 *Commission v Ireland* [2006] ECR I–4635, para 84.

the whole or part of the agreement falls within shared competence, it is not always clear to what extent the Community has exercised its competence in concluding the agreement. Some authors hold that the Community is only engaged to the extent of its exclusive competence; everything else is reserved to the Member States.[82] The Court of Justice has been more nuanced, making a link between the 'scope of Community competence' and the 'scope of Community law' and introducing the concept of a Community interest in the performance of mixed agreements.

In *Commission v Ireland* (the Berne Convention case), Ireland was charged with breach of its obligations under the EEA for not acceding to the Berne Convention;[83] it argued that intellectual property rights are a matter of Member State competence within this mixed agreement. The Court held that for a Member State to be in breach of a Community law obligation it must be shown that this provision of the agreement comes within 'the scope of Community law'.[84] It then examined the specific obligation:

> In the present case, there can be no doubt that the provisions of the Berne Convention cover an area which comes in large measure within the scope of Community competence. ... The Berne Convention thus creates rights and obligations in areas covered by Community law. That being so there is a Community interest in ensuring that all Contracting Parties to the EEA Agreement adhere to that Convention.[85]

The case is striking in that the obligation on Ireland deriving from the mixed agreement (the EEA) referred to accession to the Berne Convention, which is not itself a mixed agreement; the Community interest thus lay in ensuring that all the Member States exercised their own competence in implementing the EEA by adhering to an international agreement independently of the EC. Note the way in which, over several paragraphs, the Court starts with 'the scope of Community competence', moves on to

---

[82] For example, J Heliskoski, *Mixed Agreements as a Technique for Organizing the International Relations of the European Community and its Member States* (The Hague/ Boston, Kluwer Law International, 2001), 46–7: '... the justification for the participation of the Member States is to be found precisely in the circumstance that the Community has not decided—and upon the conclusion of a given agreement does not decide—*actually to exercise* its non-exclusive competence, which makes it possible for the Member States to act under their own powers. But this must however mean that the Community's participation is legally only relevant insofar as the Community's exclusive competence is concerned; the rest of the commitments are assumed by the Member States in their individual capacity.' (Emphasis in the original.)

[83] Under Art 5 of Protocol 28 to the EEA the Contracting Parties agreed to accede to the Berne Convention by 1 January 1995. As the EEA is a mixed agreement, Ireland is a party (alongside the EC).

[84] Case C–13/00 *Commission v Ireland* [2002] ECR I–2943 (Berne Convention case), para 13.

[85] Case C–13/00 *Commission v Ireland* [2002] ECR I–2943 (Berne Convention case), paras 16 and 19.

'areas covered by Community law' and finishes with 'there is a Community interest ...'. The reference to the Community interest is in this way linked to the fact that Community legislation overlaps with the Berne Convention, and thus that provision of the EEA in respect of which compliance was at issue.

However, in *Commission v France* (the Etang de Berre case), the ECJ held that a Member State could be in breach of its Community law obligations by failing to implement a mixed agreement, even though the alleged breach concerned an aspect of the agreement which was not actually covered by Community legislation; it was enough that the *field in general* was 'covered in large measure' by Community legislation and in such cases 'there is a Community interest in compliance by both the Community and its Member States with the commitments entered into'.[86] Rosas notes that in these cases the Court, by asking whether the field is 'covered in large measure' by Community rules, appears to be favouring the approach to competence and exclusivity developed in *Opinion 2/91*.[87] AG Maduro, in his opinion in the Sellafield case,[88] also makes the link with exercise of competence, arguing that the Court in *Commission v France* held that the Community did actually exercise a non-exclusive competence over the whole agreement when it was concluded, even though there was no existing Community legislation covering parts of it.

The conclusion by the Member States of a mixed agreement also has an effect on their relations *inter se*. In fields covered by Community law, relations between the Member States are regulated by Community law, not international law.[89] Article 292 EC is an example of that general principle,[90] expressing 'the duty of loyalty to the judicial system created by the Community Treaties'.[91] But what is the scope of the Court's jurisdictional monopoly in the context of disputes between Member States arising out of a mixed agreement? It is clear that in a multilateral agreement of this kind, the Member States have a responsibility in international law *inter se*,[92] the question is to what extent Community law constrains them in the

---

[86] Case C–239/03 *Commission v France* [2004] ECR I–9325 (Etang de Berre case), paras 29–30.

[87] A Rosas, 'International Dispute Settlement: EU Practices and Procedures' (2003) 46 *German Yearbook of International Law* 284.

[88] Case C–459/03 *Commission v Ireland* [2006] ECR I–4635, Opinion of AG Poiares Maduro 18 January 2006, para 33.

[89] See section II.A(v) above.

[90] Under Art 292 EC 'Member States undertake not to submit a dispute concerning the interpretation or application of this Treaty to any method of settlement other than those provided for therein'.

[91] Case C–459/03 *Commission v Ireland* [2006] ECR I–4635, Opinion of AG Poiares Maduro 18 January 2006, para 10.

[92] A Rosas, 'Mixed Union—Mixed Agreements' in M Koskenniemi (ed), *International Law Aspects of the European Union* (Dordrecht, Martinus Nijhoff, 1998), 142.

enforcement of those obligations and the key lies in the need to preserve the autonomy of the Community legal order.[93]

The Sellafield case in which the Commission brought an infringement action against Ireland alleging breach of Articles 10 and 292 EC illustrates the problem.[94] Ireland had sought to hold the UK to account for alleged breaches of obligations under the UN Convention on the Law of the Sea (UNCLOS), using dispute settlement procedures established by UNCLOS. The issue was whether this inter-Member-State dispute concerned 'the interpretation or application of this Treaty' (Article 292 EC). The Advocate General expressed this as a question of whether the matters brought by Ireland before the UNCLOS Arbitral Tribunal, at least in part, 'fall within the scope of Community law'.[95] Ireland argued that in concluding the UNCLOS the Community only exercised its exclusive competence (eg in matters of fisheries conservation); other areas of the agreement falling within shared competence (including its environmental dimension[96]) were concluded by the Member States. AG Maduro disagreed with this limited view of Community participation in the agreement, pointing out that the Council Decision concluding the agreement was based *inter alia* on Art 130s EC (environment policy, now Article 175(1) EC). Drawing an analogy from the Etang de Berre case considered above, he found that in concluding UNCLOS, the EC exercised not only its exclusive but also its non-exclusive competence, including in environmental fields, and that therefore these aspects are within the scope of Community law and so subject to the Court's exclusive jurisdiction.[97]

The Court largely follows this approach to the question. Taking as its starting point the proposition that since the UNCLOS was concluded by Council decision 'the provisions of that convention now form an integral part of the Community legal order',the Court holds that the first step is to determine whether the relevant provisions of the agreement 'come within

---

[93]   C–459/03 *Commission v Ireland* [2006] ECR I–4635, Opinion of AG Poiares Maduro, para 10.

[94]   C–459/03 *Commission v Ireland* [2006] ECR I–4635.

[95]   Case C–459/03 *Commission v Ireland* [2006] ECR I–4635, Opinion of AG Poiares Maduro, para 2. The Advocate General took the view that there is no threshold to the jurisdictional monopoly established by Art 292 EC: it is sufficient if part of the dispute falls within the scope of the Court's jurisdiction.

[96]   It was argued by Ireland that the environmental provisions of UNCLOS, being based on minimum standards, are not such as to affect Community rules within the meaning of *AETR*; *cf Opinion 1/92* [1993] ECR I–1061.

[97]   Case C–459/03 *Commission v Ireland* [2006] ECR I–4635, Opinion of AG Poiares Maduro, para 33. It was also argued by Commission and accepted by AG Maduro that Ireland was in breach of Art 292 by citing a number of Directives before the UNCLOS Tribunal and thereby requesting or requiring that Tribunal to rule on the interpretation of Community law: Opinion of AG Maduro, paras 44–51.

the scope of Community competence'.[98] The Court then makes it clear, quite rightly, that the conditions for determining the scope of Community competence are not the same as those which determine whether that competence is exclusive (whether, in particular, Community rules would be affected within the meaning of *AETR*). Community competence in the field of environmental protection is shared and may be exercised 'even if the specific matters covered by those agreements are not yet, or are only very partially, the subject of rules at Community level'.[99] However, in then determining whether the Community did in fact exercise its non-exclusive competence in concluding the UNCLOS, the Court relies not only on the legal base for the concluding Council Decision, but also on its interpretation of the Declaration of competence made by the EC under Annex IX of UNCLOS under which (it says) Community competence was exercised only to the extent that the field was covered by Community rules:

> that passage of the Declaration of Community competence makes the transfer of areas of shared competence subject to the existence of Community rules, even though it is not necessary that those rules be affected.
> It follows that, within the specific context of the Convention, a finding that there has been a transfer to the Community of areas of shared competence is contingent on the existence of Community rules within the areas covered by the Convention provisions in issue, irrespective of what may otherwise be the scope and nature of those rules.[100]

Although the Court's analysis is in terms of the exercise of competence—an analysis which I would argue is misplaced—its conclusions are in fact predicated on the scope of Community law (the existence of Community rules in the area). The Court is right to deny that the scope of Community law is here being used as a determinant for exclusivity.[101] However, it is not necessary to use the concept of competence at all in order to arrive at the conclusion that the relevant provisions of the UNCLOS were covered by Community law rules, and therefore within the scope of Community law and part of the Community legal order. The difficulty with an analysis based on (not only the existence but also the exercise of) external competence is first that apart from the legal base of the Council Decision concluding the agreement (which is, admittedly, important) there is no real evidence for the conclusion that non-exclusive competence was being exercised. It is arguable that the Declaration made by the EC under Annex

---

[98] Case C–459/03 *Commission v Ireland* [2006] ECR I–4635, paras 82 and 86 respectively.
[99] *Ibid*, para 95.
[100] *Ibid*, paras 106 and 108.
[101] It is not necessary that the Community rules be affected within the meaning of *AETR*, nor are their scope and nature relevant, as they would be in the application of *AETR*.

IX of UNCLOS points the other way: Churchill and Scott bring out very clearly the ambiguity of the Declaration in this respect.[102]

Second, and more importantly, the question itself is not the right one. The issue here is not to what extent the EC exercised its non-exclusive competence in concluding UNCLOS; given that there is agreement as to the existence of shared competence in the environmental field this is essentially a factual question[103] and should not bear on the issue of protection of the autonomy of the Community legal order. As both AG Maduro and the Court say, there is a great deal of Community law in the environmental field covered by UNCLOS, and the real issue is rather that a dispute under the agreement gave rise to issues within the scope of Community law. This would be so even if the Irish view had been correct and in fact the Community had *not* concluded the environmental aspects of the agreement—there would still be a threat to the Community legal order if such issues were to be submitted to non-Community dispute settlement. It is the existence of this body of law which calls into play Article 292 EC (which refers, it will be recalled, to 'the interpretation or application of this Treaty') rather than the question of either exercise of Community competence or responsibility for implementation. If this is correct then the obligation on the Member States flows from Articles 10 and 292 rather than from Article 300(7) EC. As we have seen, in relations between Member States which touch upon the scope of Community law, Community law will prevail and the extent of their mutual obligations should be defined in terms of Community law, and thus ultimately by the Court of Justice rather than an external tribunal. Article 292 creates an obligation which is essentially internal to the Community legal order; it does not tell us anything about international responsibility (who was competent to conclude an agreement, or who should be liable for implementing it).

We thus find in each of these three cases[104] an emphasis on the existence of Community law relating to the provisions of the mixed agreement raised in the case; they are all examples of the application of the Member States'

---

[102]   R Churchill and J Scott, 'The Mox Plant Litigation: The First Half-Life' (2004) 53 *ICLQ* 643, 664–6; as they point out, 'it would be possible to make a credible argument to the effect that concurrent competences have not been "transferred" to the EC. Such an argument would be credible but by no means water-tight. ... The Declaration is genuinely ambiguous.' Tomuschat, on the other hand, assumes that the Declaration is clear; see C Tomuschat, 'The International Responsibility of the European Union' in Cannizzaro (ed), *The European Union as an Actor in International Relations* (The Hague/London, Kluwer Law International, 2002), 185.

[103]   R Churchill and J Scott, 'The Mox Plant Litigation: The First Half-Life' (2004) 53 *ICLQ* 643, 663.

[104]   Case C–13/00 *Commission v Ireland* [2002] ECR I–2943 (Berne Convention case); Case C–239/03 *Commission v France* [2004] ECR I–9325 (Etang de Berre case); Case C–459/03 *Commission v Ireland* [2006] ECR I–4635.

loyalty obligation when they enter into a mixed agreement alongside the EC. As we have expressed it, the primacy of the Community legal order is the substantive expression of this principle. Clearly it is important, from the point of view of third country parties to a mixed agreement, to know the extent to which the Community has concluded the agreement and may be held responsible in international law for its implementation; the answers to these questions will depend on the existence and exercise of Community competence. Here, however, and in each of the three cases we are discussing, the issue is not one of international responsibility but rather of the extent to which performance of the agreement may be in the Community interest and enforceable as a Community law obligation. The Court clearly sees a Community interest in holding the Member States to account under Community law for the whole of a mixed agreement, at least where it is a matter of shared competence. Once the agreement has been concluded, it has become a part of the Community legal order and the Community interest is relevant to its enforcement as well as its interpretation.[105] Thus the Court's reasoning in all three cases is ultimately based on the Community interest and the scope of Community law, rather than on competence.

Taking this approach as a starting point, it would be possible to take the argument even further, and to base the application of Article 292 not on the *exercise* of competence either externally (as the Court did in the Sellafield case) or internally (as is suggested above), but rather on the scope of competence found in the Treaty.[106] Given the breadth of the potential scope of Community competence, this is a more extensive view of the limits of Article 292 EC than one based on the scope of Community law (ie on the substantive rules in the Treaty together with the actual exercise of competence through secondary legislation) and goes further than is necessary for the protection of the *acquis*.

C. The Scope of Community Law and the Limits of the Community Interest

This analysis raises the question: what are the limits of the Community interest? Here we need to make a distinction. First, there is a Community interest in ensuring that Member States, when exercising their own external competence, comply with their Community law obligations including the EC Treaty-based freedoms of movement and establishment

---

[105] On interpretation of mixed agreements see Case C–53/96 *Hermes International v FHT Marketing* [1998] ECR I–3603; Joined Cases C–300/98 and C–392/98 *Parfums Christian Dior SA v Tuk Consultancy* [2000] ECR I–11307; Case C–89/99 *Schieving-Nijstad v Groeneveld* [2001] ECR I–5851.

[106] Thanks to Robert Schütze for this suggestion.

and the principle of non-discrimination. As we have seen, this applies to bilateral agreements concluded by a Member State on its own account whatever the scope of the agreement; it also applies, a fortiori, when Member States are implementing clauses of mixed agreements within their competence.

Second is the question of the Community interest in ensuring compliance with an agreement to which the Community (as well as the Member States) is a party. I have argued above that the Community interest here is broader than the extent to which Community competence has actually been exercised. There is a Community interest in ensuring that Member States comply both with aspects of the agreement that are within Community competence and with those aspects which are within shared competence and which may be implemented either by the Community or by the Member States. However, it is important, in my view, to link the Community interest firmly to the scope of Community law. As the Court has recognised, although the whole of a mixed agreement may be part of the Community legal order, it is still necessary to determine the extent of Member States' *Community law* (as opposed to international law) obligations under the agreement, and this should depend on the scope of Community law as it relates to the subject matter of the agreement. As in the cases we have just been examining, it will be a matter of identifying Community legislation or Treaty provisions in the relevant field. Even within the limits suggested here, the Community interest will expand as Community law expands to cover more areas, giving rise to concerns that the Member States' compliance obligations towards the Community are correspondingly open-ended. It can be argued that the Member States, by choosing to enter into a mixed agreement together with the Community in a field of shared competence, have accepted a relationship of solidarity with the Community, a common defence of the Community interest which will inevitably circumscribe their freedom of action under the agreement.

The approach suggested here would imply that in the case of a provision of a mixed agreement which is clearly outside the scope of Community law, for example a CFSP-related provision, there is no Community-law-based compliance obligation on Member States. However, could it be argued that a breach by a Member State of CFSP-related provisions within a mixed agreement comes within the scope of the Community interest and Article 10 EC, on the ground that the Community has an interest in ensuring compliance with every element of an agreement to which it is a party? The argument would be that it is in the Community interest to preserve the unity of the system with respect to the outside world, and this imposes a loyalty obligation on Member States with respect to the whole agreement which is referable to the EC Treaty (Article 10) and thus reviewable by the Court. On the other hand if, as argued above, the scope of the Community interest is linked to the scope of Community law,

Member States' obligations in respect of CFSP elements of mixed agreements should be seen as referable to a *Union* interest, giving rise to an obligation derived ultimately from Article 11(2) TEU.[107] While the Union and the Community interest are clearly closely linked and should not conflict with each other (*cf* Article 3 TEU), nevertheless as long as the Union and the Community are not legally unified and indeed represent separate international legal persons (even if perhaps a single international actor) we cannot simply subsume the Community interest into the Union interest.[108]

Nevertheless, as we have seen, to link the Community interest to the scope of Community law is to accept its dynamic character and recent developments have shown that the scope of Community law appears to be moving into fields hitherto reserved for Member States, with corresponding implications for Member States' own foreign policy. In *Yusuf* and *Kadi* the CFI offers a far-reaching analysis of the relationship between the Community legal order and obligations arising out of the UN Charter.[109] It puts forward an interesting argument to the effect that the Community itself is bound to implement a UN Security Council Resolution; not only does it have the power to carry out certain of the Member States' obligations, and (under Article 307 EC) the obligation not to obstruct the Member States in the performance of their prior treaty obligations towards third countries.[110] The CFI argues that not as a matter of international law (as it is not a member of the United Nations), but *in terms of Community law itself*, the Community 'must be considered to be bound by the obligations under the Charter of the United Nations in the same way as its Member States, by virtue of the Treaty establishing it'.[111] By analogy with the arguments used in relation to the binding nature of the GATT in *International Fruit Company*, the EC Treaty is evidence of a willingness

[107]   Art 11(2) TEU imposes a loyalty obligation on the Member States in respect of the CFSP itself. Note that it is the Council that is given primary enforcement responsibility here, and on the face of it Art 11(2) TEU would not be enforceable directly by the Court of Justice: see further C Hillion and RA Wessel, 'Restraining External Competences of EU Member States under CFSP', Chapter 4, this volume.

[108]   For discussion of the issue of the unity of the Union system, see C Herrmann, 'Much Ado About Pluto? The 'Unity of the Legal Order of the European Union Revisited', Chapter 2, this volume; see also A von Bogdandy, 'The Legal Case for Unity: The European Union as a Single Organization with a Single Legal System' (1999) 36 *CML Rev* 88; RA Wessel, 'The Multilevel Constitution of European Foreign Relations' in N Tsagourias (ed), *Transnational Constitutionalism: International and European Models* (Cambridge, Cambridge University Press, 2007).

[109]   Case T–306/01 *Yusuf and Al Barakaat International Foundation* [2005] ECR II–3533, Case T–315/01 *Kadi v Council and Commission* [2005] ECR II–3649.

[110]   Thus, Art 307 EC was held in Case C–124/95 *Centro-Com* [1997] ECR I–81 to justify national measures otherwise contrary to Community law if such measures are necessary to enable a Member State to fulfil its obligations under the UN Charter.

[111]   Case T–306/01 *Yusuf* [2005] ECR II–3533, para 243.

that the Community should be so bound, and insofar as the Member States have transferred powers to the Community those powers must be used in conformity with those obligations. Its conclusion is important: that the Community is bound by the UN Charter (and therefore by UNSC Resolutions) *as a matter of Community law*:

> in so far as the powers necessary for the performance of the Member States' obligations under the Charter of the United Nations have been transferred to the Community, the Member States have undertaken, pursuant to public international law, to ensure that the Community itself should exercise those powers to that end. ... By conferring those powers on the Community, the Member States demonstrated their will to bind it by the obligations entered into by them under the Charter of the United Nations (see, by analogy, *International Fruit*, paragraph 15).

> Since the entry into force of the Treaty establishing the European Economic Community, the transfer of powers which has occurred in the relations between Member States and the Community has been put into concrete form in different ways within the framework of the performance of their obligations under the Charter of the United Nations (see, by analogy, *International Fruit*, paragraph 16).[112]

Yusuf and *Kadi* were concerned with establishing the binding nature of the UN Charter as far as the Community is concerned. However, in holding that the Charter is binding as a matter of Community law, and connecting the Charter with the Community legal order in this way, the Court opens up possible implications for the Member States. Can we now say that in implementing UN-imposed sanctions the Member States are acting within the scope of Community law? These implications were explored, to some extent, by the subsequent cases of *Ayadi* and *Hassan*.[113] In *Ayadi* the Court discusses the right, contained in Guidelines issued by the Sanctions Committee of the UN Security Council, of an individual identified on a sanctions list to present a request for review of their case to the government of the country in which they reside or of which they are nationals, for the purpose of being removed from the list. In addition to finding that the Member States are bound by these Guidelines as Members of the UN,[114] it also holds that 'particular obligations are imposed on the Member States of the Community when a request for removal from the list is addressed to them' and that the right to present a request for review 'must accordingly

---

[112] Case T–306/01 *Yusuf* [2005] ECR II–3533, paras 248–51.

[113] Cases T–253/02 *Ayadi* [2006] ECR II–2139, and T–49/04 *Hassan* [2006] ECR II–52.

[114] 'In this connection it must be observed that the Guidelines are binding on all the Member States of the United Nations by virtue of their international legal obligations, in accordance with the Security Council resolutions at issue.' Case T–253/02 *Ayadi* [2006] ECR II–2139, para 142.

be classed as a right guaranteed not only by those Guidelines but also by the Community legal order'.[115] From this certain results follow; in examining such a request,

> the Member States are bound, in accordance with Article 6 EU, to respect the fundamental rights of the persons involved, as guaranteed by the ECHR and as they result from the constitutional traditions common to the Member States, as general principles of Community law, given that the respect of those fundamental rights does not appear capable of preventing the proper performance of their obligations under the Charter of the United Nations.[116]

The Court goes on to specify in some detail what this might include, including a right to be heard (before Member State authorities), an obligation on the Member State to act promptly and the right to bring an action for judicial review 'against any wrongful refusal by the competent national authority to submit their cases to the Sanctions Committee for re-examination and, more generally, against any infringement by that national authority of the right of the persons involved to request the review of their case'.[117] The Court goes on to apply the case law of the Court of Justice with respect to the effectiveness of national remedies. Let us recall that we are not here talking about the actions of Member States in implementing a Community Regulation which itself implements a UNSC Resolution (the point at issue in *Bosphorus*). The Member States are here presented with a range of Community law obligations in respect of the position of one of their own nationals before a Committee of the United Nations, an issue linked to diplomatic protection, as the Court recognises:

> It follows that, in an action in which it is alleged that the competent national authorities have infringed the right of the persons involved to request review of their cases in order to be removed from the list at issue, it is for the national court to apply, in principle, national law while taking care to ensure the full effectiveness of Community law, which may lead it to refrain from applying, if need be, a national rule preventing that result ..., such as a rule excluding from judicial review a refusal of national authorities to take action with a view to guaranteeing the diplomatic protection of their nationals.[118]

I am not here criticising the reasoning of the CFI in ensuring that at least the procedural rights of those accused of supporting terrorism are protected, merely pointing out that the compliance obligations of Member States based on Community law reach deep into national territory.

---

[115] Case T–253/02 *Ayadi* [2006] ECR II–2139 *Ayadi*, paras 144–5.
[116] *Ibid*, para 146.
[117] *Ibid*, para 150.
[118] *Ibid*, para 152.

III. PROCEDURAL COMPLIANCE AND THE DUTY OF COOPERATION

A. The Duty of Cooperation

The duty of cooperation is a constitutional principle developed in the context of mixed agreements but of broader application and deriving from the requirement of unity in the international representation of the Community.[119] It is a practical manifestation of the loyalty obligation set out in Article 10, holding together the Community, the Member States (and possibly the Union too) in a context where competence is shared. AG Tizzano, when discussing the interpretation of mixed agreements, expresses well the link between the duty of cooperation and the Community as a 'unified system':

> ... the interpretation the Court is called upon to give represents its contribution to the fulfilment of the duty of cooperation between institutions and Member States ... The Community legal system is characterised by the simultaneous application of provisions of various origins, international, Community and national; but it nevertheless seeks to function and to represent itself to the outside world as a unified system. That is, one might say, the inherent nature of the system which, while guaranteeing the maintenance of the realities of States and of individual interests of all kinds, also seeks to achieve a unified modus operandi. Its steadfast adherence to that aim, which the Court itself has described as an obligation of solidarity, is certainly lent considerable weight by the judicial review mechanism which is defined in the Treaty and relies on the simultaneous support of the Community court and the national courts.[120]

As this passage confirms, the principle of cooperation is not limited to the Member States, and also applies to inter-institutional cooperation[121] and

---

[119] *Opinion 2/91 (re ILO Convention No 170)* [1993] ECR I–1061, paras 36–8; *Opinion 1/94 (re WTO Agreements)* [1994] ECR I–5267, para 108; P Koutrakos, 'The Elusive Quest for Uniformity in EC External Relations' (2001) 4 *Yearbook of European Law* 243, 258. See also S Hyett, 'The Duty of Cooperation: a Flexible Concept' in A Dashwood and C Hillion (eds), *The General Law of EC External Relations* (London, Sweet & Maxwell 2000). For a discussion of the duty of cooperation as one of the key principles governing the concept of coherence in the management of the EU's external relations, see C Hillion, '*Tous pour un, un pour tous!* Coherence in the External Relations of the European Union' in M Cremona (ed), *Developments in EU External Relations* (OUP, forthcoming).

[120] AG Tizzano in *Hermes*, para 21.

[121] See, eg, Case C–65/93 *European Parliament v Council* [1995] ECR I–643, para 23. In Case C–317/04 *European Parliament v Council* [2006] ECR I–4721, the Parliament argued that the Council was in breach of this duty by concluding an international agreement after the Parliament had requested an Opinion from the Court of Justice under Art 300(6) EC but before the Court had delivered its Opinion. AG Leger dismissed the argument on the ground that the Art 300(6) procedure is not designed to protect institutional prerogatives; it may be argued, however, that a dispute about legal base is not merely a question of institutional prerogative but also impacts directly on competence, which may be directly relevant to a third country (as indeed the outcome of the case demonstrates). The issue of the duty of

even to cooperation between national courts and the Court of Justice.[122] The Court has pointed out that it is by its nature a reciprocal obligation:

> Under Article 5 [now Art 10] of the Treaty, the duty to cooperate in good faith governs relations between the Member States and the institutions. It entails an obligation on the Member States to take all the measures necessary to guarantee the application and effectiveness of Community law and imposes on Member States and the Community institutions mutual duties to cooperate in good faith.[123]

Here we will focus on the position of the Member States, and the duty of cooperation as the basis for a number of procedural obligations placed on Member States, not only in the context of mixed agreements but in managing shared competence more generally when the Community interest might be at stake. As will emerge, one of the key questions in this context is the extent of the duty of cooperation: does it imply a best efforts obligation, or some form of obligation of result?

B. Cooperation in Managing Mixed Agreements

The implications of the duty of cooperation as it applies to the negotiation, conclusion and implementation of mixed agreements have been extensively explored in the literature, most notably by Heliskoski.[124] First mentioned in relation to the EAEC in 1978, it was applied by the Court to the EC Treaty in Opinion 2/91 and Opinion 1/94 in 1993 and 1994.

> At points 34 to 36 in Ruling 1/78 [1978] ECR 2151, the Court pointed out that when it appears that the subject-matter of an agreement or contract falls in part within the competence of the Community and in part within that of the Member States, it is important to ensure that there is a close association between the institutions of the Community and the Member States both in the process of negotiation and conclusion and in the fulfilment of the obligations entered into. This duty of cooperation, to which attention was drawn in the context of the

---

cooperation in this case was in reality centred on the Parliament's delay in giving its opinion under Art 300(3) to enable it to wait for the Court's Opinion, and the Council's decision to conclude the agreement without waiting for the Parliament's opinion (or, a fortiori, the Court's Opinion) given its view of the urgency of the situation. The Court did not address the issue as it decided to annul the Council act on other grounds.

[122] Joined Cases C–300/98 *Parfums Christian Dior SA v Tuk Consultancy BV* and Case C–392/98 *Assco Gerüste GmbH, Rob van Dijk v Wilhelm Layher GmbH & Co KG, Layher BV* [2000] ECR I–11307, paras 36–8.

[123] Case C–339/00 *Ireland v Commission* [2003] ECR I–11757, para 71.

[124] J Heliskoski, *Mixed Agreements as a Technique for Organizing the International Relations of the European Community and its Member States* (The Hague/Boston, Kluwer Law International, 2001).

EAEC Treaty, must also apply in the context of the EEC Treaty since it results from the requirement of unity in the international representation of the Community.[125]

In the case of the ILO, the duty of cooperation was particularly important as, although the proposed agreement fell within shared Community and Member State competence, under the Statute of the ILO the Community as such could not become a party. The duty of cooperation thus helped to resolve externally driven difficulties in managing shared competence. In parentheses we may note that this application of the duty of cooperation can also come into play where Community competence is exclusive: in *AETR*, it will be remembered that in spite of the finding of exclusive competence the Court concluded that it was in the Community interest (that being the successful conclusion of ongoing negotiations) for the Member States to continue to act:

> ... wherever a matter forms the subject of a common policy, the Member States are bound in every case to act jointly in defence of the interests of the Community. ... In such a situation it was for the two institutions whose powers were directly concerned, namely, the Council and the Commission, to reach agreement ... on the appropriate methods of cooperation with a view to ensuring most effectively the defence of the interests of the Community. ... It may therefore be accepted that, in carrying on the negotiations and concluding the agreement simultaneously in the manner decided on by the Council, the Member States acted, and continue to act, in the interest and on behalf of the Community in accordance with their obligations under Article 5 of the Treaty.[126]

In the case of the WTO, the Court referred to the duty of cooperation in refuting a Commission argument that shared competence would cause numerous difficulties in the internal administration of the agreement, including 'interminable discussions' over competence. The Commission argued that the 'Community's unity of action vis-à-vis the rest of the world will thus be undermined and its negotiating power weakened'—an argument based on the Community interest. In the Court's view, although these concerns are legitimate, they do not justify a modification of competence allocation. The Community interest may be protected by means of the duty of cooperation.[127]

Although they have not really materialised in the WTO context, 'interminable discussions' about the attribution of competence do occur in some

[125] *Opinion 2/91 (re ILO Convention No 170)* [1993] ECR I–1061, para 36.

[126] Case C–22/70 *Commission v Council* [1971] ECR 263 (AETR/ERTA case), paras 77, 87 and 90. More recently, recalling this outcome, the Court held that the AETR as a result (although not formally concluded by the Community) forms part of Community law and is subject to the interpretative jurisdiction of the Court: Case C–439/01 *Libor Cipra and Vlastimil Kvasnicka v Bezirkshauptmannschaft Mistelbach* [2003] ECR I–745, paras 23–4.

[127] *Opinion 1/94 (re WTO Agreements)* [1994] ECR I–5267, para 108.

cases, and uncertainty and disagreement as to the delimitation of competence between the Community and Member States may make it difficult to establish common ground on which cooperation may be based. The FAO fisheries agreement case is an interesting example of the duty of cooperation in action. The Court held that the arrangement between the Council and the Commission for the management of decision making under a mixed agreement was a fulfilment of the duty of cooperation between the Community and its Member States, and was intended to have legal effects:

> In the present case, section 2.3 of the Arrangement between the Council and the Commission represents fulfilment of that duty of cooperation between the Community and its Member States within the FAO. It is clear, moreover, from the terms of the Arrangement, that the two institutions intended to enter into a binding commitment towards each other. Nor has the Council contested its effect at any moment in the proceedings.[128]

In consequence the Council Decision, whereby it was decided that voting within the FAO on the draft agreement should be taken by the Member States, was annulled. In this case, then, the duty of cooperation was formalised in a binding agreement. What if there is no such agreement? To what extent does the duty of cooperation bind a Member State in its participation in a mixed agreement? This question is raised in a recent example involving Community and Member State participation in the Stockholm Convention on Persistent Organic Pollutants.[129] Sweden wished to propose the inclusion of perfluorooctane sulfonates (PFOS) in Annex A of the Convention, which imposes elimination obligations (of production, use, import and export) on parties with respect to certain organic pollutants. Agreement not being reached within the framework of consultations with the Commission and other Member States, Sweden unilaterally proposed the inclusion of PFOS in Annex A.[130] In the Commission's view, 'Proposals to amend Annexes to the Convention or the Protocol should only be done on behalf of the Community and its Member States, based on the obligation of cooperation and unity in the international representation

---

[128] Case C–25/94 *Commission v Council* [1996] ECR I–1469 (FAO Fishery Agreement case), paras 48–50. See further J Heliskoski, 'Internal Struggle for International Presence: the Exercise of Voting Rights within the FAO' in A Dashwood and C Hillion (eds), *The General Law of EC External Relations* (London, Sweet & Maxwell, 2000).

[129] See Report by the National Rapporteurs for Sweden, Anna Falk and Karin Wistrand, Ministry for Foreign Affairs, on 'External Relations of the EU and the Member States: Competence, Mixed Agreements, International Responsibility, and Effects of International Law', XXII FIDE Congress 2006, on file with the author.

[130] The use of PFOS is restricted but not eliminated under Directive 2006/122/EC, amending Council Directive 76/769/EEC on the approximation of the laws, regulations and administrative provisions of the Member States relating to restrictions on the marketing and use of certain dangerous substances and preparations (perfluorooctane sulfonates), [2006] OJ L/372/32.

of the Community that flows from Article 10 of the EC Treaty'.[131] In May 2007 the Commission initiated an action alleging infringement by Sweden of the duty of cooperation under Article 10 EC in that Sweden unilaterally proposed an amendment to Annex A of the Convention outside the joint Community/Member State process.[132] Assuming a national competence to make such a proposal,[133] and given the absence of any binding institutional agreement as to how to proceed with respect to the Convention machinery for proposing amendments, the question is the extent to which the duty of cooperation restrains the Member States in the exercise of that competence. If a Member State has tried and failed to reach a common position is it nevertheless precluded from acting? If there is indeed an obligation based on Article 10 EC to refrain from adopting a unilateral position where no EU-wide position can be reached, the duty of cooperation would appear to go beyond cooperation and to encroach on competence.

C. Negotiating National Agreements and the Duty of Cooperation

Whereas the FAO case and the PFOS case concern the management of participation in a mixed agreement, with or without an inter-institutional agreement, there has also been a case of legislation adopted with a view to managing the negotiation of international agreements by the Member States in an area of shared competence. We have already looked at Regulation 847/2004/EC on the negotiation and implementation of air services agreements between Member States and third countries, and noted that it establishes certain substantive and procedural requirements for Member States.[134] The Preamble of the Regulation (recital 4) cites the standard passage from the Court's case law on the duty of cooperation, quoted above, and refers to the Regulation as establishing a 'cooperation procedure' which is 'without prejudice to the division of competencies between the Community and Member States' (recital 5). As far as procedural obligations are concerned, the Member States are to notify the

---

[131] Proposal for a Council Decision concerning proposals, on behalf of the European Community and the Member States, for amendments to Annexes I–III of the 1998 Protocol to the 1979 Convention on Long Range Transboundary Air Pollution on Persistent Organic Pollutants and to Annexes A–C of the Stockholm Convention on Persistent Organic Pollutants, COM (2004) 537 final, Explanatory Memorandum, para 6; see also recital 5 of the proposed Decision. This proposal does not include PFOS.

[132] Case C–246/07 *Commission v Sweden*, pending, [2007] OJ C/183/19.

[133] The restrictions on the use of PFOS under Community law dates from Directive 2006/122/EC, adopted in December 2006, and thus after Sweden's proposal was made: see above, n 130.

[134] See above, section II.A.(v).

Commission about the start, process and conclusion of national negotiations, and the conclusion of the agreement is subject to authorisation, thereby allowing both the procedural and substantive obligations to be enforced.[135]

This Regulation concerned agreements in a field of shared competence but which partially fall within exclusive Community competence. However, similar procedural obligations can be derived directly from Article 10 EC and the duty of cooperation may arise with respect to national negotiations in fields of shared competence. Two examples will illustrate this, the first relating to readmission agreements, the second to bilateral agreements on inland waterways transport. Although the nature of the EC's implied competence to conclude readmission agreements with third countries on the basis of Article 63(3)(b) EC has been contested, the Commission now seems to accept the Council's view that this is a matter of shared competence.[136] In May 1999 the Council considered this question and its corollary, the constraints imposed on the Member States in the exercise of their competence in the field. Having declared that Community competence was not exclusive, the Council goes on:

> A Member State can continue to conclude readmission agreements with third States provided that the Community has not concluded an agreement with the third State concerned or has not concluded a mandate for negotiating such an agreement. In individual cases Member States may also conclude bilateral agreements after the conclusion of a Community agreement or after the opening of negotiations, for instance where the Community agreement or the negotiating mandate contains only general statements on readmission but one or more Member States require more detailed arrangements on the matter. The Member States may no longer conclude agreements if these might be detrimental to existing Community agreements.[137]

Words such as 'can' and 'may not' as well as the context suggest that the Council is talking here about limits to competence rather than procedural constraints. The emphasis in this passage is primarily on the situations in which it might be said that the Community has acted, by concluding (or even planning to conclude) a readmission agreement with a particular third country so as to give rise to pre-emptive exclusivity. There is little emphasis on the procedural mechanisms such as consultation which might be

---

[135]   Regulation 847/2004/EC, Art 1 (2)–(4), Art 4.

[136]   For a full discussion, see N Coleman, *European Readmission Policy, Third Country Interests and Refugee Rights*, thesis defended at the EUI in June 2007, citing Schieffer, 'Community Readmission Agreements with Third Countries—Objectives, Substance and Current State of Negotiations' (2003) 5 *European Journal of Migration and Law*, 343; PJ Kuijper, 'The Evolution of the Third Pillar from Maastricht to the European Constitution: Institutional Aspects' (2004) 41 *CML Rev* 609.

[137]   Conclusions of JHA Council on readmission agreements and the consequences of the entry into force of the Amsterdam Treaty, 27–28 May 1999.

necessary in order to ensure that Member State bilateral action is not harmful to EC interests, and in practice it appears that Member States have continued to conclude bilateral Readmission Agreements after the decision to negotiate a Community agreement with a particular third country, or even after its conclusion.[138] However, the Commission has so far not brought infringement actions and so the balance between competence transfer and procedural constraints in such cases is still somewhat unclear.

In our second example, by contrast, Germany and Luxembourg were found to be in breach of their obligations under Article 10 EC by concluding bilateral agreements with third countries on the transport of goods and passengers by inland waterway.[139] The bilateral agreements were concluded after a decision by the Council to authorise the Commission to negotiate a multilateral agreement with a number of third countries. In neither case did the Court accept the Commission's argument that Community competence in the field was exclusive, based on *AETR*. Existing Community legislation, the Court held, was concerned only with market access for Community carriers and thus would not be 'affected' by such a bilateral agreement. However, the Court held that the Member States were in breach of Article 10 EC ('that duty of genuine cooperation'[140]) by continuing bilateral negotiations after the mandate had been agreed in the Council without cooperating with or consulting the Commission. The adoption of the mandate is the start of a 'concerted Community action' which imposes obligations of cooperation on the Member States; this obligation may not extend to a duty of complete abstention, but does require close cooperation and consultation with the Commission in order to avoid undermining the Community's multilateral negotiation, as well to ensure consistency between the positions adopted.[141]

> The adoption of a decision authorising the Commission to negotiate a multilateral agreement on behalf of the Community marks the start of a concerted Community action at international level and requires, for that purpose, if not a duty of abstention on the part of the Member States, at the very least a duty of close cooperation between the latter and the Community institutions in order to facilitate the achievement of the Community tasks and to ensure the coherence and consistency of the action and its international representation.[142]

The Court also refers to the fact that, at the time of agreeing the mandate for the negotiation of the multilateral agreement by the Commission, the

---

[138] N Coleman, *European Readmission Policy, Third Country Interests and Refugee Rights*, thesis defended at the EUI in June 2007, 237–46.
[139] Case C–266/03 *Commission v Luxembourg* [2005] ECR I–4805; Case C–433/03 *Commission v Germany* [2005] ECR I–6985.
[140] Case C–266/03 *Commission v Luxembourg* [2005] ECR I–4805, para 58.
[141] *Ibid*, paras 57–62.
[142] *Ibid*, para 60.

Council had also agreed to apply rules of conduct set out in a 'gentlemen's agreement' which provided for close coordination between the Commission and the Member States and in particular that 'the representatives of the Member States must take no action which is likely to handicap the Commission in its work'.[143] Unlike Regulation 847/2004/EC the gentlemen's agreement was not legally binding but it was taken into account by the Court in deciding that the Member States were in breach of the duty of cooperation. Although therefore, as explicitly stated, there is no exclusive Community competence, the Member States were in fact constrained in their freedom to conclude bilateral agreements in the field. Note, however, that the obligation arose out of the decision of the Council to open Community negotiations, the start of a concerted Community action; and that the breach of Article 10 EC lay not so much in continuing bilateral negotiations as in the absence of consultation and coordination with the Community institutions (especially the Commission). Were Article 10 to require a complete halt to negotiations that would be tantamount to finding that the Member States were no longer competent to conclude the agreements, and inconsistent with the explicit ruling that there was no exclusive competence.

These cases contrast therefore with the Council Conclusions on Readmission Agreements, where the view is expressed that Member States may no longer conclude bilateral agreements once a Community negotiating mandate has been agreed. The difference illustrates that it is not always easy to determine when pre-emption has taken place so that a hitherto shared competence has become exclusive, even if only in relation to a particular type of agreement with a particular third country. More consistent with the principles of shared competence would be the position that (i) a negotiating mandate for the Community triggers the duty of cooperation but not pre-emption and loss of Member State competence; and (ii) that duty of cooperation requires consultation and coordination but not necessarily the halting of the Member State's bilateral negotiations or a bar to concluding the agreement. In the absence of a Regulation laying down specific duties, such as that on air transport services, each case ultimately requires a judgment to be made as to what the duty of cooperation requires and in some cases it might be that to continue to negotiate bilaterally would so obstruct the Community interest as to be incompatible with that duty, its extent depending not only on policy considerations but also on the nature of Community law in the field. In this way the procedural dimension of Article 10 is more flexible than the substantive dimension on which the primacy of the *acquis* is based; as we saw in Section 2, substantive compliance obligations are peremptory obligations of result.

---

[143]   *Ibid*, para 62.

Other questions pose themselves in relation to the obligation to inform and consult. Could it be taken further and applied in cases where no Community agreement was currently envisaged, or concerted action yet taken, but where the individual Member State negotiation might neverthe-less prejudice possible future action? The argument here would be that the duty applies wherever the Member State agreement falls within the scope of Community law, but would not require that a 'concerted Community action at international level' had already taken place. Could the duty be applied not only to the negotiation of agreements but to other external actions of the Member States that might intersect with Community policies and competence, individual public statements, for example? If the view proposed above is accepted—that the extent of this obligation is primarily to 'inform and consult' rather than to prohibit national action—then these more extensive applications of the duty are reasonable, in that they assist in ensuring that Member States take account of the Community interest when they engage in autonomous action.

Might Union action within the framework of the CFSP or the third pillar give rise to a duty of cooperation (loyalty obligation) on the part of the Member States to the Community legal order?[144] In *Commission v Luxembourg* the Court says that the 'duty of genuine cooperation is of general application'.[145] Arguably, Article 1 TEU (maintaining and building on the *acquis communautaire*) and Article 47 TEU (protecting the EC Treaty from being 'affected' by second or third pillar actions) would also support a view that the Member States should ensure that their actions within the second and third pillars do not undermine the Community interest. Thus, for example, a CFSP common position should not under-mine a negotiating position adopted by the Community vis-a-vis a third country. Action in breach of Article 10 EC when carried out individually or collectively could also be seen as a breach of the loyalty obligation when carried out via the institutions and actions of the CFSP. Gauttier and Gosalbo Bono have suggested that the Court might link its review powers under Article 10 EC to the requirement of consistency in Article 3 TEU which refers to the Union's external activities as a whole.[146] However, this form of the duty of cooperation legally obligates the Council rather than

---

[144] For a discussion of the extent of the Member States' loyalty obligation within the framework of the CFSP, see C Hillion and RA Wessel, 'Restraining External Competences of EU Member States under CFSP', Chapter 4, this volume.

[145] Case C–266/03 *Commission v Luxembourg* [2005] ECR I–4805, para 58.

[146] 'It seems logical that in case of overlapping competences, in accordance with the underlying rationale behind coherence, the first-pillar obligation of loyal and faithful cooperation should be applied by ricochet to the CFSP.' P Gauttier, 'Horizontal Coherence and the External Competence of the European Union' (2004)10 *ELJ* 23, 40; 'overlapping competences' in this context refers to first and second pillar competences. See also R Gosalbo Bono, 'Some Reflections on the CFSP Legal Order' (2006) 43 *CML Rev* 337, 366.

the Member States, acting as decision-maker within the CFSP and under Article 3 TEU to ensure coherence and consistency in external action. These obligations of 'horizontal coherence' are the subject of another paper altogether.[147]

D. Cooperation in Dispute Settlement

The Sellafield case[148] provides a further example of the implications of Article 10 EC as a constraint on the exercise by Member States of their external powers, in this case the ability to engage in dispute settlement procedures under a Convention to which they are party. The Commission argued that Ireland was in breach of its obligations under Articles 10 and 292 EC in submitting a dispute with the United Kingdom under the Law of the Sea Convention (UNCLOS) to dispute settlement procedures established under that Convention.[149] AG Maduro was of the view that Ireland was in breach of its obligations under Article 10 EC, independently of Article 292, by failing in its duty of cooperation. This breach was based, not on the initiation of dispute settlement proceedings per se[150] but on the failure to inform and consult with the Community institutions before initiating the UNCLOS procedure. Maduro argued that such consultation could have clarified the Community law dimension of the dispute, and could also have raised the possibility of using Community law remedies in relation to the alleged violation of the Convention (infringement proceedings against the UK). The Court agreed:

> ... the obligation of close cooperation within the framework of a mixed agreement involved, on the part of Ireland, a duty to inform and consult the competent Community institutions prior to instituting dispute-settlement proceedings concerning the MOX plant within the framework of the Convention.[151]

A recent example of prior consultation in the case of an international dispute between two Member States is provided by the Belgium/

---

[147]   C Hillion, '*Tous pour un, un pour tous!* Coherence in the External relations of the European Union' in M Cremona (ed) *Developments in EU External Relations* (OUP, forthcoming).

[148]   Case C–459/03 *Commission v Ireland* [2006] ECR I–4635.

[149]   On the application of Art 292, see above.

[150]   On this point, AG Poiares Maduro took the view that Art 292 operates as a *lex specialis* in relation to the general principle established in Art 10, and that therefore Art 10 was unnecessary as an additional ground of complaint (AG Opinion paras 54–5). The Court agreed: see Case C–459/03 *Commission v Ireland* [2006] ECR I–4635, paras 168–71.

[151]   Case C–459/03 *Commission v Ireland* [2006] ECR I–4635, para 179.

Netherlands 'Iron Rhine Arbitration'.[152] Here the Commission was consulted and accepted the Member States' view that there were no
substantive issues of Community law likely to be affected by the arbitration.[153] As in the cases discussed in the previous section, the infringement
in the Sellafield case lay in the failure to consult in advance of taking
action. This must therefore be regarded as an important requirement
placed on Member States where there is a possibility that their actions in
the external sphere might impact on the Community legal order or even on
Community policy making. There is also no reason why the obligation to
inform and consult the Commission, applied in the Sellafield case to an
inter-Member State dispute, should not also be applied where a Member
State is contemplating initiating (or is on the receiving end of) a dispute
settlement process with a third State under a mixed agreement, such as the
WTO for example.

IV. CONCLUSIONS

This Chapter has focused on the constraints imposed on the Member
States, when exercising their foreign relations powers, derived from the
loyalty principle established in Article 10 EC. This principle encompasses
both substantive and procedural dimensions, reflecting the primacy rule
and the duty of cooperation respectively. Member States may be acting in
fields where competence is shared with the Community or where competence lies with them, and it is thus the scope of Community law rather than
distribution of competences that determines the extent of the loyalty
obligation on Member States.

The substantive dimension to the loyalty obligation is based on the
primacy of Community law, and the primacy principle implies a compliance obligation that is subject only to express derogations, such as that
found in Article 307(1) EC. When exercising their competence to conclude
international agreements Member States should comply with their EC
Treaty obligations – including the obligation not to discriminate between
their own nationals and other Community nationals established in their
territory with respect to advantages resulting from international agreements. As a result, the Member States' freedom in negotiating bilateral

---

[152] The dispute on the Iron Rhine railway line was submitted to an arbitral tribunal under
the PCA in 2003 and the award was handed down in May 2005 (available on http://
www.pca-cpa.org/showpage.asp?pag_id=1155).

[153] See Award of the Arbitral Tribunal (note 152), paras 13–15. In their letter to the
Commission the Member States undertook to comply with Art 292 EC should a question of
Community law arise in the course of proceedings. In spite of this apparent agreement that
Community law was not implicated, the Tribunal devotes 15 pages of its award to a
discussion of European law, albeit concluding that neither Art 10 nor Art 292 were applicable
as interpretation of Community law was not required to determine the dispute.

agreements is circumscribed. In addition, Member States should not maintain in force international obligations (even those concluded prior to joining the EU) that conflict with their Community law obligations.

The Community has an interest in ensuring that international agreements entered into by the Community are properly performed, and hence the Member States are under a Community law obligation in respect of all aspects of the agreement (including mixed agreements) which fall within the scope of Community law. Likewise in negotiating, concluding and implementing mixed agreements the Member States and the Community institutions should act with a view to preserving the unity of the Community system with respect to third States. The use of external dispute settlement procedures is subject to the need to protect the autonomy of the Community legal order, as expressed in Article 292 EC; thus disputes between Member States which fall within the scope of Community law should not be referred to external dispute settlement. This Chapter has argued that the Community interest in such cases should not be defined in terms of the exercise by the Community of its own external competence in a particular case, but rather in terms of the scope of the Community legal order. As we have seen, for example in considering the impact of Community law on the Member States' own treaty-making power, in its approach to Article 307(2), or the effect of disconnection clauses, the Court has often been careful to separate the application of the compliance obligation from the issue of pre-emption (the exercise of competence by the Community). The distinction is less carefully drawn when the Court deals with the implications of mixed agreements, although it is argued here that the same principles should apply.

The duty of cooperation—also derived from Article 10 EC, initially in the context of mixed agreements but now of wider application in the external relations sphere—presents the Member States with procedural obligations. Defending the Community interest implies ensuring that national positions do not conflict or obstruct the policy interests of the Community, and that international negotiations by Member States do not obstruct related ongoing negotiations by the Community. It finds practical expression in more or less formal procedural arrangements for managing mixed agreements, and in the obligation to inform and consult the Commission before acting to negotiate or conclude an agreement, or before instituting dispute-settlement proceedings. If it is to be kept conceptually separate from pre-emption, as a restraint on but not a denial of Member State competence, this obligation is best seen as a 'best efforts' obligation rather than requiring Member States to refrain from acting until agreement is reached. However, the line between the duty of cooperation and pre-emption may be thin, especially where the Community is in the process of moving into a field in which it has shared competence, or where prior consultation procedures are enshrined in binding legal acts.

What purchase then does the concept of the Community interest have in this exploration of the dynamic of shared and overlapping competences? Its use by the Court in the examples we have investigated suggests that it is something more than a rhetorical expression and possesses some substantive content, with its foundation in the loyalty obligation of Article 10. The Community interest is a concept that has a number of different dimensions and is potentially very open-ended, but if it is to be used as the basis for Member State obligations based on Article 10 EC it should be linked to the demands of the Community legal order, just as Article 10 is defined in terms of the obligations imposed by the Treaty and secondary legislation, and the objectives and tasks of the Community. These imperatives include the autonomy of the Community legal order, its primacy, and a reading of its scope and nature based on *effet utile*: an orientation towards completion of its objectives. When the Member States operate within the scope of this legal order, even when exercising their own competences, they are constrained by these imperatives. Further, as we have seen, the nature of the obligation varies. The peremptory requirements of primacy, it was argued in Section II of this Chapter, refer to the need to comply with Community law in the sense of Treaty provisions, general principles of law and exercised internal or external (legislative or treaty-making) competence. Cases such as *Ayadi* demonstrate the potential reach of this principle, in holding that Member States are required to comply with human rights and procedural norms as protected by the Community legal order when acting within the framework of the UN (the review procedures of the UNSC Sanctions Committee). Nevertheless, compliance in this sense requires an identifiable Community law norm with which the Member States should comply, and not merely a not-yet-exercised capacity to act. In Section III, on the other hand, it was argued that the duty of cooperation embodies a more flexible obligation, the precise extent of which will depend on the context. This context—which has here been termed the Community interest—although it most commonly entails exercised competences and enacted legislation ('a concerted Community action'), can also include the longer-term objectives of the Community, some of which may at present take the form of competences not yet exercised either internally or externally.

6

Legal Basis and Delimitation of Competence in EU External Relations

PANOS KOUTRAKOS*

I. INTRODCUTION

THE IMPLICATIONS OF the choice of the appropriate legal basis are not only practical, that is to determine the procedures whereby secondary measures are adopted and the input of the Union institutions in decision making. As the Court of Justice pointed out in *Opinion 2/00*, 'the choice of the appropriate legal basis has constitutional significance'.[1] It indicates compliance with the principle of limited powers and determines the nature and extent of Community competence. In the words of the Court of Justice,

> to proceed on an incorrect legal basis is ... liable to invalidate the act concluding the agreement and so vitiate the Community's consent to be bound by the agreement it has signed. That is so in particular where the Treaty does not confer on the Community sufficient competence to ratify the agreement in its entirety, a situation which entails examining the allocation as between the Community and the Member States of the powers to conclude the agreement that is envisaged with non-member countries, or where the appropriate legal basis for the measure concluding the agreement lays down a legislative procedure different from that which has in fact been followed by the Community institutions.[2]

In the case of an agreement deemed to be concluded by the Community pursuant to an incorrect legal basis, the Community measure concluding the Agreement would be invalidated whilst the Agreement would be

* I am grateful to Marise Cremona for her detailed comments and suggestions. Many thanks to Francesca Martines and the other participants at the workshop, as well as Carl Fredrik Bergström and Josefin Almer.
    [1] *Opinion 2/00* [2001] ECR I–9713, para 5.
    [2] *Ibid.*

binding on the Community under international law.[3] This would necessitate not only the adoption of a new Decision but also, where appropriate, the submission of an amended declaration of competence.

It is the constitutional significance of the choice of the appropriate legal basis which this Chapter will analyse. It will do so by focusing on two specific legal provisions, namely Article 133 EC and Article 308 EC. This choice is made on grounds of significance for the general law of EU external relations as well as topicality: a host of legal questions have arisen over the years from concerted efforts to delineate the scope of the former provision, and a number of judgments delivered by the European judiciary in the last couple of years have rendered both at the centre of academic debate.

The structure of this Chapter will be as follows. First, it will outline some of the main constitutional and practical parameters of the choice of the appropriate legal basis in the context of EC external relations. Second, it will highlight the special problems raised by disputes about the choice of Article 133 EC as the appropriate legal basis and will focus on the more recent developments in the area. Third, it will discuss the creative interpretation of Article 308 EC adopted by the Court of First Instance in the area of smart sanctions in the last two years.

II. THREE PARAMETERS OF THE CHOICE OF THE APPROPIATE LEGAL BASIS

The starting point for this Chapter was to highlight the constitutional function of the choice of the appropriate legal basis. Flowing from this, three other significant aspects may be identified, all of which are interrelated. The first one is its objective nature. According to the standard formulation put forward by the Court of Justice, 'the choice of the legal basis for a Community measure must rest on objective factors amenable to judicial review'.[4] It is in the light of this principle that 'the fact that an institution wishes to participate more fully in the adoption of a given measure, the work carried out in other respects in the sphere of action covered by the measure and the context in which the measure was adopted are irrelevant'.[5]

Second, linked to the objective nature of the choice of the appropriate legal basis is the notion of the institutional balance. Based on 'a system for distributing powers among the different Community institutions, assigning

---

[3] Case C–327/91 *France v Commission* [1994] ECR I–3641, para 25.
[4] Case C–300/89 *Commission v Council* [1991] ECR I–1689 (Titanium dioxide case).
[5] Case C–269/97 *Commission v Council* (re: beef products regulation) [2000] ECR I–2257 (Beef products regulation case), para 44.

to each institution its own role in the institutional structure of the Community and the accomplishment of the tasks entrusted to the Community',[6] the principle of institutional balance is intrinsically linked to the prerogatives of the various institutions and entails that 'each of [them] must exercise its powers with due regard for the powers of the other institutions'.[7]

Third, in the case of international agreements concluded by the EC, the choice of the appropriate legal basis takes on an additional dimension in so far as the choice of legal basis is relied upon by Community institutions or Member States as a way of addressing various practical concerns about the international posture of the Community. For instance, when the Commission argued that the conclusion of GATS and TRIPS fell within the exclusive competence of the Community either pursuant to Article 133 EC or the *AETR* principle or the so-called 'necessity' principle or Articles 95 and 308 EC, it sought to rely upon the practical problems which would arise in relation to the administration of the Agreements if the Community and the Member States were to be found to share competence. Such problems relate to the long discussions necessary as to whether a given matter falls within the Community or national competence and the right of the Member States to express their views individually on matters falling within their competence in cases where no consensus would be found. These were viewed by the Commission as undermining the Community's unity of action *vis-à-vis* the rest of the world and weakening its negotiating power. Whilst viewing the above concerns as legitimate, the Court rejected the inferences made by the Commission. It pointed out that:

> any problems which may arise in implementation of the WTO Agreements and its annexes as regards the coordination necessary to ensure unity of action where the Community and the Member States participate jointly cannot modify the answer to the question of competence, that being a prior issue.[8]

This approach has also been adopted more recently. In *Opinion 2/00* it was held that 'whatever their scale, the practical difficulties associated with the implementation of mixed agreements, which are relied on by the Commission to justify recourse to Article 133 EC—conferring exclusive competence on the Community so far as concerns common commercial policy— cannot be accepted as relevant when selecting the legal basis for a Community measure'.[9]

Instead, the link between the choice of the appropriate legal basis and the delimitation of competence and all the practical problems that this may

---

[6] Case C–70/88 *European Parliament v Council* [1990] ECR I–2041, para 21.
[7] *Ibid*, para 22.
[8] *Opinion 1/94* [1994] ECR I–5267, para 107.
[9] *Opinion 2/00*, above n 1, para 41.

raise is sought to be addressed by the principle of close cooperation. Having been introduced in the late 1970s,[10] the duty of cooperation became increasingly prominent in the Court's rulings on external competence.[11] It is beyond the scope of this chapter to examine the duty of close cooperation.[12] Suffice it to point out that its scope has been interpreted widely, covering both the Community institutions and the Member States in the process of negotiation, conclusion and application of international agreements. It has also been applied to the relationship between the Court of Justice and national courts in the process of the interpretation of international agreements.[13]

III. THE DELINEATION OF COMMON COMMERCIAL POLICY—ARTICLE 133 EC

The Common Commercial Policy is one of the very few legal bases conferring express external competence which has been part of the EC Treaty since the establishment of the Community. The wording of Article 133 EC and the non-exhaustive list of policy areas which it covers are, at best, opaque in terms of both the limits and legal implications of CCP.

It was the Court of Justice which, typically, was called upon to fill in the gaps. It has done so in a twofold manner. On the one hand, the competence of the Community over the CCP is deemed to be exclusive[14] and Member States may only act pursuant to a specific authorisation granted under EC law.[15] On the other hand, the scope of the CCP was outlined in broad terms quite early on. In *Opinion 1/75* it was stated that the concept of commercial policy 'ha[s] the same content whether it is applied in the context of the international action of a State or to that of the Community'.[16] Similarly, in *Opinion 1/78* it was pointed out that 'the question of external trade must be governed from a wide point of view'.[17]

In addition to the provision for decision making by qualified majority,[18] the above normative characteristics of CCP have rendered Article 133 EC

---

[10] *Ruling 1/78* [1979] ECR 2871, paras 34–6.
[11] *Opinion 2/91* [1993] ECR I–1061, paras 36–8, *Opinion 1/94*, above n 8, paras 108–9, *Opinion 2/00*, above n 1, para 18. For applications of the duty, see Case C–25/94 *Commission v Council* [1996] ECR I–1469 (FAO case) and, more recently, Case C–459/03 *Commission v Ireland* [2006] ECR I–4635 (MOX plant case).
[12] See Chapter 5, this volume.
[13] Case C–300/98 *Dior and Others* [2000] ECR I–11307, paras 36–8.
[14] See *Opinion 1/75 (re: OECD Local Cost Standard)* [1975] ECR 1355, *Opinion 1/78* [1979] ECR 2871. Further in P Koutrakos, *EU International Relations Law* (Oxford and Portland, Hart, 2006), 11 *et seq*.
[15] Case C–41/76 *Donckerwolcke* [1976] ECR 1921.
[16] *Opinion 1/75*, above n 14, 1362.
[17] *Ibid*, para 45.
[18] Art 133(4) EC.

fertile ground for interinstitutional disputes about the choice of legal basis. One of the main issues in these disputes was whether the subject matter of a specific legislative measure or international agreement fell within the scope of CCP. Therefore, a body of case law has developed which seeks to delineate Article 133 EC from other legal bases enabling the EC to act on the international stage. As the story of the development of this body of case law has been told often and in detail,[19] this Chapter will highlight some of its main characteristics.

In the early years, the case law was characterised by its emphasis on the flexibility of the CCP, that is its ability to adjust to the evolving international economic order. When asked to adjudicate on the relationship between trade and development, in the late 1970s, the Court held that 'a coherent commercial policy would no longer be practicable if the Community were not in a position to exercise its powers also in connexion with a category of agreements which are becoming, alongside traditional commercial agreements, one of the major factors in the regulation of international trade'.[20] Rendering its ruling on the conclusion of a commodity agreement on natural rubber, the Court put forward a conception of external commercial policy broad enough to accommodate new trends in international economic relations: 'it would no longer be possible to carry on any worthwhile common commercial policy if the Community were not in a position to avail itself also of more elaborate means devised with a view to furthering the development of international trade'.[21] This dynamism was also affirmed in subsequent judgments: examining the Generalised Tariff Preferences scheme, the Court opined that 'the link between trade and development has become progressively stronger in modern international relations'.[22]

Another characteristic of the case law on Article 133 EC is its pragmatism. The specific circumstances under which an international agreement is negotiated are taken into account and inform the exercise of the Community's competence. For instance, in *Opinion 1/78* the Court ruled that, even though the Agreement on Natural Rubber fell within the Community's exclusive competence, it should be concluded by both the Community and its Member States if the latter participated in the financing of the mechanisms set up thereunder.

The above characteristics of the Court's case law on the choice of Article 133 EC as the appropriate legal basis do not define distinct periods in time

---

[19] See, eg, P Eeckhout, *External Relations of the European Union* (Oxford and New York, Oxford University Press, 2004) ch 2 and Koutrakos, above n 14, ch 2.

[20] *Opinion 1/78*, above n 14, para 43.

[21] *Ibid*, para 44.

[22] Case C–45/86 *Commission v Council* [1987] ECR 1493, para 17. The Court went on to substantiate that statement by references to UN, UNCTAD and GATT.

in a way which would facilitate their examination in neatly categorised analytical frameworks. Instead, they all apply simultaneously and shed light on the various functions that the choice of legal basis carries out and their constitutional and practical repercussions. In relation to services, for instance, whilst the starting point for its ruling in *Opinion 1/94* was the position that there was nothing in principle which would exclude them from the ambit of the CCP, the Court then went on to define most of the provisions of GATS as beyond the scope of Article 133 EC.

Furthermore, the Court has been acutely aware of the repercussions that the choice of Article 133 EC has for the exercise of national competence. In the context of the interactions between trade and foreign policy, for instance, it made it clear that the foreign policy objective of a national measure cannot remove it from the ambit of the CCP.[23] Therefore, exports of dual-use goods, that is products of both civil and military application, were deemed to fall within the scope of Article 133 EC. However, this broad construction of the scope of CCP was accompanied by an equally broad construction of the extent to which Member States were allowed to deviate from CCP measures on grounds of public security: it is for national authorities to decide whether their internal and external security requires protection by means of unilateral measures, provided that such measures are necessary and proportionate, an assessment to be made by national courts.[24]

It follows from the above that the choice of legal basis is not only constitutionally significant but also heavily charged in political terms. It is for this reason that the clarity and consistency of the relevant case law is of paramount importance. The recent case law on the relationship between external trade and environmental policy illustrates this point, albeit for all the wrong reasons.

A. Recent Tensions: Trade and Environment

Environmental policy has become increasingly prevalent and one of the main points of focus for EU external relations. In 2002, the Commission adopted a policy framework for the external dimension of the EU's strategy

---

[23] 'The specific subject-matter of commercial policy, which concerns trade with non-member countries and, according to Art 1[3]3, is based on the concept of a common policy, requires that a Member State should not be able to restrict its scope by freely deciding, in the light of its own foreign policy or security requirements, whether a measure is covered by Art 1[3]3': Case C–70/94 *Werner* [1995] ECR I–3189, para 11. See also Case C–83/94 *Leifer* [1995] ECR I–3231.

[24] See the analysis in P Koutrakos, *Trade, Foreign Policy and Defence in EU Constitutional Law* (Oxford and Portland, Hart Publishing, 2001) ch 6.

for sustainable development.[25] Following this, the Council adopted a strategy on environmental integration in the external policies. More recently, in the 18-month programme of the German, Portuguese and Slovenian presidencies, endorsed by the Council in December 2006, there was distinct emphasis on the international efforts of the EU to promote environmental protection.[26] Following up from this, the EU Member States participating in the G8 summit in Heiligendamm in June 2007 succeeded in committing the United States in negotiating the successor to the Kyoto Protocol. Finally, the mandate for the 2007 Intergovernmental Conference, agreed by the Brussels European Council in June 2007, requires that a reference be added to combating climate change by international measures in Article 174 EC.

The increasing prominence of the environmental dimension of the EU's external action raises the question of its relationship with external trade. Since 2000, the Court of Justice has delivered three judgments on the relationship between external trade and environmental policy. In *Opinion 2/00*, it was held that the Cartagena Protocol on Biosafety, adopted within the framework of the Convention on Biological Diversity, pursued an environmental objective. The Court ruled, in no uncertain terms, that the Protocol, aimed at regulating the transboundary movement of any living modified organisms resulting from modern biotechnology, was an environmental measure which affected trade with non-member countries only incidentally. A year later, the Court held that the Energy Star Agreement with the United States on the coordination of energy-efficient labelling programmes for office equipment was a trade measure which ought to have been adopted under Article 133 EC.[27]

Finally, in early 2006, it ruled on the conclusion of the Rotterdam Convention on the Prior Informed Consent Procedure (PIC) for certain hazardous chemicals and pesticides in international trade.[28] Following an annulment action brought by the Commission, it held that the Convention had been wrongly concluded on behalf of the Community under Article 175(1) EC. Instead, it should have been concluded under both Articles 133 and 175(1) EC, as it 'includes, both as regards the aims pursued and its contents, two indissociably linked components, neither of which can be regarded as secondary or indirect as compared with the other, one falling within the scope of the common commercial policy and the other within that of protection of human health and the environment'.[29]

---

[25] COM(2002) 82 fin. *Towards a global partnership for sustainable development.*
[26] 17079/06 POLGEN 125, 50–2.
[27] Case C–281/01 *Commission v Council* [2002] ECR I–12049.
[28] Case C–94/03 *Commission v Council* [2006] ECR I–1.
[29] *Ibid*, para 51. Following the Court's judgment, the Rotterdam Convention was concluded under Council Dec. 2006/730/EC [2006] OJ L/299/23 where reference to the judgment (preamble, paras 2 and 3).

Drawing the thread which would bring these judgments together is far from easy. Let us examine the more recent judgment, on the Rotterdam Convention. In Article 1 of the latter, its objective is described as follows: 'to promote shared responsibility and cooperative efforts among Parties in the international trade of certain hazardous chemicals in order to protect human health and the environment from potential harm and to contribute to their environmentally sound use'. This objective is to be achieved 'by facilitating information exchange about [the] characteristics [of those chemicals], by providing for a national decision-making process on their import and export and by disseminating these decisions to Parties'. At the very core of the Convention is the application of the PIC procedure to exports and imports of certain hazardous chemicals and pesticides. This procedure applies to products listed in an annex to the Convention as well as other 'banned or severely restricted chemicals' and 'severely hazardous pesticide formulations'. A system of information is established whereby the parties communicate, through a Secretariat, their decision to ban or severely restrict trade in hazardous chemicals and pesticides and the importing parties communicate their decision as to whether to consent to future imports of such products.

In its judgment, the Second Chamber of the Court acknowledged that the protection of human health and the environment was 'the most important concern in the mind of the signatories of the Convention', a fact which was 'clearly apparent' and 'unequivocally confirm[ed]' in the preamble and the wording of the Convention.[30] However, it went on to point out that its provisions 'also contained rules governing trade in hazardous chemicals and having direct and immediate effects on such trade'.[31] The Court noted the reference to 'trade' in the title of the Convention and observed that, whilst typically an instrument of environmental policy, the PIC procedure would be applicable to products subject to trade. Deemed to establish 'a specific link between trade and the environment',[32] the Convention was viewed by the Court as providing for a number of measures '"governing" or "regulating" international trade ... and therefore fall[ing] within the scope of the common commercial policy'.[33]

The substance of the judgment has been criticised in detail elsewhere.[34] For the purposes of this analysis, suffice it to point out that the judgment sits uncomfortably with the previous ones, on the Cartagena Protocol and

---

[30] *Ibid*, para 37.
[31] *Ibid*, para 42.
[32] *Ibid*, para 44.
[33] *Ibid*, para 46.
[34] See P Koutrakos, 'Annotation on Case C–94/03 *Commission v Council* and Case C–178/03 *Commission v Parliament and Council*', (2007) 44 *CML Rev* 171.

the Energy Star Agreement. The Court engages in a reading of the Rotterdam Convention which is as selective as it is narrow. It refers, for instance, to the preamble to the Convention, according to which 'trade and environmental policies should be mutually supportive with a view to achieving sustainable development', whilst ignoring the identically expressed provision in the preamble to the Cartagena Protocol[35] which had been held to illustrate its environmental nature. In addition, a number of statements underlying the environmental focus of the Convention are ignored by the Court.[36]

On the other hand, the judgment distinguishes the Convention from the Cartagena Protocol on the basis that, contrary to the latter, it is characterised by 'an explicit link between trade and the environment'.[37] Whilst the Rotterdam Convention is applicable to imports and exports of chemicals and the advance informed agreement procedure set out in the Cartagena Protocol is applicable to transboundary movement of living modified organisms in general, that is including, in the Court's own words, 'illegal and unintentional transboundary movements, movements for charitable or scientific purposes and movements serving the public interest', to focus on the need for this 'explicit link' is unduly formalistic. The application of the Convention to products whose movement is subject to export and import rules does not necessarily render its provisions of a trade nature. In fact, the Convention sets out a procedural framework aiming at enabling the importing countries to make an informed choice as to the harmful effects that the import and export of certain chemicals and pesticides would have on human health and the environment.[38]

Finally, in its judgment the Court ignores both the origins of the Rotterdam Convention and the policy context within which it developed. Negotiated in the context of the Rio and 2002 Johannesburg Conferences and following up from international frameworks which had been drawn up under the Food and Agriculture Organisation (namely the Code of Conduct on the Distribution and Use of Pesticides) and the United Nations Environment Programme (namely the London Guidelines for the Exchange of Information on Chemicals in International Trade), the Convention

---

[35] See ninth preambular paragraph.

[36] For instance, in the preamble to the Convention, the Parties express their 'desir[e] to ensure that hazardous chemicals that are exported from their territory are packaged and labelled in a manner that is adequately protective of human health and the environment, consistent with the principles of the Amended London Guidelines and the International Code of Conduct'.

[37] Case C–94/03 *Commission v Council*, above n 28, para 44 of the judgment.

[38] In her Opinion, AG Kokott points out that the PIC procedure can only have indirect effects on trade, either by facilitating trade in hazardous chemicals by increasing transparency of the relevant rules or by making trade more expensive for an exporter and concludes that 'no commercial policy rules' fall within the scope of the Convention' (para 39).

draws upon and develops further an incrementally developed body of principles and procedures firmly established within the sphere of environmental policy.

The narrow, selective and formalistic interpretation of the Rotterdam Convention sets the judgment apart from the other judgments on the relationship between trade and environment. In this respect, Marise Cremona writes that 'we now have three cases deciding respectively that an environmental legal base was appropriate (*Opinion 2/2000*), that the CCP base was appropriate (Case C–281/01 *Commission v Council* (the Energy Star Agreement case)) and that a dual legal base should have been used (Case 94/03 *Commission v Council*); it does not however, seem any easier to predict the outcome of a future case on the same issue'.[39] This is correct and clearly problematic. However, the Rotterdam Convention judgment is problematic not only in terms of its consistency with the case law on the interactions between trade and environmental policies but also, and more crucially, in terms of the more general tenor of the law of EC external relations. This will be analysed in the following section.

B. Legal Basis and Institutional Balance

In its judgment, the Court held that the Decision concluding the Rotterdam Convention on behalf of the Community should be annulled. In the light of the notion of institutional balance and its effects on the choice of legal basis, this was a curious position to take. It is settled case law that recourse to a dual legal basis is not possible in a case where the decision-making procedures laid down therein are incompatible with each other or liable to undermine the rights of the European Parliament.[40] Indeed, this principle was restated by the Court in the *Rotterdam Convention* judgment, which then pointed out that the addition of Article 133 EC as a legal basis along with Article 175(1) EC does not change the voting procedure (both require qualified majority voting) and does not undermine the role of the European Parliament (as the former provision sets out no formal role for it whereas the latter provides for consultation).

In the light of the above, one would have thought that the Court would reach the same conclusion in the *Rotterdam Convention* judgment. This was suggested by Advocate General Kokott who had pointed that, in accordance with Article 175 EC, the Council had adopted the Decision in

---

[39]   M Cremona, 'External Relations of the EU and the Member States: Competence, Mixed Agreements, International Responsibility, and Effects of International Law', *EUI Working Papers* LAW No 206/22, n 50.
[40]   See Titanium dioxide case, above n 4, paras 17–21.

question by qualified majority voting and the Parliament had been consulted. Nonetheless, the Court annulled the Decision concluding the Rotterdam Convention.[41] This conclusion is puzzling. The fact that recourse to a dual legal basis, rather than the single one originally envisaged, is legally possible in institutional and procedural terms does not necessarily entail the annulment of the measure in question. In *BAT*[42] and *Swedish Match*,[43] the Court ruled that Directive 2001/37 on the approximation of national rules concerning the manufacture, presentation and sale of tobacco products should have been adopted under Article 95 EC alone rather than Articles 95 and 133 EC. However, this was held not to necessitate the annulment of the Directive because 'such an error in the legal basis relied on for a Community measure is no more than a purely formal defect'[44]: both provisions required majority voting in the Council and, under the correct legal basis, the Parliament had been involved under the co-decision procedure. Put differently, recourse to the inappropriate legal basis does not question the procedure for adopting the measure in question when the legislative procedure actually followed satisfies the requirements of the legislative procedure which ought to have been applied under the correct legal basis.

Neither can the Court's conclusion be explained in the light of the judgment in Case C–178/03 *Commission v Parliament and Council*, delivered on the same day as the one in the *Rotterdam Convention* case. In that judgment, the Court held that Regulation 304/2003 implementing the *Rotterdam Convention* should also have been based on Article 133 EC along with Article 175(1) EC and, for that reason, it was necessary that it be annulled. However, the conclusion of an international agreement and the adoption of the implementing measure are two acts which may well be adopted on different legal bases: ruling on the Agreement on Agriculture, in the WTO context, the Court opined: 'The fact that the commitments entered into under that Agreement require internal measures to be adopted on the basis of Article [37] of the Treaty does not prevent the international commitments themselves from being entered into pursuant to Article [133] alone.'[45]

Therefore, compliance with the principle of institutional balance by no means explains the annulment of the Decision. The question which then

[41] See paras 52–4 with reference to Joined Cases C–164/97 and C–165/97 *Parliament v Council* [1999] ECR I–1139 (Forest protection case), para 14, and Case C–338/01 *Commission v Council* [2004] ECR I–4829, para 57.
[42] Case C–491/01 [2002] ECR I–11453.
[43] Case C–210/03 [2004] ECR I–11893.
[44] *Ibid*, para 98.
[45] *Opinion 1/94*, above n 8, para 29.

arises is whether this conclusion was adopted by the Court on the basis of any other factors, extraneous to the main parameters which define the choice of the appropriate legal basis.

C. Legal Basis and the Interests of Third Parties

In its judgment, having pointed out that recourse to a dual legal basis would not entail the application of incompatible voting procedures, neither would it undermine the prerogatives of the European Parliament, the Court ruled as follows:

> ... it is important to note that, by basing the decision approving the Convention on the dual legal basis of Article 133 EC and Article 175(1) EC, the Community is also giving indications to the other parties to the Convention both with regard to the extent of Community competence in relation to that Convention which ... falls both within the scope of the common commercial policy and within that of the Community environmental policy, and with regard to the division of competences between the Community and its Member States, a division which must also be taken into account at the stage of implementation of the agreement at Community level.[46]

The Court then ruled that the Decision concluding the Convention on behalf of the Community should be annulled. The focus of the above extract on the interests of the third parties, to such an extent as to necessitate the annulment of the Community measure concluding the Rotterdam Convention on behalf of the Community, is at variance with one of the main tenets of EC external relations, namely the internal function of the choice of the appropriate legal basis. This was articulated clearly in the late 1970s, where the Court pointed out that:

> it is not necessary to set out and determine, as regards other parties to the Convention, the division of powers ... between the Community and the Member States, particularly as it may change in the course of time. It is sufficient to state to the other contracting parties that the matter gives rise to a division of powers within the Community, it being understood that the exact nature of that division is a domestic question in which third parties have no need to intervene.[47]

The above position was later reaffirmed in *Opinion 2/00*.[48] The position that the Decision be annulled on the basis of the interests of the Community's international partners is puzzling. The internal function of the choice of legal basis for the conclusion of international agreements follows directly from the constitutional function of this choice and is related to its

---

[46]   Case C–94/03 *Commission v Council*, above n 28, para 55 of the judgment.
[47]   *Ruling 1/78 (re: Draft Convention of the International Atomic Energy on the Physical Protection of Nuclear Materials, Facilities and Transports)*, [1978] ECR 2151, para 35.
[48]   *Opinion 2/00*, above n 1, para 17.

objective nature. As outlined in the first section of this Chapter, these are the main normative characteristics of the choice of the appropriate legal basis. By introducing the interests of third parties as an additional factor in the process of the choice of legal basis, the Court rendered a process already fraught with problems even more difficult to predict. As Cremona puts it, 'there is a danger, if decisions as to legal base are seen as a signal to third countries, that the issue of choice of legal base will become even more politicised than it is already, making it more difficult to base that choice purely on "objective factors which are amenable to judicial review"'.[49]

Another way of understanding the relevant part of the Rotterdam Convention judgment may be its focus on the submission of a new declaration of competence. In this respect, the emphasis placed on the declaration of competence submitted by the Community to the UN Convention on the Law of the Sea in the *Mox Plant* judgment is interesting.[50] Therefore, the Court may be seen to suggest that more attention should be paid to the uncertainty that third parties often face when dealing with the Community and its Member States in the context of multilateral international agreements. This state of uncertainty may appear more significant as it is linked to the question of responsibility for the implementation of such agreements. However, it should be pointed out that, in fact, a declaration of competence does not always assist third countries in their understanding of who does what and who is responsible for what under EC law in the context of an international agreement. For instance, the declaration of competence submitted by the Community on its accession to the Hague Conference on Private International Law[51] is not only very long but also contains statements outlining the existence and dynamic nature of the EC external competence following AETR and *Opinion 1/76*.[52] Considering that it has taken the Community more than 30 years to clarify the precise scope, effects and repercussions of those principles—and there is still some way to go—it is rather curious that the Community's international partners should be expected to decipher them on the basis of broadly worded declarations.[53]

D. Legal Basis and Balance of Competences

The lack of clarity in the Court's case law on the relationship between trade and environmental policy, the politically charged nature of the choice

---

[49] Cremona, above n 39, 10.

[50] Above n 11.

[51] Once the amendments to its Statute allowing the accession of a regional economic integration organisation has entered into force.

[52] See Annex II to Council Dec. 2006/719/EC [2006] OJ L/297/1, 5.

[53] See also Chapter 1, this volume.

of the appropriate legal basis and its constitutional function, the wide, flexible, albeit not unlimited, and pragmatic interpretation of Article 133 EC, all suggest that the standard formulation that 'the choice of the legal basis for a Community measure must rest on objective factors' is only partly accurate: whilst the choice of legal base is not dependent upon 'an institution's conviction as to the objective pursued',[54] it becomes apparent from the Court's case law that this may not be determined on the basis of specific and easily identifiable criteria either.

A degree of uncertainty is inevitable in the process underpinning the choice of legal basis. In a legal order where the institutional balance is ill-defined and, at times, incrementally redefined, the choice of legal basis is, in any case, a potentially politicised matter.[55] However, the position of Article 133 EC in the spectrum of potential legal bases has been distinctly uneasy, shrouded in factual and normative uncertainty. This is partly due to the typically unhelpful wording of Article 133(1) EC and its procedural dimension (that is qualified majority voting) which rendered this provision both too difficult for the Commission to resist as a legal basis and too unattractive to the Council and a number of Member States.

However, what makes the lack of clarity which has started emanating from the case law disconcerting is its implications for the balance of competences in the Community legal order. It is recalled that when the Court started shaping the content, limits and normative characteristics of CCP in the early 1970s, Article 133 EC was at the very core of the Community's external relations. Being one of the very few legal bases conferring express external competence and with the principle of implied competence only a nascent pillar of the EC external powers, a widely understood CCP was essential to the effectiveness of the Community's system of external relations.

However, as time went by, the development of the doctrine of implied external competence, its acceptance as part of the mainstream EC external relations law and the introduction of new legal bases for external action at the successive amendments of the EC Treaty[56] rendered Article 133 EC a part of a system of EC external relations legal bases which was both wider in scope and more diverse in terms of institutional input. The gradual

---

[54] Case 45/86 *GSP* [1982] ECR 1493, para 11.

[55] See H Cullen and A Charlesworth, 'Diplomacy by Other Means: The Use of Legal Basis Litigation as a Political Strategy by the European Parliament and Member States', (1999) 36 *CML Rev* 1243.

[56] Art 111 on monetary and exchange rate matters, Art 170 EC on research and technical and technical development, Art 174 EC on environment, Art 181 EC on development cooperation, Art 181a on economic, financial and technical cooperation. In addition, reference is made to the possibility of fostering cooperation with third countries in the areas of education, vocational training and youth (Arts 149–50 EC), culture (Art 151 EC), and public health (Art 152 EC). International cooperation is also provided for regarding the development of trans-European networks (Art 155 EC).

establishment of this system entailed an equally gradual shift of emphasis from the need to consolidate the political and normative position of CCP to ensuring the effectiveness of the other legal bases provided in the EC Treaty.

Indeed, the ruling in *Opinion 1/94* is permeated by a concern to ensure that the definition of CCP would not encroach upon other EC Treaty provisions. In relation to trade-related intellectual property rights, for instance, it was pointed out that 'if the Community were to be recognized as having exclusive competence to enter into agreements with non-member countries to harmonize the protection of intellectual property and, at the same time, to achieve harmonization at Community level, the Community institutions would be able to escape the internal constraints to which they are subject in relation to procedures and to rules as to voting'.[57]

In a similar vein, in the *Opinion 2/00* on the conclusion of the Cartagena Protocol, to the invitation by the Commission to uphold its earlier statements about a widely construed CCP, the Court responded as follows:

> The fact that numerous international trade agreements pursue multiple objectives and the broad interpretation of the concept of common commercial policy under the Court's case-law are not such as to call into question the finding that the Protocol is an instrument falling principally within environmental policy, even if the preventive measures are liable to affect trade relating to [living modified organisms]. The Commission's interpretation, if accepted, would effectively render the specific provisions of the Treaty concerning environmental protection policy largely nugatory, since, as soon as it was established that Community action was liable to have repercussions on trade, the envisaged agreement would have to be placed in the category of agreements which fall within commercial policy. It should be noted that environmental policy is expressly referred to in Article 3(1)(l) EC, in the same way as the common commercial policy, to which reference is made in Article 3(1)(b).[58]

What is interesting about the above extract is that the wording of the ruling is identical to that used 23 years earlier when the Court sought to enhance the effectiveness of Article 133 EC. In essence, what had been deemed worthy of protection regarding CCP then became subject to manipulation in order to undermine the effectiveness of other legal bases for external action and the competence which they confer. In a mature and comprehensive system of external relations, it is vitally important that the balance of competences should be respected not as matter of political expediency but as one of constitutional significance. Whilst in *Opinion 1/94* and *Opinion 2/00* the Court appeared acutely aware of this imperative, the judgment in the *Rotterdam Convention* case ignores it and introduces doctrinal ambiguity in an area which least requires it.

---

[57] *Opinion 1/94*, above n 8, para 60.
[58] *Opinion 2/00*, above n 1, para 40.

IV. THE DELINEATION OF EC COMPETENCE—ARTICLE 308 EC

Otherwise known as the flexibility clause or *la petite revision*,[59] Article 308 EC appears to be quite broad in its scope, and has certainly been invoked by the Community institutions, with the Member States' agreement, quite widely in the past. It was famously instrumentalised by the Member States in areas such as environmental policy, where, in 1972, the Conference of Heads of State and Government, held in Paris, resolved to establish a specific policy in the area, with the suggestion that use should be made of the legal basis afforded by Articles 94 and 308 EC. The applicability of Article 308 EC in the area of external relations having been asserted in the *AETR* judgment,[60] it was then used for the conclusion of a number of environmental agreements, too.[61] In addition, prior to the introduction of Article 181 EC, the Community granted emergency food aid to non-associated states in the 1980s under Article 308 EC. In a study carried out by the Swedish Institute for European Policy Studies in 2002, it appears that between the years 1979 and 2004, that is in the course of 25 years, 74 external relations measures were adopted, a considerable number of which dealt with different aspects of aid or financial or technical assistance to third countries. From 1997 until 2006, the main part of Article 308 EC measures dealt with pre-accession strategies.[62]

Whilst politically expedient, this use of Article 308 EC has been criticised.[63] Weiler argued, 'tongue in cheek, that, on this reading defence would also be a permissible usage of Art. [308], since the common market could hardly function with the territories of the Member States under occupation.'[64] However, the wording of Article 308 EC makes it clear that

---

[59] See R Schütze, 'Organized Change towards an "Ever Closer Union": Article 308 EC and the Limits to the Community's Legislative Competence', (2003) 22 *YEL* 79.

[60] Case C–22/70 *Commission v Council* [1971] ECR 263, para 95.

[61] For instance, the Paris Convention on the Prevention of Marine Pollution from Land-Based Sources [1975] OJ L/194/5, the Barcelona Convention for the Protection of the Mediterranean Sea Against Pollution [1977] OJ L/240/5, and the Bonn Convention for the Protection of the Rhine against Chemical Pollution [1977] OJ L/240/92. It was also used, along with Art 133 EC, for the conclusion of cooperation agreements. Since the entry into force of the TEU, such agreements with developing countries have been concluded under Arts 308 and 181 EC.

[62] CF Bergström and J Almer, 'The Residual Competence: Basic Statistics on Legislation with a Legal Basis in Article 308 EC'. This was submitted to the European Convention by Lena Hjelm-Wallén to Working Group V 'Complementary Competencies' as Working Document 19 on 3 September 2002.

[63] Weiler argues that 'only a truly radical and "creative" reading of that Article could explain and justify its usage' by the Community institutions at various instances and points out that 'this wide reading ... meant that it would become virtually impossible to find an activity which could not be brought within the "objectives of the Treaty". JHH Weiler, *The Constitution of Europe* (Cambridge: Cambridge University Press, 1999), 54. He refers to the provision of emergency food aid to non-associated states.

[64] *Ibid*, 54, n 119.

reliance upon it is dependent upon three conditions: Community action should prove necessary for the attainment of one of the objectives of the Community; this should be the case in the course of the operation of the common market; there should be no other provision of the EC Treaty providing the necessary powers.

In line with the residual nature of Article 308 EC, the conditions set out therein should be interpreted strictly. As Advocate General Tizzano pointed out in his Opinion in the *Open Skies* cases, 'that article does not confine itself to requiring a measure to be necessary if Community competence is to be justified, but lays down precise conditions and procedures for the determination of that necessity and, hence, whether it is capable of founding such competence'.[65]

In terms of its applicability, a number of clarifications have been put forward by the Court over the years. First, regarding the relationship between Article 308 EC and other general legislative clauses, such as Articles 94 and 95, the latter serve as the legal basis for the harmonisation of existing provisions and the coordination of the basic provisions of future laws, whereas Article 308 EC provides the legal basis for any new act or the introduction of a new legal form. For instance, in *Opinion 1/94* it was held that the Community is competent, in the field of intellectual property, to harmonise national laws pursuant to Articles 94 EC and 95 EC and may use Article 308 EC as the basis for creating new rights superimposed on national rights such as the Community trademark.[66] In addition, the Court has enforced the residual nature of Article 308 EC at various instances.[67]

Second, in terms of endowing the Community with external competence, the Court ruled in *Opinion 1/94* that it 'cannot in itself vest exclusive competence in the Community at international level', save for the principle of necessity under *Opinion 1/76*.[68]

---

[65] Case C–467/98 *Commission v Denmark* [2992] ECR I–9591, para 53 of his Opinion. In terms of the use of Art 308 EC for the exercise of external competence, it is interesting to note that Advocate General Tizzano, in his Opinion in the *Open Skies* cases, drew a parallelism between the logic underpinning Art 308 EC and the necessity doctrine first articulated in *Opinion 1/76*. He stated that, in cases where an agreement is 'necessary to attain one of [the Community's] objectives' and the corresponding internal competence is ... lacking, the same result can be achieved ... by resorting directly to Article [308] at the tine of concluding the agreement' (para 48).

[66] This also applied to the creation of a supplementary protection certificate for medicinal products (Council Regulation (EEC) No 1768/92), as the Court pointed out in the judgment in Case C–350/92 *Spain v Council*. For a recent restatement of this position, see Case C–436/03 *European Parliament v Council* [2006] ECR I–3733 (European Cooperative Society case).

[67] For instance, Joined Cases C–51/89, C–90/89, and C–94/89 *UK v Council* [1991] ECR I–2757, para 6, *Opinion 2/92 (re: OECD)* [1995] ECR I–525, para 36. Recently in Case C–436/03 *Parliament v Council*, above n 66, para 36.

[68] Para 89.

As for its scope, the Community Courts have highlighted over the years both the limits and potential of Article 308 EC. On the other hand, it was held in *Opinion 2/94* that Article 308 'cannot serve as a basis for widening the scope of Community powers beyond the general framework created by the provisions of the Treaty as a whole and, in particular, by those that define the tasks and the activities of the Community'.[69]

The potential of Article 308 EC has been recently highlighted in a series of judgments by the Court of First Instance on smart sanctions. Given that the competence of the Community to impose sanctions on third countries had already tested the limits of the CCP up until the adoption of the Maastricht Treaty and the provision for a specific legal basis,[70] it is interesting that the imposition of smart sanctions should test the limits of Community competence and the jurisdiction of the Community judiciary.

The judgments which first examined the applicability of Article 308 EC as the appropriate legal basis for the imposition of smart sanctions targeting the assets of individuals were delivered in Case T–306/01 *Yusuf*[71] and Case T–315/01 *Kadi*.[72] Their conclusion was then repeated in three subsequent judgments, namely T–253/02 *Ayadi*,[73] T–49/04 *Hassan*[74] and T–228/02 *Organisation des Modjahedines du peuple d'Iran*.[75] These judgments are much discussed[76] and their approach to the application of

---

[69] [1996] ECR I–1759, para 30. The Court went on to point out that '[o]n any view, Article [308] cannot be used as a basis for the adoption of provisions whose effect would, in substance, be to amend the Treaty without following the procedure which it provides for that purpose'. However, this by no means clarifies the conditions under which this provision may be relied upon—in its ruling, the Court opined that the constitutional ramifications of accession by the Community to the ECHR would be such as to render reliance upon Art 308 EC impossible. In the words of Weiler and Alston, '[a]t no point in that Opinion did the Court suggest that the protection of human rights was not an objective of the Community, nor did it say that the Community lacked competence to legislate in the filed of human rights': P Alston and JHH Weiler, 'An "Ever-Closer Union" in Need of a Human Rights Policy' in P Alston *et al* (eds), *The EU and Human Rights* (Oxford, OUP, 1999) 24–5.

[70] See Koutrakos, above n 24, 58 *et seq*.

[71] [2005] ECR II–3533.

[72] [2005] ECR II–3649.

[73] [2006] ECR II–2139.

[74] [2006] ECR II–52.

[75] [2006] ECR II–4665.

[76] See C Tomuschat, 'Annotation' (2006) 43 *CML Rev* 537, N Lavranos, 'Judicial Review of UN Sanctions by the Court of First Instance', (2006) 11 *EFA Rev* 471, W Vlcek, 'Acts to Combat the Financing of Terrorism: Common Foreign and Security Policy at the European Court of Justice', (2006) 11 *EFA Rev* 491. For an interesting account of the issues raised, see T Andersson, I Cameron and K Nordback, 'EU Blacklisting: The Renaissance of Imperial Power, but on a Global Scale', (2003) 14 *EBLR* 111.

fundamental human rights in these cases is examined in another Chapter of this book.[77] This Chapter will focus on the creative interpretation of Article 308 EC.[78]

A. A Strict Interpretation of the 'Necessity' Requirement under Article 308 EC

In a manner reminiscent of the subtlety of the early judgments on the scope of CCP, the CFI interpreted Article 308 EC in both strict and wide terms. First, it focused on the requirement that reliance upon that provision was necessary for the attainment of one of the Community objectives. The CFI examined a number of objectives, namely the establishment of CCP (Article 3(1)(b)EC), the establishment of a system which would ensure that competition is not distorted (Article 3(1)(g) EC), and the abolition of obstacles to intra-Community movement of capital (Article 3(1)(c) EC). All were deemed incapable of being attained by the sanctions regime freezing funds. The CFI exercised close scrutiny as to whether, and if so how, Article 308 EC could become the appropriate legal basis on its own for freezing assets of individuals pursuant to a UN Security Council Resolution. Its approach made it clear that no general statement about the function of a measure in the context of the law of the internal market would be deemed sufficient. In relation to the need to protect undistorted competition, it added that 'a mere finding that there was a danger of disparities between the various national rules and an abstract risk of obstacles to the free movement of capital or payments or of distortions of competition liable to result therefrom' would not be sufficient to justify recourse to Article 308 EC for two reasons: on the one hand, the primary rules on competition and approximation of laws would be rendered ineffective and, on the other hand, judicial review would be rendered 'quite nugatory'.[79]

The rulings suggest that a detailed assessment of the specific function and implications of Article 308 EC is the yardstick against which reliance upon that provision would be sanctioned. Viewed from this angle, it follows the line first put forward by the Court of Justice in the *Tobacco Advertising* case where such a test was applied in relation to the suitability of another difficult-to-delineate legal basis, namely Article 95 EC.[80]

---

[77]   See Chapter 9, this volume.

[78]   As all the relevant judgments rely on the judgment in *Yusuf*, the following analysis, unless otherwise mentioned, will be referring to that judgment.

[79]   *Yusuf*, above n 71, para 147.

[80]   See Case C–376/98 *Germany v European Parliament and Council* [2001] ECR I–2247. For a comment, see G Tridimas and T Tridimas, 'The European Court of Justice and the

In fact, the CFI goes further and appears to cast doubt on the function of the measure in question and its purported aim to ensure the abolition of impediments to intra-Community movement of capital. It states that the Member States enjoy the right to impose restrictions on such movement, provided that these are necessary and proportionate in order to protect public policy or public security.[81] This is the only part of the judgment which appears to suggest an alternative course of action to that undertaken by the EU institutions, namely the adoption of unilateral measures whose implications for the functioning of the principle of free movement of capital would be addressed on the basis of Article 58(1)(b) EC. Entertaining further the idea that the sanctions regime in question could be imposed by means of national, rather than EU, measures, the CFI seems to dismiss the possibility of any serious discrepancies for the internal market arising, in the light of what it views as the clear, precise and detailed content of the Resolutions and the relatively minor measures for which they are calling. If the Member States had chosen that course of action, the Court of Justice would ensure that the national measures required for the implementation of the sanctions regime would comply with Community law in general and the principles of necessity and proportionality in particular.

B. A Strict Interpretation of EC Objectives

The Court then deals with the possibility of viewing the fight against international terrorism as a more general objective which the Community has to ensure. It is recalled that this type of argument had already been put forward by the Commission in *Opinion 2/94*, where it described respect for human rights 'as a transverse objective forming an integral part of the Community's objective'.[82] The Commission had also referred to the preamble to the SEA and its reference to respect for human rights and to the Convention.

The CFI rejects this argument on the basis of a textual approach[83]: 'nowhere in the preamble to the EC Treaty is it stated that that act pursues a wider object of safeguarding international peace and security' and there is no 'reference whatsoever to the implementation of a common foreign and security policy', the latter falling exclusively within the EU objectives. Whilst this might appear too positivist an interpretation of primary law, the judgment is actually more nuanced in so far as it does acknowledge a degree of interaction between the EC and EU objectives:

Annulment of the Tobacco Advertisement Directive: Friend of National Sovereignty or Foe of Public Health?' (2002) 14 European Journal of Law and Economics 171.
[81]   *Yusuf* , above n 71, para 146.
[82]   See Part V.2 of the ruling.
[83]   *Yusuf*, above n 71, para 155.

Admittedly, it may be asserted that that objective of the Union must inspire action by the Community in the sphere of its own competence, such as the common commercial policy.[84]

This suggests that there is a link between the first and second pillar, and that the EC external policies may not be adopted and carried out in a legal and economic vacuum, completely devoid from any other policy considerations. However, this link is limited in its effect:

[that objective of the Union] is not ... a sufficient basis for the adoption of measures under Article 308 EC, above all in spheres in which Community competence is marginal and exhaustively defined in the Treaty.[85]

The above extracts suggest that the CFI seeks to strike the balance between two interests: on the one hand, a reasonably wide external relations policy for the EC, one which would take cognisance of the EU objectives without, on the other hand, compromising the role of the conditions laid down in Article 308 EC and rendering the latter an open-ended legal basis for external action. This position is consistent with the construction of trade measures with foreign policy implications adopted by the Court of Justice. It is also consistent, and this is more relevant in practical terms, with the Court's construction of development policy. The statement in *Yusuf* mentioned above is reminiscent of the tenor of the judgment in the *India Cooperation Agreement* case, where the Court sanctioned the inclusion of a human rights clause as an essential element of the Agreement. In that case, the Court dealt with the other side of the argument with which the CFI dealt in *Yusuf*: it had been argued that the inclusion of the human rights clause and its characterisation as an essential element of the Agreement necessitated recourse to Article 308 EC. Whilst the Court rejected this approach by relying upon the reference to 'the general objective of developing and consolidating democracy and the rule of law, and to that of respecting human rights and fundamental freedoms' in Article 170(2), it also highlighted the very specific function of the clause in the Agreement with India: no specific field of cooperation between the EC and India was provided in the Agreement as a result of this clause.[86]

The CFI, then, goes on to articulate its view on the extent to which the EU objectives may inform EC actions. The relevant extract is worth citing in full:

... the coexistence of Union and Community as integrated but separate legal orders, and the constitutional architecture of the pillars, as intended by the framers of the Treaties now in force, authorise neither the institutions nor the

---

[84] *Ibid*, para 155.
[85] *Ibid*.
[86] This approach was also applied to the clause relating to energy. See Koutrakos, above n 14, 153–7.

Member States to rely on the 'flexibility clause' of Article 308 EC in order to mitigate the fact that the Community lacks the competence necessary for achievement of one of the Union's objectives. To decide otherwise would amount, in the end, to making that provision applicable to all measures falling within the CFSP and police and judicial cooperation in criminal matters (PJC), so that the Community could always take action to attain the objectives of those policies. Such an outcome would deprive many provisions of the Treaty on European Union of their ambit and would be inconsistent with the introduction of instruments specific to the CFSP (common strategies, joint actions, common positions) and to the PJC (common positions, decisions, framework decisions).[87]

This is an interesting paragraph. So far, in the few cases where the relationship between the pillars was at issue, the emphasis was distinctly on the protection of the integrity of the Community legal order. In the *Airport Transit Visa* case, for instance, the Court made it clear that policing the dividing line between the EC and the other pillars was essential in order to ensure that action adopted under the latter would not impinge upon the former: '[i]t is ... the task of the Court to ensure that acts which, according to the Council, fall within the scope of [the Title VI TEU provision] do not encroach upon the powers conferred by the EC Treaty on the Community' (para 16). Similar concerns underpinned the judgment in *Centro-Com*, where the right of Member States to carry out their foreign policy beyond the Community legal order was acknowledged, albeit in compliance with Community law.

In the judgments in *Yusuf* and *Kadi*, the Community judiciary appears prepared to assume the role of the guardian of CFSP rules, that is a set of rules excluded from its jurisdiction, whose integrity it seeks to protect against an expansive interpretation of Article 308 EC. Therefore, by highlighting the limits of Community competence, the Community judiciary appears to become not only the ultimate arbiter of constitutionality in the Community legal order but also the guardian of the Union architecture.

It is a sign of the maturity of Community law and confidence of its institutions that the ambit of its policies, as set out in some of its open-ended provisions, is defined with due regard for other external policies. This approach is linked to the effort of the Court to respect the balance of competences, examined in the previous section of this Chapter. Therefore, the balance of competences and the balance between the pillars are but two facets of the constitutional function of the choice of the appropriate legal basis within the broader European Union constitutional architecture.

---

[87]   *Yusuf*, above n 71, para 156.

C. Linking the Pillars

The balance between the pillars does not necessarily entail their distinct existence in absolute terms. A more dynamic view of the interacting pillars may be adopted; after all, such a view had already been put forward in the relevant CFI judgments themselves, when the Court suggested a wide, albeit not unlimited, reading of the EC external relations powers in the light of the EU objectives.[88]

The interaction between the pillars is suggested in the wording of the EC provisions on sanctions. According to the CFI, Articles 301 and 60 EC are 'quite special provisions of the EC Treaty' (para 160) aimed to achieve EU objectives, hence rendering 'action by the Community ... in actual fact action by the Union'.[89] This is the reason why Article 308 EC comes into play:

> the powers to impose economic and financial sanctions provided for by Articles 60 EC and 301 EC, ..., may be proved insufficient to allow the institutions to attain the objective of the CFSP, under the Treaty on European Union, in view of which those provisions were specifically introduced into the EC Treaty.[90]

Therefore, what neither Articles 60 EC and 301 EC nor Article 308 EC on their own may justify as legal bases becomes possible in legal terms pursuant to a combination of these three provisions. This formula has been viewed as 'intelligent'.[91] Indeed, it may appear to enhance the ability of the Union to impose sanctions, in conformity with the emerging international practice, whilst avoiding the pitfalls of interpreting Article 308 EC unduly widely. In other words, the effectiveness of the contested measure is sanctioned, albeit pursuant to an apparently textual reading of two exceptional EC Treaty provisions rather than a teleological interpretation of the 'flexibility clause', hence enabling the Community to act in order to pursue Union objectives.

This creative reliance upon the combination of Article 308 EC and Articles 301 and 60 EC is underpinned by the Court's distinct effort to ensure the effectiveness of the sanctions regime. This is achieved by sanctioning the choice made by the Member States to implement UN sanctions on a common basis and by relying upon the EU legal machinery. As mentioned earlier, the Court did suggest in *Yusuf* that there was an alternative: compliance with the UNSC Resolution would have been ensured by means of national measures adopted by the Member States; any problems raised in relation to the free movement of capital would be

---

[88]   *Yusuf*, above n 71, para 155.
[89]   *Ibid*, para 161.
[90]   *Ibid*, para 163.
[91]   Tomuschat, above n 76, 540.

assessed against the exceptional clause of Article 58(3) EC.[92] However, the Member States made a choice, and that involved a considerable use of the EU institutional and legal machinery. That choice was made in order to ensure the uniformity of the sanctions regime and, therefore, the effectiveness of its application. In this respect, it is interesting that the CFI, elaborating further in *Ayadi* on the combination of Articles 308, 60 and 301 EC as the necessary legal bases for the freezing of assets of individuals, addressed the issue of the application of the principle of subsidiarity. Ruling that this was not applicable in the sphere of application of Articles 301 and 60 EC, it pointed out that these rules provide for Community action when that is 'deemed necessary', and opined that, in their sphere of application, 'the EC Treaty ... confers on the Union the power to determine whether action by the Community is necessary. Such determination falls within the ambit of the exercise of discretion by the Union'.[93] The CFI went on to point out the following:

> In any event ... it is plain that the uniform implementation in the Member States of Security Council resolutions, which are binding on all members of the United Nations without distinction, can be better achieved at Community level than at national level.

> [W]ith regard to the claim that the Council compromised the Member States' freedom of choice, the Council was right when it stressed that Common Position 2002/402 reflects the unanimous assessment of the Member States that action by the Community was necessary in order to implement the freezing of funds decided on by the Security Council. As the United Kingdom points out, the Member States themselves having elected to fulfil their obligations under the Charter of the United Nations by means of a Community measure, the Council cannot be accused of having compromised their freedom of choice by complying with their intention.[94]

Therefore, it is the effectiveness of the sanctions regime which appears to be the focus of the relevant CFI judgments, an approach which is consistent with the paramount significance that the Court of Justice attaches to the effectiveness of more general sanctions regimes imposed by the Union in implementing UNSC resolutions.[95] It is entirely proper and wise that the combination of Articles 308, 60 and 301 EC should be construed in such a way as to accommodate the choice made by the Member States to rely upon EC measures in order to impose smart

---

[92] This would not have been the only case of sanctions agreed at CFSP level and then implemented by Member States at national level (eg prohibition on entry into, or transit through, the territory of Member States of certain officials of Belarus, arms embargo etc).

[93] *Ayadi*, above n 73, para 110.

[94] Ibid, paras 112–3.

[95] To that effect, see Case C–84/95 *Bosphorus* [1996] ECR I–3953 and Case C–177/95 *Ebony Maritime* [1997] ECR I–1111.

sanctions. The alternative mechanism of imposing sanctions alluded to in
Yusuf, that is by means of national implementing measures, had already
been tried by the Member States in the late 1960s and had been
characterised by inconsistencies, delays and problems. It was for this
reason that the Member States decided to have recourse to EC law, first by
instrumentalising Article 133 EC in a rather *sui generis* way, and then by
inserting the specific sanctions clauses of Articles 301 and 60 EC in the EC
Treaty at Maastricht.[96] Therefore, it was through trial and error that the
Member States chose the EC legal framework as the most appropriate
mechanism for the imposition of sanctions. It would be a retrograde step if
the Member States felt compelled to resort to national law to implement
UN sanctions: the Community legal order would be prevented from
exploring its full potential as an international actor, the Member States
would be tempted to underutilise the Community mechanism and the
effectiveness of the sanctions regimes would be undermined.

In the context of the instrumentalisation of Article 308 EC for the
imposition of smart sanctions, two further points need to be made. First,
rather than being completely distinct in legal and policy terms, the pillars
are interlinked. This position is illustrated by primary law itself: Article 3
TEU refers to 'the consistency of [the Union's] external activities as a whole
in the context of its external relations, security, economic and development
policies'. Indeed, the CFI referred to the principle of consistency in its
judgments in *Yusuf* and *Kadi*.[97] As a matter of policy, existing EC powers
are being used in order to achieve EU objectives. In the context of the
European Neighbourhood Policy, for instance, the drawing up of a
European Neighbourhood and Partnership Instrument under Articles 179
and 181a EC 'constitutes one of the general instruments providing direct
support for the European Union's external policies'.[98] Viewed from this
angle, the CFI's interpretation of Article 308 EC, along with Articles 60
and 301 EC, acknowledges the links between the pillars without compromising the limits set out in the relevant EC Treaty legal bases as to whether,
and if so under which conditions, EC powers should be utilised. In doing
so, it enhances the ability of the Union to act on the international scene.

---

[96] For an analysis of the history of sanctions imposed by Member States, see Koutrakos,
above n 24, 58–66.

[97] See *Yusuf* , above n 71, para 162.

[98] Preamble, first para of Reg 1638/2006 laying down general provisions establishing a
European Neighbourhood and Partnership Instrument [2006] OJ L/310/1. In this vein, Art
3(2) of the Regulation is noteworthy: 'Where no agreements, as mentioned in paragraph 1
[namely Partnership and Cooperation Agreements, Association Agreements and other existing
and future agreements establishing a relationship with partner countries], between the
European Union and the partner countries exist, Community assistance may be provided
when it proves useful to pursue European Union policy objectives, and shall be programmed
on the basis of such objectives'. Many thanks to Marise Cremona for drawing this to my
attention.

Second, so far, the CFI seeks to strike the balance between a number of distinct, and at times conflicting, interests: respect for the constitutional architecture of the Union and the integrity of the pillars and sanctioning of a wide and flexible external relations policy; interpreting Article 308 EC in a way which would ensure compliance with the conditions laid down therein whilst preventing its content from becoming an open-ended legal basis of external action; sanctioning the effectiveness of policy undertaken by the Member States in the context of UNSC Resolutions without rendering the constitutional constraints of EU external relations irrelevant. To strike the balance between these interests on the basis of a clearly argued and tight line of reasoning which would address the main parameters of the EU international posture is no mean feat. And it is hardly surprising that, from this exercise in judicial balancing, a paradox should emerge: whilst seeking to interpret Article 308 EC strictly and reject recourse to it in order to safeguard the integrity of CFSP, the CFI ends up interpreting Title V TEU. Indeed, it rules that 'the fight against international terrorism and its funding is unarguably one of the Union's objectives under the CFSP, as they are defined in Article 11 EU, even where it does not apply specifically to third countries or their rulers.'[99] Furthermore, in order to justify recourse to Article 308 EC, the CFI refers to the requirement of consistency laid down in Article 3 TEU, that is another TEU provision excluded from its jurisdiction pursuant to Article 46 TEU.[100]

In his Opinions in Case C-402/05 P *Kadi*[101] and Case C-415/05 P *Al Barakaat*,[102] Advocate General Maduro criticized what he viewed as the CFI's 'restrictive reading of Article 301 EC'.[103] Instead, he suggested that Articles 301 and 60 EC alone provide the adequate legal bases for the adoption of the relevant sanctions regimes. In relation to Article 308 EC in particular, he argued that it could not constitute the cross-pillar bridge which would provide the objectives to be persued under Articles 301 EC. Instead, Article 308 EC may only provide the means to enable Article 301 EC to be invoked. However, the CFI had made it clear that the objectives of the Union would be persued by the EC not pursuant to Article 308 EC but Articles 301 and 60 EC: 'under Articles 60 and 301 EC, action by the Community is therefore in actual fact action by the Union'.[104] It is also

---

[99]   *Yusuf*, above n 71, para 167.

[100]   Another paradox in the CFI's rulings is the construction of *ius cogens* and the examination of the rights to property, a fair hearing and effective judicial remedy. But this is beyond the confines of this Chapter.

[101]   Delivered on 16 January 2008.

[102]   Delivered on 23 January 2008.

[103]   Para 14 of AG Maduro Opinion in *Kadi*. As his analysis on this point is identical in both Opinions, this chapter will refer to the Opinion delivered in *Kadi*.

[104]   Para 161 of the judgment in *Yusef*.

interesting how, in rejecting what he appears to consider a broad interpretation of Article 308 EC, Advocate General Maduro puts forward a
considerably broad interpretation of Article 301 EC.

V. CONCLUSION

This Chapter focused on the interpretation of Articles 133 EC and 308 EC
in the context of the choice of the appropriate legal basis for external
action and the challenges that this raises in the light of the idiosyncrasies of
the Union's constitutional structure. Indeed, its objective nature, its ramifications for the institutional balance and its repercussions for the balance of
competences as defined in primary law are all interlinked facets of the
constitutional significance of the choice of the appropriate legal basis.
However, these factors, which are internal to the European Union, must be
assessed in the context of a rapidly evolving, increasingly interacting and
steadily widening in scope international economic environment whose
development, in the form of the negotiation and conclusion of international agreements, by no means follows the various constitutional underpinnings of the choice of the appropriate legal basis under EU law.

Viewed within this context, the choice of the appropriate legal basis
becomes even more complex and the need for clarity more compelling. On
the other hand, a degree of realism is necessary: complete clarity and
predictability are simply not possible as the politically charged character of
this process, its constitutional repercussions and the political and economic
realities of international relations render a degree of uncertainty inevitable.

In the light of the above, two concluding remarks may be made. First, all
efforts should be made to enable the Union's institutions to address the
issues underlying the choice of the appropriate legal basis at as early a
stage as possible. This is recognised by primary law, as Article 300(6) EC
enables the Community institutions and the Member States to 'obtain the
opinion of the Court as to whether an agreement envisaged is compatible
with the provisions of this Treaty'. The *raison d'être* of this provision is
deemed by the Court to forestall complications which would result from
legal disputes stemming from agreements incompatible with EC law.[105] It is
indicative of the significant function of this exceptional procedure that the
Court has construed its jurisdiction under its provision in wide terms.[106]

An example of a procedural mechanism which would help the EU
institutions address issues relating to the appropriate legal basis is provided
by the way in which the conclusion of the Passenger Name Record (PNR)

---

[105] See *Opinion 1/75*, above n 14, pp 1360 and 1361, *Opinion 3/94*, [1994] ECR I–4577,
para 16, *Opinion 2/94*, above n 69, paras 3 to 6, *Opinion 2/00*, above n 1, para 6.
[106] Koutrakos, above n 14, 186–91.

Agreement between the United States and the Community has been handled. When the Decision concluding the Agreement on behalf of the Community was submitted for consultation to the Parliament, the latter relied upon Article 300(6) EC and requested an Opinion. However, this did not prevent the Council from concluding the Agreement on grounds of urgency, following which the Parliament withdrew its request and relied upon Article 230 EC against the Council.[107] This outcome is unsatisfactory: by bypassing the exceptional procedure laid down in Article 300(6) EC, prolonged uncertainty is allowed to prevail regarding questions about competence and the choice of the appropriate legal basis. This would potentially undermine the interests of the EU in international negotiations by forcing it to adjust its position and renegotiate, following the conclusion of an agreement, under pressure and in different circumstances. In fact this was the case with the PNR Agreement: following the annulment of the Council Decision concluding it in the PNR judgment, a temporary agreement was concluded[108] whose terms were less favourable for EU citizens than the original one.[109] This chain of events illustrates how necessary it is for a mechanism to be established whereby the Court of Justice may deal with a request for an Opinion as a matter of urgency.[110]

The second concluding remark is more general. In the multilayered system of EU external relations, it is necessary that the notion of the balance of competence should become central in the choice of the appropriate legal basis and the delimitation of competence. Attention should be paid to drawing the outer limits of not only the CCP but also the other external relations legal bases in a way which would ensure that the conditions for their application do not become irrelevant. In the system of external relations set out in the Treaties there is no provision for a single legal basis to become a general external economic relations basis—all external relations legal bases are part of a system of external powers and the conditions for their application and their implications for the EU institutions should be taken seriously.

---

[107] Joined Cases C–317/04 and C–318/04 *European Parliament v Council* [2006] ECR I–4721.

[108] On behalf of the EU, this was concluded under Arts 24 and 38 TEU: Council Decision 2006/729/CFSP/JHA [2006] OJ L 298/27.

[109] See the annotation of the *PNR* judgment by M Mendez, (2007) 3 *EuConst* 127 and the measured criticism in House of Lords 21st Report of Session 2006–2007 on the PNR Agreement. A new Agreement was struck in June 2007 to replace the temporary Agreement, whose date of expiration was 30 June 2007.

[110] This point is also made in Koutrakos, above n 14, 189–90.

Part IV

Executive Accountability

7

Parliamentary Involvement in European International Relations

DANIEL THYM[*]

I. INTRODUCTION

F ROM A HISTORICAL perspective, the notion of parliamentary involvement in foreign affairs continues the struggle between the ancient prerogatives of the monarch and the novel claims for democratic self-governance. Foreign policy was one of the last strongholds of royal powers, which often seemed to be beyond the reach of democratically elected parliamentarians—as is well illustrated by the British legal concept of foreign affairs as a 'Crown prerogative'.[1] At first glance, surprisingly, the democratisation of our national constitutional orders and the recent parliamentarisation of the European Union have not fundamentally reversed the picture. Parliamentary oversight of foreign affairs continues to trail behind the role of parliaments in domestic policies. Within the European Union, this relates not only to the Common Foreign and Security Policy (CFSP), with its largely intergovernmental design, but similarly extends to various aspects of external EC policies which in many cases retain limited parliamentary involvement. Is there a monarchic relic in the Union's supranational constitutional order? Or does the analysis of parliamentary accountability of European foreign affairs rather point to an underlying conceptual specificity of external relations which justifies and guides the special constitutional treatment of EU international relations?

Any legal analysis of parliamentary powers in foreign affairs must examine principally the parliamentary control of international treaties as

* Dr iur (Berlin), LLM (London), Research Associate at the Walter Hallstein-Institute for European Constitutional Law, Humboldt University, Berlin, online at http://www.whi-berlin.de.
    [1] This corresponds to the executive prerogative in foreign affairs in many other constitutional orders and is today of course embedded in the democratic system of Westminster Parliament; for details see AW Bradley and KD Ewing, *Constitutional and Administrative Law* (13th ed, London, Longman, 2003) ch 15.

the international equivalent of domestic laws. There are, however, important differences between the rigidity of domestic legal rules, whose adoption, interpretation and change follows much stricter procedural patterns than the often dynamic, evolutionary and practice-dominated international legal regimes. An examination of parliamentary control of international treaties must take this into account (Section II). Shared competences between the Member States and the European Community are a peculiar but central feature of the European legal order, which involves national parliaments in international law-making whenever the Community and the Member States act jointly through the adoption of a 'mixed agreement'. This well-settled practice has recently been challenged by the European Union acting under the second and third pillars, with a failed attempt to take over the traditional function of the Member States and their national parliaments (Section III). The entry into force of the Lisbon Treaty would not fundamentally reverse the picture of parliamentary involvement in international treaty-making at the European and national levels—despite some important new rights for the European Parliament.

International relations are much less dominated by rule-making than domestic politics. The main regulatory instrument of the Community method are legal rules adopted by the European institutions, published in the Official Journal, transposed and implemented by national legislators and administrations, and interpreted uniformly by the European court system. International relations, however, are primarily about political positioning in favour of or against something: North Korea will not give up its nuclear weapons simply because the European Union says so in its Official Journal. Instead, foreign policy requires the identification of strategic goals, the development and constant adaptation of methods for their realisation and implementation. You may call it diplomacy, but in any case it differs substantially from domestic politics. This does not imply that parliaments should be powerless in this respect, but their channels of influence are much more indirect, centred on their control of executive actors, the tentative projection of an original 'parliamentary diplomacy', budgetary control and exceptional cases of direct involvement (Section IV). The persistence of the special treatment of the European Parliament in foreign affairs and the identification of substantive differences between domestic policies and international relations lead us to more general considerations on the underlying conceptual specificity of the European foreign affairs constitution for which the specific role of the European Parliament is an important indicator (Section V).

II. CONCLUSION OF INTERNATIONAL AGREEMENTS

The evolution of the Community's external powers is based on the 'parallelism paradigm', according to which 'the system of internal community measures may not therefore be separated from that of external relations'.[2] This parallelism between external and internal competences does not, however, extend to the institutional rules governing their exercise. While the European Parliament has been internally empowered in consecutive treaty reforms, through the introduction and extension of the co-decision procedure to ever more policy fields, the procedures for the conclusion of international agreements persistently uphold the respective prerogatives of the Commission and the Council.[3] Repeated calls for the 'parallel treatment' of domestic and international law-making have fallen on deaf ears.[4] Parliamentary consent to the conclusion of international treaties was last enhanced substantially by the Treaty of Maastricht—in obvious contrast to the extension of parliamentary co-decision in domestic European affairs in Amsterdam and Nice. The different treatment of international treaties may in many respects be rationalised by reference to the specificities of the international law of treaties, while the vitality of inter-institutional relations explains other aspects of the standard case of parliamentary consultation in accordance with Article 300 EC and the exceptions laid down for specific policy areas.

A. Standard Case: Article 300 EC

In its internal affairs, the European Union may autonomously invent new procedures which transcend the blueprint of domestic constitutional orders and international law, thereby enhancing its *sui generis* character. When it

---

[2] Case C–22/70 *AETR* [1971] ECR 263, para 19; for the evolution of the case law see M Cremona, 'External Relations and External Competence: The Emergence of an Integrated Policy' in P Craig and G de Búrca (eds), *The Evolution of EU Law* (Oxford, Oxford University Press, 1999) 137, 138–52.

[3] For the impressive extension of parliamentary oversight of domestic European affairs see B Rittberger, 'The Creation and Empowerment of the European Parliament' (2003) 41 *JCMS* 203 and A Maurer, *Parlamentarische Demokratie in der Europäischen Union* (Baden-Baden, Nomos, 2002).

[4] For a summary of the EP's call for an extension of its powers see H Krück, 'Zur parlamentarischen Legitimation des Abschlusses völkerrechtlicher Verträge der EG' in R Geiger (ed), *Neuere Probleme der parlamentarischen Legitimation im Bereich der Auswärtigen Gewalt* (Baden-Baden, Nomos, 2003) 161, 178–82.

comes to the negotiation, conclusion and evolution of international agreements, the Community is, however, integrated into the pre-existing framework of the legal and customary restraints of international relations.[5] Europe may not therefore simply project its internal procedures onto the international arena. More specifically, it must take into account the customs of international diplomatic negotiations as well as the evolutionary and practice-dominated features of the international law of treaties, which contrast with the transparency of parliamentary debate and the procedural rigidity of the Community co-decision procedure. These specificities of international treaty-making provide the background to the analysis of the standard case of parliamentary involvement in Article 300 EC. It covers the life cycle of international agreements ranging from the negotiation of new agreements (Subsection i), domestic ratification as the regular point of parliamentary involvement (Subsection ii) to specific circumstances reflecting the evolutionary character of international law (Subsection iii).

(i) Negotiations

'Being diplomatic' is proverbially different from the open and frank discussions which rightly dominate our parliamentary cultures. It is therefore not surprising that the European treaties continue the tradition of treaty negotiations as the prerogative of executive agents who are often specifically trained to manage international negotiations. Article 300(1) EC as amended in Maastricht entrusts the Commission to 'conduct these negotiations in consultation with special committees appointed by the Council to assist it in this task and within the framework of such directives as the Council may issue to it'. Official consultation of the European Parliament is not foreseen. From the sole point of view of primary law, the door of the negotiation room therefore remains closed for MEPs.

In practice, the European Parliament nonetheless has a foot in the door of the negotiation room. Based on the original 1957 version of the present Article 300 EC, the Council and the Commission have conceded limited parliamentary involvement on various occasions. The Luns I procedure (1964 on association agreements), its Luns II or Westerterp expansion (1973 on commercial and economic treaties) and the Stuttgart declaration (1983 on all 'significant' international agreements) all envisage a threefold involvement of the European Parliament during the negotiation phase: (1) the option of a plenary debate before the start of the negotiations; (2) permanent contact between the European negotiators and MEPs during the

---

[5] A survey of Europe's law and practice in this respect is presented by D Verwey, *The European Community, the European Union and the International Law of Treaties* (Den Haag, TMC Asser Press, 2004), esp 87–153.

negotiations; and (3) confidential information of the Parliament about their outcome before the signature of the agreement.[6] In its own Rules of Procedure, the European Parliament goes even further and claims far-reaching involvement. It postulates the right to suspend the opening of negotiations (Rule 83(2)), be 'regularly and thoroughly' informed (Rule 83(4)) and 'adopt recommendations and require that these be taken into account before the conclusion of the international agreement under consideration' (Rule 83(5)). It also brings forward the consultation or consent requirement to the end of the negotiation phase and prior to the signature of the agreement (Rule 83(6)).[7]

These Rules of Procedure are not binding on the other institutions of course and should therefore be read as the Parliament's vision of how it should ideally be involved.[8] It has tried, however, to put these suggestions into practice within the framework of its inter-institutional relations. Since 1995 the framework agreements concluded between the Parliament and the incoming Commission have covered the negotiation of international agreements, thereby perpetuating and enhancing the inter-institutional compromise enshrined in the original Luns, Westerterp and Stuttgart conventions.[9] The present Framework Agreement on relations between the European Parliament and the Commission was signed on 26 May 2005. It continues the earlier reassurances on the timely and comprehensive flow of information, including the 'draft negotiating directives, the adopted negotiating directives (and) the subsequent conduct of negotiations', which allow the Parliament 'to express its point of view if appropriate', which again shall be taken into account by the Commission 'as far as possible'.[10] MEPs shall even be included as observers in Community delegations negotiating multilateral agreements—with the Parliament calling for Commission support for its involvement in internal Union coordination meetings against the resistance of the Council.[11]

From a legal perspective, the framework agreement, as inter-institutional soft law, may not change the contents of primary law and the institutions

---

[6] The contents of the said interinstitutional arrangements is described and analysed by A de Walsche, 'La procédure de conclusion des accords internationaux' in M Dony and J-V Louis (eds), *Commentaire J. Mégret 12 – Relations extérieures* (2nd ed, Université libre de Bruxelles, 2005) 77, 96–106 and I MacLeod, ID Hendry and S Hyett, *The External Relations Law of the European Communities* (Oxford, Clarendon Press, 1996) 98–100.

[7] Rules of Procedure of the European Parliament, 16th ed, July 2004 ([2005] OJ L/44/1).

[8] As emphasised by the Parliament's former legal advisor Krück, above n 4, 175.

[9] On the earlier rules see Annex 2 to the Framework Agreement of 2000 ([2001] OJ C/121/128) and the Code of Conduct signed in 1995, cited by I Bosse-Platière, 'Le Parlement européen et les relations extérieures de la Communauté européenne après le Traité de Nice' (2002) 39 *RTDEur* 527, 532.

[10] Framework Agreement on relations between the European Parliament and the Commission, Annex to the EP Decision, EP doc P6_TA(2005)0194, para 19.

[11] See para 21 of the framework agreement and *ibid*, para 4.

are, at least in principle, not obliged to observe, continue or enter into these conventions unless they voluntarily decide to do so.[12] It is therefore perfectly legitimate from a legal point of view, if the Council 'recalls' after the signature of the 2005 agreements 'that the procedures enabling the European Parliament to be involved in international negotiations are governed by Article 300 of the EC Treaty'.[13] Since the framework agreement was concluded between the Commission and the Parliament, the Council is similarly right to 'stress that the undertakings entered into by these institutions cannot be enforced against it in any circumstances' and that it reserves its right to take appropriate measures, such as the initiation of legal proceedings, 'should the application of the provisions of the framework agreement impinge upon the Treaties' allocation of powers to the institutions or upon the institutional equilibrium that they create'.[14]

It is not immediately clear why the Council publicly stated its objections in 2005, given that it continues a long tradition of informal parliamentary involvement in international negotiations dating back to the 1964 Luns I procedure.[15] Its opposition is probably best understood against the background of the repeated attempts by the European Parliament to use inter-institutional arrangements as an instrument for the incremental change of the living constitution with a view to permanently enhancing its role in international relations.[16] Moreover, in parallel to the public statement of 2005, the Council was engaged in a protracted dispute with the European Parliament about the financing of the CFSP. The Parliament tried during this dispute to enhance its involvement in CFSP decision-making—and largely failed, since the Council maintained a firm approach, refusing to give way.[17] The Council's renewed opposition to parliamentary involvement in the negotiation phase of international agreements reflects a similar firmness and may even turn the institutional clock back to before the time of the original Luns, Westerterp and Stuttgart conventions.

The Luns, Westerterp and Stuttgart conventions were concluded on the basis of the original 1957 version of Article 228(1) EEC, which simply stated with regard to the negotiation phase that 'agreements shall be negotiated by the Commission'. When the Treaty of Maastricht codified

---

[12] On interinstitutional agreements the special issue of the (2007) 13 *European Law Journal*, Issue 1.

[13] Council Statement, [2005] OJC/161/1.

[14] *Ibid.*

[15] P Koutrakos, *EU International Relations Law* (Oxford, Hart Publishing, 2006), 149 suggests that it might be concerned by the disclosure of confidential documents, which the framework agreement however tries to safeguard with various special procedures.

[16] As illustrated by A Maurer, D Kietz and C Völkel, 'Interinstitutional Agreements in CFSP: Parliamentarisation through the Backdoor' (2005) 10 *EFA Rev* 175, with a view to the budgetary disputes of the 1990s.

[17] For more details see D Thym, 'Beyond Parliament's Reach? The Role of the European Parliament in the Common Foreign and Security Policy' (2006) 11 *EFA Rev* 109, 113–7.

some aspects of the Stuttgart declaration in the consent requirement of the present Article 300(3) EC, it deliberately refrained from foreseeing a role for the European Parliament during the negotiation phase.[18] Instead, it explicitly enshrined the executive prerogatives of the Council in the present version of Article 300(1) EC, which to date does not mention the European Parliament. The Amsterdam Intergovernmental Conference (IGC) confirmed the exclusion of the Parliament from the decision on the signature of the agreement.[19] Whenever the Council confronts the Parliament's renewed attempts to change constitutional practice through inter-institutional reassurances, it is worth remembering, from a legal perspective, that the wording of the Treaty prevails over the unilateral claims of the European Parliament. Legally, the negotiation room remains closed for MEPs—as enshrined in Article 300(1) EC and, *de constitutione ferenda*, Article 218(2)–(4) TFEU-Lisbon.

(ii) Conclusion

An international treaty may only bind the Community after it has established its consent to be bound at the international level, an act which Article 300(2) EC calls 'conclusion' and which is generally referred to as 'ratification'. In most constitutional orders, this process of domestic ratification is the regular point for parliamentary involvement.[20] The EC Treaty does not presently differ from the common constitutional tradition of Western European democracies. It does differ, however, in terms of the degree of parliamentary participation, which arguably constitutes a 'significant departure from the traditional parliamentary right of assent to international agreements'.[21] More specifically, the Treaty foresees mere consultation of the European Parliament as the standard case, while its consent is only required in the specific situations enumerated in the second subparagraph of Article 300(3) EC. This system was introduced in Maastricht, thereby codifying a modified version of the inter-institutional convention established by the Stuttgart declaration of 1983 mentioned above.[22] Before Maastricht, the original EEC Treaty had envisaged in most

---

[18] An overview of the evolution of the former Art 228 EEC and present Art 300 EC is provided by de Walsche, above n 6, 100–6.

[19] Art 300(2) EC again excludes the Parliament, whose consultation is only required before the adoption of the agreement—in contrast to an ongoing legal debate at the time and the former and present Rule 83(6) of the Parliament's Rules of Procedure cited above, n 7.

[20] See the comparative survey by S Riesenfeld and F Abbott (eds), *Parliamentary Participation in the Making and Operation of Treaties: A Comparative Study* (Den Haag, Kluwer, 1994).

[21] M Krajewski, 'Foreign Policy and the European Constitution' (2003) 22 *Yearbook of European Law* 435, 445.

[22] For similarities and differences between pre- and post-Maastricht rules see de Walsche, above n 6, 99–100.

cases no parliamentary consultation at all.[23] In Article 300 EC, the formulation of the consultation procedure is therefore not a relic of the early days of European integration, but a deliberate decision of the Maastricht IGC.

Consultation gives the Parliament the right to be officially informed on the substance of the agreement, debate its pros and cons, and state its opinion; only thereafter may the Council proceed with its conclusion.[24] If the Council goes ahead without parliamentary consultation, it infringes an essential procedural requirement, but it is not obliged to follow the parliamentary opinion in substance.[25] This is the obvious reason why the European Parliament has long demanded an extension of the consent requirement to all areas which fall within its domestic co-decision powers.[26] Instead, the areas of parliamentary consent under Article 300(3)(2) EC generally trail behind its powers in the respective internal decision-making procedures. The only field in which the European Parliament has gained considerable authority in theory and practice is that of association agreements, where it has withheld its consent on a number of occasions, thereby exercising real influence on the orientation of European foreign policy. Most prominent in this respect is the customs union with Turkey, where the MEPs achieved at least some symbolic improvements of the human rights situation in Turkey after the majority had repeatedly threatened to reject the agreement.[27]

In contrast, the European Parliament's role as budgetary authority and co-legislator in internal Community policies is not mirrored by Article 300(3) EC. Its consent is only required for agreements having 'important budgetary implications'. Moreover, the ECJ interpreted this phrase narrowly in the case of a fisheries agreement with Mauritania, which implied payments of approximately €250 million over five years, on the politically sensitive topic of purchasing fishing rights for the European fishing industry in the Mauritanian exclusive economic zone.[28] The asymmetry

---

[23] Art 228(1) EEC foresaw no parliamentary involvement at all, while Art 238 EEC on association agreements originally required consultation and consent after the Single European Act.

[24] Except in cases of urgency, as foreseen in the last sentence of Art 300(3)(1) EC.

[25] Cf Case C–138/79 *Roquette Frères v Council* [1980] ECR 3333.

[26] For repeated calls for the 'parallel treatment' of domestic and international law-making see Krück, above n 4, 178–82.

[27] See the case study by S Krauss, 'The European Parliament in EU External Relations: The Customs Union with Turkey' (2000) 5 *EFA Rev* 215, 223–35. Other cases of rejection are listed by K Lenaerts and P Van Nuffel, *Constitutional Law of the European Union* (2nd ed, New York, Thomson, 2005), 890–1 and C Tomuschat, 'Artikel 300 EG' in H von der Groeben and J Schwarze (eds), *EU/EG-Vertrag-Kommentar* (6th ed, Baden-Baden, Nomos, 2004), para 40.

[28] Case C–189/97 *Parliament v Council* [1999] ECR I–4741 and the more detailed analysis by Koutrakos, above n 15, 145–7. The issue has recently gained renewed significance after some development and human rights NGOs blamed EC policy to be partly responsible

between the EP's internal and external powers is, however, most evident in the rule that its consent is only required for agreements 'entailing *amendment* of an act adopted under the [co-decision] procedure'. Even if an agreement lays down detailed rules which bind the Community and preclude the *later* adoption of a different internal regulatory regime, the European Parliament is only consulted, and has therefore no substantial influence on the contents of the international rules.[29]

Regarding these constraints, there is indeed 'no compelling logic for limiting the assent requirement to such cases, as one does not see on what grounds the Parliament should be less involved in the conclusion of agreements laying down, for the first time, rules which in the internal decision-making process require co-decision'.[30] We should therefore welcome the fact that the European Convention and the subsequent IGCs agreed to an extension of the consent requirement to all 'agreements covering fields to which the ordinary legislative procedure applies, or the special legislative procedure where consent by the European Parliament is required'.[31] Since the logic of this change, which is complemented by a consent requirement for accession to the European Convention on Human Rights, is rather compelling, rightly survived the renegotiation of the Constitutional Treaty. This would align the Parliament's internal and domestic powers, while maintaining the present structure of the consent requirement which takes place after the signature of the agreement and does not grant the Parliament the right to amend individual provisions.[32]

Indeed, the binary character of the consent requirement leaves the Parliament with the choice of consent or rejection, which considerably limits its room for manoeuvre. It presents the Parliament with the outcome of negotiations undertaken behind the closed doors of the diplomatic negotiation room as a *fait accompli*.[33] This constraint on the parliamentary policy-shaping powers is particularly disappointing for the Euro-parliamentarians who are, as a 'working parliament', arguably at their best when involved in the technical debates which dominate many aspects of

---

for the decline of the Mauritanian fishing industry, thereby supporting diversification into the alternative income of shipping clandestine immigrants to the Canary Islands.

[29] A recent example how prior international agreements may restrict the regulatory autonomy of the Community institutions under the co-decision procedure is provided by ECJ, Case C–344/04 *International Air Transport Association et al* [2006] ECR I–403, paras 34–48, where *in casu* the Court, however, finds no substantial conflict between international and Community rules.

[30] P Eeckhout, *External Relations of the European Union* (Oxford and New York, Oxford University Press, 2004), 177.

[31] Article 218(6)(a)(v) TFEU-Lisbon.

[32] Cf Art 300(2) EC.

[33] C Tomuschat, 'Der Verfassungsstaat im Geflecht der internationalen Beziehungen' (1978) 36 *Veröffentlichungen der Vereinigung deutscher Staatsrechtslehrer* 7, 28.

the day-to-day management of European affairs.[34] More generally, the exclusion of parliamentary influence on the formulation of individual treaty provisions 'neither requires nor fosters a process of open deliberation and debates about policy alternatives',[35] thereby impeding the emergence of a meaningful democratic debate as the main advantage of enhanced parliamentary involvement. Of course, the European Parliament may use the threat of veto inherent in the consent requirement to bring the debate forward and influence the negotiations independently of its presence in the negotiation room.[36] But such ultimate threats may only be effective in special cases and cannot replace the regular influence on individual policy choices under the co-decision procedure.

Of course, one could theoretically extend the co-decision procedure to the conclusion of international agreements or grant the European Parliament the right to select, reject or modify individual treaty provisions. But this would not comply with the customs and laws of international relations which still consider treaty negotiations as inter-state bargaining whose compromises, especially in a multilateral context, cannot easily be unravelled. This is best illustrated with the example of the US Congress, which constitutionally holds the right to amend individual treaty provisions for purposes of domestic application. The experience of world trade negotiations, however, shows that effective multilateral bargaining only succeeds when the US Congress voluntarily surrenders its amendment rights and restricts itself to the binary assent–rejection option which characterises the parliamentary consent requirement under Article 300(3) EC.[37] Similarly, most national parliaments may only ratify or reject an international treaty as a whole, and do not hold the right to amend individual provisions for purposes of domestic application.[38]

Comparing the European Parliament to the US Congress enhances our argument in another respect: like the US Congress and contrary to the national parliaments of most EU Member States, the European Parliament enjoys widespread political autonomy from the Commission and the Council, which together form the executive of European international relations. In contrast, the parliamentary systems of most EU Member States are founded upon close cooperation between the parliamentary

---

[34] As shown convincingly by P Dann, 'European Parliament and Executive Federalism: Approaching a Parliament in a Semi-Parliamentary Democracy' (2003) 9 *ELJ* 549, 561–9.

[35] Krajewski, above n 21, 440.

[36] As underlined by R Bieber, 'Democratic Control of European Foreign Policy' (1990) 1 *EJIL* 48, 161 and illustrated by Krauss, above n 27, with the example of the customs union with Turkey.

[37] *Cf* on the current 'fast track', which Congress narrowly agreed upon in 2002 and which expires in 2007, H Shapiro and L Brainard, 'Trade Promotion Authority, formerly known as Fast Track' (2003) 35 *The George Washington International Law Review* 1.

[38] See the different contributions to Riesenfeld and Abbott, above n 20.

majority and the government, with the former usually refraining from any action which would undermine the political authority of the latter. In international relations, this support is even more pronounced than in domestic policies, where parliamentarians are more inclined to stand up for the specific interests of their constituency or social support groups.[39] The relative importance of inter-institutional control mechanisms in the European constitutional order therefore holds the potential of rendering the Parliament's consent requirement to international agreements more effective than in our domestic parliamentary systems[40]—even if the European Parliament may be inclined not to stand in the way of any agreement enhancing Europe's role in the world due to its institutional self-interest in deepening integration and the predominance of consensus politics.[41]

(iii) Evolution

As mentioned at the outset, the international law of treaties is much more evolutionary and practice-dominated than our domestic legal systems with their rather strict procedures for the adoption, interpretation, implementation and change of parliamentary statutes. The most prominent expressions of this dynamic character of international treaties are their provisional application (Article 25 Vienna Convention on the Law of Treaties (VCLT)), their suspension in response to the material breach by the other party or a fundamental change of circumstances (Articles 60, 62 VCLT) and their interpretation in the light of subsequent practice (Article 31(3)(c) VCLT). All these specificities enhance the influence of the actor which determines the position of a party in this respect. It is therefore important to note that the Amsterdam IGC decided to end the silence of the European Treaties and introduce procedural requirements for the definition of the Community's position in these circumstances. A closer look at Article 300(2) EC shows that the Parliament is deliberately only 'immediately and fully informed of any decision' in retrospect. The decision instead rests with the Council.

[39] For a classical analysis of parliamentary control of foreign policy in parliamentary systems see H Treviranus, *Außenpolitik im demokratischen Rechtsstaat* (Tübingen, Mohr Siebeck, 1966), 88–122.

[40] As highlighted by R Bieber, 'Democratic Control of International Relations of the European Union' in E Cannizzaro (ed), *The European Union as an Actor in International Relations* (Den Haag, Kluwer Law, 2002) 105, 107. In the US, the Versailles Treaty, the Nuclear Test Ban Treaty and the repeated debates about the ratification of trade agreements, including the GATT 1947, are the most prominent examples of the Congress refusing the ratification of treaties which had the support of the US President. Tellingly in Europe amendments to the founding Treaties have only failed in referenda, not in national parliaments (with the exception of the EDC during the French IVth Republic).

[41] Cf Krauss, above n 27, 219 and C Harlow, *Accountability in the European Union* (Oxford, Oxford University Press, 2002), 101–7.

Again, the position of the European Parliament does not differ from the position of most national parliaments. The provisional application of international agreements in particular has long been criticised for circumventing the constitutional prerogatives of national parliaments.[42] The provisional application may legally be terminated at any time and does not in such manner compromise the consent requirement from a dogmatic point of view; in actual fact, however, the provisional application creates a momentum in favour of the continued application of the treaty, thereby rendering parliamentary rejection more difficult.[43] Similarly, the suspension of an agreement usually involves sensitive political decisions which are often closely related to a situation of international crisis or tension, be that due to a fundamental change of circumstances, such as in the *Racke* case,[44] or due to a material breach by the other party, possibly of a human rights clause.[45] It is obvious that the European Parliament strongly opposes the fact that such fundamental foreign policy questions are decided by the Council without any formal parliamentary involvement.[46] Its exclusion is another illustration of the EC Treaty intentionally limiting the role of the European Parliament, while preserving and extending the prerogatives of the Council.[47]

International treaty regimes establishing an institutional framework for their gradual development also remain the executive prerogative of the Commission and the Council. The prominent example of association councils adopting legally binding decisions that are directly applicable in the European legal order illustrates that such international decisions may have far-reaching legislative effects.[48] It is therefore another considerable limitation of parliamentary involvement that Article 300(2) EC excludes the European Parliament from defining the European position. Although not explicitly mentioned, the rationale behind this rule suggests that it similarly applies to the position that the Community adopts within international organisations, such as the Food and Agriculture Organization

---

[42]   Eg by D Vignes, 'Une notion ambiguë: la mise en application provisoire des traités' (1972) 18 *AFDI* 181.

[43]   As is rightly noted by de Walsche, above n 6, 105.

[44]   Case C–162/96 *Racke* [1998] ECR I–3655 where the suspension was, before the introduction of Art 300(3) EC, decided by means of an autonomous Council Regulation to which the regular domestic decision-making procedure applied.

[45]   *Cf* the contribution by Päivi Leino-Sandberg in Chapter 10 of this volume.

[46]   Before the introduction of Art 300(2) EC the Parliament had interpreted the Treaty as requiring its involvement mirroring its rights in the conclusion procedure; *cf* Krück, above n 4, 167.

[47]   See Eeckhout, above n 30, 186. However, the need for swift decisions in times of crisis argues against time-consuming parliamentary involvement, as underlined by A Dashwood, 'External Relations Provisions of the Amsterdam Treaty' (1998) 35 *CML Rev* 1019, 1025 and Section V.

[48]   On the direct applicability of such decisions, Case C–192/89 *Sevince* [1990] ECR I–3461, paras 13–26.

(FAO) or the World Trade Organization (WTO).[49] The European Parliament has a right to consent to the conclusion of such agreements under Article 300(3) EC, but the definition of the European positions in the institutions or bodies thus established remains beyond Parliament's reach. The example of national parliamentary oversight of European affairs shows that alternative modes of control could be achieved without undermining the effectiveness of European foreign policy.[50]

International treaty regimes and international organisations are not only evolving through 'decisions having legal effects' (Article 300(2) EC), but similarly advance on the basis of subsequent practice and, in some cases, through international jurisprudence. Against the background of the aforementioned exclusion of the European Parliament from all evolutionary specificities of the international law of treaties, it is not surprising that international courts and subsequent practice also remain the prerogative of the Council and the Commission. Thus, the European Parliament, for example, is not involved in cases brought before the WTO Dispute Settlement Mechanism,[51] nor is it consulted before the Community agrees to summit communiqués, joint political declarations or any other form of international soft law, which by its very nature defies easy legal categorisation.[52] Only on exceptional occasions may the evolution of international treaties on the basis of subsequent practice be qualified as a substantial amendment of that treaty from the perspective of Article 300 EC, and therefore require renewed parliamentary involvement under Article 300(3) EC.[53] In such an exceptional situation, the gradual evolution of an international treaty might be linked back to the only hard constitutional

---

[49] *Cf* Tomuschat, above n 27, para 41 and MacLeod, Hendry and Hyett, above n 6, 101. An international organisation is more than a treaty regime. Moreover, for the WTO the relationship between Art 133 EC and 300(2), (3) EC remains unclear insofar as the establishment of international bodies and not mere trade agreements in general are concerned. Again, the introduction of Art 300(2) EC falls behind earlier practice, see Bosse-Platière, above n 9, 549–52.

[50] See the comparative survey by A Maurer and W Wessels (eds), *National Parliaments and their Ways to Europe: Losers or Latecomers?* (Baden-Baden, Nomos, 2001).

[51] M Hilf and F Schorkopf, 'Das Europäische Parlament in den Außenbeziehungen der Europäischen Union' (1999) 34 *Europarecht* 185, 192 deplore this exclusion.

[52] Such as the declarations during the European-Israeli dispute on the application of the association agreement with Israel to the import of farm products from the occupied territories, described in the case study by L Zemer and S Pardo, 'The Qualified Zones in Transition: Navigating the Dynamics of the Euro-Israeli Customs Dispute' (2003) 8 *EFA Rev* 51. While the EP had rejected the conclusion of a protocol to the earlier EC-Israel association agreement (see the references above, n 28), it was not involved in the dispute surrounding the application of the new agreement.

[53] As argued by the minority opinion of the German Constitutional Court in Case 2 BvE 3/92, 5, 7 & 8/93, judgment of 12 July 1994, *Auslandseinsätze*, BVerfGE 90, 286 on the Petersberg missions of NATO and WEU in line with the subsequent interpretation of their respective founding treaties which had clearly not been foreseen when the German Parliament agreed to their ratification in 1955.

right of the European Parliament in the lifecycle of international agreements: its consultation or consent to domestic ratification.

B. Exceptions: Exclusion of Parliamentary Involvement

The standard case of parliamentary involvement under Article 300 EC does not extend to the Common Commercial Policy (CCP), agreements in the field of Economic and Monetary Union (EMU) and the second and the third pillars of the EU Treaty, which fully exclude the European Parliament from the European decision-making procedure.[54] There is no inherent logic underlying the exclusion of parliamentary involvement in these policy fields. One possible explanation may be sought in considerations of political influence with the Member States maintaining control over the direction of European foreign policy to the detriment of the supranational Parliament.[55] Moreover, the intergovernmental nature of the second and third pillars in particular may be described as a *'mal nécessaire'* without which the previous IGCs would not have reached a compromise on their establishment and reform.[56] One should, however, refrain from generalised conclusions and take into account the specific circumstances of the different policy fields.

In the CCP, the persistent exclusion of the European Parliament is arguably a historic relic, since the provisions of the present Art 133 EC can be directly traced back to the original 1957 version of the EEC Treaty, when the parliamentary 'Assembly' was generally not an important institutional actor. The difficult negotiations on the extension of the CPP after the landmark Opinion 1/94 of the Court of Justice in Amsterdam and Nice were dominated by the differences among Member States, with France defending its influence on the course of the CCP. Faced with such a critical guardian of national interests, the Parliament was not heard with its call for involvement in the CPP, and the new rules in the present Article 133(5)–(7) EC do in some areas even curb its earlier powers.[57] The increased importance of international trade deals, however, gave the

---

[54] See for the CCP Art 133 EC, for EMU Art 111 EC and for the second and third pillar Art 24, 38 EU.

[55] *Cf* A Moravcsik, 'Reassessing Legitimacy in the European Union', in JHH Weiler, I Begg and J Peterson (eds), *Integration in an Expanding European Union* (New York, Blackwell Publishing, 2003), 77–97.

[56] Convincingly, B de Witte, 'The Pillar Structure and the Nature of the European Union: Greek Temple or French Gothic Cathedral?' in T Heukels, N Blokker and M Bruns (eds), *The European Union after Amsterdam* (The Hague, Kluwer Law, 1998) 51, 53. Similarly, W Schroeder, 'Verfassungsrechtliche Beziehungen zwischen Europäischer Union und Europäischen Gemeinschaften' in A von Bogdandy (ed), *Europäisches Verfassungsrecht* (Berlin, Springer, 2003) 373, 414.

[57] On the subject matters of Art 133(5)–(7) EC have hitherto been covered by the AETR principle and Art 300 EC; for more details see C Herrmann, 'Common Commercial Policy

European Parliament a powerful argument for its involvement in the ratification procedure, since its exclusion appeared more and more 'unjustifiable and stems from pre-globalization times'.[58] It is therefore not surprising and should be welcome that the Constitutional Treaty abolishes the special treatment of the CCP and aligns the procedure with the regular rules of Article III–325 ConstEU, which require parliamentary consent in areas which domestically fall under the ordinary legislative procedure.[59]

In Economic and Monetary Union the Parliament's consultative function is taken over by the European Central Bank (ECB), which is consulted before the Council concludes agreements on exchange rate systems with third countries or determines the Community position in international financial fora.[60] Of course, one may have additionally foreseen the consultation or consent of the European Parliament. But the decision not to do so reflects the general conceptualisation of EMU as a technical issue with a primary focus on price stability, the oversight of which is entrusted upon the independent ECB, which shall remain beyond direct political influences and largely escapes parliamentary control.[61]

Under the EU Treaty, the limited role of the European Parliament reflects and underlines the intergovernmental orientation of the second and third pillars. This applies to domestic decision-making and external representation alike and it is therefore not surprising that Articles 24 and 38 EU on the conclusion of international agreements do not foresee the involvement of MEPs. The Member States have not been willing to give the supranational European institutions more control in their international relations, which illustrates their desire to maintain their ultimate sovereignty as original subjects of international law.[62] Moreover, agreements in the field of CFSP and the European Security and Defence Policy (ESDP) usually do not affect the position of individuals and may therefore not be qualified as

---

After Nice: Sisyphus Would Have Done a Better Job' (2002) 39 *CML Rev* 7, 25: insofar as Art 133(6)(2) and Bosse-Platière, above n 9, 533.

[58] Eeckhout, above n 30, 188.

[59] Cf on the relevant provisions of the Constitutional Treaty M Cremona, 'The Draft Constitutional Treaty: External Relations and External Action' (2003) 40 *CML Rev* 1348, 1364, M Krajewski, 'External Trade Law and the Constitution Treaty' (2005) 42 *CML Rev* 91, 124 and B de Witte, 'The Constitutional Law of External Relations' in I Pernice and M Poiares Maduro (eds), *A Constitution for Europe. First Comments on the 2003 Draft Constitution for Europe* (Baden-Baden, Nomos, 2003) 95, 105: 'quite remarkable change'.

[60] On the unclear scope of Community competence see J-V Louis, 'Les relations extérieures de l'Union économique et monétaire' in Cannizzaro, above n 40, 77–104.

[61] Cf P Leino, 'The European Central Bank and Legitimacy: Is the ECB a Modification of or an Exception to the Principle of Democracy?' Harvard Jean Monnet Working Paper 1/01, 30–1.

[62] E Denza, *The Intergovernmental Pillars of the European Union* (New York, Oxford University Press, 2002) 19.

being legislative in character.[63] In contrast, international agreements concluded under the third pillar, such as the EU–US extradition agreement,[64] mandate state action within a core area of legislative activity whose exercise usually requires parliamentary involvement. The exclusion of the European Parliament from these areas is therefore regrettable. It should, however, be noted that national parliaments continue to exercise at least a rudimentary control function in these cases. The EU treaty-making practice shows that most agreements have been scrutinised by national parliaments after the signature and before ratification on the basis of the national constitutional scrutiny reserve of Article 24(5) EU.[65] This might not be an ideal solution, but guarantees at least formal control powers for parliamentarians in areas which directly affect the rights of individuals.

III. MIXITY: ROLE OF NATIONAL PARLIAMENTS

National parliaments have a double control function in European international relations: first, they hold their respective national governments to account for their actions within the Council; second, they exercise the original parliamentary rights regarding the autonomous foreign policy of the Member States. Since neither the European Community nor the European Union has an all-embracing 'federal' competence for foreign affairs, exercise of the national and European foreign policy powers are inherently interwoven at the international level. The infamous mixed agreements are the most renowned expression of this complementary parallelism.[66] Despite the widespread dislike of mixed agreements for their blurring of the separation of powers between the Community and its Member States, they have proved surprisingly resilient in practice and have long dominated the treaty-making practice of the Community and its Member States.[67] Indeed, mixity may positively be regarded as a tool to

---

[63] H-J Cremer, 'Anmerkungen zur GASP' (2004) 31 *Europäische Grundrechte-Zeitschrift* 587, 589–90.

[64] Agreement on extradition between the European Union and the United States of America ([2003] OJ L/181/27).

[65] See the analysis of the recent treaty-making practice in D Thym, 'Die völkerrechtlichen Verträge der Europäischen Union' (2006) 66 *Heidelberg Journal of International Law / Zeitschrift für ausländisches öffentliches Recht und Völkerrecht* 863, 889–98 and 905–8 (available online at http://www.zoerv.de two years after print publication).

[66] On mixed agreements Eeckhout, above n 30, 190–223, Koutrakos, above n 15, 150–82 and the classic collection by D O'Keeffe and H Schermers (eds), *Mixed Agreements* (The Hague, Kluwer, 1983).

[67] *Cf* Cremona, above n 2, 154; a survey of recent EC treaty-making practice indicates that mixed agreements are losing their momentum: B de Witte, 'The Emergence of a European System of Public International Law: the EU and its Member States as Strange Subjects' in E de Wet, A Nollkaemper and J Wouters (eds), *The Europeanisation of Public International Law* (2007), section 3, forthcoming.

protect Member States' legitimate interests and autonomy by preventing a gradual usurpation of their external competences by the Community without weakening the strength inherent in united action.[68] From the point of view of parliamentary accountability, they prominently involve the national parliaments in the ratification.

Against this background, recent developments in Brussels deserve our particular attention, since they call into question the long-established practice of the joint conclusion of mixed agreements by the Community and the Member States, thereby also challenging the corresponding prerogatives of national parliaments. The issue first surfaced between the autumn of 2005 and the spring of 2006 on the occasion of the negotiations for a new partnership and cooperation agreement with Thailand,[69] and most recently in relation to the potential accession of the European Union to the ASEAN Treaty of Amity and Cooperation (TAC).[70] In both cases it was not the substance of the agreement that caused a protracted inter-institutional debate, but the question of whether, and if so under what circumstances, the European Union should be a party to the agreement on the basis of Article 24 EU.[71] The motivation underlying some of the options discussed links the debate directly back to the role of national parliaments, whose necessary involvement in the ratification procedures of mixed agreements regularly entails a long waiting period before the entry into force of any mixed agreements. This waiting period is even longer now with the involvement of an increased number of Member States following the recent enlargements.[72]

To this author's knowledge, four options have been discussed within the Relex working group of the Council, the Political and Security Committee (PSC) and Coreper with a view to the Thai case: (1) the conclusion of a cross-pillar mixed agreement between the EC and the EU following the example of the agreement between the EC, the EU and Switzerland on the latter's association with the Schengen *acquis*; (2) the conclusion of separate agreements, legally connected by means of a joint declaration, between Thailand on the one side and the EC and the EU on the other side; (3) the conclusion of a traditional mixed agreement between the EC, the Member

---

[68] As proposed by JHH Weiler, 'The External Legal Relations of Non-Unitary Actors: Mixity and the Federal Principle' in JHH Weiler, *The Constitution of Europe* (Cambridge, Cambridge University Press, 1999) 185.

[69] On the political background see the Communication from the Commission: A New Strategic Partnership with South East Asia, COM(2003) 399 final.

[70] The political context is described in the Chairman's Statement of the Sixth Asia-Europe Meeting, Helsinki, 10 and 11 September 2006, Council doc of 12 Sep 2006 12775/06 (Press 253; publicly accessible).

[71] For EU agreements under Art 24 EU see above, Section 2.B.

[72] Notwithstanding the option of provisional application or the conclusion of an interim agreement covering only fields of Community competence, which is then concluded without Member State participation.

States and Thailand; (4) a novel tripartite mixed agreement between the EC, the EU, the Member States and Thailand.[73] Obviously, only options (3) and (4) would maintain a genuine role for the Member States and their parliaments, while options (1) and (2) would imply a fundamental conceptual reorientation of the constitutional law of European international relations. For the time being, Germany and the United Kingdom have resisted the pressure from the Council Secretariat, the Commission and many Member States to agree to option (1) or (2), with the eventual compromise of selecting the last option of EC, EU and (optional) Member State participation.[74]

Legally, the usual treaty provisions on political dialogue argue for the inclusion of the European Union as a separate party to future partnership and cooperation agreements. This participation, however, is not mandatory, if one maintains that no competences have been transferred to the European Union within the intergovernmental second pillar, thereby excluding the application of the supranational AETR doctrine and the pre-emption of national competences.[75] But if the Union fully replaced the Member States as a party to most mixed agreements under options (1) or (2) mentioned above, it would not only cover the political dialogue clauses, but rather all Member State competences under the current mixed agreements. While their reach is notoriously difficult to define, it remains doubtful, from a dogmatic perspective, whether the EU competences under the second and third pillars would extend to all areas covered by partnership and cooperation agreements beyond the reach of the EC Treaty.[76] Besides these dogmatic caveats, the principled departure from the long-standing tradition of Member State participation raises the conceptual question of the character of national and European international relations.

The replacement of the Member States by the European Union in mixed agreements would be an important step along the federalising avenue, further limiting Member States' independence in their international relations as a precondition for their sovereignty in the era of advanced Europeanisation.[77] The widespread frustration with tardy ratification procedures in national parliaments for most mixed agreements is certainly understandable and it is probably also correct that national parliaments do

---

[73]   See on Thailand: Council docs 12798/05, 14093/05, 9288/06 and 9745/06 and on the ASEAN TAC: Council doc 13384/06 (all not publicly accessible).

[74]   *Cf* the Draft Council authorisation, Council doc 16042/06 (not publicly accessible).

[75]   For more details on this question see Thym, above n 65, 900–12.

[76]   What about potential treaty provision on culture, education, health or any other policy where the EC Treaty lays down rather strict limits on EC competence?

[77]   See Denza, above n 62, 19 and C Hillgruber, 'Der Nationalstaat in der überstaatlichen Verflechtung' in J Isensee and P Kirchhof (eds), *Handbuch des Staatsrechts, Band II* (3rd ed, Heidelberg, CF Müller, 2004), ch 32 para 91.

not even exercise their constitutional scrutiny powers in practice, effectively nodding through most mixed agreements without substantive scrutiny or debate. But from a theoretical perspective, the continued practice of mixed agreements, with their genuine role for national parliaments, is an important expression of Europe's principled ambiguity between federal- and con-federalism, which not even the Constitutional Treaty would have altered.[78] Against this background, the continued participation of the Member States and their parliaments in mixed agreements is an important expression of the unique character of European international relations, with complementary roles for the Community, the Union and the Member States based on cooperation instead of subordination.

IV. DIPLOMACY

The development of European foreign policy during the past 35 years has rightly been described as a process of legalisation or judicialisation, whereby foreign policy formulation has been gradually integrated into formalised standards of behaviour and is ultimately subject to judicial review.[79] Indeed, the experience of external Community policies suggests that the treaties' institutional rules are an important framework and catalyst for the progressive realisation of common policies.[80] Conceptually, this extends to the development of the Community's external powers based upon the 'parallelism paradigm', which construes Europe's role in the world as the other side of its internal development.[81] The success of the Community method over the past 50 years argues strongly for its extension to most areas of Union activity, including foreign affairs. But a closer look at the constitutional role of the European Parliament in the CFSP reveals a continuous special treatment. Here, the role of the European Parliament lags even further behind its already limited involvement in international treaty-making. This does not imply that the MEPs are powerless, but their channels of influence are much more indirect, centred on their influence on

[78] The European Convention considered a codification of the practice of mixed agreements (see the Final Report of Working Group III 'Legal Personality', 1 Oct 2002, CONV doc 305/02, paras 22–8), but eventually decided to continue the present silence of the primary law; de Witte, *supra* note 59, 101 contrasts this silence with the elaborate provisions of Art III–227 ConstEU (formerly Art 300 EC) on the conclusion of international EC agreements.

[79] See the analytical account by M Smith, *Europe's Common Foreign and Security Policy* (Cambridge, Cambridge University Press, 2004) and, similarly his 'Diplomacy by Decree: The Legalization of Foreign Policy' (2001) 39 *JCMS* 79.

[80] On domestic EC policies the classic standpoint by A Stone Sweet, *The Judicial Construction of Europe* (Oxford, Oxford University Press, 2004).

[81] *Cf* Case C–22/70 *AETR* [1971] ECR 263 and the analysis of the Court's case law by Cremona, above n 2, 138–52.

the relevant executive actors, the tentative projection of a genuine 'parliamentary diplomacy' and budgetary control powers, which shall be the subject of scrutiny in this section.

I suggest that the special institutional structure of the CFSP does not contradict the supranational structure of Community integration, but complements it with a sector-specific adaptation. The CFSP, much less than the external policies of the first pillar, is dominated by rule-making. Instead, foreign policy and international relations are by their nature strategic. They require the identification of strategic goals and the development and constant adaptation of methods of their realisation and implementation. The Community method is characterised by the adoption of legal rules at European level, their transposition and implementation by the Member States and uniform interpretation by the courts. But foreign policy is primarily about political positioning in favour of or against something. As mentioned at the outset, North Korea will not give up its nuclear weapons only because the European Union says so in its Official Journal. Foreign policy requires strategic thinking through the development and adaptation of political goals and methods for their realisation. One may call it diplomacy, but in any case it differs substantially from domestic politics. Moreover, the limited foreign policy resources of the European Union, besides the financial and human resources of the Community budget and administration, calls for the integration of the experiences, contacts and clout of national foreign ministries and the hardware of national military and civilian personnel for ESDP missions, leaving a definite sphere of influence for national parliaments.

A. Formal Control Powers

Article 21 EU upholds the intergovernmental nature of the CFSP by limiting the involvement of the European Parliament to being 'regularly informed' and 'consulted on the main aspects and basic choices' of the CFSP—with an additional obligation of the Council Presidency to 'ensure that the views of the European Parliament are duly taken into account'. It should be noted that these information and consultation rights do not cover individual common positions or joint actions, but only the 'main aspects and basic choices', thereby trailing behind the consultation procedure under the first pillar as the standard case for the conclusion of international agreements under Article 300(2) EC. It should also be noted that the European Parliament maintains that it should generally be informed about future projects and was considering a legal challenge before the Council agreed to forward-looking reporting in 2006.[82] Leaving aside the outcome of this renewed inter-institutional quarrel, the Parliament's general exclusion from individual CFSP measures is not coincidental, but is rather the deliberate choice of various IGCs which have consciously refrained from extending parliamentary oversight. The present 'parliamentary vacuum' dates back to the Single European Act, which already contained a corresponding provision and kept the adoption of individual foreign policy decisions beyond the Parliament's reach.[83]

Not even the entry into force of the Lisbon Treaty would change much in this respect, since it continues the custom of almost exclusive deliberation and decision-making in the Council without direct parliamentary participation.[84] Rather surprisingly, not even the Convention's working group on external action, with its primarily parliamentary composition, proposed substantial changes; it concluded that the present rules 'were satisfactory'.[85] Anticipatory obedience towards the presumed wishes of the ultimate decision-makers in the IGC may have played a role in this respect, with the Convention trying to avoid any proposal which might have served as a pretext for the IGC to depart substantially from its draft; but the parallel extension of the parliamentary consent requirement to international agreements indicates that the EP's consistent exclusion from the CFSP over the past 20 years is also based on underlying conceptual considerations.[86] Indeed, the European Convention refrained from any substantive 'supranationalisation' of the CFSP and focused on practical arrangements through the merger of both the pillars and the executive functions of the Commission and the Council, while maintaining the specificity of its competences, procedural rules and legal instruments.[87]

---

[82] Cf the Report on the Main Aspects and Basic Choices of CFSP (Rapporteur: Elmar Brok), 1 Dec 2005, EP doc A6–0389/2005, para 2 and the explanatory statement. The Treaty does not specify whether the information and consultation on major developments in the field of CFSP under Art 21 TEU concerns *past* actions or *future* projects. The 2006 IIA now foresees a regular *a priori* consultation in line with the Parliament's demands; see section 4.B below.

[83] Art 30(4) of the Single European Act and the additional Decision of the Foreign Ministers of the Member States meeting within the European Political Cooperation on the Occasion of the Signature of the Single European Act on 28 February 1986 already comprised the features of the present Art 21 TEU, which is identical with Maastricht's Art J.7 EU.

[84] Art 24(1), 36 TFEU-Lisbon officially extend parliamentary consultation to defence policy, establish the foreign minister as the institutional interface between Council and Parliament and double the number of general debates.

[85] Recommendation 10 of Working Group VII 'External Action', Final Report, 16 Dec 2002, doc CONV 459/02.

[86] On various proposals to strengthen the parliamentary oversight in the CFSP see J Mittag, 'Die Parlamentarische Dimension der ESVP: Optionen für den Verfassungsvertrag' (2003) 26 *Integration* 152, 157–60 and D Thym, 'Reforming Europe's Common Foreign and Security Policy' (2004) 10 *ELJ* 5, 13–15.

[87] Cf de Witte, above n 59, 97–9, Cremona, above n 59, 1352–9 and Thym, above n 86, 6–8.

Parliamentary accountability of governmental action does of course transcend involvement in the decision-making process. Indeed, the primary elective function and the secondary control powers culminating in the right to recall the government or its ministers through a motion of censure are crucial components of parliamentary accountability of executive actors.[88] The political dramas over the departure of the Santer Commission and the nomination of the Barroso Commission are good illustrations of the effectiveness of the Parliament's powers vis-a-vis the Commission in this respect. Regarding the CFSP, the Commission's limited role as an associate actor within the CFSP under Article 27 EU, however, entails a corresponding weakness of the Parliament's elective and control functions—even though the Commissioner for external relations, Benita Ferrero-Waldner, promised to 'develop the closest possible working relations with the EP' and 'to pay very careful attention to all observations and recommendations of the EP [in the field of CFSP]' during her nomination hearing in the EP.[89] Instead, the Parliament will set its sights on the control of the CFSP executive dominated by the Council's Secretary-General and CFSP High Representative (SG/HR) and the respective Council Presidency.

Javier Solana, the current SG/HR, however, evades parliamentary scrutiny as far as his election and possible recall is concerned. His appointment was by unanimous decision of the Council, in accordance with Article 207(2) EC, without prior consultation of the EP, let alone requiring that its consent mirror the Commission investiture. The EP's Rules of Procedure may self-consciously foresee a hearing of the candidate designate, but his renomination in June 2004 and identification as future EU Minister for Foreign Affairs took place behind the closed doors of the Council's Justus Lipsius building, frustrating the Parliament's expectation of influence.[90] Interestingly, the IGC which drafted the final version of the Constitutional Treaty even detached the institutional fate of the future minister for foreign affairs from the political survival of the Commission by making clear that only the European Council, not the Parliament, may officially end its tenure as far as the 'CFSP hat' is concerned, even if the minister for foreign affairs must lay down his or her Community hat as Commissioner for external relations after a successful motion of censure by the EP.[91] This exclusion of parliamentary appointment and recall powers extends to EU special representatives and heads of Commission delegations, where both

---

[88] Cf Dann, above n 34, 557–61 and Harlow, above n 41, 94–6.

[89] See her answers to the general question no 7 and the specific question no 4 in deliberate avoidance of the promise to act as a spokesperson for the EP's CFSP proposals in the Council, online at http://www.europarl.eu.int/press/audicom2004/index_en.htm.

[90] See Art 85 of the EP's Rules of Procedure in contrast to the Council Press Release on the meeting of Heads of State or Government on 29 June 2004, Council doc 10995/04.

[91] Art I–26(7), I–28(1) ConstEU and Art 18(1) TEU-Lisbon; on the 'double-hatted' structure of the foreign minister Thym, above n 86, 18–22.

the Council and the Commission reject the EP's call for the introduction of appointment hearings reflecting US-style senatorial hearings of future ambassadors.[92]

Of course, the absence of parliamentary participation in the nomination procedure for the SG/HR and other senior CFSP personnel does not exclude regular contact and debate, be it on the basis of the Parliament's information and consultation rights under Article 21 EU or through voluntary cooperation schemes. During the fifth legislature from 1999–2004 the SG/HR Solana attended 10 meetings of the Committee on Foreign Affairs AFET (French acronym for *affaires étrangères*), including a high-profile debate on the draft European Security Strategy, and complemented these meetings with 11 appearances before the EP plenary. Moreover, the former Commissioner for External Relations, Christopher Patten, appeared 22 times before the AFET, national foreign or defence ministers attended on 54 occasions and EU Special Representatives eight times. A closer look at the frequency of hearings and debates shows increased activities towards the end of the legislature, signalling a reinforced focus on the CFSP. This trend will be further enhanced by the creation of a new AFET Sub-Committee for Security and Defence (SEDE). Even though the MEPs only officially hold information and consultation rights, the regularity of debate ideally results in effective scrutiny through intensity,[93] although the exact degree of influence is of course difficult to measure.

B. Budgetary Blackmail?

Budgetary powers are the European Parliament's only 'hard powers' in the CFSP. According to Article 28 EU, administrative CFSP expenditure shall be charged to the EC budget, while the Council may decide to finance operative expenditure by alternative means, in particular national contributions. It is not surprising that the EP tried to use its budgetary prerogatives as a leverage for more influence on CFSP decision-making. It has indeed obtained some minor improvements as the result of a protracted quarrel with the Council in the 1990s.[94] In 1997, the Parliament,

---

[92] Art 86 of the EP's Rules of Procedure foresees a hearing of EU Special Representatives in contrast to Art 18(5) EU; Commissioner Ferrero-Waldner rejected the EP's plea for parliamentary hearings of the heads of Commission delegations in her answer to specific question no 3, above n 89.

[93] Various commentators underline the importance of parliamentary influence on ministers through personal contact and debate, eg Denza, above n 77, 323–4, J Mittag, 'Escaping the Legitimacy-Accountability-Trap?', ZEI Discussion Paper C161 2006, 17–18 and U Diedrichs, 'The European Parliament in CFSP: More than a Marginal Player?', The International Spectator 2/2004, 36–8.

[94] See J Monar, 'The Finances of the Union's Intergovernmental Pillars—Tortuous Experiments with the Community Budget' (1997) 35 *JCMS* 57, E Dardenne, 'Le Parlement européen

the Council and the Commission signed an inter-institutional agreement (IIA) on the issue, which was later integrated into the 1999 IIA on the last financial perspective. On both occasions, the Parliament conceded modest financial resources for the CFSP in return for a reinforcement of its information rights.[95] In 2002 and 2003, the rapid realisation of the ESDP and the corresponding calls for an increase of the CFSP budget caused renewed inter-institutional tensions, with the European Parliament obtaining further minimal concessions from the Council.[96] Most recently, the IIA of 17 May 2006 on the next financial perspective codified and further extended the Parliament's respective powers. The MEPs are still not consulted before the adoption of individual CFSP measures, but are promised a 'forward-looking Council document' on the main aspects and basic choices of the CFSP as well as regular joint consultation meetings at least five times a year in the framework of the regular political dialogue on the CFSP.[97]

In return for the consolidation of its information and consolidation rights, the Parliament agreed to a considerable increase in the CFSP budget.[98] However, the CFSP budget will still amount to only 3.5 per cent of the EC's overall budget for external action, reflecting the way in which the external EC policies with the corresponding institutional prerogatives of the Parliament remain the financial backbone of European foreign policy.[99] Arguably, this indirect financial weakening of the CFSP to the benefit of external Community policies, with a potential thematic overlap with the CFSP, is the main success of the EP's budgetary power game.[100] Within the CFSP, however, the Parliament's 'democratic blackmail' provoked counter-reactions by the Council. Being frustrated with the tardy and scarce flow of financial resources, the Council reinforced extra-budgetary means of financing, in particular through recourse to separate national contributions (for instance, for the European Defence Agency)

---

et le financement de la PESC' in M Dony (ed), *L'Union européenne et le monde après Amsterdam* (Université libre de Bruxelles, 1999), 291–313, R Wessel, *The European Union's Foreign and Security Policy* (The Hague, Kluwer Law, 1999) 220–3 and Maurer, Kietz and Völkel, above n 16, 175–95.

[95] See points 39–40 of the 1999 IIA, [1999] OJ C/172/1, and its analysis in Thym, above n 17, 114–15; the 1997 IIA may be found in [1997] OJ C/286/80.

[96] More details in Thym, above n 95, 115–16.

[97] Cf point 43 of the 2006 IIA, [2006] OJ C/139/1.

[98] Point 42 of the 2006 IIA, *ibid*, foresees at least €250 million per annum on average, considerably more than the €63 million in 2005.

[99] Annex 1 to the 2006 IIA, *ibid*, apportions €49,463 million for 2007–13 to the budget heading 'EU as a Global Player'.

[100] The adoption of the EC policies on the promotion of human rights and democracy is an excellent example of the Commission and the Parliament using the financial muscle to extend their reach to areas which had temporarily become important fields of CFSP activities; cf I Pernice and D Thym, 'A New Institutional Balance for European Foreign Policy?' (2002) 7 *EFA Rev* 369, 387.

and new budgetary Union instruments (such as the ATHENA mechanism for military operations).[101] Arguably, the European Parliament's financial 'greed' even played a role in the decision of the European Convention and the subsequent IGC not to extend the Parliament's formal powers in the CFSP. A closer look at Article III–313(3) ConstEU and Article 41(3) TEU-Lisbon reveals that the new Constitutional Treaty even limits the Parliament's budgetary powers by granting the Council a right of unilateral recourse to the EC budget without parliamentary veto rights for 'urgent financing of (CFSP) initiatives'.

C. Projection of 'Parliamentary Diplomacy'

No constitutional document is set in stone, but evolves dynamically in the course of time. Foreign policy is no exception in this respect. Indeed, the European Parliament has always played a genuine role in foreign policy independently of its information, consultation and control rights under the EC and the EU Treaties. Its effective use of regular dialogue with the political actors of the CFSP, such as Javier Solana, is a primary illustration of its attempt to reach beyond its formal powers.[102] Its impact on the real world is reinforced, moreover, by the projection of a tentative 'parliamentary diplomacy' in its own right through the public debate of important foreign policy developments and periodic contact with representatives of third countries and international organisations. For third-country politicians, media representatives and citizens who are not fully aware of the idiosyncrasies of the EU's institutional balance, with its asymmetric distribution of parliamentary powers in different policy areas, the influence of the European Parliament in foreign policy issues is arguably even more accentuated.

Indeed, a closer survey of the Parliament's activities during the past legislature shows numerous senior representatives of third states and international organisations appearing before the EP plenary or exchanging their political views with AFET. The Parliament's guests include the NATO Secretary-General on three occasions, the UN High Commissioner for Human Rights and the President of the International Criminal Court. On 26 October 2006, the annual Sakharov Prize for Freedom of Thought was awarded to Alexander Milinkevich, leader of the political opposition in

---

[101] Thym, above n 17, 116–17 for more details.
[102] See section IV.A above.

Belarus.[103] Mirroring diplomatic relations in the narrow sense, the inter-parliamentary delegations even constitute a genuine element of 'parliamentary diplomacy', in the context of which MEPs feel free to voice their opinions plainly without being constrained by diplomatic customs or the prior, and often cumbersome, alignment of national positions in the Council. The 'Taiwan policy' of the EP is a telling example in this respect.[104]

Any citizen or journalist visiting the AFET website will come across the Parliament's various policy reports, which covered Europe's strategic relations with all important international actors in 2006: Russia, China, the US and Latin America.[105] Legally speaking, most of these reports are own-initiative reports and therefore not part of a formal consultation procedure.[106] One may thus speak of a 'virtual' parliamentary foreign policy, since AFET reports on CFSP-related policy topics are not officially linked to Council decision making. In practice, however, the foreign policy positions of the Parliament carry the weight of its institutional legitimacy.[107] They may be considered by civil servants in the Council Secretariat, national foreign ministers and the Commission's directorates-general dealing with external relations. In this way, they have an indirect impact on CFSP decision making. Parliament's influence in the real world is further increased by the publicity of its debates and the easy electronic accessibility of its reports, which contrasts with the 'secretive' decision making in the Council. Thus, 'parliamentary diplomacy' may in reality reach further than the rules of the European Treaties suggest.

D. Defence: Cooperation with National Parliaments

From a traditional intergovernmentalist standpoint, the persistent limitations of the role of the European Parliament in foreign policy follow the intergovernmental integration logic, which regards national parliaments as being better positioned to scrutinise national foreign ministers on the basis

---

[103] On the development of the EP's 'human rights diplomacy' see Smith, above n 79, 171 and Bieber, above n 36, 166–7.

[104] See the case study by Y Lan, 'The European Parliament and the China-Taiwan Issue: An Empirical Approach' (2004) 9 *EFA Rev* 115.

[105] Online at http://www.europarl.europa.eu/committees/afet_home_en.htm. Mittag, above n 93, 18–20 and Diedrichs, above n 93, 36–8 underline the influence of quality reports.

[106] Own initiative reports are not explicitly foreseen in the Treaty and one might argue from the strict point of view of delegated powers that these reports have no legal base, but it is nowadays accepted that such autonomous initiatives fall within the wider political responsibilities of the EP; cf Hilf/Schorkopf, above n 51, 197–8.

[107] As emphasised by de Witte, above n 59, 104 and T Grunert, 'Die verfassungsvertragliche Rolle der Organe der Europäischen Union in den Außenbeziehungen' in P-C Müller-Graff (ed), *Die Rolle der erweiterten Europäischen Union in der Welt* (Baden-Baden, Nomos, 2006) 25, 32.

of their respective constitutional control powers.[108] But even if one does not subscribe to this argument in general, the present treaty regime clearly follows the intergovernmental path in questions of 'war and peace' related to the realisation of the ESDP. Here, the exclusion of the European Parliament is at least partly compensated by national parliamentary prerogatives for the deployment of military personnel in many Member States.[109] In ESDP, national parliamentary powers are particularly effective, since the general public will usually pay close attention to any parliamentary debate and, moreover, the launch of an ESDP mission does not legally prejudge the autonomous national decision (not) to second military personnel, since any rejection by a national parliament does not block the mission as long as other Member States provide sufficient troops.

National parliaments also retain the primary responsibility over national defence spending which remains outside the realm of the EC budget under Article 28(3) EU—even if the reinforced coordination of public defence procurement and armaments policy at European level through the European Armament Organization (OCCAR) and the European Defence Agency (EDA) constrains the practical autonomy of national parliaments which are confronted with intergovernmental defence deals that may not be legally binding on them but nonetheless exercise pressure to pay the bill in order not to stand in the way of the joint undertaking.[110] In exercising their control functions, national parliaments may of course agree on various forms of horizontal and vertical cooperation with the parliaments of other Member States and the European Parliament, building upon the cooperation among national European affairs committees in the Conference of Community and European Affairs Committees of Parliaments of the European Union (COSAC).[111] But eventually their combined influence will legally not transcend their cumulative powers under the European treaties and the national constitutions.

---

[108] See amongst others A Moravcsik, 'Reassessing Legitimacy in the European Union' in Weiler, Begg and Peterson, above n 55, 77–98 and with a view to the second pillar Denza, above n 77, 325.

[109] For more details see Thym, above n 17, 121–3.

[110] On the protracted procurement of the A400M military transport aircraft, where the governments of Germany and Portugal in particular agreed to the purchase of more aircraft than the national parliaments were willing to finance see again Thym, above n 109, 122.

[111] As foreseen by Art 10 of the Protocol (No 1) on the Role of National Parliaments annexed to the ConstEU; for COSAC see online at http://www.cosac.eu.

V. CONCEPTUAL FOUNDATIONS OF EU INTERNATIONAL RELATIONS

The special treatment of the European Parliament in Europe's international relations is an important indicator for the underlying conceptual specificities of the constitutional fundamentals of European foreign affairs. Its limited role in the negotiation, conclusion and evolution of international agreements and the wide executive prerogatives in non-contractual international diplomacy stand in obvious contrast to the Parliament's empowerment in domestic European policies in recent years. Why did the Parliament not become an equal player in inter-institutional decision making in foreign affairs? Based on the preceding analysis of the Parliament's role in the different categories of external action, this section focuses on the conceptual foundations of the role of the European Parliament in the European foreign policy constitution. Its origins are either specific to the European model of government as laid down in the European Treaties or reflect the abstract character of international relations in general terms. This section, as a sketch of ideas flowing from the analysis of the Parliament's constitutional powers, makes no claim to completeness.

As mentioned at the outset, the argument regarding the parliamentary accountability of foreign affairs continues, from a historical perspective, the struggle between the ancient prerogatives of the monarch and the novel claims for democratic self-governance. In the 19th century, greater parliamentary involvement in foreign affairs indeed implied an enhancement of democratic legitimacy to the detriment of hereditary monarchy. This led many observers to the conclusion that only an unlimited parliamentary hold over foreign affairs completes the process of democratisation.[112] But this correlation is not imperative. The dual claims for legitimacy underlying the monarchic-parliamentary stand-off have given way to a uniform democratic justification of public authority, at least in Europe. Parliamentarians may well be more directly linked back to citizens, but the executive agents in the Council and the Commission are nonetheless democratically elected and controlled—independently of how we position ourselves in the dispute over the democratic legitimacy of the different European institutions.[113] Enhancing the role of the European Parliament in foreign affairs may therefore entail a strengthening of democratic legitimacy, but its continued limitation to the contrary no longer implies undemocratic

---

[112]   See in the German context the famous dispute between W Grewe and E Menzel in 'Die auswärtige Gewalt der Bundesrepublik' (1954) 12 *Veröffentlichungen der Vereinigung deutscher Staatsrechtslehrer* 129.

[113]   With the intergovernmentalist standpoint arguing that the Council, not the European Parliament, enjoys greater democratic legitimacy through its direct integration in our national political systems; cf above n 108.

standards. The argument about parliamentary involvement in foreign affairs is therefore not only about democratic legitimacy, but also about the effective exercise and control of state functions.

In this respect, the European situation does not differ from the national context where the same arguments underlie the limited role of most national parliaments in foreign policy. The example of Germany and Italy deserve particular attention in this respect, since both countries redrafted their constitutions after the traumatic experience of the Nazi and fascist periods in a deliberate attempt to establish the institutional foundation of a viable democracy; they refrained from a widespread parliamentarisation of foreign affairs.[114] In the same vein, the new constitutions of the Central and Eastern European states following the fall of the Berlin Wall have not embraced a full-scale parliamentarisation of foreign policy.[115] Of course, a rough comparative survey of positive constitutional rules does not give any definitive answers about the underlying constitutional concepts for foreign relations, but it nonetheless indicates that the European model follows the constitutional mainstream. At the same time, the variety of detailed rules on the role of parliaments in foreign affairs shows that the common thread of limited parliamentary involvement does not translate into an institutional blueprint which the European Union might follow indiscriminately.[116] Instead, the EU also needs to develop its specific and unique inter-institutional system and the respective provisions of the Treaty have to be interpreted autonomously.[117]

The preceding analysis has shown that the EU's specific constitutional model of parliamentary involvement in foreign affairs laid down in the European treaties is the result of recurring debates. Various IGCs and the European Convention deliberately refrained from a substantial enhancement of parliamentary powers in foreign affairs, in obvious contrast to its continued empowerment in domestic policy areas. As a result, both Article 300 EC on the conclusion of international agreements and Article 24 EU on the CFSP maintain a decidedly executive orientation (Sections 2 and 4 above). Similarly, the Parliament's attempt to change the institutional practice in its favour has largely been unsuccessful despite repeated

---

[114] For Germany, the historic *Menzel v Grewe* dispute, *ibid*, and, most recently, C Calliess, 'Auswärtige Gewalt' in Isensee and Kirchhof, above n 77, 589.

[115] See the comparative survey of judicial control with corollary remarks on parliamentary accountability by T Giegerich, 'Verfassungsgerichtliche Kontrolle der auswärtigen Gewalt im europäisch-atlantischen Verfassungsstaat' (1997) 57 *ZaöRV* 409, available online at http://www.zaoerv.de.

[116] See again the study by Riesenfeld and Abbott, above n 20.

[117] Case C–189/97 *Parliament v Council* [1999] ECR I–4741, para 34 rejects the argument of a wide interpretation of the EP's powers under the present Art 300(3) EC, whose interpretation cannot 'be affected by the extent of the powers available to national parliaments.'

endeavours to get a foot in the negotiation room of international agreements and use its budgetary powers as a leverage to be involved in the elaboration of the CFSP (Sections 2.A.1 and 4.C). Generally speaking, these developments show that the 'parallelism paradigm' of EU external relations does not extend to the institutional involvement of the European Parliament. As lawyers, we have to accept this constitutional status quo as a legal fact of life—whether we like it or not.

I suggest that there is a conceptual logic underlying the current constitutional role of the European Parliament in EU international relations—even if many treaty rules and the pillar structure are the result of political compromises rather than the realisation of a constitutional master plan.[118] More specifically, we should complement the 'parallelism paradigm' which continues to dominate the academic analysis of EU external relations and embed Europe's foreign policy constitution into the international context. The international relations of the European Union are no mere continuation of its internal integration process, projecting its domestic competences, procedures and integration method towards the external dimension. Instead, analysis of the treaty provisions on parliamentary involvement in Europe's international relations illustrates the need to combine the internal perspective with the external viewpoint. Parliament's role in foreign affairs constitution combines the constitutional essentials of Europe's domestic system of government with the requirements of the laws and customs of international relations. In this respect, Parliament's role in foreign affairs is a generic expression of the constitutional fundamentals of Europe's foreign affairs.

Four findings of the preceding analysis support this argument. First, the treaty rules governing the negotiation, conclusion and evolution of international agreements repeatedly take into account the customs of diplomatic relations and the evolutionary and practice-dominated features of the international law of treaties (Section 2.A). Second, foreign policy in general and the CFSP in particular are by nature strategic, much less dominated than domestic politics are by rule-making with the corresponding rights of parliaments (Section 4). Third, the realisation of the ESDP requires Union access to civilian and military personnel of the Member States, whose organisation and deployment remains a constitutional prerogative of the Member States, controlled primarily by national parliaments (Section 4.D). Eventually, the continued statehood of the Member States under international law argues for their authentic place at the international level beside and together with the widespread powers of the European Community—as illustrated by the maintenance of Member State participation in mixed agreements with genuine role for national parliaments (Section 3).

---

[118]   As remarked by de Witte, above n 56, 51.

My theses on the conceptual specificity of Europe's foreign affairs constitution are based on the current provisions of the European treaties. I do not imply that the Parliament's current constitutional status is or should be set in stone. The reform steps envisaged in the Lisbon Treaty indicate that there is room for change within the above-mentioned conceptual understanding of Europe's foreign affairs constitution.[119] Moreover, the international context itself is undergoing a fundamental transformation which might lead to a conceptual reassessment of parliamentary involvement in foreign affairs and eventually translate into new constitutional rules: international law, not only within the WTO, is increasingly effecting the position of individuals, reinforcing the call for more parliamentary accountability.[120] With the emergence of non-state actors, which facilitate a pluralist representation of public interests through parliamentary involvement, sovereign nation-states are losing their monopoly as the principal actors in international relations.[121] International law has abandoned its neutrality towards the internal system of government and the EU itself is actively promoting the spread of democracy, which again argues for more parliamentary rights in foreign affairs.[122] Europe's repeated call for 'effective multilateralism' might eventually also lead towards more parliamentary rights, effectively exporting some features of the European supranational model to the international level.[123]

VI. CONCLUSION

Europe's international relations continue the tradition of executive dominance in foreign affairs. The impressive empowerment of the European Parliament in domestic policies does not extend to the external activities of the European Union. Instead, repeated calls for an enhancement of parliamentary involvement have fallen on deaf ears. This is apparent in the

---

[119] Art 218 TFEU-Lisbon. See sections II.A and B.

[120] See R Uerpmann-Wittzack, 'The Constitutional Role of Multilateral Treaty Systems' in A von Bogdandy and J Bast (eds), *Principles of European Constitutional Law* (Oxford, Hart Publishing, 2006) 145; and E-U Petersmann, 'Human Rights in European and Global Integration Law: Principles for Constitutionalizing the World Economy' in Studies in Transnational Economic Law in Honour of Claus-Dieter Ehlermann (The Hague, Kluwer Law, 2002) 383.

[121] If national governments loose their former monopoly as primary agents of international relations through the increased importance of NGOs and multilateral companies, it becomes easier for national parliaments to complement the unitary position of the executive with pluralistic parliamentary debate.

[122] See de Witte, above n 59, 105 and P Eeckhout, *Does Europe's Constitution Stop at the Water's Edge? Law and Policy in the EU's External Relations* (Leuven, Europa Law Publishing, 2005), 4.

[123] Cremona, above n 2, 148 and L Azoulai, 'The Acquis of the European Union and International Organisations' (2005) 11 *ELJ* 196.

rules governing the negotiation, conclusion and evolution of international agreements, where the standard case of parliamentary involvement is limited to parliamentary consultation or consent under Article 300(3) EC. In obvious contrast to the parliamentary policy-shaping powers under the co-decision procedure, the diplomatic negotiation room remains closed for MEPs, whose options are limited to the binary rejection or approval of agreements. Evolutionary features of the international law of treaties, such as the suspension of rights or the adoption of implementing decisions, are even quite beyond the Parliament's reach, as are some policy areas such as the Common Commercial Policy. The Lisbon Treaty would not fundamentally reverse this picture of limited parliamentary involvement in international law making, despite some important new rights for the European Parliament.

Limited parliamentary involvement extends to the non-contractual 'diplomatic' dimension of foreign policy, which is particularly pronounced under the CFSP, with its almost complete exclusion of formal parliamentary oversight—this, however, is in practice complemented by the tentative projection of a genuine parliamentary diplomacy, with the European Parliament trying to influence foreign affairs as a foreign policy actor in its own right. Corresponding with the constitutional character of the European Union, national parliaments maintain a genuine function in European foreign affairs with regard to defence policy and the ratification of mixed agreements. Their maintenance should be welcomed as a principled expression of Europe's constitutional singularity, despite recent calls for their replacement by cross-pillar EU/EC agreements. The persistence of the special treatment of the European Parliament is an important indicator of the specificities of Europe's foreign affairs constitution. The EU's international relations are no mere continuation of its internal integration process, which projects its domestic integration method to the external dimension. Instead, an analysis of the Treaty provisions on parliamentary involvement illustrates the accommodation of Europe's domestic constitutional model with the requirements of the laws and customs of international relations.

8

Fundamental What? The Difficult Relationship between Foreign Policy and Fundamental Rights

ELEANOR SPAVENTA*

I. INTRODUCTION

IN THE PAST years we have witnessed an increased activity in the field of EU foreign policy. In particular, following the terrorist attacks in the United States first, and in Europe later, the EU has adopted a series of measures which directly affect individuals. In some instances, those measures were aimed at implementing Security Council resolutions which imposed sanctions on named individuals and/or alleged terrorist organisations; in other cases, following the general Security Council Resolution on terrorism,[1] the EU adopted its own measures. The 'fight against terror' has also led to an increased activity in the field of cooperation in the criminal sphere, and most notably in the adoption of the framework decision on terrorism and the framework decision on the arrest warrant.[2]

The increased activity in fields which affect individual rights raises important problems in relation to fundamental rights protection. In this

---

* Department of Law, Durham University, and Durham European Law Institute. I am grateful to Marise Cremona and Bruno de Witte for organising a very stimulating workshop and for their comments on an earlier version of this paper. I am also grateful to the other participants for a very lively and interesting discussion on these issues, and to Andrés Delgado Casteleiro for having very kindly brought to my attention the Spanish Supreme Court's ruling in the *Segi* case. The usual disclaimer applies.

[1] UN Security Council Resolution 1373(2001).

[2] Council Framework Decision on Combating Terrorism 2002/475/JHA, [2002] OJ L/164/3, and Council Framework Decision 2002/584/JHA on the European arrest warrant and the surrender procedure between Member States, [2002] OJ L/190/1. The latter measure has been the focus of much controversy with national courts clearly not being all that confident that it is consistent with fundamental rights; eg Case C–303/05 *Advocaten voor de Wereld v Council*, judgment of 5 May 2007, referred by the Belgian Court of Arbitration. See also the ruling by the German Constitutional Court, *Bundesverfassunsgericht*, 18/7/05, 2 BvR 2236/04.

respect, the EU shows a considerable degree of schizophrenia: on the one hand, it seeks to reassure its citizens, as well as its international partners, as to its sincere commitment to fundamental rights through the adoption of the Charter,[3] its action in the field of discrimination,[4] the creation of the fundamental rights agency,[5] as well as the considerable improvements that would have been introduced by the Constitutional Treaty.[6] On the other hand, the fundamental rights agency lacks powers in relation to cooperation in criminal matters and common and foreign security policy, the areas in which fundamental rights scrutiny would have been most needed and useful,[7] and, generally speaking, the Union seems incapable of ensuring even that minimum standard of protection required (from the Member States) by the European Convention on Human Rights. Nor should one consider this schizophrenia as simply the result of an inherent pathological condition stemming from the European Union's institutional and constitutional structure. After all, whilst it is true that the second and third pillars are ill-equipped to afford even a minimum level of democratic and judicial accountability, it is also true that action at Union level was not essential, and the Member States could have well refrained from using Union instruments until that moment in which a more healthy institutional structure had been put into place. And even should one consider that coordinated Member States' action would have not been sufficient and that therefore Union activity in these fields was an absolute necessity, it should be noted that there are instances, some of which will be examined in detail below, where the Union and (some) Member States could have chosen a different path to reach the same result, whilst being more respectful of both their citizens and their own constitutional obligations.

In this Chapter I will analyse some of these problems. In particular, after having given a brief account of the Union's institutional structure, I will analyse, from a fundamental rights perspective, the problems arising from the adoption of 'terrorist lists'. In this respect it is necessary to distinguish between the *Taliban* list,[8] which is of UN derivation and which does not

---

[3] [2000] OJ C/364/1, and amended version in Part II of the Constitutional Treaty, [2004] OJ C/310/1.

[4] Directive 2000/43 implementing the principle of equal treatment between persons irrespective of racial and ethnic origin, [2000] OJ L/180/22; Directive 2000/78 establishing a general framework for equal treatment in employment and occupation, [2000] OJ L/303/16.

[5] Regulation 168/2007 establishing a European Agency for Fundamental Rights [2007] OJ L/53/2.

[6] Eg the CT would have made the Charter legally binding; and would have extended the jurisdiction of the Court to the third pillar, as well as to CFSP action when such action affected individuals.

[7] In this respect, see the statement by the Italian Government concerning the Regulation establishing a European Agency for Fundamental Rights, Annex 6166/07, available on statewatch.org; www.statewatch.org/news/2007/feb/eu-hra-6166-07.pdf.

[8] Common Position 2002/402/CFSP concerning restrictive measures against Usama bin Laden, members of the Al-Qaeda organisation and the Taliban and other individuals, groups,

leave any discretion to the EU as to who should be included in the list, and the EU's own list.[9] The latter is further divided into two types of listing: foreign-linked alleged terrorists, and those alleged terrorists who do not have any link with outside the EU.[10] My overall conclusion is that we are witnessing a progressive erosion of the very guarantees that were at the foundation of post-war nation states, a result which is perhaps inevitable once concepts which are inherently political, and to a certain extent subjective, such as the definition of terrorism,[11] are transformed into objective and unquestionable legal 'truths' via the medium of international executive action.

II. THE EUROPEAN UNION'S INSTITUTIONAL STRUCTURE AND FUNDAMENTAL RIGHTS

Action in the field of Common and Foreign Security Policy is pursued through joint actions and common positions, whilst the general agenda is set through general guidelines and common strategies. Joint actions address specific situations and 'commit the Member States in the positions they adopt and in the conduct of their activity'.[12] Common positions, on the other hand, define the approach of the Union to 'a particular matter of a geographical or thematic nature'.[13] Unanimity is required for both instruments, although qualified majority is sufficient when the instrument is adopted on the basis of a common strategy. In any event, however, if a Member State opposes Union action for reasons of national policy, the instrument can be adopted only following a unanimous vote.[14] The role of the European Parliament is limited to the right to be consulted by the Presidency on the main aspects and basic choices concerning the CFSP. The

undertakings and entities associated with them and repealing Common Positions 96/746/ CFSP, 1999/727/CFSP, 2001/154/CFSP and 2001/771/CFSP, [2002] OJ L/169/4 (Hereinafter Common Position 2002/402, or the Anti-Taliban Common Position). The assets of those identified at UN level are frozen pursuant to Council Regulation 881/2002 imposing certain specific restrictive measures directed against certain persons and entities associated with Usama bin Laden, the Al-Qaeda network and the Taliban (...), [2002] OJ L/139/9, as updated regularly (hereinafter Council Regulation 881/2002, or the Anti-Taliban Regulation).

[9] Council Common Position 2001/931/CFSP on the application of specific measures to combat terrorism, [2001] OJ L/344/93, as updated regularly (hereinafter Common Position 2001/931 or the EU list).

[10] For the sake of convenience I will refer to alleged terrorists and terrorist organisations simply as 'terrorists'; I will also refer to 'foreign linked' terrorists as 'foreign terrorists', even though their status has nothing to do with nationality. And I will refer to those who have no link with outside the EU as 'home-terrorists'.

[11] It is not by coincidence that the UN could not reach an agreement on the definition of 'terrorism' in its anti-terrorism Resolution ((1373)2001).

[12] Art 14 TEU.
[13] Art 15 TEU.
[14] Art 23 TEU.

Presidency must then ensure that Parliament's views are taken into due consideration; and Parliament must be 'regularly informed' in relation to the Union's foreign policy.[15]

The Union can also adopt international agreements in relation to both Common and Foreign Security Policy and in relation to fields falling within the scope of police and judicial cooperation in criminal matters (Title VI). In relation to those agreements Article 24(5) TEU provides that 'no agreement shall be binding on a Member State whose representative in the Council states that it has to comply with the requirements of its own constitutional procedure', even though the other Member States might decide that the agreement shall nonetheless apply provisionally. The 'constitutional safeguard' suggests that the agreement concluded by the Union is binding upon the Member States, unless they have made the declaration.

The jurisdiction of the European Court of Justice is excluded in relation to second pillar instruments, which, in any case, cannot have direct effect unless the Community takes action by using the 'passerelle clause' contained in Article 60 EC read together with Article 301 EC. The latter states that when it is provided in a CFSP common position or joint action that the Community should take action to 'interrupt or reduce, in part or completely, economic relations with one or more third countries', the Council must take the necessary measures. And Article 60 EC empowers the Community to take the 'necessary urgent measures on the movement of capital and payments as regards the third countries concerned'. Moreover, the Court of First Instance has clarified that Article 60 EC and 301 EC can be read together with Article 308 EC, in order to establish competence to adopt measures for the freezing of assets even when there is no direct connection with a third 'state'. This is the case despite the fact that Article 60 EC provides for the competence to adopt urgent measures in the field of the free movement of capital in relation to 'third countries'.[16]

In relation to action in the field of police and judicial cooperation in criminal matters, the two main instruments that can be used are common positions and framework decisions. The former define the approach of the Union to a particular matter, whilst the latter are akin to directives in the

---

[15]   Art 21 TEU.

[16]   *Cf* the CFI ruling in Case T–306/01 *Yusuf* [2005] ECR II–3533, now under appeal in Case C–415/05 P, case pending. See also Case T–315/01 *Kadi* [2005] II–3649, under appeal in Case C–402/05 P, case pending. The Community competence to enact freezing Regulations in respect of individuals and organisations not having a specific link to a third country is by no means uncontroversial; see, eg, E Spaventa, 'Fundamental Rights and the Interface between Second and Third Pillar' in A Dashwood and M Maresceau (eds), *Law and Practice of EU External Relations* (Cambridge: Cambridge University Press, forthcoming); in favour of such an interpretation see C Tomuschat 'Annotation of the *Yusuf* and *Kadi* judgments' (2006) 43 *CML Rev* 537.

first pillar, but for the explicit exclusion of the possibility of direct effect.[17] Common positions are adopted by the Council without consultation with the European Parliament, and the European Court of Justice does not have any jurisdiction (but for the possibility of policing whether the act should have been adopted at Community level).[18] Framework decisions are adopted after consultation with the European Parliament and there is limited jurisdiction of the European Court of Justice. In particular, the Court's jurisdiction is voluntary, i.e. dependent upon an explicit declaration by the Member State,[19] and is excluded in relation to the review of proportionality of operations carried out by the police or other law enforcement body.[20] The ECJ also has jurisdiction to assess the legality of a framework decision in review proceedings: however, only the Commission and the Member States can bring such proceedings, to the exclusion not only of individuals, but also of the European Parliament.

And, as has been noted before, the Union can also enter into international agreements in matters covered by Title VI by using the competence provided for in Article 24 TEU as provided in Article 38 TEU.[21] It should be noted, however, that in relation to cooperation in criminal matters there is no equivalent to the 'passerelle clause' provided in Articles 60 and 301 EC for the CFSP. Therefore, the use of third-pillar competence cannot trigger, or be complemented by, Community action.

It is clear that the institutional framework provided for in relation to the CFSP, with its limitation of democratic accountability and the exclusion of any judicial protection, is inadequate to meet the basic demands of fundamental rights protection once action taken at Union level affects individuals. The same can be said in relation to international agreements adopted pursuant to Articles 24 and 38 TEU, and in relation to mixed second and third pillar instruments, especially when the instrument is

---

[17] Art 34 TEU.

[18] See, by analogy, Case C–170/96, *Commission v Council* [1998] ECR I–2763 (Airport Transit Visas case). It is likely that litigation as to the correct legal basis is on the increase; see, eg, Case C–176/03, *Commission v Council* [2005] ECR I–7879.

[19] Art 35 TEU. Before the Bulgarian and Romanian accession, 14 out of 25 Member States had made such a declaration. See 'Information concerning the declarations by the French Republic and the Republic of Hungary on their acceptance of the jurisdiction of the Court of Justice to give preliminary rulings on the acts referred to in Article 35 of the Treaty on European Union' [2005] OJ L/327/19.

[20] Art 35(5) TEU.

[21] Eg *Agreement on Extradition between the European Union and the United States of America* [2003] OJ L/181/27; see also *Agreement on Mutual Legal Assistance between the European Union and the United States of America* [2003] OJ L/181/34; *Agreement between the European Union and the United States of America on the processing and transferring of passenger name record (PNR) data by air carriers to the United States* [2006] OJ L/298/29. For a rather critical appraisal of the agreement see the debate before the plenary session of the European Parliament, *Use of Passenger Data*, debate of 11/10/06, Document of 16/10/06, 13991/06 PE 326.

adopted through the use of a common position thus excluding any possibility of review by the European Court of Justice. We shall now turn to analyse the problems arising from the use of Union competence to identify individuals and organisations as 'terrorists'.

III. THE UN DERIVED TERRORIST LIST: FROM *YUSUF* TO *AYADI*

As mentioned above, terrorist lists have been adopted by the EU in two instruments: Common Position 2002/402, which implements the Anti-Taliban UN Security Council Resolution by imposing sanctions on those designated by the UN Sanctions Committee as being associated with the Taliban, Bin Laden, Al-Qaeda and the like[22]; and Common Position 2001/931, which contains a list of those identified by the Council as being connected with terrorism. The format for both types of Acts is the same: the Union adopts a Common Position which is then given effect, as far as the freezing of assets is concerned, through a Community Regulation adopted on the basis of Articles 60, 301 and 308 EC.[23] However, in the case of the UN related list, the Common Position is taken on the basis of Article 15 TEU alone,[24] and the duty to update the list in the Regulation falls upon the Commission, which simply has regard to the UN list.

In the case of the 'home-decided' lists, the relevant instrument is Common Position 2001/931/CFSP, which has been adopted using a mixed second and third pillar legal basis. As we shall see in more detail later, the mixity is due to the fact that Common Position 2001/931 identifies two categories of terrorists: those who have some link with outside the EU, and 'home terrorists', whose alleged terrorist activities are confined to within the EU boundaries. For this latter category of people, the Council and Commission found that there was no competence for enacting a freezing Regulation since there was not even a remote link to a third country which would justify the use of CFSP competence and of the passerelle clause contained in Articles 301 and 60 EC.[25] For this reason, this category of people and organisations are not subject to EU-wide freezing orders. The

---

[22]   UN Security Council Resolution 1390(2002).

[23]   Council Regulation 881/2002 (the Anti-Taliban Regulation); and Council Regulation 2580/2001 on specific restrictive measures directed against certain persons and entities with a view to combating terrorism, [2001] OJ L/344/70.

[24]   Common Position 2002/402/CFSP concerning restrictive measures against Usama bin Laden, members of the Al-Qaeda organization and the Taliban and other individuals, groups, undertakings and entities associated with them and repealing Common Positions 96/746/CFSP, 1999/727/CFSP, 2001/154/CFSP and 2001/771/CFSP, [2002] OJ L/169/4.

[25]   It has been argued that the existence of the general anti-terrorist Resolution would have been enough to trigger CFSP competence; on the relationship between the UN anti-terrorist Resolution and Regulation 2580/2001 see several obiter in Case T–228/02 *Organisation des Modjahedines du peuple d'Iran (OMPI) v Council*, judgment of 12 December 2006, nyr.

list in the Annex to the Common Position is updated regularly and, since in this case it is not a mere replication of the UN list, it falls upon the Council to do so voting unanimously.

The legality of both lists has been called into question; since the lists raise different legal problems we will first analyse the UN-derived list, then consider the EU list. As has been mentioned above, the Anti-Taliban Common Position and Regulation are entirely of UN derivation and the Community institutions limit themselves to implement what is decided at UN level. The list is drawn up by a UN Sanctions Committee, and unanimity is required in order both to place people and organisations on the list and to strike them off. Those who have been included have no possibility of seeking redress in front of the UN Sanctions Committee. Rather, the only avenue open to those affected is to persuade one of the Member States (either that of residence or that of nationality) to make representations in front of the UN Committee on their behalf; however, since unanimity is required to strike people off the list, such a remedy is not particularly effective. Furthermore, the UN Sanctions Committee is a governmental, not a judicial body. It is not surprising, then, that those included in the list might attempt to seek a judicial (and less partial) review of their case in front of a national court. In the Community context, since the UN list is implemented through a Regulation, the only competent courts to assess the validity of the Regulation are the European courts. One such challenge was brought in the *Yusuf* case.[26]

Mr Yusuf had been placed on the list of those whose assets would be frozen following his inclusion in the UN Anti-Taliban list. He brought proceedings for annulment of Regulation 881/2002,[27] on the grounds, inter alia, of breach of fundamental rights. In particular, the applicant sought to challenge his inclusion in the Regulation by relying on the breach of the right to property and, more importantly, on the breach of his right to a fair hearing. In relation to the latter claim, Mr Yusuf stressed how he had not been told the reasons which led to the imposition of sanctions against him or the evidence which had been relied upon against him; nor had he been given the opportunity to explain himself. Given that both the adoption of Regulation 881/2002, and the inclusion of Mr Yusuf in the list annexed therein, were a direct consequence of the UN Anti-Taliban Resolution,[28] the Court of First Instance felt it necessary to start by

---

[26] *Cf* CFI ruling in Case T–306/01 *Yusuf* [2005] ECR II–3533, now under appeal in Case C–415/05 P, case pending. See also Case T–315/01 *Kadi* [2005] ECR II–3649, under appeal in Case C–402/05 P, case pending.

[27] The original claim related to preceding Regulations and was later adjusted when the latter were repealed and substituted by Regulation 881/2002.

[28] UN Security Council Resolution 1390(2002).

assessing the extent of its own jurisdiction to review a Community instrument adopted in order to comply with UN obligations.

The Court found that there were 'structural limits' imposed to the review it could carry out in relation to the Regulation at issue. In particular, since the Council did not have any autonomous discretion, a review of the Regulation would imply a review of the UN Security Council Resolution, a power that the CFI felt it lacked, both as a matter of international law and as a matter of Community law. However, the CFI accepted that it could scrutinise the Regulation—and indirectly the Security Council Resolution—in relation to *jus cogens*, since such principles also bind the Security Council. As a result, the applicable standard of human rights protection is the lower *jus cogens* standard. In this respect, the Court found that the right to property had been adequately safeguarded since, following new Resolutions as implemented in Community law, the national authorities could (and can) declare that the freezing of funds does not apply to funds essential for ordinary expenses (food, medicines, rent etc). More importantly, however, the CFI found that the UN Sanctions Committee was under no duty to hear the applicant before his inclusion in the list; and that, in any event, the Security Council, by providing for the possibility for individuals to petition their State of nationality or of residence to make representations to the Sanctions Committee on their behalf, 'intended to take into account, as far as possible,' the fundamental rights of individuals. Short of errors in the identification of the persons concerned, which the CFI seems to be ready to scrutinise, there is thus no substantive review at Community level of the soundness of the reasons that led to inclusion in the UN list.

The *Yusuf* ruling has been criticised for several reasons: the CFI's view of the relationship between UN Resolutions and Community law not only reflects an absolute monist understanding of the relationship between the two systems, but it also introduces something akin to direct effect of international norms within the Community and national legal systems.[29] This debatable choice also redefines the effect of international law in domestic constitutional systems, rendering UN Resolutions directly effective, and unquestionable, in domestic systems through the medium of Community law.[30] Furthermore, such pervasive effects in domestic constitutional law have been achieved by means of an extensive interpretation of Community competence. The result of the Court's ruling in *Yusuf* is

---

[29] It is also a matter of debate whether the *Yusuf* understanding of the relationship between UN Resolutions and Community law is consistent with the ECJ decision in Case C–84/95 *Bosphorus* [1996] ECR I–3953, where the Court had no problem in scrutinising a UN Security Council Resolution with the general principles of Community law; see also Case of *Bosphorus etc v Ireland* (Appl No 45036/98), judgment of 30/6/05.

[30] On those issues see also N Lavranos, 'Judicial Review of UN Sanctions by the Court of First Instance' (2006) 11 *European Foreign Affairs Review* 471.

ultimately to leave a substantial gap in fundamental rights protection, by allowing representatives of the executive to impose sanctions on individuals without any guarantee as to how such individuals are chosen; and without there being any possibility of an independent (if not judicial) assessment of the, at least prima facie, evidence relied upon to justify such pervasive measures. Thus, the effect of the ruling is to deprive the claimant to any meaningful access to review of his/her inclusion in the UN list.

This said, the approach of the Court is more nuanced than what might appear at first sight. First, as we shall see below, it indicates the Court's readiness to impose a more intensive scrutiny for EU produced lists; secondly, in *Yusuf*, the Court indicated in an obiter that it would be open to an applicant to bring judicial review proceedings, based either on domestic law or indirectly on Regulation 881/2002, of the national authorities' refusal to make representations on behalf of the listed individual in front of the Sanctions Committee.[31] In the subsequent case of *Ayadi*,[32] the CFI clarified that, as a matter of Community law, the Member States have an obligation to respect the claimant's fundamental rights when dealing with her/his application for review of their case with the aim of triggering the procedure for de-listing in front of the Sanctions Committee. The obligation to respect fundamental rights also applies in relation to all matters concerning the de-listing procedure (ie even in relation to the Member State's negotiations with other States); and judicial review of the Member State's refusal to consider the applicant's case must be ensured as a matter of Community law.

The reasoning of the CFI is persuasive: the UN Sanctions Committee has, in its guidelines, acknowledged that the Resolution in question confers a right on individuals to request a review of their case to their State for the purposes of being removed from the list. The Community Regulation giving effect to the UN Resolution then needs to be interpreted in conformity with the Committee's guidelines; however, since it is a Regulation that gives effect to the sanctions, such right should be seen as guaranteed not only by the Guidelines but also by the Community legal order itself. Thus, when the Member State examines the request for review, and when the Member State consults other States in the context of the procedure that might lead to de-listing, the Member State is bound by Article 6 TEU, and by fundamental rights as general principles of Community law. Respect for those obligations does not affect the Member State's performance of its UN obligations, and therefore the *Yusuf* reasoning does not apply to the de-listing procedure. Furthermore, the CFI also made clear that, insofar as that is allowed by the UN Resolution/Sanctions Committee,

---

[31] Case T–306/01 *Yusuf* [2005] ECR II–3533, para 317.
[32] Case T–253/02 *Ayadi* [2006] ECR II–2139.

the national authorities must act proportionately in relation to the freezing order: thus, refusing a taxi driver's licence to the applicant without regard to 'his needs (...) and without consulting the Sanctions Committee' is a misrepresentation or misapplication of the Regulation concerned.[33]

The effect of *Ayadi* is a welcome qualification of the *Yusuf* ruling: whilst the CFI has confirmed the *Yusuf* interpretation in relation to the hierarchy between UN Resolutions and Community law, and whilst it has reaffirmed the exclusion of a possibility of review of inclusion in the list, it has imposed upon Member States a substantive Community law obligation to respect fundamental rights and the other general principles of Community law whenever dealing with those aspects of the Regulation about which the Member States (or indeed the Community) enjoy any discretion. Thus, even though the CFI does not impose an *automatic* duty upon Member States to make representations on behalf of individuals, it makes denial to do so much more difficult. In dealing with applications for review with the view of triggering the de-listing procedure, the national authorities have now, as a matter of Community law, several obligations, such as:

(i) a duty to take into account the difficulties that individuals might face in protecting themselves, especially given that the person might not know why he/she has been put on the list; and might have no knowledge of the evidence relied upon against him/her. Thus, the fact that individuals might not be able to provide precise and relevant information to support their case should not be conclusive;

(ii) a duty to act 'promptly' whenever re-examination seems to be justified; and

(iii) the decision refusing to make representations on behalf of the individual must be reviewable as a matter of Community law, even when it would not be so in national law.

The *Ayadi* ruling is a clear attempt to afford the best protection possible, given the circumstances, to the individual. In this respect the principle of supremacy and direct effect of Community fundamental rights, together with ample discretion left to the national authorities to ensure as effective a protection as possible, narrows the gap in fundamental rights protection opened by the use of Community competence to implement UN individual sanctions. The irony now lies in the fact that those included in the EU list might well find themselves in a worse position that those included in the UN list.

---

[33] On the duties falling upon national authorities see also Case T–47/03 R R *Sison v Council* (Interim relief) [2003] ECR II–2047.

IV THE EU LISTS—THE IDENTIFICATION OF THE 'TERRORISTS'

As mentioned above, the Union has also drafted its 'own' list of terrorists in Common Position 2001/931/CFSP. The latter Common Position has been adopted in order to implement UN Security Council Resolution 1373(2001) on terrorism (the Anti-terrorist Resolution) which, inter alia, provides that States must freeze the assets of terrorist organisations and individuals; of entities controlled by terrorist organisations/individuals; of persons acting on behalf of terrorist organisations/individuals. The UN Security Council Resolution, however, fails to identify such entities, and it does not provide a list like the one adopted in relation to the Taliban Resolution. Furthermore, the Resolution fails to define what is meant by 'terrorist' act, offence etc, since agreement could not be reached on that point. Common Position 2001/931, on the other hand, gives a rather broad definition of terrorist act (which was later duplicated in the Framework decision on terrorism),[34] and provides that the list of those identified as terrorist shall be drawn up on the 'basis of precise information or material in the relevant file which indicates that a decision has been taken by a competent authority' in relation to those groups. The competent authority 'shall mean a judicial authority, or, where judicial authorities have no competence (...) an equivalent competent authority in that area'.[35] The first issue for consideration relates, then, to how those who are included in the list are actually chosen.

First of all, it should be noted that Common Position 2001/931 does not give any indication as to what an 'equivalent' competent authority is: in this respect, Tappeiner has remarked how, despite what might appear at first sight, the relevant 'authority' might not only not be a judicial authority, but the criterion of 'equivalence' might be interpreted in a rather loose way to admit simple (unchecked) intelligence.[36]

Second, it should be noted that the Common Position does not explicitly refer to the fact that the authority in question must be that of a Member State, thus leaving the avenue open for the possibility that the relevant decision might have been taken by an authority outside the European Union. And indeed, the fact that Article 1(4) Common Position 2001/931 refers to the possibility of including in the list those identified by the UN seems to support the view that the authority in question need not be a

---

[34] Council Framework Decision on combating terrorism 2002/475/JHA, [2002] OJ L/164/3.

[35] Art 1(4) Common Position 2001/931/CFSP.

[36] I Tappeiner, 'The Fight against Terrorism. The Lists and the Gaps' (2005) 1 *Utrecht Law Review* 97, and on line at www.utrechtlawreview.org. See also Case T–228/02 *Organisation des Modjahedines du peuple d'Iran (OMPI) v Council*, judgment of 12 December 2006, nyr, where Council and the United Kingdom refused to (or could not) identify the authority the decision of which led to the inclusion of the applicant in the list.

domestic one. And at least in one case, it seems that inclusion on the list of one of those individuals might have stemmed from political pressure exercised by a foreign country (whether this might in certain cases be the only criterion is impossible to say given the secrecy that surrounds the entire exercise).[37] The fact that a decision of a non-EU country might be given such pan-European effects is clearly problematic: the fundamental rights standard of the country in question might fall short of those (which should be) applied by the Union; and there is an increased danger that inclusion on the list might be the result of a foreign policy decision rather than the result of an independent assessment as to whether the individual and/or the organisation in question is actually connected to terrorism.

Third, it is impossible to say whether the Council exercises any control over the names suggested by Member States. Whilst inclusion in the list needs to be unanimously agreed by the Council, there is the possibility that the Council does not in fact exercise a real scrutiny over the names suggested by the Member States, and that it merely rubber-stamps the decision of other Member States. A recent decision of the Court of First Instance seems to have legitimised a 'rubber-stumping' approach. In the *OMPI* case, in relation to the list contained in Regulation 2580/2001, the Court held that the Council has no other duty than to assess whether there exists a decision by a competent authority, excluding the Council's duty not only to assess whether the national procedure was conducted correctly, but even 'whether the fundamental rights of the party concerned were respected by the national authorities'.[38] In this way, the CFI has accepted that a national decision, even when not judicial, can be given pan-European effect regardless of whether the minimum guarantees of fundamental rights protection required by Article 6 TEU and by the general principles of Union law have been respected. This is all the more worrying given that, as said above, there is no guarantee that the decision at stake would have been adopted by a European Union authority.[39]

---

[37] See the transcript of comments on combating the financing of terrorism made by Alan P Larson, Under-Secretary for Economic, Business, and Agricultural Affairs, in testimony before the House (Congress) Committee on Financial Services on 19 September 2002, http://useu.usmission.gov/Dossiers/Terrorist_Financing/Sep1902_Larson_Testimony.asp; 'The European Union has worked with us to ensure that nearly every terrorist individual and entity designated by the United States has also been designated by the European Union', and also the testimony of Juan C Zarate (Deputy Assistant Secretary, Executive Office) *Terrorist financing and financial crime*, US Department of the Treasury, Senate Foreign Relations Committee, 18 March 2003, JS-139 (http://www.ustreas.gov/press/releases/js139.htm).

[38] Case T–228/02 *Organisation des Modjahedines du peuple d'Iran (OMPI) v Council*, judgment of 12 December 2006, nyr, para 121.

[39] And, following the recent reports on the Member States' complacency in relation to 'extraordinary renditions', and given that the equivalent authority needs not to be a judicial one, it is hardly for the Union and its Member States to claim the moral high ground on such matters. See European Parliament Resolution on the alleged use of European countries by the CIA for the transportation and illegal detention of prisoners (2006/2200); Report *CIA*

Furthermore, given the possibility of lack of scrutiny by the Council, there is a real risk that inclusion in the list might be politically motivated. In this respect, the Amnesty International report on counter-terrorism and EU criminal law refers to the case of *Segi*. As we shall see in more detail below, SEGI, an organisation supporting Basque independence, has been included in the list of 'home-terrorists'. This notwithstanding, the French *Cour de Cassation* upheld the French Court of Appeal's decision not to surrender to the Spanish authorities the spokesperson for SEGI on the grounds that part of the alleged offence had been carried out in France. However, the French authorities have never taken any action to prosecute the alleged offences.[40] This reinforces the suspicion that the list might serve to introduce a pan-European proscription of organisations even when inclusion might be, if not altogether politically motivated, at least deeply rooted in the political problems/conflict/reality of one single Member State.

Fourth, it should be noted that the entire listing process is, not surprisingly, surrounded by secrecy. Thus, it is very difficult for an individual to obtain any meaningful information as to why his/her name has been included in the list. In the case of *Sison*,[41] one such person requested access to the documents which had led the Council to include his name in the list by relying on Regulation 1049/2001 on pubic access to documents.[42] The Council refused even partial access to those documents, relying on the fact that disclosure would undermine public security and international relations; and it also refused to disclose the identity of the States that had provided the information on the grounds that the originating authority opposed disclosure. Both the CFI and the ECJ have upheld the Council's decision, thus excluding that Regulation 1049/2001 can ever apply to the information relating to inclusion in the list. The ruling might well be justified having regard to the public security exception since, were the principle of open access to apply to such documents, it would most likely have to apply *erga omnes*, ie so that anyone could access such documents, something that might undoubtedly contrast with the public interest of both the Union and the Member State which instigated the

Activities in Europe, 14 February 2007; Council of Europe, *Committee on Legal Affairs and Human Rights, Alleged secret detentions and unlawful inter-state transfers involving Council of Europe Member States*, available on statewatch.org.

[40] Amnesty International Report (EU Office) *Human Rights dissolving at the borders? Counter-terrorism and EU criminal law*, 31/5/05, AI Index: IOR 61/013/2005, also available on http://web.amnesty.org/library/index/engior610132005, p 15. For the text of the decision see Council documents, *Comments of the French delegation, presenting the main decisions handed down by the Supreme Court of Appeal on the European Arrest Warrant*, 2/09/05, doc. No. 11902/05, COPEN 133, EJN 52, EUROJUST 56.

[41] Joined Cases T–110/03, T–150/03 and T–405/03 *Sison v Council* [2005] ECR II–1429, upheld in Case C–266/05 P *Sison v Council*, judgment of 1 February 2007, nyr.

[42] Regulation No 1049/2001 regarding public access to European Parliament, Council and Commission documents [2001] OJ L/145/43.

listing. This said, in the above-mentioned *OMPI* case,[43] the Court of First Instance has held that the duty to state reasons and the right to a fair hearing apply, at least to a certain extent, to the Council's decision to include someone on the list. Following the decision, the Council has indicated that it will provide those listed with such reasons[44]; it remains to be seen, however, whether the Council will be willing to go much beyond a formal compliance with such duty. Given that inclusion in the list is at the request of the Member States, there is a not-insignificant risk that the statement of reasons might, at best, simply identify the national authority's decision (when indeed there is one) which has triggered the listing.

Lastly, it should be noted that in the context of the EU list, there is no procedure in place to request a Member State to review one's case and make representations to the Council with a view to de-listing. This means that the only avenue open to a listed individual/organisation is a legal challenge to the legality of the inclusion of his/her name on the list. We will consider the problems arising in relation to such challenge in the next section. However, in the meanwhile, it should be noted how, in any event, 'home-terrorists' are deprived of any access to judicial review at European level, since the European Courts do not have jurisdiction over Common Positions. The lack of a de-listing procedure then leaves such applicants without even those minimal remedies afforded to those who are included in the UN list. We will deal with this issue further below.

V THE EU FOREIGN TERRORISTS' LIST AND JUDICIAL REVIEW: SOME STRUCTURAL DIFFICULTIES

As said above, Common Position 2001/931/CFSP provides for two types of 'terrorists', those with a connection to third countries, and entirely EU-based terrorists. It is only in relation to the former that freezing measures can be taken at Community level since the list of home terrorists is adopted using Title VI competence and therefore cannot benefit from the passerelle clause contained in Articles 60 and 301 EC.

Regulation 2580/2001 implements Common Position 2001/931/CFSP and provides for the freezing of assets of those listed in the Common Position as regularly amended by the Council. According to Article 1(6) of Common Position 2001/931, the list must be updated by means of a

---

[43] Case T–228/02 *Organisation des Modjahedines du peuple d'Iran (OMPI) v Council*, judgment of 12 December 2006, nyr.

[44] See Notice for the attention of those persons/groups/entities that have been included by Council Decision 2006/1008/EC of 21 December on the list of persons, groups and entities to which Regulation 2580/2001 applies, [2006] OJ C/320/02.

Common Position at least every six months[45]; the Article applies also to the Regulation and in relation to that instrument the list is updated by means of a Council Decision. The reason for the duplication is that the latter instrument is that applicable in relation to the Regulation, whilst the former, which contains both home and foreign terrorists, is the general CFSP one (which consequently cannot have direct effect).

The Council Decision which lists the individuals subject to the freezing of assets provided for by the Regulation is naturally of direct and individual concern to those who are identified in the Decision and therefore can be reviewed under Article 230 EC.[46] There is no doubt that cases concerning inclusion in the list could also be referred by national courts on a preliminary ruling. In any case, however, since we are within the ambit of Community law, the *Foto-Frost* principle should apply and the only courts to have jurisdiction to declare the nullity of the applicant's inclusion in the list are the Community courts.[47] This might create significant problems, given that it is not obvious that the Rules of Procedure are suitable for accommodating such complex proceedings where sensitive evidence might have to be discussed.[48] Furthermore, the duty to justify inclusion on the list would fall upon the Council; however, the intelligence upon which inclusion on the list is based is national (if not altogether external to the EU) and not all of it might have been disclosed to the Council for inclusion in the relevant file. This might lead to some difficulties since, presumably, and unless the relevant Member State is prepared to grant access to fuller intelligence, the case might fall to be decided, if at all, on the incomplete evidence contained in the file. The situation is even worse should the case reach the Court through means of a preliminary ruling since those proceedings are not adversarial in nature and, in relation to those proceedings, the right of the defence might well be compromised.[49]

---

[45] This time limit was at the time of writing being ignored by the Council; the last amendment was on 29 May 2006, Common Position 2006/380/CFSP and Council Decision 2006/379/EC.

[46] Case T–229/02 *Kurdistan Workers' Party (PKK) and Kurdistan National Congress (KNK) v Council* [2005] ECR II–539, para 27. In this case the CFI nonetheless found that the applicant, a Mr Ocalan, who claimed to act on behalf of the PKK, did not have standing since he could not claim to be the legal representative of an organisation which had ceased to exist. The flaws in the CFI's argument have been fully exposed by AG Kokott in her Opinion on the appeal to the CFI ruling, Opinion of 27/09/2006 in Case C–229/05 P *Kurdistan Workers' Party (PKK) and Kurdistan National Congress (KNK) v Council*. The Court has agreed with the AG and has quashed the CFI ruling, Case C–229/05 P *Kurdistan Workers' Party (PKK) and Kurdistan National Congress (KNK) v Council* [2007] ECR I–445.

[47] Case C–314/85 *Foto-Frost v Hauptzollamt Lübeck-Ost* [1987] ECR 4199.

[48] Cf also obiter at para 158 of Case T–228/02 *Organisation des Modjahedines du peuple d'Iran (OMPI) v Council*, judgment of 12 December 2006, nyr.

[49] The situation would be incredibly difficult also given that the Council would not be formally part of the proceedings even though it would of course be open to it to intervene.

But even leaving aside the procedural difficulties in having the Community courts dealing with those cases, the real issue relates to the extent to which those courts are willing to conduct a substantive review of the Council Decision to include someone on the list. A recent case might serve to illustrate the problem inherent in entrusting the Community courts with judicial review in such matters. In the above mentioned *OMPI* ruling,[50] one of the organisations which had been listed in both the Common Position and in the Community list, and whose assets had consequently been frozen, brought an action for annulment in front of the CFI. The *OMPI* relied, inter alia, on infringement of a right to a fair hearing; infringement of the duty to state reasons; and on the infringement of the right to effective judicial protection. The Council had failed to hear the applicant either before or after its inclusion in the list; and it had refused to communicate the reasons which led to the decision to include it in the list, and the authority which had instigated such inclusion.

The Court found that the right to a fair hearing, the duty to state reasons and the right to effective judicial protection all applied to the contested decision; however, it refused to engage in the substantive review of the reasons which led to the applicant's inclusion in the list. Thus, it held that the right to be heard is limited to the opportunity for applicants to make known their views as to 'the legal conditions of application of the Community measure in question', ie as to whether there is specific information or material in the file which shows that a decision meeting the definition in Article 1(4) of Common Position 2001/931 has been taken by a competent national authority, and in the case in which the case concerns the decision to maintain someone on the list, whether there is a justification for so doing. The Court also clarified that issues relating to the well-foundedness and appropriateness of the decision to include someone in the list can 'only be raised at national level'. And as mentioned before, the Court indicated that the Council bears no duty to investigate whether the national authority's decision was adopted in proceedings conducted correctly or whether the fundamental rights of the parties concerned were respected by such authority. In its abdication of judicial responsibility, the Court went even further, stating that even though one of the conditions for the legality of inclusion in the list is that the decision must have been based 'on serious and credible evidence', those affected by such decisions do not have a right to be heard in respect of such matters. Thus, in the Court's view, 'it would be *inappropriate*, in the light of the principle of sincere cooperation referred to in Article 10 EC, to make it subject to the exercise

---

[50] Case T–228/02 *Organisation des Modjahedines du peuple d'Iran (OMPI) v Council*, judgment of 12 December 2006, nyr.

of a fair hearing at Community level'.[51] The only exception to this principle arises when the Council based its decision to 'freeze funds on information or evidence communicated to it by representatives of the Member States without it having being assessed by the competent national authority'. Whilst this qualification might at first sight look reassuring, since it might introduce a right to be heard in relation to the substance of the allegations, at closer scrutiny it constitutes a worrying indication that the Court might be willing to extend the Council's power beyond the, very limited, procedural requirements provided for in Article 1(4) Common Position 2001/931. That provision states that 'The list in the Annex shall be drawn up on the basis of precise information or material in the relevant file which indicates that a decision has been taken by a competent authority (...)'. Article 1(4) is phrased in mandatory terms and does not seem to confer upon the Council the power to include someone in the list *regardless* of a prior national authority's decision. Yet, the Court seems to indicate that that would be possible.

In the *OMPI* case, the CFI also recognised that, after the first order for the freezing of funds has taken place, those concerned have a right to be notified of the evidence adduced against them and a right to request a re-examination of the initial decision. However, the Court again qualified such a right by stating that a hearing in such circumstances is not 'automatically required' since those concerned have in any event the right to bring judicial proceedings for annulment in front of the Community courts. The Council has also an obligation to state reasons which in these cases entail an obligation 'to state the matters of fact and law which constitute the legal basis of [the Council's] decision and the considerations which led it to adopt that decision'.[52] In any event, however, those rights are subject to the public security/interest caveat so that the Council is entitled to refuse disclosure of evidence and of information contained in the file to protect such interests. As to the extent to which 'effective judicial protection' is guaranteed by the Court, the ruling contains contradictory statements. Thus the Court first stated that the Community courts must be able to review both the lawfulness and the *merits* of the decision to freeze funds, without the Council being entitled to refuse disclosure of the evidence, then concluded that since it is not for the judiciary to substitute its assessment for that of the Council, the Court's review must be restricted to 'checking that the rules governing procedure and the statement of

---

[51] Case T–228/02 *Organisation des Modjahedines du peuple d'Iran (OMPI) v Council*, judgment of 12 December 2006, nyr, para 122, emphasis added.
[52] Case T–228/02 *Organisation des Modjahedines du peuple d'Iran (OMPI) v Council*, judgment of 12 December 2006, nyr, para 143.

reasons have been complied with, that the facts are materially accurate, and that there has been no manifest error of assessment of the facts or misuse of powers'.[53]

The *OMPI* case seems to indicate the Court's unwillingness to engage with the substantive issues which determined inclusion in the list, preferring it to leave such issues to the competent national authority, thus ensuring that such decisions can be given pan-European effect without the need for further scrutiny.[54] Furthermore, it should be remembered that there is no guarantee that the decision would have been taken by a judicial authority (something which admittedly would make things less bleak from a fundamental rights perspective); that neither Common Position 2001/931 nor the Court have defined what is to be intended for authority 'equivalent' to a judicial one; and that the Court indicates that such a decision does not in any event represent an essential procedural or substantive requirement for the legality of inclusion. This surrender of jurisdiction is legally questionable: once an individual or an organisation has been placed on the EU list, then the matter becomes one governed by European Union law, and therefore subject to the conditions of legality imposed by such system including fundamental rights protection. The Court's deference to national process is therefore puzzling: the standards upon which Union action must be assessed is that set by European Union law, not that set by national law. Moreover, the Court's indication that not even the Council should perform any substantive scrutiny seems to be inconsistent with the Council's duties as provided by Article 6 TEU.

The other thorny question relating to the list concerns whether the freezing of assets is properly defined as a criminal charge which should trigger the guarantees provided in Article 6 ECHR. The issue was argued in the *Sison* access to documents case,[55] but the CFI decided that it was not relevant for that case, rather being an issue for consideration in the related case for annulment, which is still pending.[56] In the *OMPI* case the Court did not analyse this matter even though, given the low standard of review imposed on the Council's decision, one might infer that the Court does not believe that such guarantees are necessary in relation to such cases.

Finally, it should be noted that the Council seems not to be willing to respect the Court's authority. In the *OMPI* case, the CFI annulled the inclusion of the applicant in the list; this notwithstanding, the Council has

---

[53] *Ibid*, paras 155 and 159 respectively.

[54] It could also be queried whether the *OMPI* ruling is consistent with the ruling in *Ayadi*, where, as we have seen above, the Court relied on the discretion conferred upon the Community legislature and upon national authorities to impose substantive duties upon the national authorities. It is puzzling then that the Community institutions should be subject to (arguably) lower standards than those imposed upon national authorities.

[55] Joined Cases T–110/03, T–150/03 and T–405/03 *Sison v Council* [2005] ECR II–1429.

[56] Case T–47/03 *Sison v Council*, case pending.

failed to give effect to the ruling and the *OMPI*'s assets are still frozen. This is the case, even though, subsequent to the ruling, the Council adopted a new Common Position and a new decision in order to add more individuals and organisations to its lists.[57] Furthermore, the Council has also indicated that it does not believe that the ruling affects the list annexed to the Common Position, since the CFI did not annul the inclusion of the applicant in that list.[58] The reason why the CFI did not do so is of course because it did not have jurisdiction to review the Common Position. Given that the Council is bound by fundamental rights regardless of whether it acts as a Community or a Union institution, and given that the CFI found that the applicant's fundamental rights had been infringed, the Council's position is not only untenable but in blatant defiance of the rule of law.

VI. HOME-MADE TERRORISTS AND EFFECTIVE JUDICIAL PROTECTION

It is now time to consider the EU list of 'home-terrorists', ie those whose assets cannot be frozen.[59] This area does not squarely fall within the scope of this contribution since it is only remotely connected to foreign policy. Yet, in order to give a more complete picture of the status of fundamental rights protection in the Union, it might be useful to make some remarks. This part of the list, like the foreign terrorist list, was adopted to give effect to the general anti-terrorism Resolution which, as mentioned before,

[57] Council Decision 2006/1008 of implementing Art 2(3) of Regulation 2580/2001 on specific restrictive measures directed against certain persons and entities with a view to combating terrorism [2006] OJ L/379/123. It should also be noted that at the time of writing the Council has failed to update the existing list, even though more than nine months have elapsed since the last update, thus also infringing Art 1(6) of Common Position 2001/931, which provides in mandatory terms the duty to review the list at least every six months. In the writer's opinion such infringement constitutes infringement of an essential procedural (and substantive) requirement which should render the entire list void. On these issues see E Spaventa, 'Fundamental Rights and the Interface between the Second and Third Pillar' in A Dashwood and M Maresceau (eds), *Law and Practice of EU External Relations* (Cambridge: Cambridge University Press, forthcoming).

[58] EU Council Secretariat Factsheet *Judgment of the Court of First Instance in the OMPI Case T–228/02*, para 3. The only concession the Council has made to the ruling is to undertake to provide a statement of reasons for those whose assets have been frozen and to establish a clearer and more transparent procedure for reconsideration. See also Notice for the attention of those persons/groups/entities that have been included by Council Decision 2006/1008/EC of 21 December on the list of persons, groups and entities to which Regulation 2580/2001 applies, [2006] OJ C/320/02.

[59] The remarks in this section of course also apply to the 'foreign' terrorists insofar as they are listed in the Common Position. However, and as seen above, those have access to the court because of the freezing Regulation. Following the remarks of the Council to the effect that annulment of the decision to include someone in the Regulation does not affect their inclusion in the list annexed to the Common Position, it cannot be excluded that even foreign terrorists might find themselves in this legal limbo.

requires States to take action (including the freezing of funds) against those identified as terrorists or involved in supporting terrorism. Despite the clear UN mandate, the European Union institutions have limited themselves to a mere identification of those who should be considered as terrorists, without requiring the Member States to take any further action. Thus, the domestic part of the list has been adopted by means of a Title VI Common Position, an instrument which simply sets policy objectives for the Union, and it is not explicitly binding upon Member States (albeit the duty of loyal cooperation would apply). Furthermore, the Common Position demands no specific action from the Member States which are just required to 'fully exploit their powers' in relation to requests from other Member States authorities.

The choice of a Common Position is therefore puzzling: on the one hand, it seems to put the Union in a questionable position from an international law viewpoint, since if those identified in the list are indeed terrorists, the Union and its Member States have an international law obligation to take action. And yet, the Common Position does not require Member States to freeze the assets of those therein identified therefore raising suspicions as to whether inclusion in the EU domestic list might not be politically motivated.

On the other hand, the fact that the list has been adopted in a Common Position might give rise to the suspicion that such a choice might have been instrumental to the desire to evade any judicial (and democratic) accountability since, as said above, common positions are not subject to the jurisdiction of the ECJ. This leads to the very concrete possibility that a person listed as 'home-terrorist' might find him/herself in a limbo where access to any judicial review is prevented. This issue has been raised before both the European Court of Human Rights and the Community courts by SEGI, an organisation supporting Basque independence and included in the list of home terrorists. Before the European Court of Human Rights, SEGI complained of a breach of several Convention rights, including the presumption of innocence, freedom of expression and freedom of association. The European Court of Human Rights refused to hear the case on the grounds that there had been only a *potential* rather than an actual breach of the Convention.[60] SEGI then brought an action for damages before the CFI, which dismissed the case since it has no jurisdiction to review

---

[60] Decision declaring the inadmissibility of the case *Segi and Gestoras pro-Amnistía v 15 States of the European Union*, Appl No 6422/02, and 9916/02, 23 May 2002. The ECtHR decision seems also to have been driven by the mistaken certainty that in any case the Community courts would have jurisdiction.

common positions. As a result, and as acknowledged by the CFI itself, the claimant was left without any judicial remedy.[61]

As far as de-listing is concerned, two solutions might be considered. First, one should consider the possibility for a national court to grant an injunction against the State requiring it to make representations in Council on behalf of the applicant, regardless of whether such possibility is provided for in the Common Position. Furthermore, it could be argued that even where such a possibility is not provided by national law, the national court might still, applying by analogy the principles elaborated in the context of the first pillar, and especially those elaborated in *Ayadi*, be under a Union law obligation to create a remedy to ensure that the principle of effective judicial protection is complied with.

Second, in relation to national courts in those Member States which have accepted the jurisdiction of the Court pursuant to Article 35 TEU, the possibility should be considered that it would be open to the national court to assess whether the Common Position is not in fact a decision. According to Article 34 TEU a common position defines the 'approach' of the Union to a particular matter. An instrument which identifies named individuals and requires Member States to engage in third-pillar cooperation in relation to those individuals is not merely defining the approach of the Union. Whilst it could be that the choice of instrument was dictated by the desire to save both words and legal instruments, it could be said that the list concerning home-terrorists is in fact a decision. Since the definition that the institutions give to an act is not conclusive, the national court could depart from it and make a preliminary reference to the ECJ to assess both whether the common position is in fact a decision and, should that be the case, whether inclusion of the applicant in the list is justified. This finding seems to find support in the European Court of Justice's ruling in the appeal to the SEGI case.[62] There, the Court held that the Court's jurisdiction under Article 35 TEU, according to which framework decisions and decisions might be the subject of a preliminary ruling, is intended to ensure jurisdiction in relation to those acts which might produce legal effects in relation to third parties. A Common Position producing such effects might have a scope going beyond what was provided for in Article 34 TEU, and the national court should feel empowered to make a preliminary reference to enquire if such is actually the case. Whilst the ECJ ruling is to be welcomed, it is also going to raise considerable issues of interpretation because of the reference to the need for the Common Position to produce legal effects vis-a-vis third parties. It is not clear that a

---

[61] Case T–338/02, *Segi et al v Council* [2004] ECR II–1647, para 39; upheld in Case C–355/04 P *Segi et al v Council*, judgment of 27 February 2007, nyr. See also the interesting opinion of AG Mengozzi, delivered on 26 October 2006.

[62] Case C–355/04 P *Segi et al v Council*, judgment of 27 February 2007, nyr.

Common Position might in itself produce such effects: whilst the prejudice to those therein listed is clear, there is no 'legal' consequence, strictly speaking, following from inclusion in such a list. It would therefore have been better if the Court had simply focused on the nature of the act, regardless of the 'legal' effects to third parties.

VII CONCLUSIONS

In this Chapter I have tried to voice some concerns over the increasing use of Union competence in fields which affect individual rights. This is particularly worrying in those cases where judicial scrutiny is more limited. In this respect, I would argue that the failure in the Union institutional structure to provide for effective judicial (and democratic) accountability might push the standard of fundamental rights protection below the minimum guarantees provided by the ECHR. Truth be told, the same could be said with many of the developments that have occurred as a result of the 'war on terror'. Whilst the UN smart sanctions might have been a reasonable response to the need to isolate 'nasty' regimes, the practice of identifying individuals as 'terrorists' without having put into place any system aimed at counterchecking a decision which is, at the end of the day, exclusively executive-based is extremely worrying. The CFI ruling in *Yusuf*, even when tamed by the ruling in *Ayadi*, constitutes an uncritical, and therefore dangerous, reception of the status quo. The same can be said about the ruling in the *OMPI* case. The latter, despite appearances, falls short of even those minimum guarantees established in *Ayadi*.

The abdication of judicial responsibility in this field is particularly worrying, not least since the very definition of what, and who, constitutes a terrorist is politically motivated. And it is in the realm of politics, not of law, that any a priori definition should apply. The debate as to whether we should entertain relations with a Hamas-led government in Palestine, with the PKK, or even with the IRA or ETA, is a political debate. But the realm of the law is different: by definition, we are not concerned with a priori assessments. We are concerned only with whether a crime, even a broadly defined one, has been committed. If so, prosecution should ensue regardless of any political assessment and with all the guarantees afforded to the defendant. But, other than that, we should resist any temptation to justify the sacrifice of our fundamental rights on the altar of that undefined god who is fighting the 'war on terror' on our behalf. That said, it seems that the Member States are taking a rather different view on the matter; the guarantees which we once knew as standard are not so any longer. There is neither democratic nor clear judicial accountability for those decisions. Rather, international and inter-governmental action is being used as a shelter. It is for this reason that judicial activism is needed. But we should be conscious of the fact that judicial activism is only a palliative treatment for such an acute endemic disease in the European Union. The only appropriate treatment lies with a Treaty amendment, as it would have been provided by the Constitutional Treaty. Lacking such a step, the Member States should refrain (and can indeed refrain) from acting at Union level in matters that affect individual rights.

Part V

EU Foreign Relations, Human Rights and International Law

9

The Journey Towards All that is Good and Beautiful: Human Rights and 'Common Values' as Guiding Principles of EU Foreign Relations Law

PÄIVI LEINO*

I. THE VISION

MUCH IN THE world changed around the time when the Berlin Wall fell. The Cold War had involved two competing conceptions of the political: both of them deadly serious; and both fundamentally incompatible with each other.[1] The views and actions of the West were balanced by counteractions of the Eastern bloc; as a result there was no clear, universally accepted idea of the 'right' or of the 'good'. The world after the fall of the Berlin Wall was a different one, with Western ideas of rights and individuals now coming to occupy the centre of international legal debates. The language of universal human rights flourished—after all, now it had no clear competitors.[2] The new era carried a promise of freedom, democracy, human rights, rule of law and free markets, all defined along Western lines. But the problem is this: the

* Doctor of Laws, Centre of Excellence for Global Governance Research, the Erik Castrén Institute for International Law and Human Rights, University of Helsinki, Finland. Many thanks to Katja Keinänen for good discussions over lunch.

[1] On this, see eg PW Kahn, 'American Hegemony and International Law. Speaking Law to Power: Popular Sovereignty, Human Rights, and the New International Order', (2000) 1 *Chicago Journal of International Law* 1, 7–8.

[2] As Barber has found, during the 1990s liberal democracy became such a powerful model that apparent alternatives to it are absent for 'those seeking other legitimate forms of politics'. This leaves the Western states 'with no standard against which to measure their own liberal politics and with no ideal by which to modify them, should they wish to do so'. BR Barber, *Strong Democracy. Participatory Politics for a New Age* (Berkeley, University of California Press, 2003) 3.

absence of the 'other' to contest Western policies does not necessarily imply that they would now be universally accepted and embraced, or that no alternatives or discussion of their contents would be needed.

The universality of rights has always formed the basis of the Union human rights policies.[3] Human rights provide Europe with a mission and a purpose, reflected in the following declaration by the European Council adopted in 1991:

> The Community and its Member States undertake to pursue their policy of promoting and safeguarding human rights and fundamental freedoms through- out the world. This is the legitimate duty of the world community and of all States acting individually or collectively. [...] The European Community and its Member States seek universal respect for human rights.[4]

The European vision of human rights goes as follows. We believe that human rights values were our discovery. Thus, we know that these values are *good*. And because these values are good, and because we wish to do good, then everyone else should enjoy our beautiful values—so let's change the world. Nothing in the universalist ideas of today is new: it is universalism that is actually closely attached to our own personal and cultural understanding of morals or values.[5] Earlier this mission was carried out by the great imperial powers; today the EU has assumed much the same role. Thus, it is not without precedent that in today's world politics the EU wishes increasingly to be profiled as a 'messenger of good values'.[6]

---

[3] See eg the EU Fundamental Rights Charter, which proclaims that 'conscious of its spiritual and moral heritage, the Union is based on indivisible and universal values'. This, of course, reflects the Kantian vision best illustrated in I Kant, 'Idea for a Universal History with a Cosmopolitan Purpose' in H Reiss (ed), *Kant's Political Writings* (Cambridge, Cambridge University Press, 1991) 41.

[4] Declaration on human rights, adopted by the European Council, [1991] 6 Bull EC 17, point 1.45. See also Statement on human rights, adopted by the Foreign Ministers meeting in political cooperation in Brussels on 21 July 1986, [1986] 7/8 Bull EC 100, point 2.4.4. See also the Foreign Ministers' Statement on Human Rights, 21 July 1986, Bull EC 7/8–1986, 100, point 2.4.4: '*The Twelve seek the universal observance of human rights. The protection of human rights is the legitimate and continuous duty of the world community and of nations individually.*' The same vision is continued in 'The European Union and the External Dimension of Human Rights Policy. From Rome to Maastricht and Beyond', Communication from the Commission to the Council and European Parliament, Brussels 22.11.1995, COM (95) 567 final.

[5] On this, see eg GW Gong, *The Standard of 'Civilization' in International Society* (Oxford, Clarendon Press, 1984); A Anghie, 'Time Present and Time Past: Globalization, International Financial Institutions, and the Third World', (2000) 32 *New York University Journal of International Law and Politics* 243; B Kingsbury, 'Confronting Difference: The Puzzling Durability of Gentili's Combination of Pragmatic Pluralism and Normative Judg- ment', (1998) 92(4) *American Journal of International Law* 713, 723. For a discussion of this in the context of the EU, see P Leino, 'European Universalism? The EU and Human Rights Conditionality', (2005) 24 *Yearbook of European Law* 330.

[6] See also the New Transnational Agenda, adopted jointly by the EU and the US in Madrid on 3 December 1995.

Europe's common values enjoy a central position in EU parlance. For example, the Lisbon Treaty emphasises the position of values as central objectives of Union action both within and outside its own borders. According to Article 49 EU (as amended by the Lisbon treaty), '[t]he Union shall be open to all European States which respect its values and are committed to promoting them together'. Common values thus have a crucial task: they are believed to guide Union action.[7] The EU speaks equally bravely of its *own* common values in relation to third states. According to Article 21 EU (as amended by the Lisbon Treaty),

> The Union's action on the international scene shall be guided by the principles which have inspired its own creation, development and enlargement, and which it seeks to advance in the wider world: democracy, the rule of law, the universality and indivisibility of human rights and fundamental freedoms, respect for human dignity, the principles of equality and solidarity, and respect for the principles of the United Nations Charter and international law.

The Constitution further establishes that the Union shall seek to develop relations and build partnerships with third countries and organisations that share these principles.[8] In practice, this is realised both through the mainstreaming of human rights into EU foreign policy and by making human rights considerations an aspect of external trade and development assistance.[9] The EU implements a specific suspension mechanism, the human rights clause, included in Community agreements negotiated with third countries, which makes it possible for the Union to suspend the implementation of the agreement or trade concessions and put its aid programmes on ice if its trade partners fail to respect human rights.[10] Human rights have played a role in the enlargement of the Union eastwards as one of the formal membership criteria and with a human rights clause included in the Europe Agreements in force with these

---

[7] 'The Union's aim is to promote peace, its values and the well-being of its peoples' (the Union's objectives I–3).

[8] Article 21 EU, second subparagraph (as amended by the Lisbon Treaty).

[9] See 'The European Union and the External Dimension of Human Rights Policy: From Rome to Maastricht and Beyond', Communication from the Commission to the Council and European Parliament, Brussels 22.11.1995, COM (95) 567 final, para 34.

[10] In more detail, see P Leino, 'European Universalism? The EU and Human Rights Conditionality', above n 5. Agreements with human rights clauses are in force with more than 120 countries, including the states of Central and Eastern Europe, the developing world including the 78 ACP States, Morocco, Tunisia, South Korea, Nepal, former Soviet Union states, India, Sri Lanka, Israel, Brazil, Venezuela, Colombia, Ecuador, Peru, Bolivia (Andean Pact), Tunisia, Vietnam, Laos, Cambodia, Egypt, Jordan and Lebanon. Cuba became the 79th ACP state in December 2000 but does not yet participate in the partnership agreement.

States.[11] In addition, human rights conditionality applies to financial assistance given by the Community,[12] and is closely tied to the use of economic sanctions.[13]

Today 'common values' enjoy a pivotal position in the various areas of EU foreign relations. For example the theme of the recent EU–India Summit, organised on 13 October 2006 in Helsinki, was 'Shared values, mutual interests'.[14] Similarly, the EU Strategy for Africa, adopted in December 2005, underlines how 'the EU and Africa share basic values and objectives'.[15] The EU-Caribbean Partnership, based on a Communication adopted by the Commission in March 2006, declares that the 'strategy is articulated around a shared vision of the future based on a history of shared values [...]'.[16] Not surprisingly, the EU's privileged relationship with its neighbours (covered by the European Neighbourhood Policy) is also based on the 'common values' of the parties; however, 'the degree of ambition of the EU's relationships with its neighbours will take into account the extent to which these values are indeed shared'.[17]

For the Union, emphasising the position of Europe's 'common values' as universal human rights[18] has been a necessary instrument for avoiding the charge of neo-colonialism associated with its policies. The EU approach is,

[11]   See P Leino, 'Rights, Rules and Democracy in the EU Enlargement Process: Between Universalism and Identity', (2002) 7 *Austrian Review of International and European Law* 53.

[12]   See eg Reg (EC) 1638/2006 of 24 October 2006 laying down general provisions establishing a European Neighbourhood and Partnership instrument, [2006] OJ L/310/1; Reg (EC) 1085/2006 establishing an instrument for pre-Accession Assistance, [2006] OJ L/210/82; Reg (EC) 1905/2006 establishing a financing instrument for development cooperation, [2006] OJ L/378/41.

[13]   See Article 215 TFEU (as amended by the Lisbon Treaty).

[14]   See the Commission external relations website http://ec.europa.eu/news/external_relations/061013_3_en.htm. Follow-up from 'An EU-India Strategic Partnership', Communication from the Commission to the Council, the European Parliament and Social Committee, Brussels, 16.6.2004 COM(2004) 430 final.

[15]   See Communication from the Commission to the Council, the European Parliament and the European Economic and Social Committee. 'EU Strategy for Africa: Towards a Euro-African pact to accelerate Africa's development', Brussels 12.10.2005, COM(2005) 489 final, 19.

[16]   See 'Communication from the Commission to the Council, the European Parliament and the European Economic and Social Committee. An EU-Caribbean Partnership for growth, stability and development'. Brussels 2.3.2006, COM(2006) 86 final, 2.

[17]   See 'Governance in the European Consensus on Development. Towards a harmonised approach within the European Union', Communication from the Commission, COM(2006) 421 final, Brussels, 30.8.2006, 15–16. In fact, Asia seems to be the main area with which the EU does not make reference to 'common values'; while there is on the EU side 'an overall commitment' to support these values, the relationship is influenced by Asia's 'great political, economic, social and cultural diversity'. *Ibid*, 18.

[18]   For the EU, the 'universal' invoked as a justification for its external human rights policies is embodied in the Universal Declaration of Human Rights and its 'confirmation' by the Vienna Human Rights Conference in 1993. See eg 'The European Union and the External Dimension of Human Rights Policy: From Rome to Maastricht and Beyond', Communication from the Commission to the Council and European Parliament, Brussels 22.11.1995, COM (95) 567 final, 10.

after all, not to be seen 'as imposing conditions, but in the spirit of a joint undertaking to respect and promote universal values'.[19] In the EU vision, serious human rights problems are linked with political and institutional instability,[20] while progress with democracy, the rule of law and human rights functions as a 'prerequisite for stable trade relations and the orderly implementation of trade agreements', and trade conditionality and sanctions serve as a powerful means in the promotion of human rights worldwide.[21] Instead of being just an EU concern, human rights are presented as 'a subject of shared interest'.[22] The association of a language of universality with human rights conditionality thus achieves—rhetorically—the outcome that the actor exercising conditionality does not appear to impose Western values on other countries, but simply uses its 'influence to bring the practice of other governments more into line with *their own* professed values (which we share)'.[23]

Despite the obvious appeal of associating policy objectives with the 'good', there are various problems with this approach. First, even though the values the EU proclaims were indeed universal, their universality seems to abide more in their purported logic of aspiration, rather than in the reality of attainment.[24] More than anything else, universal human rights offer a horizon; 'an ever expanding set of objectives waiting to be realized'.[25] As the universal only exists at an abstract level and escapes definition, articulating it in any specific manner is impossible.[26] Thus even the Union's 'common values' are difficult to define in practice. One example of this ambiguity is reflected in the recently adopted regulation establishing a financial instrument for promoting human rights worldwide, where the reference to 'common values' is tied to numerous (though unspecified) UN and regional human rights instruments:

> The Community's contribution to the development and consolidation of democracy and the rule of law, and of respect for human rights and fundamental

---

[19] 'The European Union and the External Dimension of Human Rights Policy: From Rome to Maastricht and Beyond', Communication from the Commission to the Council and European Parliament, Brussels 22.11.1995, COM (95) 567 final, para 63.

[20] A Rosas, 'Human Rights in the External Trade Policy of the European Union' in Publications de l'Institut International des Droits de l'Homme, *World Trade and the Protection of Human Rights. Human Rights in Face of Global Economic Challenges* (Brussels, Bruyland, 2001) 193, 207.

[21] *Ibid* 205.

[22] *Ibid.*

[23] J Donnelly, *Universal Human Rights in Theory and Practice* (Ithaca and London, Cornell University Press, 1989) 234 (emphasis in original).

[24] U Baxi, *The Future of Human Rights* (New Delhi, Oxford University Press, 2002) 101.

[25] S Kothari and H Sethi, 'Introduction' in S Kothari and H Sethi (eds), *Rethinking Human Rights. Challenges for Theory and Action* (Delhi, New Horizons Press and Lokayan, 1989) 1, 9.

[26] For a further discussion, see P Leino, 'European Universalism? The EU and Human Rights Conditionality', above n 5.

freedoms is rooted in the general principles established in the International Bill of Rights, and any other Universal Human Rights Instrument adopted within the framework of the United Nations, as well as relevant regional human rights instruments.[27]

On the website of the Office for the UN High Commissioner for Human Rights, a total of 102 documents are listed as belonging to the category of 'Universal Human Rights Instruments'—conventions, declarations and resolutions, only a few of which provide for actual enforcement of any kind.[28] As to their substantive scope, it would seem that there are very few aspects of good life that would not be covered by one of the universal or regional instruments. The argument made here relates to the objectives expressed in this reference: a policy designed to promote absolutely everything good and beautiful cannot but remain void in substantive direction.

Second, even if it was true that certain values indeed are 'universal', it is by no means clear that the EU would be entitled to speak for them[29] and thus take unilateral action to enforce them. On a theoretical level, the EU's strategy aims at connecting the particular (the European, the Western) with the universal. The universal does not have a representative of its own, because there is no actor with an absolutely universal coverage; it is thus necessarily represented by a particular.[30] In practice, this situation can be observed in the way in which human rights argumentation has been used in historical contexts, with the claim for the 'universal' often tending to reveal a particular policy.[31] If this is the case, then the universality of rights just appears to support the supremacy of one group over others, with a

---

[27] Regulation (EC) 1889/2006 of 20 December 2006 on establishing a financial instrument for the promotion of democracy and human rights worldwide, [2006] OJ L/386/1, preamble, para 6.

[28] See http://www.ohchr.org/english/law/index.htm, site last visited 22 October 2006. Instruments that are mentioned include, in addition to the more well-known ones, various other instruments, such as the Declaration on the Use of Scientific and Technological Progress in the Interests of Peace and for the Benefit of Mankind and the Declaration on Social Progress and Development, the contents of which seem to be much less generally known. The European Parliament Resolution (2006)0056 on the human rights and democracy clauses in European Union agreements includes an almost equally wide list of references: the UDHR, the two International Covenants, 'and the internationally recognised UN covenants and legal norms of the jus cogens' (para 7(b)). Unlike the Commission, the EP underlines that it refers to 'international obligations which have already been ratified'.

[29] In more detail, see P Leino, 'European Universalism? The EU and Human Rights Conditionality', above n 5, 368–79.

[30] On this, see S Žižek, 'Class Struggle or Postmodernism? Yes, please!' in J Butler, E Laclau and S Žižek (eds), *Contingency, Hegemony, Universality. Contemporary Dialogues on the Left* (London and New York, Verso, 2000) 90, 111.

[31] For the classic account of universal principles, see EH Carr, who argued that absolute universal principles are really the 'unconscious reflections of national policy based on a particular interpretation of national interests at a particular time'. According to Carr, the true nature of these principles as disguises of selfish vested interests is revealed as soon as an attempt is made to apply these supposedly abstract principles to a concrete political situation.

'particular' dressed to look as if it were the 'universal'.[32] In the actual case this would be so if it appeared that the particular (the EU) uses the universal language mainly in order to promote its own objectives. This could suggest that in referring to universality the EU is, in fact, not representing that which is genuinely shared, but a false universal.

The argument made here is that while it is self-evident that Union policies should respect 'good values',[33] it is quite another thing how these values should be realised in practice: the abstraction of values hides from sight the degree to which we disagree on how these values should be turned into political practice. None of these ideas is detailed enough to provide much substantive indication about its contents[34]: in their openness, the Union's 'common values' allow quite different, even opposite readings. For this reason, they have little capacity to be policy-guiding, which is the role allocated to them in EU external policies. EU external human rights policy functions in two principal ways: it is based on political dialogue and conditions and sanctions.[35] Nevertheless, since even policies based on conditionality include political dialogue on the implementation of human rights, 'dialogue' on human rights has a key function in EU relations with nearly all third states.[36] Indeed, 'dialogue' as the process through which the

EH Carr, *The Twenty Years' Crisis 1919–1939: An Introduction to the Study of International Relations* (first published 1946) (London and Basingstoke, Macmillan Press, 1983) 87–88.

[32] See M Koskenniemi, 'Human Rights, Politics and Love', (2001) 4 *Mennesker & Rettigheter* 33, 41.

[33] Such as those defined in Article 2 EU (as amended by the Lisbon Treaty): 'human dignity, freedom, democracy, equality, the rule of law and respect for human rights, including the rights of persons belonging to minorities'.

[34] This also applies to the conception of rights in the European Union Member States themselves. For example, even if we all are for 'equality' and 'solidarity', we disagree on whether health care should be defined in terms of an individual right or simply as a general policy objective; we agree on the principle that everyone should have the right to a 'freedom of expression', but disagree on how people should be entitled to exercise that right and where its limits should be drawn. See P Leino, 'A European Approach to Human Rights? Universality Explored', (2002) 71(4) *Nordic Journal of International Law* 455.

[35] The Cotonou Convention provides an excellent example of this approach. See the Partnership agreement between the members of the African, Caribbean and Pacific Group of States of the one part, and the European Community and its Member States of the other part, signed in Cotonou on 23 June 2000, published in [2000] OJ L/317/3. See in particular Art 8 on political dialogue and Art 96 on the formal consultation procedure. Both Articles were revised in the context of the 2005 revision process. See [2005] OJ L/209/26 and [2005] OJ L/287/1. The revised agreement is currently subject to ratification.

[36] I have discussed the conditionality side of the EU human rights policies in P Leino, 'European Universalism? The EU and Human Rights Conditionality', above n 5. In short, serious doubts have been expressed about the usefulness of attaching sanctions to the implementation of human rights. See eg 'The relationship between economic sanctions and respect for economic, social and cultural rights', General Comment No. 8 (1997) adopted by the UN Committee on Economic, Social and Cultural Rights, E/C.12/1997/8. For the classic critical piece analysing the effectiveness of sanctions, see J Galtung, 'On the Effects of International Economic Sanctions. With Examples from the Case of Rhodesia', (1967) 19(3) *World Politics* 378.

'common values' are implemented is of a high significance in guaranteeing that the 'common values' are not simply another name for the EU's own political objectives.

II. DIALOGUE

The most obvious point of departure for an analysis of the EU understanding of the meaning of dialogue is offered by the 'EU guidelines on human rights dialogues' adopted by the Council in 2001 with the objectives of providing greater coherence and consistency, furthering the integration of human rights into all EU action, improving the openness of EU policies and in order to identify priority areas of EU action.[37] Based on this document, the EU's purpose of having a dialogue seems to be this: dialogue is used either in order to share broadly converging views, as with Western states, or in order to achieve change in a third state based on the concerns and wishes of the EU.[38] The EU's guidelines make no provision for the adjustment of its own stance: they are not open to the possibility that the 'other' does not wish to change, or that occasionally, the EU might itself need to adjust its stance in the face of divergent views. In short, either we are the same at the beginning of the dialogue, or then you should be more like us.

There is certainly no lack of alternative definitions for 'dialogue'.[39] For Korhonen, 'dialogue' should by definition be about an exchange of rational ideas based on respect for each other's value and norm systems.[40] In general, the idea behind the concept of 'dialogue' focuses on the 'meeting of different positions', not a merging or assimilation of them.[41] In

---

[37] See the European Union guidelines on human rights dialogues, adopted by the Council of the EU on 13 December 2001.

[38] On the Commission website, the following description of the dialogue is given: 'In general, the human rights dialogues aim at seeking information about the human rights situation in the country concerned, expressing EU concerns about the country's human rights record and identifying practical steps to improve it, in particular through co-operation projects, and discussing questions of mutual interest and enhancing co-operation on human rights in multinational fora such as the United Nations. Moreover, human rights dialogues can at an early stage identify problems likely to lead to conflicts in the future. They can also be useful in exposing governments to international human rights standards and EU practices.' See http://ec.europa.eu/comm/external_relations/human_rights/intro/index.htm, section 5.

[39] See O Korhonen, 'Voidaanko ihmisoikeuksien ja uskonnon suhde ratkaista poliittisen keskustelun kautta?' in K Kouros and S Villa (eds), *Ihmisoikeudet ja islam* (Keuruu, Like, 2004) 339, 340–1.

[40] *Ibid*, 340–2.

[41] See O Korhonen, 'Dialogue among Civilizations: International Law, Human Rights and Difference' in L Hannikainen and SK Sajjadpour, *Dialogue among Civilizations. The Case of Finnish-Iranian Human Rights Expert Dialogue* (Rovaniemi, The Northern Institute for Environmental and Minority Law, University of Lapland, 2002) 30, 33.

fact, genuine dialogue should start and end with disagreement[42]—something that questions its usefulness in the context of policies based on conditionality. Otherwise, Korhonen argues, there is a great risk of dialogue narrowing down to a monologue, in which only one position and one opinion prevails.[43] The idea of dialogue among civilisations presumes the existence of two distinct but interacting positions.[44] Successful dialogue also presumes that both parties acknowledge each other's equal value.[45] A similar understanding of 'dialogue' is reflected in the definition of intercultural dialogue offered by the UN General Assembly:

> Dialogue among civilizations is a process between and within civilizations, founded on inclusion, and a collective desire to learn, uncover and examine assumptions, unfold shared meaning and core values and integrate multiple perspectives through dialogue.[46]

Dialogue does not, however, presume that 'anything goes': The reference to different civilisations and cultural backgrounds does not legitimise any practices with reference to cultures:

> By virtue of being 'cultural' no practice is automatically valuable. The practical, social and personal consequences to its subjects will always have to be scrutinized to be able to say anything about its value.[47]

Having a dialogue is not enough; in running the dialogue, attention needs to be given to the social consequences of the questions being discussed.[48] In the EU, this dimension is extremely visible:

> Dialogue must be the preferred means of encouraging countries to embark on reforms. Unilaterally imposing new conditions must be avoided. Dialogue must have a substantial preventive dimension and permit the discussion of often politically sensitive issues [...]. Sanctions may nevertheless prove necessary in serious cases. In such instances incentive approaches must also be developed to remedy the problems identified.[49]

---

[42] *Ibid*, 33.

[43] *Ibid*.

[44] *Ibid*, 30.

[45] E Tuomioja, 'Sivilisaatioiden välinen dialogi ja kansainväliset ihmisoikeudet' in K Kouros and S Villa (eds), above n 39, 345. See also the resolution on the ACP–EU political dialogue adopted by the ACP–EU Parliamentary Assembly, which stresses that political dialogue should be a reciprocal process between equal partners based on mutual trust, which places the ACP countries in a position to call in particular for the coherence of EU policies and their impact on the ACP countries to be examined. [2005] OJ C/80/17, para 26.

[46] 'Global Agenda for Dialogue among Civilizations', A/RES/56/6, adopted on 21 November 2001, Art 1.

[47] O Korhonen, 'Dialogue among Civilizations: International Law, Human Rights and Difference', above n 41, 36.

[48] *Ibid*, 38.

[49] Communication from the Commission to the Council, the European Parliament, the European Economic and Social Committee and the Committee of the Regions. 'Governance

For the EU, dialogue is essentially a tool for persuasion, rather than an element of negotiation. However, genuine dialogue would seem to require that the EU would need to forget about imposing conditions; after all, their contents should also correspond to the wishes of the other party.

Thus, on the theoretical level, the EU understanding of 'dialogue' appears as somewhat problematic. The practical implementation of the EU guidelines witnesses a similar confusion. In relation to some third states political dialogue conducted by the Union forms a part of the diplomatic discussions between the parties without any formal basis in an agreement between them; this is the case with 'strong states' such as the Western industrialised countries and other states with significant political negotiating positions.[50] With some of these states, such as China and Iran, dialogue focuses specifically on human rights. The EU has also conducted informal *ad hoc* dialogues with certain states, such as Cuba or Sudan. As with China, with these states the emphasis is less on 'common values' since the deviating positions of the parties are acknowledged; the purpose of the dialogue is to transmit the positions of the parties.[51] The main significance of dialogue in these cases is underlining that values are not irrelevant for the EU: in particular, dialogue is not linked to political conditionality.[52] However, for example, the dialogue with China has often been criticised as insufficient: the EU has not seemed to care much about the actual attainment of the human rights objectives it purports to aim at. In fact, it is recognised that human rights, the rule of law and political reforms are 'sensitive for China'.[53] For this reason:

---

in the European Consensus on Development. Towards a harmonised approach within the European Union' Brussels 30.8.2006, COM(2006) 421 final, 7.

[50] For the purposes of this Chapter, I use the terms 'weak' and 'strong' states. Another possible characterisation would be 'industrialised' and 'developing' states. However, while Russia, for example, is not necessarily an 'industrialised' state comparable to Japan or the US, it is definitely a 'strong' state, for example, in terms of geopolitical and bargaining power. Therefore, the use of terms 'strong' and 'weak' seem more appropriate. See also P Leino, 'European Universalism? The EU and Human Rights Conditionality', above n 5.

[51] The descriptions of the dialogues run with China and Iran included in the 2006 EU Annual Human Rights Report provide good examples of this. In relation to China, the Report states, '[a]s always, the EU handed over a list of individual cases of concern, on which China provided replies in writing.' Following this, a number of concerns were raised by the EU. Then the 'Chinese side informed the EU of a number of legislative reforms taken or under way' (at 18). With Iran, the Report notes that 'since the start of the dialogue there has been little or no progress against the EU's benchmarks'. The dialogue had included a broad range of participants, including the government, the judiciary, academics, and civil society. The Report acknowledges, 'engaging with Iran is a way to encourage those who want to promote reforms there' (at 19).

[52] See eg the Commission Policy Paper for Transmission to the Council and the European Parliament. 'A Maturing partnership—shared interests and challenges in EU–China relations', Brussels 10.9 2003, COM (2003) 533 final.

[53] *Ibid*, 7.

Dialogue and co-operation should continue to constitute the main EU approach to improving the human rights situation in China, although this should not exclude expressing comments and observations in other appropriate fora.[54]

Thus in relation to China, dialogue 'is the Union's preferred channel for working to improve the situation in areas of concern to it'.[55] The Council's conclusion is somehow surprising, recalling that it is talking about *dialogue*: 'The European Union urges China to contribute to this exchange too.'[56]

In the EU guidelines, a particular position in the context of human rights policies is allocated to those Western states with whom the EU believes it shares the same 'common values', such as the EEA countries, the United States and Canada.[57] With these countries the dialogue on values mainly focuses on how the 'common values' of the parties would be best promoted globally.[58] The assumption is that the positions of the parties are similar, and thus dialogue functions as the tool for asserting the joint position.

Dialogue can also form a part of an agreement, take regulated forms and be linked to political conditionality. This is the case with the weak states—the EU's candidate states, the 77 African, Caribbean and Pacific (ACP) states, the Latin American countries, the Mediterranean states and the countries of the Western Balkans. Considering developing states, 'common values' figure in the Community's unilateral scheme of generalised tariff preferences (GSP)[59] and in the Community development policy through the Cotonou Convention, which contains a long and rather elaborate human rights clause.[60] The EU places particular emphasis on

[54] *Ibid*, 13.
[55] See the Conclusions of General Affairs Council 2,327th Council Meeting, 'EU–China dialogue on human rights', Brussels 22–23 January 2001, para 6.
[56] *Ibid*, para 7.
[57] On this, see P Leino, 'Dialogia vai fraseologiaa? "Yhteiset arvot" EU:n ja kolmansien maiden välisissä suhteissa' in S Pohjonen (ed), *Ennakoiva oikeus* (Helsinki, Talentum, 2005) 226.
[58] For descriptions of discussions with like-minded countries, see the EU Annual Human Rights Report 2006, 20. For Canada, cooperation in the UN Human Rights Council and coordination between like-minded countries was mentioned; with New Zealand, discussions on strengthening cooperation were held; in relation to the Candidate countries, information about future EU initiatives was provided with a request for support for them. The death penalty was discussed with Japan, as it was discussed with the US together with topics relating to counter-terrorism; however, it seems that little conclusions were drawn from these discussions on the EU side.
[59] Council regulation (EC) No 980/2005 of 27 June 2005 applying a scheme of generalised tariff preferences, [2005] OJ L/169/1.
[60] See Art 186 and 212 TFEU. See also the Partnership agreement between the members of the African, Caribbean and Pacific Group of States of the one part, and the European Community and its Member States of the other part, signed in Cotonou on 23 June 2000, published in [2000] OJ L/317/3. See esp. Art 9 on 'Essential Element and Fundamental Element'.

'dialogue' in its relations with the developing world; this is visible in the recent Communication on the EU Strategy for Africa:

> it is crucial that the EU's relations with Africa should be increasingly pervaded by a culture of dialogue. The importance of a permanent, frank and constructive political dialogue can hardly be underestimated.[61]

With most of the weak states, despite the rhetorical reference to 'common values' as a basis for the relationship, the EU would seem to assume that the approaches of its partners to human rights differ from those of its own.[62] The main purpose of dialogue is to guide their development. The direction is clear: the third countries are to follow the EU's model.[63]

The recent Communication by the Commission on the relations between the EU and Latin America can serve as an example of this vision.[64] The Communication starts by describing how the EU as a world actor needs to consolidate its relations with its closest partners, including Latin America

> with which we share a common commitment to human rights, democracy and multilateralism. Europe needs all its friends in order to assert these common values. Few regions in the world offer so many reasons to build a genuine alliance.[65]

Then the Commission moves on to describe the economic significance of the partnership: the EU is not only the largest foreign investor in Latin America; it is the largest donor and the primary trading partner for many countries in the region. While most of these countries have adopted democratic systems, they face major challenges due to various destabilising factors. It is here that the EU comes in: 'The EU could draw on its experience to help strengthen stability and security and bring sustainable development to Latin America.'[66] However, this comes at a cost: if Europe is ready to commit itself further to Latin America, it also expects a firm

---

[61] See Communication from the Commission to the Council, the European Parliament and the European Economic and Social Committee, 'EU Strategy for Africa: Towards a Euro-African pact to accelerate Africa's development'. Brussels 12.10.2005, COM(2005) 489 final, point 2.2.3.

[62] Even if the starting point of the relationship between the EU and its Candidate States was their 'common values', in the view of the EU, the Candidate States had a long way to go in this area. The Candidate States needed to both embrace the 'common values' and implement them following an EU agenda before their membership of the Union was deemed possible. See P Leino, 'Rights, Rules and Democracy in the EU Enlargement Process: Between Universalism and Identity', above n 11.

[63] The same pattern was visible in the enlargement process of the EU eastwards: see P Leino, *ibid*.

[64] Communication from the Commission to the Council and the European Parliament, 'A stronger partnership between the European Union and Latin America', Brussels 8.12.2005 COM(2005) 636 final.

[65] *Ibid*, 5.

[66] *Ibid*.

commitment in return.[67] This presumes development in two areas in particular: first, stepping up and focusing political dialogue, and second, creating a climate that is more favourable to trade and development[68]—the latter, of course, being a quite straightforward acknowledgement of how the prosperity of Europe relies on trade and the openness of markets.[69] Thus, the message of the Communication is clear: the EU is happy to assist others in implementing its own home-grown best practices. A similar understanding of the meaning of dialogue is reflected in the Commission's recent Communication on an EU-Caribbean Partnership:

> A strong political partnership between the EU and the Caribbean—founded on shared values—is central to further enhancing EU–Caribbean relations and responding collectively to the political challenges facing the Caribbean region.[70]

Against the background of the definitions of dialogue cited in the beginning of this section, the EU understanding of its meaning seems awkward; after all, it mainly aims at changing the other party. Dialogue in this sense does not aim at the development of both parties, but at securing the development of one of them towards a certain objective, the attainment of which is monitored and assessed by the other party; one with a deeper understanding of the meaning of the 'common values'. This is problematic—after all, dialogue should be a means towards a genuinely jointly defined end, which requires that both parties are willing to adjust their direction and courses of action.

In principle, there is no reason why the EU could not sometimes represent an interest that is universally recognised and accepted. But how to know whether this is the case? Promoting one's own objectives might do little harm, presuming that those objectives are good and compatible with the objectives of others—after all, the universal is always rooted in and coloured by some particular content without having an independent

---

[67] *Ibid.*

[68] *Ibid*, 10. The Commission also mentions support to the countries in the region and more effective cooperation as specific areas requiring improvement.

[69] See 'Bilateral Agreements in EU trade policy', speech given by Peter Mandelson at the London School of Economics on 9 October 2006; available at http://ec.europa.eu/commission_barroso/mandelson/speeches_articles/sppm118_en.htm.

[70] See Communication from the Commission to the Council, the European Parliament and the European Economic and Social Committee, 'An EU-Caribbean Partnership for growth, stability and development'. Brussels 2.3.2006, COM(2006) 86 final. See also the Joint statement by the Council and the representatives of the governments of the Member States meeting within the Council, the European Parliament and the Commission on European Union Development Policy: 'The European Consensus', [2006] OJ C/46/1, para 17 'An in-depth political dialogue': 'Political dialogue is an important way in which to further development objectives. In the framework of the political dialogue conducted by the Member States and by the European Union institutions [...] the respect for good governance, human rights, democratic principles and the rule of law will be regularly assessed with a view to forming a shared understanding and identifying supporting measures. This dialogue has an important preventive dimension and aims to ensure these principles are upheld.'

substance.[71] Since the universal does not have a representative of its own, it can only be present through the particular; thus, a preference is not necessarily wrong just because it is particular. For this reason, it becomes necessary to observe the functioning of argumentation based on 'common values' in practice. The central question here is what happens to those states that, despite perhaps sharing the EU's 'common values' at some abstract level, prefer their own understanding of them at the expense of the EU's reading, or have a different understanding of how these values should be turned into practical measures. Recalling the purposes of genuine dialogue, such an outcome should be possible—but how is this to be combined with the political context in which the EU invokes dialogue?

III. COMMON VALUES IN ACTION: THE DEVELOPMENT CONTEXT

These questions can be usefully explored in the context of the long-standing discussion on the 'right to development' between the industrialised states and the developing world. On this matter, there have always been two discourses that do not meet, reflecting the difficult clash between the wish of the developing countries for increased autonomy and self-reliance on one hand, and the donors' fear for misuse or mismanagement of funds on the other.[72] For developing states, the entitlement to receive aid has been the most central part of this right.[73] The industrialised states, however, have never accepted a *duty* to provide assistance; instead, development assistance must remain an act of charity on their part.

Of relevance for this question is the joint statement entitled 'The European Consensus on Development' adopted in December 2005 by the European Parliament, the Council and the Commission, which is naturally based on the 'common values' that the EU partnership and dialogue with third countries is designed to promote.[74] In this document the three institutions lay down the traditional cornerstones of European development policies—that the developing countries have the prime responsibility for their own development, but that 'sustainable development includes

---

[71] Generally, see S Žižek, above n 30, 110.

[72] For the latter argument, see 'Evaluating co-ordination and complementarity of country strategy paper with national development priorities', study conducted by the Evaluation Service of the Department for International Development, and commissioned by the Evaluation services of the European Union 2006, 14.

[73] See eg the UN General Assembly resolution of 4 December 2002 on the right to development, A/RES/57/223, para 15, reaffirming the commitment of developed countries to give 0.7% of their GNP for official development assistance to developing countries.

[74] These include the beautiful values of 'respect of human rights, fundamental freedoms, peace, democracy, good governance, gender equality, the rule of law, solidarity and justice'. *Ibid*, para 13.

good governance, human rights and political, economic, social and environmental aspects'.[75] In short, development is understood in following terms:

> Successful development requires: adherence to human rights, democratic principles and the rule of law; and effective, well-governed states; and strong efficient institutions.[76]

The approach follows logically from that taken already in 1991, when the Council of Ministers adopted a resolution on development and human rights, underlining the need for positive measures and increased assistance to countries that respect human rights.[77] Some 15 years later, this vision is dressed in following terms:

> Progress in the protection of human rights, good governance and democratisation is fundamental for poverty reduction and sustainable development. All people should enjoy all human rights in line with international agreements. The Community will on this basis promote the respect for human rights of all people in cooperation with both states and non-state actors in partner countries.[78]

Faithful to the liberal tradition, both the 1991 resolution and the 'European Consensus' approach human rights and democracy as a precondition for development. However, the idea of a 'European consensus' symbolises many of the problems it embodies: already the thought that a consensus on the essence of development could be reached on the European continent, without any participation of those most affected by the matter, seems odd.

Sadly, this might not be far from the truth. As King has argued, the EU's understanding implies in practice that it claims a right to supervise the domestic implementation of the right to development:

> If aid is to be given to promote development, and development can occur only in a democratic society guaranteeing human rights, in order to ensure that

---

[75] *Ibid*, paras 2, 7. The same vision can, of course, be found in various rather general instruments of global nature. However, the 'European Consensus' differs from them in making explicit whose task it is to enforce these goals in practice.

[76] See also 'The EU and Africa: Towards a strategic partnership' adopted by the European Council on 15 and 16 December 2005, para 5. On the approach in general, see S Seppänen, *Possibilities and Challenges of the Human Rights-Based Approach to Development* (Helsinki, The Erik Castrén Institute Research Reports 17/2005, 2005).

[77] [1991] 6 Bull EC, para 1.45, Art 8. 'Positive measures' have been gradually introduced to the EC development cooperation. See especially Council Reg 975/1999 of 29 April 1999 laying down the requirements for the implementation of development cooperations which contribute to the general objective of developing and consolidating democracy and the rule of law and to that of respecting human rights and fundamental freedoms, [1999] OJ L/120/1.

[78] Joint statement by the Council and the representatives of the governments of the Member States meeting within the Council, the European Parliament and the Commission on European Union Development Policy: 'The European Consensus', [2006] OJ C/46/1, para 86.

individuals are able to realise their right to development the Community must be entitled to take measures to promote democracy and human rights.[79]

The problem with this logic is that the right to development, which initially was a tool used by the developing states to justify increased amounts of development assistance, turns into a tool for the developed countries that use it to justify far-reaching domestic adjustments by recipient states, which traditionally would have been considered to fall within the domestic jurisdiction of the latter.[80] While the right to development forms a central element of universal human rights for the developing world,[81] the EU as their 'partner' wishes to address the two as separate questions. Instead of being an entitlement to a right, development is merely an objective, and aid remains linked to performance, EU standards and the need of the developing state.[82] With the right to development thus quite transformed, the EU has adopted its own reading of it, and then declared itself responsible for supervising its implementation—thus speaking as the voice of the 'universal'.

This underlines how the abstract nature of the language of 'common values' actually hides from sight quite a fundamental disagreement relating to their implementation. Despite these opposite understandings, the two worlds have recently managed to include their views into the same document. The Cairo Declaration incorporates a reference to the 'shared values' of the parties but by making specific reference to the right to development:

> We reaffirm our commitment to promote and protect all human rights including the right to development and fundamental freedoms taking into account their universal, interdependent and indivisible character, as confirmed by our commitment to the Charter of the United Nations and the Universal Declaration on Human Rights.[83]

However, on the whole, the Cairo Declaration approaches this from a different starting point:

---

[79] T King, 'Human Rights in the Development Policy of the European Community: Towards a European World Order?', (1997) XXVIII *Netherlands Yearbook of International Law* 51, 66–67.

[80] *Ibid*, 67.

[81] For one view from a developing state, see K Kibwana, *Fundamental Rights and Freedoms in Kenya* (Nairobi, Oxford University Press, 1990), Kibwana argues: 'for a developing country to secure the [first and second generation] rights for her people, it is also necessary that such a country enjoys third generation group rights [...]'. *Ibid*, 92.

[82] Especially after the Cotonou agreement, allocation of aid is no longer automatic but based on needs and performance. See K Arts, 'ACP–EU Relations in a New Era: The Cotonou Agreement', (2003) 40 CML Rev 95, 100. See also K Arts, *Integrating Human Rights into Development Cooperation: The Case of the Lomé Convention* (The Hague, Kluwer Law International, 2000), 44.

[83] Cairo declaration adopted by the Africa Europe Summit under the Aegis of the OAU and the EU, Cairo, 3–4 April 2000, para 43.

We deplore the intolerable fact that more than half of all Africans are living in absolute poverty and agree to intensify the fight against poverty. The primary responsibility for alleviating poverty lies at home with each country, but this does not diminish the importance of the international dimension in the war against poverty.[84]

The central position given to poverty reduction points at a practical difficulty with the EU's human rights based approach to development: little clear added value can be attributed to development strategies based on human rights as compared to, for example, poverty reduction strategies.[85] Moreover, while the implementation of human rights are presented as a precondition for development, this is occasionally contradicted by findings in the field, showing how many of the fastest growing states have actually been dictatorships and not democracies.[86] While it is commonly proclaimed that there is a positive correlation between human rights and development, there is also plenty of evidence to the contrary.[87] This provokes various fundamental questions relating to the EU development policies. Most crucially, while our policies seem to promise that the reforms we insist upon will automatically lead to a certain outcome (development), this is not necessarily the case: our recipe for development is only one among various options. This is because there is from a technical point of view no consensus on how to bring about 'development'; thus, political choices between different alternatives need to be made.[88] The question is who should make these decisions.

In the development context it is also apparent that while human rights offer objectives, they do not provide for solutions.[89] The assertion that development is based on human rights includes no guidance for prioritising different human rights or needs; and the idea of prioritisation remains equally alien to human rights law at large. As Seppänen has shown, no matter how large the development budget, choices still need to be made between different sectors and projects.[90] Development issues often involve either grass-roots issues or large structural questions, such as integration to the world economy; and on both of these human rights law remains

---

[84] *Ibid*, para 87.

[85] S Seppänen, *Possibilities and Challenges of the Human Rights-Based Approach to Development*, above n 76, 96.

[86] See S Seppänen, *Good Governance in International Law* (Helsinki, The Erik Castrén Institute Research Reports 13/2003, 2003) 24.

[87] S Seppänen, *Possibilities and Challenges of the Human Rights-Based Approach to Development*, above n 76, 96–8.

[88] See D Kennedy, 'Laws and Developments' in A Perry and J Hatchard (eds), *Contemplating Complexity, Law and Development in the 21st Century* (London, Cavendish Publishing: 2003).

[89] S Seppänen, *Possibilities and Challenges of the Human Rights-Based Approach to Development*, above n 76.

[90] *Ibid*, eg at 97.

silent.[91] In the real world, few decisions relating to the implementation of particular development projects are for everybody's good: instead, when somebody wins, somebody else loses. 'Common values' cannot alone justify specific policy choices or guide those solving day-to-day problems at the grass-roots level; still, in implementing these values, choices need to be made. This suggests that it is not impossible to give rights more specified meanings. However, the more concrete and policy-guiding rights become, the less universal they are. Their interpretation becomes dependent on a specific situation; a specific time and place. By seeing assistance as subject to its own discretion, the EU arrogates this choice to itself. As the donor, it can decide.

This suggests that human rights are seldom 'automatically' realised. Their implementation requires divergent interpretations or priorities under the surface of the universal language. In practice, the EU view prevails, because it is the actor with the economic and financial resources. This results in the EU defining what the underlying 'common values' require in a particular situation; thus, quite often their charm turns against those states that are at the receiving end. Far too often, the

> actual contents of the universalist arguments are determined by those who implement them on the ground. If one is not in such a position, universalist arguments are best left unused.[92]

The more indeterminate the EU standards are, the more the Commission (or whoever applies the standards) has political discretion to say whether some state does (or does not) fulfil them. The abstraction of rights turns human rights into a matter of institutional politics, and their interpretation becomes dependent on who has the power to implement them in particular cases. The actual meaning of the 'common values' comes to be decided in administrative processes, not by politicians but by bureaucrats.

The right to development thus offers a good example of the contradictions inherent in the discussion of universal human rights or 'common values'. While there is no doubt of the need for action and enhanced efforts in order to achieve development, the right itself is a symbol of balancing between rhetoric and reality; universal rights and agnosticism. As both resources and political will are limited, the rhetoric of universal declarations alone will achieve little. If, however, the right to development were a truly universal right, then much would need to happen: the West would need to treat its wealth on a completely different basis and be prepared to

---

[91]   *Ibid*, 96–8.
[92]   For this argument relating to good governance as a 'universal' principle, S Seppänen, *Good Governance in International Law*, above n 86, 122.

distribute it in terms of more genuine solidarity,[93] so that the developing states would also be able to exercise an economic power equal to the West. In this way, the right to development is an example of universalism in an agnostic world, which endures a lack of resources and lacks a voice that would be genuinely universal. As such, it articulates the agnostic reality of the world, but also shows how quickly universalism turns into paternalism. Recalling that the EU is today the world's greatest donor and half of the public aid received by the developing world comes from the Union, the actual functioning of the 'dialogue' on the 'common values' in this context and its effects on the substance or conditions of the relationship is quite crucial.

IV. QUESTIONS OF PROCESS

As regards the choices made in the context of the EU policies relating to the 'right to development', the most obvious context for their exploration is the relationship between the EU and the ACP states under the Cotonou Convention. Even though the human rights clause included in the Convention possesses a more specific form than many others, the human rights agenda set by the Convention remains rather general in nature:

> The rough contours of standards to be met are provided, but these by no means extend to a roadmap ready for implementation at the national level. Obviously, this was done on purpose, so as to create the necessary space for national prioritising and own policy choices.[94]

Partly for this reason the ACP-EC Council of Ministers adopted guidelines for human rights dialogues in May 2003 with the aim of providing a more detailed framework for political dialogue established by the Agreement.[95] Unfortunately, in referring to the need to maintain principles like 'flexibility', 'transparency', 'inclusiveness', 'legitimacy' and 'process approach', the

---

[93] For an alternative vision stressing the global collective responsibility, see the United Nations Millennium Declaration adopted by the United Nations General Assembly on 18 September 2000, A/RES/55/2. For a scheme creating a Global Resources Dividend, aiming at global economic justice, see TW Pogge, *World Poverty and Human Rights. Cosmopolitan Responsibilities and Reforms* (Cambridge, Polity Press, 2002). For six critiques of the present global public order and the same number of visions for a just world order for the future, see BS Chimni, 'Alternative Visions of Just World Order: Six Tales from India' (2005) 46(2) *Harvard International Law Journal* 389–402.

[94] K Arts, 'Political dialogue requires investment: meeting the human rights commitment of the Cotonou Agreement' in (2003) 200 *The Courier ACP–EU* 21.

[95] See the Guidelines for ACP–EU Political Dialogue (Art 8) as adopted by the joint ACP–EU Council of Ministers at its 76th session in Brussels in May 2003.

guidelines add little to the actual Convention.[96] Since the relevant provisions of the Convention are too general to provide substantive direction for policies, much of the actual implementation of the human rights objectives in regard to each developing country has taken place through the country strategy papers, which have been used by the Community as a tool for improving the planning and management of its development since the late 1990s. However, even the strategy papers have not really contributed to the aims they were thought to promote. Instead, a recent study suggests that they have, in fact, had the effect of restraining the possibilities for dialogue at the local level by limiting the possibility to adjust the aid management process.[97] This is largely due to the dominant position of Brussels officials in the decision-making. While strategy papers had been endorsed by the partner country Government in the formal sense, their comments often appeared more a procedural requirement to be fulfilled rather than an opportunity of dialogue and debate between the parties.[98]

The difficulties experienced by the weaker state have been frequently pointed out in the context of EU policies: the standards implemented are open to various possible interpretations, and the process is entirely based on the interests of the stronger party—after all, in practice the procedure relating to the usage of the human rights clause only works one way,[99] and is ultimately based on a unilateral decision made by one party with reference to its own prerogatives.[100] Recently, the European Parliament also has called for greater transparency and objectivity as concerns the criteria to be invoked,[101] stressing that:

[96] Instead of repeating the obvious, they could, for example, have elaborated on the role of civil society in the process, and on the relationship of the Cotonou Convention to other ongoing development processes. K Arts, 'Political dialogue requires investment: meeting the human rights commitment of the Cotonou Agreement' in (2003) 200 *The Courier ACP–EU* 21, 23.

[97] 'Evaluating co-ordination and complementarity of country strategy paper with national development priorities', study conducted by the Evaluation Service of the Department for International Development, and commissioned by the Evaluation services of the European Union 2006, 16. In fact, the Report argues that the strategy papers had even limited the promotion of alignment, co-ordination and complementarity of aid.

[98] *Ibid*, 47.

[99] On this see, eg, K Arts, *Integrating Human Rights into Development Cooperation: The Case of the Lomé Convention*, above n 82, 193.

[100] However, in the new GSP regulation, Art 16 lays down the rules on temporary withdrawal, ie based on serious and systematic violations of principles included in 16 core human and labour rights conventions adopted under the UN and ILO regimes. What is new here is that the process of withdrawal has been made conditional on the conclusions of the relevant monitoring body and is thus ultimately not merely an independent EU decision. Council Reg (EC) No 980/2005 of 27 June 2005 applying a scheme of generalised tariff preferences, [2005] OJ L/169/1.

[101] The European Parliament resolution (2006)0056 on the human rights and democracy clause in European Union agreements, para 15.

one of the factors which have compromised the application of the clause is the generic nature of its wording, since this does not spell out detailed procedures for 'positive' and 'negative' interventions under EU/third country cooperation, leaving the Council and Member States' national imperatives to hold sway over the more general requirements of human rights.[102]

While the Parliament proposed adding human rights clauses to all new EU agreements and formulating them in greater detail,[103] this would not seem to be enough to solve the most fundamental problem relating to the operation of the clause. This problem relates to the abstraction of human rights, which is transferred to the EU's policies and the conditions it invokes, which become equally unable to imply any substantive criteria.[104] This ambiguity allows the stronger party to determine at the stage of implementation what is actually aimed at.

Today, the EU understanding of the meaning and purpose of running a dialogue is very closely linked to promoting its own views and positions, which, however, are defended as if they were non-political and neutral; for the 'good' of everybody. However, in practice, defending your own economic and commercial interests is often difficult to combine with the interests of others. For example, it is difficult to find solutions that would be equally beneficial for an EU-based transnational corporation operating in global markets and the citizens of a developing state. The question is not simply about what is good for everybody but about making choices that are in fact political in nature.

The relationship between the EU and weaker states is characterised by a lack of such dialogue that could actually bring about substantive changes. This is closely linked to the underlying assumptions of the purpose of dialogue on the EU side, but also has a practical side to it. The lack of dialogue is strongly built into the EU's own internal methods of functioning: the EU position is at the opening stage of external negotiations already relatively final as a result of lengthy intra-EU negotiations. Therefore, the re-opening of its negotiating position at the stage when external negotiations are launched is a practical impossibility, which makes the EU structurally unable to engage in such dialogue that could actively affect the outcome. Quite recently, certain Articles of the Cotonou Convention have been revised in order to reflect basic principles that the EU wishes to underline with the agreement (equality, partnership and ownership), the idea being that 'a formal, structured dialogue should be held systematically

---

[102] *Ibid*, para 4.

[103] *Ibid*, paras 8, 10.

[104] While the open-ended wording of the human rights clause is politically convenient for the Community, it leaves legal uncertainty both as to the scope and reach of the clauses and to their mechanisms of interpretation and application. For a further discussion, see, eg, E Fierro Sedano, *The EU's Approach to Human Rights Conditionality in Practice* (The Hague, Martinus Nijhoff Publishers, 2003).

with each country'.[105] This would seem to require much greater investment in such dialogue: keeping in mind that there are 77 ACP countries, it is obvious that the Union has insufficient resources for such an undertaking at any satisfactory level. But most crucially, it should be kept in mind that when 'common values' are implemented, they have effects at local level. For this reason, the implementation of these values also provokes the question of political responsibility, not only in relation to the European electorate, which has so far been the main consideration, but those much more directly affected by our foreign policy decisions.

A recent study on the Community support given to further good governance formulated the challenge as one of playing 'a positive, pro-active role in supporting governance while avoiding the "conditionality gap"'.[106] The report argues that the EU's political response capacity ought to be strengthened in order to deal properly with the *politics* of EU governance support. Among other things, this would require a greater understanding of the nature and dynamics of political and societal trans-formation processes in different contexts, and much greater willingness to engage in multi-actor political dialogue on governance priorities.[107] Instead of providing largely imported agendas, priority should be given to

> the elaboration, negotiation, adoption and implementation of home-grown governance agendas, owned by the different stakeholders (through an enlarged political dialogue) and properly articulated with the various levels of governance (local, national, regional).[108]

Following this, the focus of policies should be widened from a technical approach to a much more solid institutional development approach, which takes into consideration a wider scope of questions relating to culture, leadership, incentives, organisational behaviour and incentives for change.[109] Since questions relating to the sound management of finances form a key area in the relations between the donor and the recipient, genuine dialogue should be extended to cover these questions as well, using the partnership as a forum for committing 'the partners to new ways of solving examples of fraud in amicable ways'.[110]

---

[105]   See the 'Information Note on the Revision of the Cotonou Agreement' on the round of negotiations concluded on 23 February issued by the Commission and available on its website. The revised agreement is published in [2005] OJ L/209/26 and [2005] OJ L/287/1.
[106]   Thematic evaluation of the EC support to good governance. Final report Volume 1 Synthesis report, Evaluation for the European Commission, June 2006, 7.
[107]   *Ibid*, 9.
[108]   *Ibid*.
[109]   *Ibid*, 9–10.
[110]   'Evaluating co-ordination and complementarity of country strategy paper with national development priorities', study conducted by the Evaluation Service of the Department for International Development, and commissioned by the Evaluation services of the European Union 2006, 18.

For this reason, a much more political understanding of development policy objectives would also be needed.[111] This points at a need to understand the process of setting and implementing development policy objectives as a political, rather than technical, exercise. To the extent 'common values' exist, finding agreement on their content requires genuine discussion and a fair process, which gives a possibility to speak to all parties concerned. 'Common values' are no substitute for political debate but require discussion, because their contents are contested.[112] Thus, even the contents of terms like 'freedom', 'justice', 'equality' or 'right' should receive their meaning through political deliberation, since they have little independent meaning outside a particular context.[113] For this reason, when seeking the limits of what is genuinely shared or universal, openness in relation to its exclusions and inclusions should be fundamental. As Žižek has argued, universality that is 'living' and 'concrete' presumes a

> permanent process of the questioning and the renegotiation of its own "official" content. Universality becomes "actual" precisely and only by rendering thematic the exclusions on which it is grounded, by continuously questioning, renegotiating, displacing them, that is, by assuming the gap between its own form and content, by conceiving itself as unaccomplished in its very notion.[114]

Dialogue is a precondition for the emergence of universal values: to the extent that human rights represent an 'emerging consensus', they mainly provide

> an opportunity for a debate on the manner in which the norms that are contained in international declarations and conventions can best be implemented. Such a debate, and the consensus that, it is hoped, may emerge from that debate, are indispensable conditions for arriving at a greater respect for human rights in all parts of the world.[115]

More than a set of criteria that could be used as conditions, universality of rights refers to a general direction for government policies, a horizon, and calls for dialogue and inclusion. However, genuine universality in its requirement of dialogue is also more complex—after all, intercultural dialogue on rights questions becomes far more complicated if all cultures are allowed to participate as equals instead of one view dominating the

---

[111] On this, see also D Kennedy, *The Dark Sides of Virtue. Reassessing International Humanitarianism* (Princeton and Oxford, Princeton University Press, 2004) 329.

[112] For discussion on this, see J Klabbers, 'Redemption Song? Human Rights Versus Community-building in East Timor', (2003) 16 *Leiden J of Intl Law* 367, at 373–376.

[113] See BR Barber, *Strong Democracy. Participatory Politics for a New Age* (University of California Press, 1984/2003) 157.

[114] S Žižek , 'Class Struggle or Postmodernism? Yes, please!' above n 30, 162.

[115] PR Baehr, *Human Rights. Universality in Practice* (Basingstoke, Palgrave Macmillan, 2001) 18.

discussion.[116] A good development policy is not about the adoption of someone else's best practices, but about building capacity for contestation about the terms of the policy, its costs, the potential winners and losers of the policy and its cultural consequences.[117] In short, '[i]t is too easy to assume that those who do not agree with us suffer from false consciousness'—even this is an assumption that can be tested in genuine dialogue.[118]

The process for implementing the 'common values' is of utmost importance in guaranteeing that when substantive choices are made, the decision process is open to all on something approaching an equal basis and those taking the decisions are accountable to those whose interests are affected.[119] Even values should receive their meaning in the same political process by being properly identified, weighed, and accommodated.[120] This is where the necessity of conducting a genuine dialogue with others steps in: it is not possible to reach a true consensus without symmetrical relations between all the participants. This presumes

> relations of mutual recognition, mutual role-taking, a shared willingness to consider one's own tradition with the eyes of the stranger and to learn from one another, and so forth.[121]

Solving these questions belongs to the people most closely affected by the decision; thus they have their proper place in the political processes in the recipient state and are not to be settled by the 'Brussels bureaucrats' as technical questions. Greater efforts should be made to promote capacity building of partner country institutions and increased local ownership. Based on the report quoted above, as a first step, instead of directing policies from Brussels, more power should be given to the local level to control funds and set priorities. More flexible guidelines should be used to enable the adaptation of policies to local opportunities through local

---

[116] M Ignatieff, *Human Rights as Politics and Idolatry* (introduced and edited by A Gutmann), (Princeton, Princeton University Press, 2001) 63.

[117] See D Kennedy, above n 111, 354.

[118] O Korhonen, above n 41, 43.

[119] On this, see JH Ely, *Democracy and Distrust. A Theory of Judicial Review* (Cambridge, Harvard University Press, 1980/2001) 74 [emphasis omitted], who uses this argument when analysing judgments of the US Constitutional Court. The argument, however, seems to be equally applicable here.

[120] *Ibid*, 77.

[121] See J Habermas, 'Remarks on Legitimation through Human Rights' in J Habermas, *The Postnational Constellation: Political Essays*, translated, edited, and with an introduction by Max Pensky (Cambridge, MIT Press, 2001) 113, 129.

dialogue.[122] Moreover, instead of setting the key policies with governments, which in many developing countries are not known for their accountability to the people, future policies ought to be presented to the civil society, and then brought to the parliaments in the partner states for approval, since in the 'new, weak democracies these processes are cornerstones in the construction of the political process'.[123] In this context, the absence of support to political society from among the EU democracy support programmes has also been pointed out.[124] As concerns the participation of civil society in the process, so far non-state actors have participated in the programming of aid.[125] However, actual dialogue concerning the implementation of the programmes presents a challenge to established practice, since the association of non-state actors with dialogue on political issues has been sensitive and for governments in difficult circumstances problematic. Consequently, the involvement of civil society has so far not been systematic at country level and thus greater efforts would need to be made in this respect.[126] Since the current funding procedures, known for their rigidity and inflexibility, exceed the capacity of most organisations at local level, they should be simplified so as to avoid the current outcome that large international NGOs with few linkages to local communities act as the main beneficiaries of EC resources.[127]

In this context, it is equally crucial to keep in mind that the attempts at external imposition of human rights, democracy and good governance could well also be counter-productive. This is because a government may lose its democratic legitimacy if it continually responds to the wishes of external actors: 'Good governance is accountability to the governed, not to the donors.'[128] In EU policy, our societal model (Western, liberal market economy) has often been presented as the 'final destination' at which other

---

[122] 'Evaluating co-ordination and complementarity of country strategy paper with national development priorities', study conducted by the Evaluation Service of the Department for International Development, and commissioned by the Evaluation services of the European Union 2006, 46.

[123] *Ibid*, 95.

[124] See 'No lasting Peace and Prosperity without Democracy and Human Rights. Harnessing debates on the EU's future Financial Instruments'. Report commissioned by the European Parliament; carried out under the auspices of the Netherlands Institute for Multiparty Democracy, July 2005, 15–16.

[125] L Stathopoulos, 'Political dialogue under Art 8 reflects the normal state of affairs in relations between the Community and the ACP states', (2003) 200 *The Courier ACP–EU* 18, 19.

[126] *Ibid*.

[127] See 'No lasting Peace and Prosperity without Democracy and Human Rights. Harnessing debates on the EU's future Financial Instruments'. Report commissioned by the European Parliament; carried out under the auspices of the Netherlands Institute for Multiparty Democracy, July 2005, 14.

[128] P Nherere, 'Conditionality, Human Rights and Good Governance: a Dialogue of Unequal Partners' in K Ginther *et al* (eds), *Sustainable Development and Good Governance* (Dordrecht, Martinus Nijhoff Publishers, 1995) 289, 306.

countries should aim. This seems to disregard both the need for political contestation and transformation through a democratic process within the third countries themselves and the sense of process that is, after all, central to the idea of human rights.[129] Imposing Western human rights norms from the outside denies the process through which rights have traditionally been gained in Western societies, ie through struggle, and questions whether external bodies are even equipped to administer human rights in developing states.[130] In more than one way, the international human rights movement contributes to the impoverishment of local political discourse.[131] This is because 'meaningful and lasting changes can only come from within'.[132] After all,

> Universal standards and local democracy—local power—are, by definition, contradictory objectives.[133]

This idea is visible in the preamble of the recent regulation establishing a financial instrument replacing Regulation 975/1999:

> Human rights may be considered in the light of universally accepted international norms, but democracy has also to be seen as a process, developing from within, involving all sections of society and a range of institutions, in particular national democratic parliaments, that should ensure participation, representation, responsiveness and accountability. The task of building and sustaining a culture of human rights and making democracy work for citizens, though especially urgent and difficult in emerging democracies, is essentially a continuous challenge, belonging first and foremost to the people of the country concerned but without diminishing the commitment of the international community.[134]

---

[129] For example, the EU's main reference, the Universal Declaration for Human Rights, presents human rights in its Preamble as a 'common standard of achievement' that all peoples and nations 'shall strive' for.

[130] MRR Lister, 'Rebalancing Lomé: Human Rights, South Africa and the Future' (1991) 25 *Journal of World Trade* 21, 24.

[131] D Kennedy, 'The International Human Rights Movement: Part of the Problem?' (2001) 3 *European Human Rights Law Review* 245, 258. In the EU, it has 'proven difficult to select strategic initiatives that could potentially contribute to transformational change in third countries, and to avoid assistance to projects which could actually harm locally driven reform processes and simply shore up non-reformist elites'. 'No lasting Peace and Prosperity without Democracy and Human Rights. Harnessing debates on the EU's future Financial Instruments'. Report commissioned by the European Parliament; carried out under the auspices of the Netherlands Institute for Multiparty Democracy, July 2005, 14.

[132] P Alston, 'International Trade as an Instrument of Positive Human Rights Policy', (1982) 4 *Human Rights Quarterly* 155, 169.

[133] S Seppänen, *Good Governance in International Law*, above n 86, 121.

[134] Regulation (EC) 1889/2006 of 20 December 2006 on establishing a financial instrument for the promotion of democracy and human rights worldwide, [2006] OJ L 386/1, preamble, para 9. A similar tone can be found in Communication from the Commission to the Council, the European Parliament, the European Economic and Social Committee and the

Though it is nice to have this perspective acknowledged, it is clear that a preambular reference in a regulation is by no means sufficient. Instead, this principle should be turned operative and into a cornerstone of all Union external policies which make reference to human rights objectives. Alternatively, if there is no real interest in interaction and discussion of positions, then any dialogue will remain empty in meaning. If there is no possibility of running a genuine dialogue, then conditionality should be more openly attached to the EU's own political objectives.

V. THE DIFFICULT JOURNEY TOWARDS THE GOOD AND BEAUTIFUL

The promise of universal human rights is a beautiful one: that all human beings are equal in their value and should have all their human rights protected. In principle, it is an enchanting idea— though not particularly new—to link your policies with good values. But the question is not about whether Europe should promote ideas like 'liberty' or 'solidarity' both within and outside its borders—of course, Europe should do both. In running our policies we ought to keep in mind the history of human rights as a 'shield of false universality',[135] which relates to the malfunction of values in guiding a policy. Values receive their substance only when placed in a particular context. For this reason, the most important question relates to the process in which rights receive their meaning. The problem is thus not whether some rights are or are not universally shared—on which there is persistent disagreement—but that actions are based on an agenda that reflects primarily the interests of the stronger party. This is exactly what happens in the context of EU policies: the ambiguity of 'common values' means that their contents are defined by the EU. This suggests that in the worst case, the idea of 'common values' makes 'us'—in speaking the language of universal human rights—strong, and those whose rights we are claiming to protect weak.

In this way good intentions sometimes create bad outcomes: the objectives we believe are inevitably good are not actually that good when implemented in practice.[136] An originally emancipatory language becomes a legitimising screen over bureaucratic patterns and elitism, for instance. It is precisely in that regard that some aspects of EU practice should be

---

Committee of the Regions. Governance in the European Consensus on Development. Towards a harmonised approach within the European Union, Brussels 30.8.2006 COM(2006) 421 final.

[135] See J Habermas, 'Remarks on Legitimation through Human Rights' in J Habermas, above n 121, 120.

[136] On this, see especially D Kennedy, above n 111. In his book, Kennedy encourages searching: questioning is good because instead of weakening and undermining the 'project', it in fact makes human rights stronger.

reconsidered. The EU's closed reading of human rights leaves little room for differing views and perceptions, highlighting the most fundamental problem relating to the EU's pursuit of universality: its limited view of the purpose of having a dialogue with a third state. The malfunction with the language of 'common values' does not lie so much in a failure to implement them than in the purposes for which they are invoked. Often it seems that the lack of political dialogue is compensated by the establishment of legal 'criteria'—criteria that end up being so vague or incoherent that they in fact merely legitimate the use of discretion by the EU institution with the competence to 'apply' them. At the same time, it appears difficult to trace any notion of political responsibility in the application of such criteria.

Much of the confusion around the meaning of human rights relates to the gap between their promise and actual achievements; the level of ideal and the level of reality. As Susan Marks has put it, while human rights clearly seem to make some difference, they do not make *all* the difference. These

> two visions, coexisting uneasily, reflect the real state of human rights: at once empowering and cruelly deceiving; at once decisive and irrelevant; at once critical of, and apologist for, governments. [...] [H]uman rights, if they are to be worth anything, must promise a lot, even while guaranteeing little.[137]

At a more theoretical level the problems relating to the EU's policies can be linked to confusion between the notions and implications of moral rights, on the one hand, and legal rights, on the other. The human rights of modern liberal states—and by extension, the EU—belong to the latter group and receive their legal form in international human rights instruments. In other words, the legal conception of human rights does not originate in morality; instead, it has been modelled after the modern concept of individual liberties and is firmly based in legal positivism (at least nominally), thus making the conception 'distinctly judicial in character'.[138] This form of validity points out how human rights as legal rights require the existence of 'law' for their enforcement; thus they are tied to an existing national, international or global legal order, in which their protection is possible.[139] The moral idea behind human rights, and the theory and argument behind them, again, is abstract in nature and

---

[137] S Marks, 'Nightmare and Noble Dream; the 1993 World Conference on Human Rights', (1994) 53 *Cambridge Law Journal* 54, 62.
[138] J Habermas, 'Kant's Idea of Perpetual Peace, with the Benefit of Two Hundred Years' Hindsight' in J Bohman and M Lutz-Bachmann (eds), *Perpetual Peace. Essays on Kant's Cosmopolitan Ideal* (Cambridge, The MIT Press, 1997) 113, 137.
[139] *Ibid*, 140.

expresses a 'universal aspiration'.[140] This creates a peculiar tension between the universal meaning of rights and the local conditions that are required for their realisation: while human rights promise universal validity, they do not specify how this is to be achieved.[141] When this universal aspiration takes the form of a legal text, it becomes closely attached to a particular society, historical period or set of cultural resonances.[142] This entails that once human rights are implemented in a particular situation they lose much of their universality: they are no longer applicable to all possible situations. Universality of rights—meaningful as an 'aspiration'—is often defended with reference to the embeddedness of rights in morality. But the problem here is that there is no structure within which moral rights could be enforced; thus they remain an aspiration, a horizon. Legal rights, again, irrespective of the universal validity that they claim, have 'an unambiguously positive form only within the national legal order of the democratic state'.[143] Their validity in international law is currently weak, and its strengthening would require their institutionalisation as a part of a truly cosmopolitan order.[144] That this has so far not taken place explains many of the problems in the enforcement of legal rights.

While there is much reason to criticise what Habermas calls 'the shameless instrumentalisation of human rights that conceals particular interests behind a universalist mask', Habermas also warns against the false assumption that the meaning of human rights would be 'exhausted by their misuse'.[145] Instead, human rights provide politics (be it local, national

---

[140] On this, see J Waldron: 'Nonsense upon Stilts?—a Reply' in J Waldron (ed), *'Nonsense upon Stilts'. Bentham, Burke and Marx on the Rights of Man* (London and New York, Methuen, 1987) 155, 179.

[141] J Habermas, 'Remarks on Legitimation through Human Rights' in J Habermas, above n 121, 113, 118.

[142] J Waldron, above n 140, 179; K Günther, 'The Legacies of Injustice and Fear: A European Approach to Human Rights and their Effects on Political Culture' in P Alston *et al* (eds), *The EU and Human Rights* (Oxford and New York, Oxford University Press, 1999) 117, 127.

[143] J Habermas, 'Kant's Idea of Perpetual Peace, with the Benefit of Two Hundred Years' Hindsight', above n 138, 140. For a similar point, see also C Brown, 'Universal Human Rights: a Critique' in T Dunne and NJ Wheeler (eds), *Human Rights in Global Politics* (Cambridge, Cambridge University Press 1999) 120. See also H Arendt, *The Origins of Totalitarianism* (New York, Harcourt Brace & Company 1973). Arendt underlines that human rights presume belonging to a specific community, as 'the fundamental deprivation of human rights is manifested first and above all in the deprivation of a place in the world which makes opinions significant and actions effective'. *Ibid*, 290–302, especially at 296.

[144] See J Habermas, *ibid*. According to Habermas, such an order would entail, among other things, that human rights violations would be prosecuted as criminal acts according to institutionalised legal procedures. An individual actor's (like the EU's) actions would seem to fall outside this vision. See also J Habermas, 'Remarks on Legitimation through Human Rights' in J Habermas, above n 121, 118–19.

[145] J Habermas, 'Remarks on Legitimation through Human Rights' in J Habermas, above n 121, 129.

or international in nature) with a permanent trace of critique. While the focus of this Chapter has been on the more negative uses of human rights language, EU policies also provide for many situations in which human rights play their proper role. On 17 January 2007 the EU adopted a declaration on the release of five student leaders by the authorities of Burma/Myanmar.[146] In the same context, the EU took positive note of the decision to grant amnesty to around 50 prisoners of conscience. Two days later the EU adopted another declaration welcoming the decision acquitting five accused persons in Burundi.[147] Three days later the Council adopted conclusions on the death sentence given to five Bulgarian nurses and one Palestinian doctor in Libya.[148] All of these are examples of contexts in which human rights language plays its original function in giving a voice to the weak against the abuse of power by the state. These cases remind us that 'human rights vocabulary has become the most accepted political form in which to couch protest against the state and international institutions.'[149] The function of human rights is mainly in empowering individuals with a language they can use against their own governments by offering a language of hope or aspiration; empowerment and contestation. Universality, again, mainly refers to an objective, while still giving a rather wide margin of discretion to national governments. After all, a principle can be of a universal significance without being a ready-made solution to all questions.[150]

The argument made here is that while the EU is today both capable and willing to do 'good', many of its actions appear ineffective, badly justified, or simply arrogant and ought to be re-evaluated. One should aim at keeping simultaneously in mind the historical legacy of universal human rights, but also their 'character as an ideal, transformatory tool and executive promise, always "to come"'.[151] The criticism presented should be understood as encouragement to re-evaluate our understanding of what 'common values' or 'universal human rights' mean in practice—without necessarily forgetting the objective. Instead of understanding rights as neutral or independent standards, human rights should be regarded as a commonly shared basis for political discussion. Because 'common values' have little automatic content or consequences, they ought to receive their meaning through political discussion. Therefore, simply adding more

---

[146]   Brussels, 17 January 2007, 5264/1/07 REV 1.

[147]   Brussels, 19 January 2007, 5467/07.

[148]   Brussels, 22 January 2007. Conclusions adopted in the 2276th External Relations Council meeting.

[149]   BS Chimni, 'Alternative Visions of Just World Order: Six Tales from India', (2005) 46(2) *Harvard International Law Journal* 389, 401.

[150]   In relation to democracy, S Marks, *The Riddle of All Constitutions. International Law, Democracy, and the Critique of Ideology* (Oxford, Oxford University Press, 2000) 150–51.

[151]   *Ibid.*

references to 'rights' or introducing new 'human rights criteria' gives few answers. In fact, often it has the opposite effect to that sought for, seeming to diminish further the possibility of thinking about problems in a genuinely political way. For example, in EU-ACP relations, instead of inspiring change, human rights language has simply been used to re-describe the setting between Europe and its colonies in new, less questionable terms. The strength of human rights is in the wide platform that they offer for discussion; the inspiration they should provide for breaking loose from bad and oppressive politics. On the whole, there seems to be much less need for fixed criteria and standards, unilaterally applied by the EU, than for dialogue, accommodation, and a debate concerning priorities. After all, everything that is 'good' about human rights depends on the politics through which such rights are recognised and applied.

Even if we Europeans embark on our journeys in order to speak about the beauties of living in a democratic society, we forget about the difficulties of democracy; we forget what makes democracy a beautiful principle: the need to discuss priorities, debate and contest. Quite often, it might be that it is more important to travel together than to reach any particular destination.[152] If we believe in our values, then we should keep on talking about them. However, we ought to keep in mind that there is little that is automatic or generally accepted in our values. And we should also keep in mind that we ourselves could be wrong—and need to change accordingly.

---

[152] Or as Douzinas has put it, human rights are about 'not yet', because 'no right can earn me the full recognition and love of the other and no Bill of Rights can complete the struggle for a just society'. C Douzinas, *The End of Human Rights* (Oxford and Portland, Oregon, Hart Publishing, 2000) 318. Therefore, '[t]he end of human rights comes when they lose their utopian end'. *Ibid*, 380.

10

Effects of International Agreements in the EU Legal Order

CHRISTINE KADDOUS

I. INTRODUCTION

THE QUESTION OF the effects of international agreements in the
EU legal order raises the more general problem of the relationship
between international and EU law. It relates to two different
theoretical conceptions: dualism and monism. As is well known, states as
well as other international actors such as the EU may decide autonomously
how to regulate the relations between international and domestic law as
long as the fundamental principle *pacta sunt servanda* of the 1969 Vienna
Convention on the Law of Treaties (Article 26) is respected.[1] The main
purpose of this Chapter is to provide a survey of recent developments
rather than to discuss theoretically at greater length or depth the effects of
different sources of international law in the EU legal order. We will first
deal with the status of international agreements to which the Community
is solely a party (I.A); then mixed agreements, to which the Community
and its Member States are parties (I.B); then agreements to which the
Community is not a party, but one or more Member States are (I.C); and
finally agreements to which the EU is a party (I.D). We will also consider
the ways these agreements penetrate the EU legal order with regard to the
questions of direct effect (II) and interpretation (III) as well as to their place
in the hierarchy of the sources of EU law. Not only provisions of
international agreements act as sources of EU law. Mention must be made
of the general principles of Community law, among which the Court of

---

[1] See the Vienna Convention of 23 May 1969 on the Law of Treaties (in force since 27
January 1980), published in UNTS No 58 (1980) vol III; Vienna Convention of 21 March
1986 on the Law of Treaties between States and International Organisations or between
International Organisations.

Justice includes fundamental rights, as guaranteed *inter alia* by the European Convention on Human Rights (ECHR),[2] principles of customary international law[3] as well as of international law,[4] which the Court takes into account when interpreting and applying Community law.

II. STATUS OF INTERNATIONAL AGREEMENT IN THE EC/EU LEGAL ORDER

A. Community Agreements

International agreements concluded by the Community shall be binding on the institutions and on Member States according to Article 300(7) EC. Whereas only the Community is a party to these agreements, these imply consequences for the institutions as well as for the Member States.

It is incumbent upon the Community institutions, as well as upon the Member States, to ensure compliance with the obligations arising from such agreements. The measures needed to implement the provisions of an agreement concluded by the Community are to be adopted, according to the state of Community law for the time being in the areas affected by the provisions of the agreement, either by the Community institutions or by

---

[2] See, eg, Case C–224/84 *Johnston* [1986] ECR 1651; Case C–46/87 *Hoechst* [1989] ECR 2869; Case C–5/88 *Wachauf* [1989] ECR 2609; 4; more recently Case C–540/03 *Parliament v Council* [2006] ECR I–5769, para 38. The Court has held since 1969 that fundamental human rights are enshrined among the general principles of Community law and protected by the Court. Since then, the formula has been extended in order to take into account as inspiration sources the constitutional traditions common to the Member States and as guidelines the international treaties for the protection of human rights on which the Member States have collaborated or of which they are signatories (Case C–4/73 *Nold* [1974] ECR 491, para 13). In addition to the ECHR the Court has regard to the 1966 International Covenant on Civil and Political Rights (ICCPR) and other international agreements as well as the Charter of Fundamental Rights of the European Union proclaimed by the European Parliament, the Council and the Commission in 2000.

[3] Case C–286/90 *Poulsen* [1992] ECR I–6019; Case C–162/96 *Racke* [1998] ECR I–3655; Case C–344/04 *International Air Transport Association and Others (IATA)* [2006] ECR I–403, para 40; Case T–315/01 *Kadi* [2005] ECR I–3649, paras 182, 227, 231; Case T–306/01 *Yusuf* [2005] ECR II–3533, paras 232, 278, 282. A notable example of customary international rules to which the Court refers are the rules of the "law of treaties" codified in the Vienna Conventions mentioned above.

[4] For the principle of international law according to which a State is precluded from refusing its own nationals the right of entry to its territory, see, eg, Case C–41/74 *Van Duyn* [1974] ECR 1337, para 22; Case C–171/96 *Pereira Roque* [1998] ECR I–4607, para 38; Case C–416/96 *El-Yassini* [1999] ECR I–1209, para 45; Case C–257/99 *Barkoci and Malik* [2001] ECR I–6557, para 81; Case C–235/99 *Kondova* [2001] ECR I–6427, para 84; Case C–63/99 *Gloszczuk* [2001] ECR I–6369, para 79. For the principle of territoriality, a general principle of public international law which the Community must observe in the exercise of its powers, see, eg, Case C–286/90 *Poulsen* [1992] ECR I–6019, para 9; Case T–102/96 *Gencor v Commission* [1999] ECR II–753, para 50.

the Member States.[5] In accordance with the Court's case law, in ensuring respect for commitments arising from an agreement concluded by the Community institutions the Member States fulfil an obligation not only in relation to the non-Member State concerned but also and above all in relation to the Community which has assumed responsibility for the due performance of the agreement.[6] In this respect Article 300(7) is also an expression of the vital principle of loyalty defined in Article 10 EC, which obliges the institutions and the Member States to assist the Community in the achievement of its tasks. An infringement by the Member States of the agreements concluded by the Community may form the basis of actions for failing to fulfil Treaty obligations according to Article 226 EC. The European Commission, which made use of this provision quite often, helped the Court in ensuring the respect of international agreements by the Member States.[7]

On the basis of Article 300(7) EC, the Court pointed out that agreements concluded by the Community, as of their entry into force, form an integral part of Community law in accordance with the *Haegeman* judgment[8] and they prevail over provisions of secondary Community legislation.[9] In that respect, Article 300(7) can be read as a confirmation of the monist approach towards international law, as there is no need for any particular act of transposition.[10] However, this approach is not always clear in the Court's case law, particularly in relation to the statement that an agreement is, in so far as concerns the Community, an act of one of the institutions of the Community and the related consequences in the case of annulment procedures.[11] It seems that the traditional dogmatic approach has progressively given precedence to a more empirical analysis of the legal reality.[12]

---

[5] Case C–104/81 *Kupferberg* [1982] ECR 3641, paras 11–12.

[6] Case C–104/81 *Kupferberg* [1982] ECR 3641, para 13.

[7] Recently see, eg, Case C–13/00 *Commission v Ireland* [2002] ECR I–2943; Case C–239/03 *Commission v France* [2004] ECR I–9325. These examples concern mixed agreements but the same point is relevant for Community agreements.

[8] Case C–181/73 *Haegeman* [1974] ECR 449.

[9] Case C–61/94 *Commission v Germany* [1996] ECR I–3989, para 52; Case C–286/02 *Bellio F.lli* [2004] ECR I–3465, para 33; Case C–344/04 *International Air Transport Association and Others (IATA)* [2006] ECR I–403, para 35.

[10] On monism and dualism, see, eg, FG Jacobs and S Roberts (eds), *The Effect of Treaties in Domestic Law* (London, Sweet & Maxwell, 1987), xxiv; P Pescatore, 'L'application judiciaire des traités internationaux dans la Communauté européenne et dans ses Etats membres' in *Mélanges offerts à Pierre-Henry Teitgen* (Paris, Pedone, 1984), 355–406.

[11] On this question, see, eg, C Kaddous, 'Le droit des relations extérieures dans la jurisprudence de la Cour de justice des Communautés européennes' in *Dossier de droit européen* No 6 (Geneva, Helbing/Brussels, Bruylant, 1998) 271–2.

[12] For a general discussion of these issues, see, eg, GC Rodriguez Iglesias, 'Quelques reflexions sur la singularité des rapports du droit communautaire avec d'autres ordres juridiques' in *Mélanges J-V Louis* (Brussels, Editions de Université Libre de Bruxelles, 2003) 389, 390.

B. Mixed Agreements

In principle mixed agreements have the same status in the Community legal order as Community agreements, especially as concerns provisions falling under Community competence.[13] If they do not fall under the Community competence, the question is: do these provisions form an integral part of Community law or not? This issue was studied for the first time in the *Demirel* judgment[14] in relation to the Court's jurisdiction to interpret provisions on free movement of workers in the Association Agreement with Turkey. In that case, the German and British Governments took the view that, in the case of mixed agreements, the Court's interpretative jurisdiction does not extend to provisions whereby Member States have entered into a commitment with regard to Turkey in the exercise of their own powers, which they argued was the case with the provisions on freedom of movement for workers. However, the Court stated that, since the agreement in question was an association agreement creating special, privileged links with a non-Member State which must, at least to a certain extent, take part in the Community system, Article 310 EC must necessarily empower the Community to guarantee its commitments towards non-Member States in all the fields covered by the Treaty. Since freedom of movement for workers is, by virtue of Articles 39 *et seq* EC, one of the fields covered by that Treaty, it follows that commitments regarding freedom of movement fall within the powers conferred on the Community by Article 310 EC. Thus the Court concluded that the question, as to whether it has jurisdiction to rule on the interpretation of a provision in a mixed agreement regarding an obligation which only the Member States could enter into in the sphere of their own powers, did not arise. Furthermore, it added that its jurisdiction cannot be called into question by virtue of the fact that in the field of freedom of movement for workers, as Community law now stands; it is for the Member States to lay down the rules which are necessary to give effect in their territory to the provisions of the agreements or the decisions to be adopted by the association council. It also emphasised that in ensuring respect for commitments arising from an agreement concluded by the Community institutions, Member States fulfil, within the Community system, an obligation in relation to the

---

[13]   See Case C–13/00 *Commission v Ireland* [2002] ECR I–2943, para 14; Case C–459/03 *Commission v Ireland* [2006] ECR I–4635, para 84. On mixed agreements, see, eg, A Rosas, 'Mixed Union—Mixed Agreements' in M Koskenniemi (ed), *International Law Aspects of the European Union* (The Hague and Boston, Kluwer Law International, 1998), 125–49; J Heliskoski, *Mixed Agreements as a Technique for Organizing the International Relations of the European Community and Its Member States* (The Hague and Boston, Kluwer Law International, 2001); M Dony, 'Les accords mixtes' in *Commentaire J Mégret* vol 12 (Brussels, Editions de l'Université Libre de Bruxelles, 2005) 167.

[14]   Case C–12/86 *Demirel* [1987] ECR 3719.

Community, which has assumed responsibility for the due performance of the agreement. Consequently the Court held itself competent to interpret the provisions of the Agreement on free movement for workers. Its jurisdiction was not determined by the question of who is finally competent to implement the agreement.

We consider appropriate the position adopted by the Court in this ruling concerning mixed agreements.[15] It is indeed difficult to conceive that the status of provisions, being part of an agreement, could vary according to the fact that these provisions fall under Community competence or under the competence of the Member States. This would run counter to the principle of uniform application of agreements in the EU that the Court should ensure. While the Court asserted in the *Dior* judgment[16] that, acting in cooperation with the courts and tribunals of the Member States pursuant to Article 234 EC, it is in a position to ensure a uniform interpretation of Article 50 of the TRIPs,[17] it took an ambivalent position on the question of the recognition of direct effect in establishing a distinction in terms of whether it concerned a field 'to which TRIPs applies and in respect of which the Community has already legislated' or a field 'in respect of which the Community has not yet legislated and which consequently falls within the competence of the Member States'.[18] In this last hypothesis, it allows potentially divergent positions by the Member States on the question of the direct effect of TRIPs provisions and seems therefore to accept a breach in the principle of the uniform application of mixed agreements.

More recently, in *Commission v Ireland*, the Court had to decide whether Ireland failed to fulfil its obligations under Article 300(7) EC in conjunction with Article 5 of Protocol 28 to the Agreement on the European Economic Area (EEA Agreement), according to which the contracting parties are obliged to adhere to the 1971 Berne Convention for the Protection of Literary and Artistic Works.[19] In accordance with the *Demirel* case, it was held that the provisions of the Berne Convention cover an area which comes in large measure within the scope of Community competence. It was added that the protection of literary and artistic works is to a very great extent governed by Community legislation.[20] It follows that the requirement of adherence to the Berne Convention which Article 5

---

[15] The ECJ confirmed its position in Case C–53/96 *Hermès* [1998] ECR I–3603. The question was whether the provisional measures adopted in order to put an end to the sale of counterfeit ties of the trademark *Hermès* fell within the scope of the definition of 'provisional measure' provided for in Art 50 of TRIPs.

[16] Joint Cases C–300/98 and C–392/98, *Dior* [2000] ECR I–11307.

[17] *Ibid*, para 38.

[18] *Ibid*, para 39.

[19] Case C 13/00 *Commission v Ireland* [2002] ECR I–2943.

[20] *Ibid*, paras 16–17.

of the Protocol imposes on the contracting parties comes within the Community framework, given that it features in a mixed agreement concluded by the Community and its Member States and relates to an area covered in large measure by the Treaty. Therefore it was accepted that the Commission was competent to assess compliance with that requirement, subject to review by the Court.[21]

Accordingly, in *Commission v France*, the question was raised whether France failed to fulfil its obligations under specific provisions of the 1976 Convention for the protection of the Mediterranean Sea against pollution. The Court first stated that the provisions of the Convention cover a field which falls in large measure within Community competence and added that environmental protection, which is the subject-matter of the Convention, is in very large measure regulated by Community legislation. Furthermore, since the Convention creates rights and obligations in a field covered in large measure by Community legislation, there is a Community interest in compliance by both the Community and its Member States with the commitments entered into under those instruments. The Court asserted jurisdiction and held that the fact that discharges of fresh water and alluvia into the marine environment, which were at issue in the present action, had not yet been subject of Community legislation was not capable of calling that finding into question.[22]

Even if certain inconsistencies may appear in the Court's case law, it is true that the tendency consists in admitting that mixed agreements have in principle the same status as Community agreements in the Community legal order. They form an integral part of it from the moment of their entry into force and the Court has jurisdiction to interpret them as a whole.

C. Agreements of Member States with Third States

Many agreements concluded by the Member States with third States may have effects in the Community legal order. However, a distinction must be made between agreements concluded after the EEC Treaty entered into force and those concluded before that moment.

(i) Agreements Concluded after the EEC Treaty Entered into Force

The EC Treaty does not preclude international competence on the part of the Member States in respect of matters which do not fall within the

---

[21] *Ibid*, para 20. In the same perspective, the Advocate General emphasised that the Berne Convention is not divisible, in the sense that a Member State cannot adhere to it in part, Opinion of AG Mischo, para 48.

[22] Case C–239/03 *Commission v France* [2004] ECR I–9325, paras 27–30.

exclusive competence of the EC. Consequently such agreements may be concluded in matters which fall either within the exclusive competence of the Member States or within a shared competence of the EC and the Member States.

In matters for which the EC has exclusive competence, there is in principle no more space for the conclusion of international agreements by Member States. If such cases arise, however, an action for infringement of EC law could be launched by the Commission according to Article 226 EC.

Agreements which Member States conclude with third States or international organisations are not binding on the EC and the Court has no jurisdiction to interpret them, except when the EC substituted itself for the Member States.[23]

The conclusion of such agreements obliges the Member States to respect the duty of cooperation in good faith,[24] enshrined in Article 10 EC which requires the Member States to facilitate the achievement of the Community's tasks and to abstain from any measure which could jeopardise the attainment of the objectives of the Treaty. In the area of external relations, it is well known that the Community's tasks and the objectives of the EC Treaty would be compromised if Member States were able to enter into international commitments containing rules capable of affecting rules adopted by the Community or of altering their scope.[25]

(ii) Agreements Concluded before the EEC Treaty Entered into Force

The legal effects of agreements concluded by Member States with third States or international organisations before the entry into force of the EC Treaty are covered by Article 307 EC. This provision applies also to those agreements concluded by new Member States before the date of their accession.

Article 307 EC is of a general scope and applies to any international agreement, irrespective of subject-matter, which is capable of affecting application of the EC Treaty.[26] The purpose of Article 307(1) is to make clear, in accordance with the principles of international law, that the

---

[23] Joined Cases C–21–24/72 *International Fruit* [1972] ECR 1219.

[24] See, eg, Joined Cases C–176/97 and C–177/97 *Commission v Belgium and Luxembourg* [1998] ECR I–3557.

[25] *Opinion 2/91* [1993] ECR I–1061, para 11; Case C–22/70 *ERTA* [1971] ECR 263, paras 21–2. See also the Open Skies cases, ie Case C–475/98 *Commission v Austria* [2002] ECR I–9797, paras 124–5; *Opinion 1/03* [2006] ECR I–1145, para 119.

[26] Case C–812/79 *Burgoa* [1980] ECR 2787, para 6; Case C–158/91 *Lévy* [1993] ECR I–4300, para 11; Case C–466/98 *Commission v United Kingdom* [2002] ECR I–9427, para 23. On this question, see M Cremona, 'Defending the Community Interest: the Duties of Cooperation and Compliance', Chapter 6, this volume; J-V Louis, 'Les accords antérieurs conclus par les Etats membres et le droit communautaire' in *Commentaire J Mégret* vol 12 (Brussels, Editions de l'Université Libre de Bruxelles, 2005) 201.

application of the EC Treaty does not affect the duty of the Member States to respect the rights of non-Member States under a prior agreement and to perform their obligations thereunder.[27] Consequently, this provision preserves the rights of third States. In the event of a conflict between Community law and a pre-existing agreement between a Member State and a third country, the EC Treaty ensures that the international obligation is complied with.

Article 307(2) EC provides that, to the extent that agreements concluded by Member States are not compatible with the EC Treaty, the Member State or States concerned shall take all appropriate steps to eliminate the incompatibilities established. Member States shall, where necessary, assist each other to this end and shall, where appropriate, adopt a common attitude. Consequently, the Member State or States in question should start negotiations in order to adapt the prior non-compatible agreements and, if such negotiations are not successful, terminate these agreements. According to the Court, the obligation to have recourse to denunciation constitutes an exceptional obligation. However, although the Member States have a choice as to the appropriate steps to be taken in the context of Article 307, they are nevertheless under an obligation to eliminate any incompatibilities existing between a pre-existing agreement and the EC Treaty. If a Member State encounters difficulties which make adjustment of an agreement impossible, an obligation to denounce that agreement cannot therefore be excluded.[28] The failure to comply with this obligation may be considered as a breach of the obligations of a Member State under Community law, which may be condemned by the Court on the basis of the Article 226 EC procedure.[29] Article 307 implies a balance between the foreign-policy interests of a Member State and the Community interests, which is not easy to apply due to the fact that these issues are subject to a variety of factors that cannot be easily categorised because of their evolving character. It appears from the case law that the Commission is pretty much willing to take initiatives in order to push the Member States to eliminate incompatibilities with Community law, enshrined in pre-existing agreements with third States.

Finally, one example of agreements concluded by the Member States before the establishment of the EEC must be mentioned even though it does not relate directly to the application of Article 307 EC. The GATT 1947 was concluded by the Member States and the EC was never a contracting party to it. However, its provisions became an integral part of

---

[27] See, in that connection, Art 30(4)(b) of the Convention on the Law of Treaties signed in Vienna on 23 May 1969.
[28] Case C–62/98 *Commission v Portugal* [2000] ECR I–5171, paras 48–9; Case C–84/98 *Commission v Portugal* [2000] ECR I–5215, paras 57–8.
[29] *Ibid.*

Community law on the basis that the EC gained exclusive competence over trade policy and assumed, since that time, the powers previously exercised by the Member States in the area governed by the GATT. Therefore the provisions of the GATT were deemed binding on the Community.[30] Since the creation of the WTO in 1994, both the EC and the Member States are members and the question of 'substitution' is no longer relevant.

D. EU Agreements

Whereas the EU Treaty does not expressly endow the EU with legal personality, it is today commonly accepted that it has such personality under international law. By virtue of Articles 24 and 38 EU, the EU has the capacity to conclude international agreements with third States and international organisations. Such agreements in the second (CFSP) and third pillar (PJC) of the EU are concluded by the Council and shall be binding on the institutions of the Union according to Article 24(6) EU. This formula is similar to that of Article 300(7) EC, but it does not specify that these agreements are binding on the EU Member States. The legal effects of such agreements are largely unknown because of the lack of relevant case law. The Court has not rendered rulings similar to those of *Haegeman* or *Commission v Ireland*. However, this does not mean that these agreements have no effect in the EU legal order. At the same time it must be emphasised that according to Article 46 EU, the Court has no jurisdiction to interpret and apply the agreements concluded in the fields of CFSP and PJC unless the question concerns the limits between the pillars.[31]

As it is well known, the role of the Court varies according to the pillars: complete jurisdiction in the Community field,[32] a less extensive jurisdiction in the third pillar (PJC) and no jurisdiction in the second pillar (CFSP). This situation will without any doubt raise sensitive questions in the case of agreements covering more than one pillar.[33] The Court could be asked to interpret and apply 'cross-pillar' agreements and decide on its jurisdiction in relation to such texts, the content of which can be found for

---

[30] Joined Cases C–21–24/72 *International Fruit* [1972] ECR 1219, paras 16–18. See also by analogy the position of the CFI in case T-306/01 *Yusef* [2005] ECR II-3533, para 253

[31] Case C–170/96 *Commission and Parliament v Council* [1998] ECR I–2763, para 16: 'it is the task of the Court to ensure that acts which, according to the Council, fall within the scope of Art K.3(2) of the Treaty on European Union do not encroach upon the powers conferred by the EC Treaty on the Community.' See also Case C–176/03 *Commission v Council* [2005] ECR I–7879, para 39.

[32] It must, however, be noted that the ECJ has special competences in accordance with Art 68 EC.

[33] On this question, see C Kaddous, 'La place des accords bilatéraux II dans l'ordre juridique de l'Union européenne' in C Kaddous and M Jametti Greiner (eds), *Accords bilatéraux II Suisse-UE et autres accords récents*, Dossier de droit européen No 16 (Geneva, Helbing/Brussels, Bruylant/Paris, LGDJ, 2006), pp 63–92, p 83.

example in both the Community and the third pillar of the EU Treaty. An example of this new phenomenon of cross-pillar mixity is given by the Swiss Schengen Association Agreement, to which the EU and the EC are parties.[34] The proposals for decisions on the signature of this agreement which indicate, through a reference to Council Decision 1999/436,[35] the parts of the Schengen *acquis* covered by the agreement fall under the scope of the EU Treaty and the ones which fall under the EC Treaty could be useful to the Court of Justice in order to determine the scope of its jurisdiction.

On the other hand, the Treaty regime allows Member States not to be bound by an agreement concluded on behalf of the Union before it is ratified in their national legal system. According to Article 24(5) EU, no agreements shall be binding on those States whose representatives in the Council stated that it has to comply with the requirements of their own constitutional procedure. However, this does not affect either the signature of such agreements nor in principle their conclusion. The lifting of these reservations may take time and the other members of the Council are authorised to agree that the agreements shall nevertheless apply provisionally. It is interesting to note that no Member State has made use of the possibility to make reservations with respect to CFSP matters whereas in the case of PJC agreements, the majority of the Member States have declared it necessary to comply with their national constitutional rules.[36]

---

[34] This Agreement entered into force on 1 March 2008. Following the approach of the Commission, the Council adopted two decisions: Council Decision 2008/146 of 28 January 2008 on the conclusion, on behalf of the European Community, of the Agreement between European Union, the European Community and the Swiss Confederation concerning the latter's association with the implementation, application and development of the Schengen *acquis*, [2008] OJ L 53/1, and Council Decision of 28 January 2008 on the conclusion on behalf of the European Union, of the Agreement between the European Union, the European Community and the Swiss Confederation concering the latter's association with the implementation, application and development of the Schengen *acquis*, [2008] OJ L 53/50.

[35] Council Decision 1999/436 of 20 May 1999 determining, in conformity with the relevant provisions of the Treaty establishing the European Community and the Treaty on European Union, the legal basis for each of the provisions and decisions which constitute the Schengen *acquis*, [1999] OJ L/176/17.

[36] Outcome of the proceedings of JHA Council of 6 June 2003, doc 10409/03 of 13 June 2003. For example this issue was raised in the case of the Schengen Association Agreement with Switzerland by Sweden, Germany, Denmark, Italy, the Netherlands, Czech Republic, Greece and Belgium. See, eg, S Marquardt, 'The Conclusion of International Agreements under Art 24 of the Treaty on European Union' in V Kroneneberger (ed), *The European Union and the International Legal Order: Discord or Harmony?* (The Hague, Asser Press, 2001) 333; RA Wessel, 'The EU as a Party to International Agreements: Shared Competences? Mixed Responsibilities?' in A Dashwood and M Maresceau (eds), *Recent Trends in the External Relations of the Union* (Cambridge: Cambridge University Press, forthcoming).

III. DIRECT EFFECT OF INTERNATIONAL AGREEMENTS

The doctrine of direct effect (or direct applicability) in EC law has been set down by the Court of Justice in the *Van Gend en Loos* judgment of 1963.[37] Direct effect can be defined as a characteristic of a Community rule which confers the capacity to create rights and obligations upon individuals.

The question of direct effect is of great importance because if an agreement is interpreted as only creating rights and obligations between the contracting parties, its effectiveness is obviously more limited than if it were to create rights and obligations that individuals could enforce before their national authorities.

According to settled case law, the Court considers that a provision of an international agreement must be regarded as having direct effect when, 'regard being had to its wording and the purpose and nature of the agreement itself, the provision contains a clear and precise obligation which is not subject, in its implementation or effects, to the adoption of any subsequent measure'.[38] These principles are applicable to agreements to which the Community is a party,[39] including mixed agreements,[40] as well as to decisions of association councils adopted under the agreements.[41]

The Court has accepted on a very broad basis the direct effect of provisions of free trade agreements, ACP agreements, association agreements, cooperation agreements and the EEA Agreement,[42] whereas it denied as early as 1972 the direct effect of the GATT in *International Fruit Company*,[43] and many years later it reached the same conclusion in relation to provisions of the WTO agreements.[44]

---

[37] Case C–26/62 *Van Gend en Loos* [1963] ECR 6.

[38] Case C–12/86 *Demirel* [1987] ECR 3719, para 14.

[39] Case C–270/80 *Polydor* [1982] ECR 329; Case C–104/81 *Kupferberg* [1982] ECR 3641.

[40] See, eg, Case C–87/75 *Bresciani* [1976] ECR 129; Case C–17/81 *Pabst* [1982] ECR 1331; Case C–18/90 *Kziber* [1991] ECR I–221.

[41] Case C–192/89 *Sevince* [1990] ECR I–3461; more recently Case C–502/04 *Torun* [2006] ECR I–157; Case C–4/05 *Güzeli* [2006] ECR I–10279.

[42] Case T–115/94 *Opel Austria* [1997] ECR II–39.

[43] Joined Cases C–21–24/72 *International Fruit Company* [1972] ECR 1219.

[44] Case C–149/96 *Portugal v Council* [1999] ECR I–4973; Joined Cases C–300/98 and C–392/98 *Dior* [2000] I–11307; Case T–19/01 *Chiquita* [2005] ECR II–315. On GATT and WTO law, see, eg, M Cremona, 'Neutrality or Discrimination? The WTO, the EU and External Trade' in G de Búrca and J Scott (eds), *The EU and the WTO: Legal and Constitutional Issues* (Oxford and Portland, Hart Publishing 2001); P Eeckhout, *External Relations of the European Union, Legal and Constitutional Foundations* (Oxford and New York, Oxford University Press 2003), 292–314; C Kaddous, 'La politique commerciale commune' (2004) *Annuaire de droit européen* 710, 717; P Koutrakos, *European Union International Relations Law* (Oxford and Portland, Hart Publishing, 2006), 251–99.

A. Association, Partnership and Cooperation Agreements

In the recent case law related to association as well as to partnership and cooperation agreements, the Court seems to pursue its open approach to granting direct effect, and in the case of *Simutenkov* it has gone even further than in previous judgments.

As to the Europe Association Agreements, the Court acknowledged in *Bakoci and Malik, Jany, Gloszczuk and Kondova* the direct effect of provisions which concerned the right to work and to take up an activity as a self-employed person taking into consideration the nature and the structure of these agreements, the purpose of which is to provide an appropriate framework for the gradual integration of these states into the Community, and ultimately their accession to the EU.[45] In other cases, the question of direct effect was related to the non-discrimination principle enshrined in the Association Agreements with Poland and Slovakia as well as in the Partnership and cooperation Agreement with Russia.[46]

In the *Pokrzeptowicz-Meyer* case, the question was raised whether Article 37(1) of the Europe Agreement should be construed as precluding the application to Polish nationals of a national provision according to which positions for foreign-language assistants may be filled by means of fixed-term contracts of employment, whereas, for other teaching staff performing special duties, recourse to such contracts must be individually justified by an objective reason. In order to answer the question, it was necessary to consider whether this provision may be relied upon by an individual before a national court and, if so, to determine the scope of the principle of non-discrimination. In that case, the Court did not follow the opinion of the Advocate General, according to which the reference in Article 37(1) to the conditions and modalities applicable in each Member State should have been understood as a reminder that, since the conditions of access to the labour markets of the Member States remain in principle a matter of national law, the right to equal treatment in employment applies only to Polish migrant workers who satisfy the procedural and substantive conditions for entry and stay on the territory laid down by the relevant national rules.[47] Basing itself on the settled case law, the Court came rather to the conclusion that Article 37(1) lays down, in clear, precise and unconditional terms, a prohibition preventing each Member State from discriminating in relation to its own nationals, on grounds of their

---

[45] See, eg, Case C–257/99 *Bakoci and Malik* [2001] ECR I–6557; Case C–268/99 *Jany and Others* [2001] ECR I–8615; Case C–63/99 *Gloszczuk* [2001] ECR I–6369; Case C–235/99 *Kondova* [2001] ECR I–6427.

[46] Case C–162/00 *Pokrzeptowicz-Meyer* [2002] ECR I–1049; Case C–438/00 *Kolpak* [2003] ECR I–4135; Case C–265/03 *Simutenkov* [2005] ECR I–2579.

[47] Opinion of AG Jacobs, para 44.

nationality, against Polish nationals covered by that provision as far as their conditions of employment, remuneration and dismissal are concerned. According to the Court, Polish nationals who are entitled to the benefit of that provision are those who, having been previously granted the right to stay in a Member State, are legally employed there. It added that the rule of equal treatment enshrined in Article 37(1) lays down a precise obligation to produce a specific result and can be relied on by an individual to apply to a national court to set aside the discriminatory provisions of a Member State's legislation, without any further implementing measures being required for that purpose.[48] The terms 'subject to the conditions and modalities applicable in each Member State' should not be interpreted in such a way as to allow the Member States to subject the principle of non-discrimination to conditions or discretionary limitations because such an interpretation would render the provision meaningless and deprive it of any practical effect.[49] It further held that the conclusion that the principle of non-discrimination laid down in Article 37(1) is capable of directly governing the situation of individuals is not invalidated by the examination of the purpose and nature of that agreement, of which that provision forms part.

In the *Simutenkov* case of 2005, the Court had to decide whether the non-discrimination principle in the Partnership and Cooperation Agreement with Russia is to be construed as precluding the application to a professional sportsman of Russian nationality, who is lawfully employed by a club established in a Member State, of a rule drawn up by a sports federation of that state which provides that clubs may field in competitions at national level only a limited number of players from countries which are not parties to the EEA Agreement. In order to answer this question it was necessary first to examine whether that provision may be recognised as having direct effect and second to determine the scope of the non-discrimination principle which that provision enshrines.[50] The Court held that Article 23(1) lays down, in clear, precise and unconditional terms, a prohibition precluding any Member State from discriminating, on grounds of nationality, against Russian workers, vis-a-vis their own nationals, so far as their conditions of employment, remuneration and dismissal are concerned and that such a rule does not require any further implementing measures.[51] It added that this interpretation cannot be brought into question by the words '[s]ubject to the laws, conditions and procedures applicable in each Member State', which feature at the beginning of Article

---

[48]   Case C–162/00 *Pokrzeptowicz-Meyer* [2002] ECR I–1049, para 22.
[49]   *Ibid*, para 24.
[50]   Case C–265/03 *Simutenkov* [2005] ECR I–2579.
[51]   *Ibid*, paras 22–23. See also Case C–162/00 *Pokrzeptowicz-Meyer* [2002] ECR I–1049, para 22, and Case C–171/01 *Wählergruppe Gemeinsam* [2003] ECR I–4301, para 58.

23(1) of the Partnership Agreement, or by Article 48 of that Agreement. Those provisions cannot be construed as allowing the Member States to subject application of the non-discrimination principle to discretionary limitations, which would have the effect of rendering that provision meaningless and thus depriving it of any practical effect.[52] In addition the fact that Article 27 of the Agreement provides that Article 23 is to be implemented on the basis of recommendations by the Cooperation Council does not make the applicability of Article 23, in its implementation or effects, subject to the adoption of any subsequent measure. The role which Article 27 confers on that council is to facilitate compliance with the prohibition of discrimination but cannot be regarded as limiting the immediate application of that prohibition.[53]

Two observations may be made. First, the approach adopted by the Court is rather different from the one it developed in the *Demirel* judgment in which it denied direct effect to provisions of the Association Agreement with Turkey in the absence of Association Council decisions in relation to the provision under examination.[54] Second, according to well-established case law, the test the Court applies when it has to determine if a provision of an international agreement has direct effect consists first of examining the issue related to the purpose and nature of the agreement as a whole before looking at the precise wording of one of its provisions. In *Pokrzeptowicz-Meyer* as well as in *Simutenkov* it did the contrary and this approach might be criticised.[55] What would be the logic if the Court were to admit that a specific provision is capable of direct effect because it is sufficiently clear and precise but then had to state that the agreement *as a whole* is not apt to have direct effect. These two issues should be examined the other way around, as indeed was the practice in previous case law.

B. Cooperation and Euro-Mediterranean Agreements

With regard to cooperation agreements and Euro-Mediterranean agreements, the Court accepted in *El-Yassini* that the non-discrimination principle of the Cooperation Agreement with Morocco had direct effect.[56] This approach was confirmed in *Gattoussi* as to the corresponding provision of

---

[52] Case C–265/03 *Simutenkov* [2005] ECR I–2579, para 25. For a contrary position, see Case C–18/90 *Kziber* [1991] ECR I–199, para 19; Case C–262/96 *Sürül* [1999] ECR I–2685, para 66.

[53] Case C–265/03 *Simutenkov* [2005] ECR I–2579, para 28. The Court referred to its previous case law in *Kziber* [1991] ECR I–199, para 21, Case C–113/97 *Babahenini* [1998] ECR I–183, para 17, and Case C–162/96 *Racke* [1998] ECR I–3655, paras 34–6.

[54] Case C–12/86 *Demirel* [1987] ECR 3719.

[55] It followed the same reasoning in relation to the Cooperation Agreement with Morocco in Case C–416/96 *El-Yassini* [1999] ECR I–1209.

[56] Case C–416/96 *El-Yassini* [1999] ECR I–1209.

the Tunisia Euro-Mediterranean Agreement whose wording was almost identical to the one in the Morocco Cooperation Agreement. Taking into account the purpose and nature of the Euro-Mediterranean Agreement, the Court stressed that by contrast with the Morocco Agreement, it establishes an association between the Community and its Member States of the one part, and Tunisia of the other part.[57]

In its recent case law the Court has granted direct effect without distinguishing on the basis of the purposes of the agreement at issue, whether it concerned a pre-accession agreement or a purely cooperation agreement (*Simutenkov*). However, even though it decided identically in *El-Yassini* and *Gattoussi*, it placed more emphasis in the latter case on the difference in their nature and purpose between a cooperation and a Euro-Mediterranean association agreement. Therefore, it is difficult to assert that the category of agreement in question no longer has any impact on the granting of direct effect.

IV. INTERPRETATION OF INTERNATIONAL AGREEMENTS

In the fundamental *Haegeman* case of 1974, the Court held that an international agreement is, in so far as concerns the Community, an act of one of the institutions of the Community within the meaning of Article 234 EC. However, the scope of this approach goes well beyond the procedure for a preliminary ruling which was at issue in *Haegeman* since the Court may have to construe international agreements in actions for annulment, actions for failure to act, actions for infringement of Community law, objections for illegality or opinions on the compatibility of an international agreement with the provisions of the EC Treaty.

The Court has proceeded to such interpretations without distinguishing on the basis of the nature of international agreements. It has accepted jurisdiction to interpret Community agreements, mixed agreements, agreements binding on the Community as well as acts and decisions of organs established by these agreements. However, the Court's jurisdiction to interpret these agreements applies solely with regard to the Community. The Court has no jurisdiction to rule on the interpretation of these agreements as regards their application in the third states.[58]

The main issue remains whether the Court has the tendency to interpret provisions of agreements with third States in the same way as corresponding provisions of the EC Treaty. In the *Polydor* judgment of 1982 the Court stated that the similarity between the terms used in Articles 30 and 36 EEC and those in Articles 14 and 23 of the FTA between the EEC and

---

[57] Case C–97/05 *Gattoussi* [2006] ECR I–11917, paras 26–8.
[58] Case C–321/97 *Andersson* [1999] ECR I–3551, para 28.

Portugal was not a sufficient reason for transposing to the provisions of the Agreement the case law of the Court which determines in the context of the Community the relationship between the protection of industrial and commercial property rights and the rules on the free movement of goods. The purposes of the Agreement and of the EEC Treaty were different.[59] This approach was confirmed in *Kupferberg* and *Metalsa*.[60] However, in other judgments in relation to FTAs an identical interpretation was given to the provision of the international agreement and of the one of the EC Treaty on the basis of the 'effet utile' principle (*Legros, EurimPharm, Commission v Italy* and *Aprile*).[61]

A. Cooperation and Euro-Mediterranean Agreements

As far as cooperation agreements are concerned, the extension of the interpretation of a provision of the EC Treaty to a corresponding provision of an international agreement depends mainly on the political objectives of the EC Treaty and on the more limited purposes of the agreements concluded by the Community. It seems that the case law has been rendered step by step without paying enough attention to the coherence of the general approach. If one looks at the cooperation agreements concluded with Algeria and Morocco, the Court decided in *Kziber* that the concept of social security had to be understood by analogy with the identical concept in Community law, in particular Regulation No. 1408/71 on the application of social security schemes to employed persons.[62] This approach was confirmed in *Yousfi, Hallouzi-Choho, Krid* and *Babahenini* with a difference in relation to the scope *ratione personae* with the result that the case law in which a distinction is drawn between the derived rights and the personal rights of the members of the migrant worker's family in the context of Regulation No. 1408/71 cannot be applied in the context of the agreement.[63]

In *El-Yassini* the Court compared the Morocco Cooperation Agreement with the Association Agreement with Turkey in relation to the scope of the non-discrimination principle. It referred to Article 31 of the 1969 Vienna Convention on the Law of Treaties, which provides that a treaty is to be

---

[59]   Case C–270/80 *Polydor* [1982] ECR 329.

[60]   Case C–104/81 *Kupferberg* [1982] ECR 3641; Case C–312/91 *Metalsa* [1993] ECR I–3769.

[61]   Case C–163/90 *Legros* [1992] ECR I–4625; Case C–207/91 *Eurim Pham* [1993] ECR I–3723; Case C–228/91 *Commission v Italy* [1993] ECR I–2701; Case C–125/94 *Aprile* [1995] ECR 2919.

[62]   Case C–18/90 *Kziber* [1991] ECR I–199, para 25.

[63]   Case C–58/93 *Yousfi* [1994] ECR I–1353; Case C–126/95 *Hallouzi-Choho* [1996] ECR I–4829; Case C–103/94 *Krid* [1995] ECR I–719; Case C–113/97 *Babahenini* [1998] ECR I–183; Case C–23/02 *Alami* [2003] ECR I–1399.

interpreted in good faith in accordance with the ordinary meaning to be given to its terms in their context and in the light of its object and purpose.[64] It concluded that there were substantial differences in the wording as well as in the object and purposes of the two agreements. The latter provides for a possibility of accession and intends progressively to secure freedom of movement for workers whereas the agreement with Morocco does not. Moreover, the Court underlined that the EC–Morocco Cooperation Council had not adopted any decision containing a provision analogous to the one in Decision no 1/80 of the EC–Turkey Association Council.[65] Therefore, according to the Court, the case law on the rules governing the Turkey Agreement cannot be applied by analogy to the Morocco Agreement. It is interesting to note that in this case a comparison was established between two agreements and not between an agreement and the EC Treaty which was the key question in earlier case law.

In *Gattoussi* the question was raised whether it was appropriate to apply the approach adopted by the Court in *El-Yassani* to the Tunisia Euro-Mediterranean Agreement and whether Article 64 of this last agreement precludes the host Member State from curtailing the period of validity of the residence permit of a Tunisian national, to whom it had granted leave to remain in its territory for a specified period and to undertake gainful employment there for a period of indefinite duration, in the case where the original justification for his right to remain lapses before the date on which the validity of his residence permit expires. Having stated that the circumstances in the proceedings are comparable to those examined in *El-Yassini*, the Court held that the Euro-Mediterranean Agreement, like the Morocco Cooperation Agreement, is not designed to secure freedom of movement for workers. The Tunisia Agreement does not in principle prohibit a Member State from taking measures concerning the right to remain of a Tunisian national whom it had previously authorised to enter its territory and to engage in gainful employment. However, the situation would be different if, in the absence of grounds relating to the protection of a legitimate national interest, such as public policy, public security or public health, that refusal were to affect the right to engage in employment conferred on the person concerned in that Member State by a work permit duly granted by the competent national authorities for a period exceeding that of his residence permit.[66] The Court stressed that it does not follow from that interpretation that a Tunisian national will never be able to rely on the prohibition of discrimination laid down in Article 64 for the purposes of contesting a measure taken by a Member State in limitation of

---

[64] Case C–416/96 *El-Yassini* [1999] ECR I–1209, para 47, with references to *Opinion 1/91* [1991] ECR I–6079, para. 14; Case C–312/91 *Metalsa* [1993] ECR I–3751, para 12.
[65] Case C–416/96 *El-Yassini* [1999] ECR I–1209, paras 49–61.
[66] Case C–97/05 *Gattoussi* [2006] ECR I–11917, paras 29–31.

his right to remain. According to the Court, it would be unacceptable for the Member States to deal with the non-discrimination principle of the Agreement by using provisions of national law to limit its effectiveness. This would undermine the provisions of an agreement entered into by the Community and its Member States and would jeopardise the uniform application of that principle.[67]

B. Association, Partnership and Cooperation Agreements

In the case of Europe Association agreements, it was recalled in *Gloszczuk* that the extension of the interpretation of a provision in the EC Treaty to a comparably, similarly or even identically worded provision of an agreement concluded by the Community with a non-Member State depends on, *inter alia*, the aim pursued by each provision in its own particular context. A comparison between the objectives and context of the agreement and those of the Treaty is of considerable importance in that regard.[68] The question was whether the right to establishment enshrined in the Agreement with Poland comprised the right of entry and residence as corollaries. The Court started by referring to the different aims of, on the one hand, the agreement designed simply to create an appropriate framework for a gradual integration of Poland into the Community and, on the other, of the EC Treaty creating an internal market. It held that the rights of entry and residence conferred on Polish nationals as corollaries of the right of establishment are not absolute privileges, inasmuch as their exercise may, where appropriate, be limited by the rules of the host Member State concerning entry, stay and establishment of Polish nationals. Consequently the interpretation of Article 43 EC, as reflected in the case law, cannot be extended to Article 44(3) of the Association Agreement.[69] This approach was confirmed in *Kondova* and *Barkoci and Malik* in which the Court recognised that the freedom of establishment enshrined in the Europe agreements could be restricted by the host Member State.[70]

In the *Jany* case, the question was raised whether the concept of activities as self-employed persons has the same meaning in Article 43 EC as in the Europe Agreements with Poland and the Czech Republic.[71] Referring to Article 31 of the Vienna Convention on the Law of Treaties, the Court held that the purposes of the two agreements were to establish an association designed to promote the expansion of trade and harmonious

---

[67] *Ibid*, paras 38–9.
[68] Case C–63/99 *Gloszczuk* [2001] ECR I–6369.
[69] *Ibid*, paras 51–2.
[70] Case C–235/99 *Kondova* [2001] ECR I–6427; Case C–257/99 *Barkoci and Malik* [2001] ECR I–6557.
[71] Case C–268/99 *Jany and Others* [2001] ECR I–8615.

economic relations between the contracting parties in order to foster dynamic economic development and prosperity in these two non-Member States, with a view to facilitating their accession to the Union. It came to the conclusion that the provisions in the Europe agreements had to be construed to the effect that the concept of economic activities as self-employed persons has the same meaning and scope as the activities as self-employed persons referred to in Article 43 EC. The activity of prostitution, which was in issue in this case, pursued in a self-employed capacity can be regarded as a service provided for remuneration and is therefore covered by both those expressions.[72]

In direct line with this judgment, the Court gave the same interpretation as in Article 39 EC to the non-discrimination principle in the context of the free movement of workers in the Agreement with Poland. In *Pokzeptowicz-Meyer* it looked at the wording of the two provisions as well as to the aims of the Agreement and of the EC Treaty and held there was no reason to give a different construction to the two provisions.[73] In the field of sport a similar approach was adopted by the Court in the *Kolpak* case in relation to the non-discrimination principle of the Association Agreement with Slovakia.[74] It is interesting to note the readiness of the Court to give similar meaning to a provision of the Partnership and Cooperation Agreement with Russia in *Simutenkov*.[75] It noted that the question raised was similar to the one put in the *Kolpak* case in which it interpreted the non-discrimination principle of the Europe Association Agreement with Slovakia as precluding the application to a professional sportsman of Slovak nationality, who was lawfully employed by a club established in a Member State, of a rule drawn up by a sports federation in that State under which clubs were authorised to field, during league or cup matches, only a limited number of players from non-Member States that are not parties to the EEA Agreement.[76] The Court stated that the wording of the provision in the Russia Partnership Agreement was very similar to the one of the Slovakia Association Agreement and that the difference in drafting was not a bar to the transposition to the provision of the Partnership Agreement of the interpretation upheld in *Kolpak*.[77] Whereas the Court considered that unlike the Slovakia Association Agreement, the Russia Partnership Agreement is not intended to establish an association with a view to the gradual integration of that non-Member State into the European Union but is designed rather to bring about 'the gradual

---

72 *Ibid*, paras 36–7.
73 Case C–162/00 *Pokzeptowicz-Meyer* [2002] ECR I–1049, para 44.
74 Case C–438/00 *Kolpak* [2003] ECR I–4135.
75 Case C–265/03 *Simutenkov* [2005] ECR I–2579.
76 Case C–438/00 *Kolpak* [2003] ECR I–4135.
77 Case C–265/03 *Simutenkov* [2005] ECR I–2579, para 34.

integration between Russia and a wider area of cooperation in Europe', it held that it does not follow from the context or purpose of that Partnership Agreement that it intended to give to the prohibition of 'discrimination based on nationality, as regards working conditions ... any meaning other than that which follows from the ordinary sense of those words. Consequently, in a manner similar to Article 38(1) of the Slovakia Association Agreement, the provision of the Russia Partnership Agreement establishes, for the benefit of Russian workers lawfully employed in the territory of a Member State, a right to equal treatment in working conditions of the same scope as that which, in similar terms, nationals of Member States are recognised as having under the EC Treaty, which precludes any limitation based on nationality, such as the Court established in similar circumstances in the *Bosman* and *Kolpak* judgments.[78]

C. Decisions of Organs Established by Agreements

The Court's case law on decisions of organs established by agreements is very rich. It has been admitted in *Sevince* that a provision in a decision of such an organ must be regarded as having direct effect when, regard being had to its wording and to the purpose and nature of the decision of which it forms part and of the agreement to which it relates, that provision contains a clear and precise obligation which is not subject, in its implementation or effects, to the adoption of any subsequent measure.[79]

Accordingly, the Court adopted an open approach in *Bozkurt* concerning the interpretation of such provisions.[80] In the *Wählergruppe Gemeinsam* case, also related to Turkey Association Council decisions, the Court applied the principles laid down in connection with the freedom of movement for workers who are nationals of a Member State by analogy to Turkish workers enjoying the rights conferred by Decision no 1/80.[81] It referred to the aim and broad logic of this Decision, which intends to secure progressively freedom of movement for workers and to promote the integration in the host Member State of Turkish workers who satisfy the conditions laid down in that decision. According to the Court, granting Turkish workers legally employed in the territory of a Member State entitlement to the same conditions of work as those enjoyed by workers

---

[78]   Case C–265/03 *Simutenkov* [2005] ECR I–2579, para 36.

[79]   Case C–192/89 *Sevince* [1990] ECR I–3461, para 15; Case C–171/01 *Wählergruppe Gemeinsam* [2003] ECR I–4301, paras 54–55.

[80]   Case C–434/93 *Bozkurt* [1995] ECR I–1475; Case C–171/95 *Tetik* [1997] ECR I–329, paras 20 and 28.

[81]   Case C–171/01 *Wählergruppe Gemeinsam* [2003] ECR I–4301. This approach was confirmed in Case C–275/02 *Ayaz* [2004] ECR I–8765, para 44, and Case C–467/02 *Cetinkaya* [2004] ECR I–895, para 42.

who are nationals of the Member States was an important step towards creating an appropriate framework for the gradual integration of migrant Turkish workers.[82] In the same line, the Court held in *Dörr and Ünal* that Articles 8 and 9 of Directive 64/221 may be regarded as capable of extension to Turkish workers who enjoy the rights recognised by Decision no 1/80.[83]

It appears that the Court does not make any difference between a provision in an agreement and a provision in a decision of an organ established by an agreement when it is asked to interpret them. It applies the same criteria in both cases whether the question put to it concerns direct effect or interpretation by analogy of the decision's provision with the corresponding provision of EC law.

V. CONCLUSIONS

In recent years the Court has adopted a very open approach to the effects of international agreements within the EU legal order. The agreements entered into by the Community are binding on the Community institutions and take precedence over secondary legislation.[84] The legal effects of agreements concluded by the EU are still largely unknown whereas they are binding on the institutions. The Court has not yet had the opportunity to render judgment on the effects of a cross-pillar agreement.

The Court has very largely granted direct effect to provisions of international agreements, with the important exception of GATT and WTO agreements. No difference has been made on the basis of the purposes of the agreements. It has accepted direct effect of provisions in free trade agreements, cooperation agreements, association agreements, Europe agreements, Euro-Mediterranean agreements, cooperation and partnership agreements as well as decisions of organs established by agreements, if the provision is clear, precise and unconditional. In general, one may observe that in recent cases an important element which is increasingly taken into consideration by the Court and which seems to take precedence over the nature of the agreement analysed is the capacity of the provision to govern the position of individuals. However, there is a divergence with the GATT and WTO case law. According to the Court, the grounds for denying direct effect lie in the structure and nature of the GATT, which are different from the other agreements concluded by the

---

[82] Case C–171/01 *Wählergruppe Gemeinsam* [2003] ECR I–4301, para 79.

[83] Case C–136/03 *Dörr and Ünal* [2005] ECR I–4759, para 65.

[84] Case C–61/94 *Commission v Germany* [1996] ECR I–3989, para 52; Case C–286/02 *Bellio F.lli* [2004] ECR I–3465, para 33; Case C–311/04 *Algemene Scheeps Agentuur Dordrecht* [2006] ECR I–609, para 25; Joined Cases C–447/05 and C–448/05 *Thomson and Vestel France*, judgment of 8 March 2007, para 30.

Community. The GATT was considered as too flexible to be given direct effect. A further line of reasoning had to be developed as to the WTO agreements, involving the principle of reciprocity, insofar as the Community's main trading partners do not recognise the direct effect of these provisions. Another rationale was added in relation to the role of the EU political institutions (Council and Commission), to which scope of manoeuvre must be left in their dealings and negotiations with the other WTO members in order to determine the legal effects of the agreements in the Community legal order. For these reasons, the Court's approach to GATT and WTO agreements is more "closed" than to the other agreements concluded by the Community.

As to the interpretation issue the Court has more often than in the past accepted the application of the same interpretation to a provision of an international agreement as has been developed for a corresponding rule on the EC Treaty. In some cases, the Court had to decide whether to give the same interpretation to similar provisions enshrined in two different categories of agreements. In the 1999 *El-Yassini* judgment it made a difference between the Morocco Cooperation Agreement and the Association Agreement with Turkey. More recently in 2005 it gave in *Simutenkov* the same interpretation to a provision enshrined in the Partnership and Cooperation Agreement with Russia as it has developed for the Europe Association Agreement with Poland. There are still differences in the case law and it remains difficult to determine to what extent the nature of the agreements will be taken into consideration.

Despite these uncertainties the open approach of the Court to the questions of direct effect and interpretation is clearly positive because it tends to give the fullest effect to the Community's international obligations in favour of individuals and to create the most uniform legal order possible in extending interpretations given internally to Community principles to similar concepts enshrined in international agreements concluded with third states. The agreements discussed in this paper all, to a greater or lesser extent, seek to extend rules that are similar or identical to Community rules towards third states and their nationals. This is not the case of the WTO agreements, in which no extension of Community rules is envisaged. The WTO rather seeks to create an "alternative" system of rules, to be applied between more than 150 Member States and to which the EC has committed itself. One might consider this as an explanation, among others, for the Court's different approach towards integration of WTO norms into the Community legal order justifying that the principle of uniformity in the interpretation and application of the agreements bears some exceptions. The picture emerging from the analysis in this Chapter shows how difficult it is to classify the EU as a monist or dualist system.

Index

Introductory Note

References such as '178–9' indicate (not necessarily continuous) discussion of a topic across a range of pages. Wherever possible in the case of topics with many references, these have either been divided into sub-topics or the most significant discussions of the topic are indicated by page numbers in bold. Because the entire volume is about the 'EC', 'EU', 'foreign relations' and the 'Common Foreign and Security Policy (CFSP)', the use of these terms as entry points has been minimised. Information will be found under the corresponding detailed topics.